The Book of Habakkuk:
An Exegetical-Theological Commentary on the Hebrew Text

A Teleioteti Old Testament Commentary

J. Alexander Rutherford

Unless otherwise indicated, all Scripture quotations from the Book of Habakkuk are the author's own translation.

Unless otherwise indicated, all other Scripture quotations are from The Holy Bible, English Standard Version® (ESV®), copyright © 2001 by Crossway Bibles, a publishing ministry of Good News Publishers. Used by permission. All rights reserved.

Copyright © 2019 James Alexander Rutherford
Teleioteti publishing, Vancouver, B.C.
All rights reserved.

ISBN-13: 978-1-989560-00-6

DEDICATION

This book is dedicated to my glorious God and Saviour Jesus Christ, in whom is my faith and through whom I have life—and that in abundance. It is dedicated also to my ever patient and loving wife, Nicole, who constantly challenges me to be a more faithful follower of Jesus, to live constantly in dependence upon the Holy Spirit, and to trust God my Father more and more every day. Finally it is dedicated to our church family over the last 5 years in Vancouver, first at the Bridge and then at Christ City Church Kitsilano. We have truly felt at home over these last 5 years as we shared coffees, meals, heartbreaks, and joys. Thank you for your love, friendship, and support.

CONTENTS

Dedication iii
Contents v
Acknowledgments xi
Preface xiii
I. An Introduction to Habakkuk 1
    Overview 3
    Outline 4
        The Parties involved in Habakkuk 6
        The Identity of the Vision 10
    Canonical Position 14
        The Prophets 18
        The Twelve 21
        The Larger Story 25
    Habakkuk in the New Testament 30
        Habakkuk 1:5 in Acts 13:41 30
        Habakkuk 2:4 in Romans 1:17 32
        Habakkuk 2:4 in Galatians 3:11 34
        Habakkuk 2:3-4 in Hebrews 10:37-39 36
    Style and Text 38

The Text of Habakkuk 39
The Hebrew of Habakkuk's Poetry 42
Habakkuk's use of Structure and Vocabulary 47

II. A Translation of The Book of Habakkuk 53
III. Commentary 61

1. The Oracle of Habakkuk (1:1-2:20) 63

A. Superscription (1:1) 65

Exegesis of Verse 1 66

B. Habakkuk's Complaints and Yahweh's Responses (1:2-2:20) 69

i. Habakkuk's First Complaint (1:2-4) 71

Exegesis of Verses 2-4 72
Exposition **78**

ii. Yahweh's Response to Habakkuk's First Complaint (1:5-11) 81

Exegesis of Verses 5-6b 82
Exegesis of Verses 6c-7 89
Exegesis of Verses 8-9 91
Exegesis of Verses 10-11 94
Exposition **97**

iii. Habakkuk's Second Complaint (1:12-2:1) 101

Exegesis of Verses 12-13 102
Exegesis of Verses 14-17 109
Exegesis of Chapter 2, Verse 1 114
Exposition **116**

iv. Yahweh's Final Response (2:2-2:20) 119

1. A Reply for the People: the Question of Righteousness (2:2-4) 120

Exegesis of Verses 2-4 121
Exposition **137**

2. A Reply for Babylon: They Will Receive My Cup (2:5-2:19) 139

Exegesis of Verse 5-6c 142
Exegesis of Verse 6d-8 146

Exegesis of Verse 9-11 147
Exegesis of Verse 12-14 149
Exegesis of Verse 15-17 151
Exegesis of Verse 18-20 155
Exposition **157**

C. Conclusion: Let all the earth be silent (2:20) 163

Exposition **163**

2. Habakkuk's Prayer of Faith in Response to the Oracle (3:1-19) 167

A. Superscription (3:1) 169

Exegesis of Verse 1 169

B. Habakkuk's Prayer of Faith in Response to the Oracle from God (3:2-19c) 171

i. Strophe 1: Bring Your Deed to Life (3:2-3B) 173

Exegesis of Verses 2-3B 174
Exposition **177**

ii. Strophe 2: God Comes Forth (3:3c-9b) 179

Exegesis of Stanza 1: God Comes in Glorious Power (3c-5) 180
Exegesis of Stanza 2: The World Responds to His Coming (6-7) 183
Exegesis of Stanza 3: God is Ready for War (8-9b) 185
Exposition **187**

iii. Strophe 3: Yahweh Arrives (3:9c-13) 191

Exegesis of Stanza 1: The Waters Join Your Assault (9c-10d) 193
Exegesis of Stanza 2: The Luminaries Strengthen Your Weapons (11-12) 194
Exegesis of Stanza 3: You Come for Salvation with His Anointed (13) 196
Exposition **198**

iv. Strophe 4: Habakkuk's Response of Faith (3:14-19d) 203

Exegesis of Stanza 1: With the Anointed One's Weapons You Strike Me (14-15) 205

   Exegesis of Stanza 2: Though Terrified, I Will Wait For Him (16) 207
   Exegesis of Stanza 3: When All Fails, I Will Rejoice in Yahweh (17-19c) 208
   Exposition **210**

 C. Conclusion: Musical Instructions (3:19d) 213

   Exegesis of Verse 19d 213
   Exposition **215**

IV. Appendices – Further Theological and Exegetical Meditations 217

 Introduction to the Appendices 219
 Appendix 1 – On Context 221

  Case Study in Context: Habakkuk 224
  Layers of biblical context: 225

   The Context of the whole Bible: 225
   The context of a distinct work: 225

 Appendix 2 – Canonical Context and Meaning 227
 Appendix 3 – On the Use And Abuse of Historical Background 235

  The Uses of Extra-Biblical Evidence 237
  The Challenge of Using Extra-Biblical Data 239
  Objections 240

 Appendix 4 – On Emendations and Lexical Meaning 243
 Appendix 5 - Knowing Bible Translations 247

  Bible Translation 248
  Translation Theories 250
  Bible Translations 252

   ESV 253
   KJV 253
   NASB 254
   NET 255
   NIV 255
   NLT 258
   NRSV 258
   The Message 258
   Further Reading 259

Appendix 6 - On the Translation of Habakkuk 2:2c in the Septuagint 261
Appendix 7 - Habakkuk 2:4 in Romans 1:17 265
    Overview of Romans 265
    Introduction to 1:1-17 267
    Romans 1:16-17 270

        Verse 16 270
        Verse 17 271

        The Righteousness of God 271
        The Gospel is God's Righteousness for Salvation Completely by Faith 273

    Conclusion 278

Appendix 8– Towards a Biblical Theology of Imputation: A Consideration of an Old Testament Root for Christ's Imputed Righteousness in Romans 279

    Covenant Fulfillment in the Letter to the Romans 280
    Imputed Righteousness in Romans 282

        God's Righteousness as Imputed Righteousness in 1:16-17 282
        Imputation in Romans 1:18-3:20 282
        Imputation in the Argument of Romans 3:21-4:25 283

    Genesis 15:6 as an Old Testament Root for the Doctrine of Imputation 285
    Excurse: Is Imputation Confused Nonsense? 287

Bibliography 289

    About Teleioteti 307

        Other Books by J. Alexander Rutherford 307

ACKNOWLEDGMENTS

There are hundreds of men and women whose support, encouragement, and timely rebukes have been used by God to make me the man I am today, and so—directly or indirectly—have led to the writing of this commentary. Without the God-centred upbringing provided by my parents Ernie and Carolyn, this project would not have been possible: I am ever thankful to God for providing them as my parents. I would not have the passion for God's word that I have today if it were not for the wise teaching and friendship of Brad Copp, whom God has used in immeasurable ways to shape me and my reading of the Bible. Lastly, to Fred Eaton, my pastor at Christ City Church Kitsilano, and all my friends who have stood by me and encouraged me—first at Pacific Life Bible College and then at Regent College—I am ever grateful for your friendships. To name but a few, Aaron Dickey, Aaron Fraser, Chris Leckman, Dan Pederson, Joel Nafziger, Jon Hawes, John DesRoches, Matt Nickerson, and Raphael Hauser, your friendships have been well treasured.

PREFACE

First things first, it is pronounced Ha-ba-kook. With that out of the way, we can discuss what is really pressing: why in the world do we need another Old Testament commentary, and why one on an obscure book such as Habakkuk? The idea for this commentary emerged from the nexus of two experiences: first, as I studied Habakkuk intensively for a paper at Regent College, I found that the Holy Spirit was continually giving me insights into this wonderful book and a growing love for it. This birthed in me a desire to dig deeper and study the book further. In doing so, I experienced something rather unfortunate. Digging through piles of scholarly and pastoral commentaries on the book, I discovered that none of them were seeing what I was seeing. When they did, they failed to carry these insights to their logical conclusion. With one or two exceptions, every commentary I opened spent more time ripping apart the Hebrew text and declaring it unacceptable than wrestling with the text and trying to understand it.

This meant that many commentaries ignored the questions that I was asking—leaving me with no easy answers—and, as a result, spent very little time wrestling with the theological conundrums facing Habakkuk, issues tremendously relevant for us today. This commentary is the result of my time wrestling with the Hebrew text of Habakkuk, of going through it line by line, building a translation from the ground up, and drawing together the insights from the myriad of commentators that have come before me. This is not my first book on Habakkuk; in 2018 I published a Bible study Guide, *Believe the Unbelievable: A Study in Habakkuk*, which I intended to help the reader reflect upon the message of the book and apply it to their lives. This commentary will go far deeper than that study guide, explaining why I have translated the book as I have, the insight it holds for our culture, and how it communicates its message.

The result is hopefully not a novel commentary: I am not interesting in being "new" or "innovative," especially not for their own sake—as is commonly the case today. There may be some points in your reading of this commentary when you will find an insight that I have been unable to trace to another author, but these are rare and in as much as they are correct, all credit must go to the Holy Spirit for guiding my reading. In most cases, I have built on the insights of many godly men who have written about Habakkuk before me, my own contribution being merely to bring together their insights into a cohesive interpretation and to apply it to my culture.

I have ultimately sought to be faithful to God by honouring His word in my writing and thinking. My vision for putting my insights on paper is to see God's people—pastors, scholars, and every Christian—growing in their faith and understanding of God our Father and His Son Jesus Christ. It would probably be wise to orient you to some of the presuppositions that have led to this commentary's style, lest you find yourself disappointed and left with no answer to the questions you are asking.

In calling this a exegetical-theological commentary, I am purposefully putting distance between myself and two common streams of biblical interpretation prevalent today.[1] The first is that of "theological interpretation." This title is used for many different approaches to reading the Bible, many of them not quite different from what I am attempting here. But there is among those who practice theological interpretation a growing number who are seeking to re-appropriate the allegorical interpretive method of the Church Fathers. One such author questions whether there is any objective meaning in the biblical texts. I am deeply troubled by this movement, for it in effect leaves man as the autonomous judge of right or wrong interpretation and doctrine. For all its claims of antiquity, it is really a capitulation to post-modern tendencies in the church—clothed in ancient garb—and leaves the Christian in the same place as those addressed by Nietzsche's madman:

> What were we doing when we unchained this earth from its sun? Where is it moving to now? Where are we moving to? Away from all suns? Are we not continually falling? And backwards, sidewards, forwards, in all directions? Is there still an up and a down? Aren't we straying as though through an infinite nothing?[2]

In depriving God's word of its authority to speak truth clearly, it is as if we

---

[1] For more on the exegetical approach embodied in this commentary, see my series *God's Gifts for the Christian Life*, especially Volume 2, *The Gift of Reading Part 1: Reading the Bible in Submission to God* (Vancouver: Teleioteti, 2019) & *The Gift of Reading Part 2: A Biblical Perspective on Hermeneutics* (Vancouver: Teleioteti, 2019).

[2] Friedrich Nietzsche, *The Gay Science* in Friedrich Wilhelm Nietzsche and Walter Kaufmann, *Basic Writings of Nietzsche*, Modern Library ed. (New York: Modern Library, 2000), 120.

have detached the earth from the sun and been flung to the outer reaches of space with no anchor to stop our flight. But I digress; even more pressing on my heart than this capitulation to the authority vacuum our society propagates is the way this rips God's word away from the people for whom it was intended. If Scripture is left in the hands of the elite only—those mature enough to probe the spiritual insights of allegorical "interpretation"—how then can the young man struggling with sin keep his ways according to God's word (Psalm 119:9), how can he meditate on YHWH's precepts (v. 15), think over them day and night (Psalm 1:2)? How can Christians be sanctified in God's truth (John 17:19) when it is inaccessible to them?

The second trend in biblical interpretation that I seek to avoid is that of rampant historical criticism, those approaches that see a need to ground every interpretation not in the Scriptures God has given us but in reconstructions of the audience, author, and purpose of the books making up the Bible. That is, the methods of interpretation that treat Scripture as a collection of historical documents, the primary value of which is the window they give us into history by which we might see what God has done and so be able to re-appropriate that work for our lives today. This, like allegorical interpretation, severs us from our moorings and leaves us like a ship tossed about in the wicked seas of the Atlantic. How can we be sure that our reconstructions are accurate—are correct—or that our preferred backgrounds are the right ones? This danger is compounded when we come to a book such as Habakkuk (or Hebrews, or Job, or Samuel, etc.) concerning which we know almost nothing about the author, the audience, the date of writing, or the situation within which it was penned. Now, this is not to say that historical background is not helpful in our interpretation of Scripture—surely it is!—but to guard against the error of making this context normative for our interpretation. Graeme Goldsworthy aptly addresses this point in relation to New Testament studies when he writes,

> Among some contemporary scholars there is an emphasis on Jewish interpretations, including those of the Dead Sea Scrolls, as the background that explains much of the interpretation of the Old Testament in the New. While we may gain from the understanding of this cultural context, we need to remember that the New Testament itself and not its Jewish context is the norm, and that Jesus was not noted for his conformity to standard Jewish interpretation.[3]

---

[3] Graeme Goldsworthy, *Gospel-Centered Hermeneutics: Foundations and Principles of Evangelical Biblical Interpretation* (Downers Grove: InterVarsity Press, 2006), 92.

The dangers here are innumerable, but just as with allegorical interpretation, Scripture is separated by an unbridgeable gap from the average Christian. Only the elite professional scholar is sufficient to understand God's revelation. Furthermore, the many different options available for supposed historical backgrounds has allowed many interpreters to escape the awkwardness of an uncomfortable teaching by explaining it away with the background of his or her choice. The problem is evident as one observes the variation among the backgrounds suggested by each commentator.

Thus, by calling this commentary an "exegetical-theological" commentary, I intend to convey the heart of my approach to the Word of God. I have sought to perform solid exegesis, wrestling with the Hebrew text and the other versions, employing the best lexica and resources available, and staring at the text multiple times a day for months on end. I have, above all, sought to justify my readings by the whole of Scripture. I have not based any reading of the text of Habakkuk merely on historical background. Where helpful, I have drawn on the wealth of data archaeology has uncovered, but I have only done so as a tool to illuminate the meaning I arrived at from a detailed search of the canon of Scripture, the Book of the Twelve (Minor Prophets), and Habakkuk. In many more cases than the reader may expect, I have arrived at syntactically and contextually appropriate readings for the difficult parts of Habakkuk without resorting to historical/archeological data as the background against which to read the text. This is what I intend when I say "exegetical."

By "theological," I intend that I have sought to relate all of Habakkuk to the greater context of Scripture so to understand how it contributes to the worldview (systematic theology) and redemptive historical story (biblical theology) of the Bible. With John Frame, I affirm that theology is essentially application. Writing theology is not an attempt to say better something concealed by Scripture: by doing theology, we are trying to take what was clearly said in Scripture and clearly say it now in light of our cultural customs and questions. This is the goal of translation, theology, and commentaries; this is, therefore, what I have attempted to do here.[4] I have discussed the exegetical approach employed here and alternate methods in my books *The Gift of Reading Part 1 & Part 2*. I direct the interested reader to these books for a further discussion.

Having bored you with this prefatory material, it is about time we turned to the matter at hand, the great gift God has given us in the book of

---

[4] John M. Frame, *The Doctrine of the Knowledge of God*, A Theology of Lordship (Phillipsburg: P&R Publishing, 1987), 81–85, 93–98.

Habakkuk. The Book of Habakkuk is breathtaking in the beauty of its poetry, the vividness of its language, and the horror of God's deed unveiled therein; yet like all good theology, it reaches a crescendo in the heartfelt confession of praise that pours forth from Habakkuk's lips:

> [17]Even when the fig tree does not bear fruit,
>   and there is no yield of the vine;
> the labour done for olives fails,
>   and the fields do not produce food;
> the flocks are cut from the fold,
>   and there are no cattle in the stalls,
> [18]I will rejoice in YHWH,
>   I will exult in the God of my salvation.
> [19]The Lord YHWH is my strength;
>   He sets my feet like a doe
>   and causes me to tread upon high places.

Before we begin our expository journey together, let us pray for God's wisdom and discernment in our reading of Habakkuk,

> O God of Truth,
> I thank thee for the holy Scriptures,
>   their precepts, promises, directions, light.
> In them may I learn more of Christ,
>   be enabled to retain his truth
>   and have grace to follow it....
>
> By his aid may I be enabled to explore
>   all its truths,
>   love them will all my heart,
>   embrace them will all my power,
>   engraft them into my life....
>
> Help me to gain profit by what I read,
>   as treasure beyond all treasure,
>   a fountain which can replenish my dry heart,
>   its waters flowing through me as a perennial river
>   on-drawn by thy Holy Spirit....
>
> Then write thy own words upon my heart
>   and inscribe them on my lips;
> So shall all glory be to thee

in my reading of thy Word![5]

Soli Deo Gloria,
    J. Alexander Rutherford

---

[5] *Valley of Vision*, 346-347

I. AN INTRODUCTION TO HABAKKUK

As with most commentaries, we shall begin with an introduction to the Book of Habakkuk. The purpose of an introduction is to help our reading by providing us with valuable information for interpretation, a road map (outline) for navigating the text, and an introduction to key themes and major areas of interest or dispute in a book. Alerting the reader to these issues is immensely helpful, yet the criteria we use to determine what should and should not be in an introduction is dependent largely on one's interpretive approach. If one is convinced that truth is best achieved by mediating scholarly opinion, an introduction will focus mainly on contemporary scholarly debate, alerting one to the positions and trying to navigate them with a *via media* that does justice to all that the experts say. This is not that kind of introduction.

I have already played my hand in the preface, revealing in brief my interpretive approach in contrast with theological interpretation and historical criticism. Most Evangelical commentaries practice a mild form of historical criticism—grammatical-historical exegesis—and so focus their introductions mainly on author, date, and audience along with thematic overviews.[1] The purpose of providing this information is not for the sake of the often interesting debates that ensue but for aiding the reader in interpreting the book. I am not convinced that this information is as helpful as is supposed. Even if I were, we know none of this with certainty when it

---

[1] This is sometimes called "special introduction."

comes to Habakkuk. If you are looking for information on the author, about all we can say is that Habakkuk may or may not have been a Levite.[2]

What follows will not be a historical introduction to Habakkuk. In its place, I am going to provide what I am convinced is the most valuable information for our exposition of the book. Because I have already laid out in detail my approach to exegesis—biblical interpretation—elsewhere (*The Gift of Reading Part 1 & Part 2*),[3] I will not go over it here. I have introduced some of my presuppositions in the preface and provide in the appendices some theoretical discussions that underlie my approach. I believe this approach will speak for itself as we proceed, but if the reader is interested in learning more, I direct them to the above mentioned books.

In this introduction, we will begin by examining the book of Habakkuk as a whole, its major themes, purpose, and argument. Following that, I will provide what I propose to be the outline of the book of Habakkuk along with discussions of two key issues concerning the way one reads the book, namely, the number and identity of the parties involved in the book and the identity of the vision mentioned in 2:2-3. In the two sections following, we will look at the role of Habakkuk within the greater storyline of Scripture, the impact that Habakkuk's canonical placement has on our interpretation of it, and the way Habakkuk has been used in the New Testament. This will alert us to key themes to watch for and give us an appreciation for Habakkuk's role in biblical and systematic theology, as well as beginning to unpack some of the ways that Habakkuk speaks of Jesus Christ (cf. Luke 24:27, 44; John 5:46). In the last part of this introduction, we will examine the style of Habakkuk's writing and the state of the text of Habakkuk.

---

[2] Some commentators come to this conclusion through the prayer song that ends the book. The Levitical or priestly office is linked with musical worship in the OT and the reference to "my stringed instruments" in 3:19 is thought to suggest that Habakkuk had role in the liturgical music of the temple. I do not put much stock in this argument and do not think it matters either way. C.F. Keil and F. Delitzsch, *Commentary on the Old Testament in Ten Volumes: Minor Prophets; Two Volumes in One*, trans. James Martin, Reprint., vol. 10.2 (Grand Rapids: Eerdmans, 1978), 412.

[3] J. Alexander Rutherford, *The Gift of Reading - Part 1: Reading the Bible in Submission to God*, God's Gifts for the Christian Life Part 1 Vol. 2a (Vancouver: Teleioteti, 2019); J. Alexander Rutherford, *The Gift of Reading - Part 2: A Biblical Perspective on Hermeneutics*, God's Gifts for the Christian Life Part 1 Vol. 2b (Vancouver: Teleioteti, 2019).

Overview

The nature of Habakkuk is unique in the Old Testament, being a sustained dialogue between Habakkuk and Yahweh. One is first struck by similarities to Job, yet in Job God does not answer his concerns; God questions Job and leaves him to confess and repent, for he has spoken things he did not understand (Job 42:3). Whereas in Job we could say that God's answer is His inscrutability, in Habakkuk it is His unfailing trustworthiness. Despite the rather bold posture Habakkuk adopts (2:1), God is quite patient with him, answering his concerns—though not quite in the way Habakkuk expected.

The book opens with a complaint on Habakkuk's part (1:2-4), God then responds (1:5-11). There is one more question/answer exchange (1:12-2:20) before Habakkuk submits to God in humble faith and praise (ch. 3). Each of Habakkuk's complaints addresses the apparent inconsistencies between Habakkuk's experiences and God's character. God's responses serve to adjust Habakkuk's view so that he may see how God is at work to fulfill His purposes and that he may come to a place of submission and faith in Yahweh. We witness in Habakkuk's response a gradual submission and acceptance of God's purpose: at first, he acknowledges God's deed (1:12e-f) yet is not content—questions remain. But in the end, he praises God for this same act (3:2, 17-19).

With many commentators, I see the central theme of the book as the question of God's character in the light of the realities His people face— that is, *theodicy*. But the question of theodicy, a defense of God's character in the face of a seeming difficulty, is not expounded as an apologetic endeavor—to rid some doubt in the mind of the reader. Instead, Habakkuk addresses God's character in the face of difficulties to draw attention to the attitude God would have from all His people. God commands unwavering faith in His goodness and character, trust in Him that defies the difficulties of life in a fallen world and ventures to rejoice in the face of even His most terrifying deeds.

We could then summarize the purpose of Habakkuk, as I see it, as a re-orientation of the believer. It is meant to lead the reader to a deeper faith in and understanding of the God they worship. The reader is to be led from shock when confronted by God's deed (1:5), through an acknowledgment of it, to the full realization of God's character and a solidifying of the faith that has led him or her to read the book in the first place. The themes unpacked towards this end include God's sovereignty among the nations, the nature of the people of God, prayer, and faith. It is Habakkuk's discussion of faith and the nature of God's people that catches the eye of the New Testament writers and becomes its main contribution to the progression of God's revelation in

Scripture (Rom 1:17, Gal 3:11, Heb 10:37-38—the quotation in Acts is the exception, 13:41).

Outline

I. ***THE ORACLE OF HABAKKUK THE PROPHET***
   1. SUPERSCRIPTION (1:1)
   2. HABAKKUK'S COMPLAINTS AND YAHWEH'S RESPONSES (1:2-2:20)
      A. Habakkuk's First Complaint (1:2-4)
      B. Yahweh's Response to Habakkuk's Complaint (the Vision) (1:5-11)
         a. A Call to See God's Answer Among the Nations: Chaldea (1:5-6b)
         b. A Description of the Chaldeans (1:6c-11)
            i. They come with ferocity, bitter and brash (6c-9)
               a) They are bitter (6c-7)
               b) They are brash (8-9c)
            ii. In their arrogance they transgress (10-11)
      C. Habakkuk's Second Complaint (1:12-2:1)
         a. Habakkuk Acknowledges God's Deed and Complains (12-17)
            i. *Habakkuk acknowledges God's answer (12)*
            ii. *Habakkuk complains about God's deed on account of His character (13-17)*
               a) How can you allow a wicked nation to consume the more righteous? (13)
               b) Will you allow the Chaldeans to continue forever? (14-17)
         b. Transition: Habakkuk will wait (2:1)
      D. YHWH's Response to Habakkuk's Second Complaint (2:2-20)
         a. A Reply for Israel: the Question of Righteousness (2:2-4)[4]
            i. The test: write it down clearly, incite a response (2:2-3)
               a) *God's command: Make it clear on tablets (2:2a-c)*
               b) *God's purpose: That the one reading will run (2:2d)*

---

[4] The structure here is not able to be sufficiently displayed in a linear outline, see commentary on vv. 2-5.

     c) *God's Reason: For the vision will not let up but come (2:3)*
   ii. Diagnosis: the arrogant and the believing (2:4)
     a) *The one who runs is crooked (2:4a)*
     b) *But those who are right will live by trusting in me (2:4b)*
  b. <u>A Reply for Babylon: They Will Receive My Cup</u> (2:5-2:19)
   i. If I have dealt with your injustice, how much more so will Babylon receive judgment? (2:5)
   ii. The oppressed speak a word against their oppressor *(2:6-19)*
     a) *Introduction of the taunt-song (2:6a)*
     b) *The taunt-song: five woes for the Chaldean (2:6c-19)*
      1) The first woe: to the One who accumulates an unpayable debt (6d-8b)

      Refrain (8c-d)

      2) The second woe: to the one who tries to Build His House (9-11)
      3) The third woe: to the one who builds his kingdom in wickedness (12-14)
      4) The fourth woe: to he who shames himself (15-17b)

      Refrain (17c-d)

      5) The fifth woe: to the one who creates dumb idols (18-19)
 3. CONCLUSION: LET ALL THE EARTH BE SILENT BEFORE THE TRUE GOD (2:20)

II. HABAKKUK'S PRAYER OF FAITH IN RESPONSE TO THE ORACLE FROM GOD (3:1-19)
 1. SUPERSCRIPTION: A PRAYER OF HABAKKUK (3:1)
 2. STROPHE 1: BRING YOUR DEED TO LIFE (3:2-3B)
  A. <u>God, Despite My Fear, Bring This Deed to Life (3:2)</u>
  B. <u>God Comes From Edom (3a-b)</u>
 3. STROPHE 2: THE DIVINE WARRIOR COMES FORTH (3:3C-9B)
  A. <u>Stanza 1: God Comes in Glorious Power (3c-5)</u>
  B. <u>Stanza 2: The World Responds to His Coming (6-7)</u>
  C. <u>Stanza 3: YHWH is Ready for War (8-9)</u>
 4. STROPHE 3: THE DIVINE WARRIOR ARRIVES (3:9C-13)
  A. <u>Stanza 1: The Waters Join Your Assault (9c-10d)</u>
  B. <u>Stanza 2: The Luminaries Illumine Your Weapons (11-12)</u>

      C. <u>Stanza 3: You Come forth for Salvation with Your Anointed (13)</u>
5. STROPHE 4: HABAKKUK'S RESPONSE OF FAITH (3:14-19D)
      A. <u>Stanza 1: With the Anointed One's Weapons You Strike Me (14-15)</u>
      B. <u>Stanza 2: Though Terrified, I Will Wait For Him (16)</u>
      C. <u>Stanza 3: When All Fails, I Will Rejoice in YHWH (17-19c)</u>
6. CONCLUSION: MUSICAL INSTRUCTIONS (19D)

The Parties involved in Habakkuk

The above outline has assumed that there are two additional parties considered in the book of Habakkuk, apart from Habakkuk and God. Though this is a widespread view, it does not enjoy universal recognition; it is in fact an area of serious dispute among commentators on the book. When their existence is acknowledged, the identity of these two parties is further debated. Among the various positions here, I judge that two alternatives are worth considering in the space we have.

The first argues that there is in fact only one additional party considered in the book, the Chaldeans. In this view, 1:5-11 does not present God's response to Habakkuk's prayer in 2-4. It is, instead, the cause of it. The Chaldeans are the party that has led to Habakkuk's initial outcry, therefore the rest of the book records Habakkuk gradual acceptance of God's actions as expressed in 1:5-11.[5] Some commentators argue that in verses 5-11 Habakkuk is quoting the word of God that originally led him to cry out the prayer recorded in 1:1-4.[6] The reasons given for this position are three. There is a theological objection, that it does not make sense to read 1:5-11 as God's answer to Habakkuk's prayer in 1:1-4. They also argue from conspicuous absence: there is no indication that Judahites are responsible for the terrible

---

    [5] We will not consider the variation of this position that sees a need to move verses 5-11 elsewhere in the book.

    [6] See, Michael H. Floyd, *Minor Prophets. Part 2*, The Forms of the Old Testament literature v. 22 (Grand Rapids: Eerdmans, 2000), 82, 95–96; David Cleaver-Bartholomew, "An Alternative Reading of Hab 1 and 2," *Proceedings, Eastern Great Lakes and Midwest Bible Societies* 24 (2004): 45–59; Marvin A. Sweeney, "Structure, Genre, and Intent in the Book of Habakkuk," *Vetus Testamentum* 41, no. 1 (January 1991): 63–83; M.A. Sweeney, *The Twelve Prophets*, ed. David W. Cotter, vol. 2, Berit Olam (Collegeville, Minn.: The Liturgical Press, 2000), 455.

things in 1:1-4. Lastly, they argue from word usage: the party in 1:1-4 is said to do violence (חָמָס, *ḥāmās*), as are the Chaldeans in verse 9.[7]

Others agree with my proposed reading in seeing Chaldea as a separate party than those in 1:1-4 but identify these initial oppressors as some party other than Judah.[8] I do not find any of the proffered arguments convincing; I maintain that Judah is the party in 1:1-4 and that in 1:5-11 Chaldea is God's answer to Habakkuk's prayer. Instead of directly addressing their arguments, I will put forward here the case for my position in brief, answering all these objections by doing so, and trust that the translation and commentary below will justify this position further.[9] In support of the position I am defending, let us consider three points.

First, the word usage employed by Habakkuk in 1:1-4 suggests that he has Judah in view.[10] To begin with, Habakkuk mentions תּוֹרָה (*tôrāh*, "Law") in verse 4. Unlike in verse 7, referring to the Chaldeans, Habakkuk here identifies the specific miscarriage of justice occurring as "the Law is numb." The Law, Torah, refers most often to the Law of Moses recorded in the Pentateuch; this is without a doubt the case here. The Law is the binding document governing God's people under His covenant: Torah is unique to God's people Israel. That those in verses 1-4 are presented as failing to enact Torah—causing it to be numb, ineffective—without a doubt demonstrates that they are Judahites, probably the leadership.[11]

---

[7] Cleaver-Bartholomew, "An Alternative Reading of Hab 1 and 2," 45–46; Sweeney, "Structure, Genre, and Intent in the Book of Habakkuk," 455; ibid., 67; Floyd, *Minor Prophets. Part 2*, 82, 95–96.

[8] E.g. Marshall D Johnson, "The Paralysis of Torah in Habakkuk 1:4," *Vetus Testamentum* 35, no. 3 (July 1985): 260–261.

[9] For the interpretation I have adopted, see also O. Palmer Robertson, *The Books of Nahum, Habakkuk, and Zephaniah*, NICOT (Grand Rapids: W.B. Eerdmans, 1990); John Goldingay and Pamela J Scalise, *Minor Prophets II* (Peabody: Hendrickson, 2009), 47–49, 54–55; Richard Duane Patterson, *Nahum, Habakkuk, Zephaniah*, The Wycliffe Exegetical Commentary (Chicago: Moody Press, 1991); Dennis Leroy Bomgaars, "Habakkuk: Some Introductory and Literary Issues" (Master's Thesis, Reformed Theological Seminary, 1984), 8–9.

[10] These points could likewise apply to Israel, but—among other indicators—that the Babylonians are the secondary antagonist in the book indicates that it is the Southern Kingdom being addressed.

[11] See Waldemar Neufeld, "An Exegetical and Theological Study of Habakkuk 2:4-5," *Master of Art Theology Thesis* (May 1, 1990): 7,

Furthermore, in verse 3c Habakkuk describes the initial conditions under the oppression of the party in 1:1-4 as being characterized by שֹׁד and חָמָס (*šōd*, havoc, and *ḥāmās*, violence). These two words occur together four other times in the Bible (in the reverse order), in each instance they are linked by ו (*vav*, and). Each of these occurrences is in the Prophets (the second section of the Hebrew Canon) and describes Judah. Together these words form a hendiadys, a single idea; "havoc and violence" is similar to our "death and destruction," though usually on a social level—that is, within a community as opposed to between nations.[12] Their occurrence together here should immediately lead us to think of Judah, especially in consideration of the use of this word pair in Amos 3:10 to describe the sin of Judah—the sin that is now being addressed with judgment. With Habakkuk placed later than Amos in the Book of the Twelve and introducing judgement against Judah for sins already described in detail, this intertextual association is strong (See below on the canonical placement of Habakkuk).[13]

As our last vocabulary consideration, we should note that using similar words for the oppressive leaders of Judah and for the Chaldeans does not necessarily suggest that the same party is being referred to. It could—and read in the context of the book, does—provide significant support for our interpretation. Habakkuk intentionally uses similar language throughout the book to describe both Chaldea and the wicked Judahites in order to support the argument that the wicked of Judah are just as responsible, wicked, and worthy of judgment as the horrible pagan Chaldeans (1:4, 9; 1;4, 7, 13d-e; 2:4a, 5; 2:10-13, 3:13c-d; 1:4, 3:14).

Second, there are immediate markers that identify those in 1:1-4 as a different group than those in 1:5-11. Those who argue that Chaldea is

---

http://scholar.csl.edu/ ma_th/10; Bomgaars, "Habakkuk," 9–10. I am giving less weight to the mention of Torah here than Johnson and Watts, both of whom see the numbness as an intrinsic weakness in Torah. However true that may be theologically, I do not see any evidence that this is Habakkuk's point. See the commentary below for further discussion. Rikki E. Watts, "'For I Am Not Ashamed of the Gospel': Romans 1:16-17 and Habakkuk 2:4," in *Romans and the People of God*, ed. Sven K. Soderlund and N.T. Wright (Grand Rapids: Eerdmans, 1999); Johnson, "The Paralysis of Torah in Habakkuk 1."

[12] HALOT notes the English idiom, the rest of the analysis is my own.Ludwig Koehler et al., *The Hebrew and Aramaic Lexicon of the Old Testament*, electronic ed. (Leiden; New York: Brill, 1999), 1418.

[13] Cf. Bomgaars, "Habakkuk," 9.

referred to in both these sections suggest that verses 5-11 are a quotation, yet there is no indication in the text that this is the case. The immediate change in speaker, from addressing God to a command towards God's people, suggests, rather, an interruption. Habakkuk is mid-prayer when God breaks in with the answer he has been asking for. God calls Habakkuk to look among the nations and see His deed (1:5), the answer He has prepared. It is objected that this cannot be God's answer: it would be against God's character to respond in this way.[14] Yet this objection ignores the fact that Habakkuk's response addresses this very issue of God's character (1:12-17). Furthermore, Habakkuk acknowledges in his response that Chaldea, for all their terror, is God's answer (12d-e). The astounded complaint by Habakkuk and the questions he asks in his response presuppose that 1:5-11 are in fact God's answer to his prayer. The theological tension here does not make this interpretation unlikely: it is this tension that drives the rest of the book.[15]

Third, building on our previous point, the whole flow of the book's argument requires part of Judah to be the group complained against in 1:1-4. This point will be unpacked below, but a few key details can be brought up here to establish this. To begin with, 2:2-4 differentiates the wicked and righteous among God's covenant people. On the basis of their response to God's vision, these two are demarcated. This division explains why, in 1:13d-e, Habakkuk does not complain about the wicked swallowing the righteous: he complains instead about the wicked swallowing up those *more righteous* than they are. That is, Habakkuk's complaint is not that the Chaldeans are raised for a rebuke of a righteous people but that God is using a pagan, wicked nation to judge a wicked nation that is in covenant with Himself. This finds further support in the transition between 2:4 and 5: Habakkuk's use of a lesser to the greater argument means that the gluttonous wicked in 2:2-4 are different—and of a lesser degree of wickedness—than the gluttonous Chaldeans of 2:5ff.

Turning at last to chapter 3, we find the most significant support for seeing those in 1:1-4 as the wicked Judahites. In this chapter—against most commentators—we do not read of God judging the Chaldeans: we find in Habakkuk's song a celebration of God's use of His anointed, of the Chaldean, to bring salvation to Judah by crushing its wicked leadership (3:13-14). Among other features within this chapter, the fact that Habakkuk prays to God to show mercy in the midst of his deed (3:2, cf. 1:5) reveals that this is so. Habakkuk would not ask for mercy to be shown to the Chaldeans (cf.

---

[14] E.g. Cleaver-Bartholomew, "An Alternative Reading of Hab 1 and 2," 45.

[15] Cf. Bomgaars, "Habakkuk," 10.

1:12-17, 2:5-19), but he would seek it for his own people. Furthermore, the root פעל (p'l; deed) shows up three times in Habakkuk, twice in 1:5 (I am *doing* a *deed*) and once in 3:2 (your *deed*). This firmly links the deed Habakkuk asks to be made alive with the deed that God reveals in 1:5—the coming of the Chaldeans. Habakkuk is waiting patiently for "a people to attack" him (3:16): he waits for God to come for salvation with His anointed (3:13, 18). This is God's answer to the seeming lack of action Habakkuk complained about (1:2). Habakkuk sought salvation in light of the violence with which he was faced; God showed him that Chaldea was His salvific provision for the righteous of Judah. In the conclusion of the book, Habakkuk submits to this purpose and praises God for His salvific deed, wrought through the hand of His anointed (1:2, 1:5, 2:4, 3:13, 3:18-19).[16]

From these three points we can see that there are very good reasons to follow the classic interpretation: the wicked Judahite leadership are the concern in 1:1-4, and Chaldea is God's answer in 1:5-11 and throughout the book.[17] In my own study, I have found the reasons given above compelling, but more so has been the coherence and sense this reading makes of the entire book. This can only be seen by reading through the book itself; I trust that as we proceed on our expository journey, the explanatory power of this interpretation will become abundantly clear.

The Identity of the Vision

The second issue that needs be addressed regarding the outline I have given

---

[16] There is a sense of circularity involved in my argument above and that below: in citing evidence from the book itself, I am supporting my conclusions with interpretations of verses that presuppose them (one would not read 2:2-4 as a contrast between the wicked and righteous within Judah if he were convinced that only the righteous of Judah were involved). This should not be a concern, however: good exegetical argumentation will be inherently circular. An interpreter will use interpreted texts to support his or her interpretation.

[17] Cf. Theodore, *Commentary on the Twelve Prophets*, ed. Robert C. Hill, The Fathers of the Church: The Writings of Augustine 108 (Washington D.C.: Catholic University of America Press, 2004), 266, 270; Matthew Henry, *Matthew Henry's Commentary on the Whole Bible: Complete and Unabridged in One Volume* (Peabody, Mass.: Hendrickson, 1994), 1550; John Calvin, *Commentaries on the Twelve Minor Prophtes; Habakkuk, Zephaniah, Haggai, Zechariah, Malachi*, trans. John Owen, vol. 4, Calvin's Commentaries XV (Grand Rapids: Baker, 1996), XIV.

is the identity of the vision mentioned in 2:2-3. Contemporary commentaries are divided amongst themselves whether the vision should be identified as some portion of chapter two, often 2:4-5,[18] or with chapter 3.[19] Rarely is the vision identified with the contents of chapter 1, as I contend.[20] Despite the unanimous disagreement, I see no good reason to make the identifications these authors have and many reasons for identifying 1:5-11 as the vision. The most compelling reason for my interpretation is the sense it makes of the book—the overall coherent picture it paints—and so will be unpacked below in the notes. Here, I will identify three specific reasons for identifying the vision with 1:5-11: the content of 1:5-11, the function of the vision and 1:5-11 within the book, and function of the vision within 2:2-4 all identify it as the "vision."

First, the content of 5-11—of all the sections of Habakkuk—suggests that it is the vision. We can begin by considering its visual nature.[21] God

---

[18] Andersen identifies the vision with the woe oracles of 2:6-20, Bomgaars with 2:4-20, Calvin v. 4ff, Janzen 2:2-4, Johnson 2:2-5, Neufeld part of ch. 2, Nogalski 2:4-5, Patterson 2:4, Robertson 2:4-5, and Sweeney 2:4. Francis I. Andersen, ed., *Habakkuk: A New Translation with Introduction and Commentary*, 1st ed., Anchor Bible 25 (New York: Doubleday, 2001), 204; Bomgaars, "Habakkuk," 45–46; Calvin, *Commentaries on the Twelve Minor Prophtes; Habakkuk, Zephaniah, Haggai, Zechariah, Malachi*, 4:66; J. Gerald Janzen, "Habakkuk 2:2-4 in the Light of Recent Philological Advances," *Harvard Theological Review* 73 (1980): 76; Johnson, "The Paralysis of Torah in Habakkuk 1," 257; Neufeld, "An Exegetical and Theological Study of Habakkuk 2," 10–13; James D. Nogalski, *The Book of the Twelve: Micah-Malachi*, Smyth & Helwys Bible Commentary (Macon, Ga: Smyth & Helwys Publishing, 2011), 668; Patterson, *Nahum, Habakkuk, Zephaniah*, 171–172; Robertson, *The Books of Nahum, Habakkuk, and Zephaniah*, 168; Sweeney, "Structure, Genre, and Intent in the Book of Habakkuk," 71.

[19] Bruce identifies the vision with 3:3-16, Goldingay with God's coming in ch. 3. F. F. Bruce, "Habakkuk," in *The Minor Prophets: An Exegetical and Expository Commentary*, ed. Thomas Edward McComiskey (Grand Rapids: Baker Book House, 1992), 859; Goldingay and Scalise, *Minor Prophets II*, vii, 78.

[20] Cf. Henry, *Commentary on the Whole Bible*, 1360; Cleaver-Bartholomew, "An Alternative Reading of Hab 1 and 2."

[21] Though we translate חָזוֹן (ḥāzôn) as "vision," many rightly note that the content of a ḥāzôn does not have to be visual. As with many Hebrew words that refer to the sense of sight, it can also refer to a broad range of sensory experiences. It may be, at times, better-translated "revelation," that is, an audio or visual sensory experience given by God. Yet, there are times when it clearly retains the visual

breaks into Habakkuk's complaint and calls him to look! He is told to pay attention to what God is doing. God's speech does not end with a command but goes on to describe vividly the actions of the Chaldeans, those God is raising up. God's revelation itself functions to give the reader a view among the nations: He directs Habakkuk where he should look and paints for him the picture he should see. Furthermore, when we look at the command itself, we see that verses 5-11 are not directed narrowly to Habakkuk: he is included in the command, but it is addressed more widely.

To whom is it addressed? Because it describes YHWH's deed of raising up the Chaldeans in response to a righteous Judahites' prayers, the only plausible addressees for the command are the Judahites. This is exactly what we would expect if 1:5-11 were the vision. In fact, this is the only section of Habakkuk that is addressed to the people in general. We can add to this the interjectory nature of this unit: God breaks in and reveals something drastic to Habakkuk, the answer to His prayers. The interjectory force suggests an immediate, vivid, and vital revelation from God.

The last evidence we can draw from the nature of this passage is that it is the longest section where God speaks. It may be objected that 2:5-19 (the woe oracle) is longer, but this section has God putting the condemnation of Chaldea in the mouth of the nations (2:6). Chapter 3 is a psalm containing Habakkuk's description of God's arrival; it does not present Habakkuk as receiving or revealing a revelation from God. Therefore, we see from the nature of verses 1:5-11 that they are a perfect fit for the vision mentioned in 2:2-3.

Second, 1:5-11 is the turning point of the whole book. Though it appears at the beginning of Habakkuk, this unit is the reference point for all that follows. Consider the following: Habakkuk's complaint in 1:12-2:1 addresses the theological difficulties 1:5-11 seems to raise. 2:2-4 differentiates between the righteous and wicked of God's people on the basis of their response to this revelation. 2:5-20 details the judgment God will bring upon

---

sense (e.g. Dan 1:17, 9:21; Isa 29:7); most of the other occurrences are ambiguous. We should, therefore, be alert for visual revelation associated with this term but not confine it to this sense alone. Koehler et al., *HALOT*, 301; Francis Brown et al., *The Brown-Driver-Briggs Hebrew and English Lexicon* (Peabody: Hendrickson, 1996), 302; Patterson, *Nahum, Habakkuk, Zephaniah*, 173; Robert D. Culver, "Ḥāzâ," ed. R. Laird Harris, Archer Jr. Gleason L., and Bruce K. Waltke, *Theological Wordbook of the Old Testament* (Chicago: The Moody Bible Institute, 1980), 274–275.

those in 1:5-11, paralleling the ideas there (idolatry, transgression, gathering). And chapter 3 praises God for and unpacks His salvific action first revealed in 1:5-11. The vision mentioned in 2:2-4 is central to the book; the only section of the book that is equally central, and so qualifies as the vision, is 1:5-11.

Furthermore, when you read the text and arrive at word "vision" in 2:2, it seems as if it already has been given: there is no indication that Habakkuk for it to be its revealing only it's fulfillment.[22] 1:5-11 is exactly what we would expect for the vision God has given Habakkuk, and nothing else quite fits the bill. Someone might suggest that הִנֵּה (*hinnēh*, behold) in verse 4 signals the beginning of the prophecy, yet there is a better explanation for its function, as I argue in the notes below.

Third, the details of the vision given in 2:2-4 suggest that it is to be identified with 1:5-11. Our first consideration here is the nature of the vision as suggested by these verses. Some commentators identify the vision as good news of great joy—Babylon will fall (2:5-20, ch. 3) or the righteous will live (2:4)—yet there is no evidence in the context to suggest this.[23] One may appeal to verse 3: it is to be awaited, suggesting that the Judahites are to anticipate it. From this, it may be surmised that they are of course to await the destruction of Babylon, spoken of in 2:5-19. Yet, this misses the point of the book: the destruction of Babylon is an important vindication of God's justice but not the central theme. The answer to Habakkuk's prayer, the expected salvation for which he is to await, is God coming through Babylon to crush Judah. In 3:16, Habakkuk uses a synonym for the word translated "wait" in 2:3 to describe his waiting for "a people to attack us," which is God coming forth "for salvation with your anointed" (3:13)—here, Chaldea.

---

[22] It may be objected that there is no article on the vision, suggesting an indefinite vision, one not yet apprehended by Habakkuk's mind. It should be observed, in response, that most translations rightly identify it as definite. The reason for this is that the omission of the article is common in Hebrew poetry, of which much Hebrew prophecy consists (cf. 2:3, Ezek 7:13). Bruce K. Waltke and Michael Patrick O'Connor, *An Introduction to Hebrew Syntax* (Winona Lake, Ind.: Eisenbrauns, 1990), 250.

[23] For those who make such a claim, see e.g. Ebenezer Henderson, *The Twelve Minor Prophets* (Grand Rapids: Baker, 1980), 301; David W. Baker, *Nahum, Habakkuk and Zephaniah: An Introduction and Commentary*, Tyndale Old Testament Commentaries 27 (Nottingham; Downers Grove: Inter-Varsity Press; IVP Academic, 2009), 59.

Instead of joyous news, the vision is portrayed as one that will incite a bad response among the wicked Judahites: they will run,[24] respond impetuously, to God's revelation, thus revealing their crooked and bloated desires. But the righteous of Judah will live by faith, by trusting in God and His character and so waiting for the vision's fulfillment, despite the terror it invokes (2:2-4). This attitude of the righteous is perfectly expressed by Habakkuk in chapter 3, especially verses 16-19. We can add to this evidence that the only occurrence of the root אמן (*'mn*) other than "faith" in 2:4 is the description of God's act as unbelievable in 1:5. The righteous of Judah are to believe God even though they are faced with an unbelievable, terrifying vision of the Chaldeans: though rot may enter their bones in fear (3:16-17), they are to trust in God who is their strength (3:18-19).

The evidence we have so far seen shows that the vision spoken of in 2:2-3 is to be identified with the revelation of God's deed in 1:5-11. This reading coheres best with the book, the language employed, the flow of the argument, and with the contexts of both 2:2-3 and 1:5-11. I hope that the value of this identification will become even more clear as we see God's message to Habakkuk unpacked throughout the book

Canonical Position

So far we have been examining Habakkuk on its own, looking at its purpose, its themes, and its structure. Yet this is not sufficient information for an Biblical interpretation of Habakkuk. To achieve a biblically faithful interpretation and truly grasp the significance of Habakkuk for the Church today, we must turn our eyes beyond Habakkuk to consider its place in the completed body of Scriptures, the canon. In their significant work on Biblical Theology, Stephen J. Wellum and Peter J. Gentry identify three horizons, or contexts, that must be taken into account for any interpretation of Scripture.[25]

---

[24] On which, see the notes below.

[25] Cf. Peter J. Gentry and Stephen J. Wellum, *Kingdom Through Covenant: A Biblical-Theological Understanding of the Covenants* (Wheaton, Ill: Crossway, 2012), 92–93. It should be observed that all three of these "horizons" encompass the same ground, the entire Bible, but explain the function of the Bible in different ways. The *textual horizon* focuses on text and grammar, how the context of the Bible helps

We have spent our time so far addressing the first of these horizons, the textual horizon. With Edmund Clowney, we may identify the second horizon as the epochal horizon, that is, where the text is found in the context of God's redemptive historical plan.[26] The third horizon could be called the canonical horizon, the book considered in light of the whole Canon.[27] These horizons give us three necessary contexts in which we have to consider our book: we must first understand each verse of Habakkuk in light of the whole, asking how it contributes to the book and seeking answers to interpretive questions in the immediate context.

When considering the textual horizon of Habakkuk, I suggest that we must look beyond just the bounds of the book itself to the greater corpus in which it occurs. Considering Habakkuk, God has placed it in the Book of the Twelve (Minor Prophets), which is part of the Prophets—the second section of the Hebrew Bible. The Book of the Twelve will give us immediate textual and thematic clues for our interpretation of Habakkuk; the Prophets provides us with a thematic perspective on God's Covenant that can help us get our orientation for reading Habakkuk. That Habakkuk occurs in the Old Testament will lead us to read the book not in light of the New Covenant in Christ but the Abrahamic, Mosaic (or Sinaitic), and Davidic covenants and their promises—all which look forward to the coming of Christ in the New Testament.

Turning from the textual context, we have the Epochal horizon to consider. There is significant overlap between what I have included under the textual horizon above and what we will consider here. The difference could be identified as a synchronic versus diachronic emphasis. Considering the textual horizon of the Twelve and the Prophets, we are not so much

---

us interpret the words and sentences on the page. The *epochal horizon* considers the metanarrative or story told by the Bible and the place of a text within it. The *canonical horizon* asks how the teaching of the rest of Scripture informs our application or use of the text in question.

[26] Referenced in Richard Lints, *The Fabric of Theology: A Prolegomenon to Evangelical Theology* (Grand Rapids: Eerdmans, 1993), 293.

[27] These last two horizons correspond to Sailhamer's diachronic (reading through time) and synchronic (reading all together) approaches to Old Testament theology. By the *Canon*, I refer to the books that form the protestant Bible. *Canon* is then a synonym with *Scripture* and *Bible*, but it emphasizes the parts that make up the whole. By using the word *Canon*, I also emphasize the shape of the Bible—the order of the parts. Gentry and Wellum, *Kingdom Through Covenant*, 97–100; John H. Sailhamer, *Introduction to Old Testament Theology: A Canonical Approach* (Grand Rapids: Zondervan, 1995), 184–196.

considering the storyline unpacked across these books but thematic and linguistic parallels that shed light on our reading. Considering the Epochal horizon, we look to the unfolding of God's redemptive story.

We do not consider Habakkuk merely as part of the Old Testament, but as a book that takes place during the critical time of God's judgment upon Israel and Judah for their apostasy. Thus we detect the curses of Deuteronomy 28-29 in the prophetic literature, God's righteous justice poured out against His sinful people. We understand the judgment of Israel not as a general act of God's providence among the nations but as a specific act of judgment for covenant disobedience. Reading in this way will raise important biblical theological questions, questions that are dealt with in the New Testament.

The last horizon we must consider is that of the Canon as a whole. This context is often considered in systematic theology—taking into account all God's revelation as it pertains to a specific subject—and is invaluable and necessary for our exegesis as well. Gentry and Wellum emphasize the importance of this oft-neglected horizon, writing,

> We cannot adequately interpret and apply Scripture if we ignore the canonical level.… In fact, to read the Bible canonically is not merely a matter of how the church has read Scripture, it best corresponds to what the bible actually is. That is why, "To read the Bible as unified Scripture is not just one interpretative interest among others, but the interpretative strategy that best corresponds to the nature of the text itself, given its divine inspiration."[28]

A discussion of the canonical horizon of Scripture could span dozens of pages, yet here I hope only to consider some of the ways we must read Habakkuk—all the Bible—canonically. Protestants have long recognized the need to employ the analogy of faith, that is, to interpret all Scripture by Scripture.[29] If God is wise and true, and all Scripture is authored by Him,

---

[28] Quoting Kevin J. Vanhoozer, Gentry and Wellum, *Kingdom Through Covenant*, 99.

[29] The analogy of faith is often called "the analogy of Scripture" in order to distinguish this phrase the Roman Catholic epistemological method of the same name. Goldsworthy, *Gospel-Centered Hermeneutics*, 117–118. Cf. Rutherford, *The Gift of Reading - Part 2*.

then it follows that all Scripture will speak a coherent message, a message free from contradiction and deceit: it will all be useful (Psalm 119; Prov 30:5-6; John 17:17; 2 Tim 3:16-17; 2 Pet 1:20-21).[30] A canonical reading of Scripture means that, minimally, we will not read scripture in contradiction with other Scripture—at least as interpreted within its Epochal Horizon.[31] A canonical reading of Scripture will also make use of the themes of the rest of Scripture to shed light on the application of specific passage to our present day.[32] Lastly, a canonical reading will take into account intertextuality and turn to the rest of the Bible as the best resource God has provided for solving the problems presented by difficult texts. Taking into account intertextuality, we will see how the rest of Scripture has shaped Habakkuk, how allusions to it and its use of allusion illumine our reading.

More significantly, we will consider the New Testament uses of the Old Testament, understood within their own context, and use this as a tool for better understanding how God would have us to read and understand His Scriptures. When interpreting difficult texts, a canonical reading will acknowledge that the best resource we have is Scripture itself. For example,

---

[30] The doctrine of Scripture, so essential to the Christian faith, is under intense attack today. Here are a few recent volumes worth consulting that defend the authority, unity, and truthfulness of God's word:,John M. Frame, *The Doctrine of the Word of God*, A Theology of Lordship (Phillipsburg: P&R Publishing, 2010); D. A. Carson and John D. Woodbridge, eds., *Hermeneutics, Authority, and Canon* (Grand Rapids: Academie Books, 1986); D. A. Carson and John D. Woodbridge, eds., *Scripture and Truth* (Grand Rapids: Baker Book House, 1992); John D. Woodbridge, *Biblical Authority: A Critique of the Rogers/McKim Proposal* (Grand Rapids: Zondervan, 1982). Cf. J. Alexander Rutherford, *The Gift of Knowing: A Biblical Perspective on Knowing and Truth*, God's Gifts for the Christian Life Part 1 Vol. 1 (Vancouver: Teleioteti, 2019).

[31] Though Scripture is free from contradiction — saying something is true when elsewhere, it is said to be false—it is not free from tension, especially as introduced through progressive revelation. There is a tension within the Old Testament between works and faith that is only finally resolved in the New Testament; this tension is not a contradiction but an intentional feature God has written into His progressive revelation, leading us ever towards Christ even when He is not explicitly mentioned in the Old Testament. In my master's thesis on Samuel, I gave referred to such tensions as *prophetic expectation*. J. Alexander Rutherford, *God's Kingdom Through His Priest-King: An Analysis of the Book of Samuel in the Light of the Davidic Covenant* (Vancouver; Teleioteti, 2019), 82-83.

[32] For a discussion of "application" and "meaning," see Rutherford, *The Gift of Reading - Part 1*; Rutherford, *The Gift of Reading - Part 2*.

the entire Canon provides us various uses of different word roots to help ascertain the meaning of hapax legomenon (words occurring only once in Scripture) and rare words; the Canon also contains many texts with similar themes to shed light on obscure texts (e.g. reading Genesis 15 with Jer 34:18-19). Scripture also provides us with allusions and quotations in the New Testament that help us to interpret Old Testament texts in light of the coming of Jesus.

With a view to these three horizons, we will now consider Habakkuk in the context of the larger story of Scripture, in the textual horizon of the Prophets, in the textual horizon of the Twelve, and we will consider the four quotations of Habakkuk in the New Testament.

The Prophets

It goes without saying that Habakkuk can be found in the Old Testament, but what is not so clear for readers of the English Bible is Habakkuk's place in one of the three divisions of the Hebrew Bible. From early in the formation of the Hebrew Bible, three groupings of books were recognized. These were known as the Law (*Torah*), the Prophets (*Nevi'im*), and the Writings (*Ketuvim*). Many of those seeking to read the bible canonically recognize that these groups are significant for interpretation and have biblical precedence (e.g. Luke 24:20), over against the orders of the Septuagint and most English bibles, which adopt a more logical ordering of the Biblical books.[33]

---

[33] Now, this does not mean that the order of the Septuagint or of English bibles are not helpful but that they do not have the same precedence, and so interpretive priority, as the Hebrew order. See further Rutherford, *The Gift of Reading - Part 1*; Rutherford, *The Gift of Reading - Part 2*. John Sailhamer employs the analogy of a film montage to explain how all the different orders of the Old Testament (Rabbinic, MT, English, LXX, etc.) contribute to interpretation. By juxtaposing different books, each order draws the reader's attention to different features of the text.

Noteworthy in identifying the canon of the OT by the time of the New Testament is the prologue of Ben Sirach (c. 2nd cent. BC), which speaks of the Law, the Prophets, and the other books. A similar reference is found in Josephus, *Against Apion* 1.40. Jesus in Luke 24:44 identifies the Old Testament as the Law, Prophets, and Psalms; Qumran 4QMMTC, line 10, says similarly, "the book of Moses [and] the book[s of the pr]ophets and Davi[d…]." Flavius Josephus, "Against Apion," in *The Works of Josephus: Complete and Unabridged*, trans. William Whiston (Peabody, Mass.: Hendrickson, 1987); Florentino García Martínez and Eibert J. C. Tigchelaar, *The Dead Sea Scrolls Study Edition (Translations)*, vol. 2, 2 vols. (Leiden; New York:

Though there are historical reasons for making this decision, what are most important are the internal clues found in the Bible that suggest this. We can observe the way the New Testament refers to the Old. There is a consistent pattern in the New Testament in which the Old Testament is summarized as the "Law" or the "Law and the Prophets" (Matt 5:17, 7:12, 11:13, 22:40; Luke 16:16; John 1:45; Acts 13:15, 24:14, 28:23; Rom 3:21), using the first or first two groupings as a synecdoche for all three of the divisions found in the Hebrew Canon. In one key instance, when Jesus speaks of the whole of Scripture pointing to Himself, he speaks of "the Law of Moses and the Prophets and the Psalms" (Luke 24:44), referring to this trifold division.

Considering these three divisions, all three overlap to some extent in the types of literature of which they are made—e.g. historical narratives—but are distinguished by their predominant text type. For the Torah, there is a large quantity of legal material, the foundation of the covenant: these legal

---

Brill, 1997).

There many resources that discuss what we should make of the Canon and its order; I have found Miles Van Pelt's work most illuminating. In my critical review of Stephen Dempster's *Dominion and* Dynasty, I summarize some of the external and internal evidence for the tripartite OT Canon. J. Alexander Rutherford, "A Critical Review of Stephen Dempster's Dominion and Dynasty" (Teleioteti, 2017), accessed January 23, 2018, https://teleioteti.ca/2017/10/13/a-critical-review-of-dempsters-dominion-and-dynasty/. Cf. Roger T. Beckwith, *The Old Testament Canon of the New Testament Church and Its Background in Early Judaism* (Grand Rapids: Eerdmans, 1986); Stephen G. Dempster, "An 'Extraordinary Fact': Torah and Temple and the Contours of the Hebrew Canon Part 2," *Tyndale Bulletin* 48, no. 2 (1997): 191–218; Stephen G. Dempster, "An 'Extraordinary Fact': Torah and Temple and the Contours of the Hebrew Canon Part 1," *Tyndale Bulletin* 48, no. 1 (1997): 23–56; Stephen G. Dempster, "From Many Texts to One: The Formation of the Hebrew Bible," in *The World of the Aramaeans*, ed. P. M. Michèle Daviau et al., Journal for the Study of the Old Testament 324–326 (Sheffield: Sheffield Academic Press, 2001); Stephen G. Dempster, "The Prophets, the Canon and a Canonical Approach: No Empty Word," in *Canon and Biblical Interpretation*, ed. Craig G. Bartholomew et al., Scripture and Hermeneutics Series v. 7 (Grand Rapids: Zondervan, 2006), 303–311; David G. Dunbar, "The Biblical Canon," in *Hermeneutics, Authority, and Canon*, ed. D. A. Carson and John D. Woodbridge (Grand Rapids: Academie Books, 1986); Gentry and Wellum, *Kingdom Through Covenant*, 135–139; Sailhamer, *Introduction to Old Testament Theology*, 213; Miles Van Pelt, *A Biblical-Theological Introduction to the Old Testament: The Gospel Promised*, ed. Miles Van Pelt (Wheaton: Crossway, 2016), 24–41.

provisions are especially dominant the later four books. In the prophets, the primary text-type is prophecy; for the writings, it is poetic literature.[34]

Each section shows a further thematic consistency: Van Pelt has describe the thematic consistency of each section by the way it addresses Israel as God's covenant people. He describes the three sections of the Old Testament as the Covenant (The Law), Covenant History (the Prophets), and Covenant Life (Writings).[35] According to this schema, the Law lays out the covenant, with its regulations, expectations, and its accompanying blessings and curses. The prophets take a theological/historical approach to the Covenant.

The Prophets describe Israel's failure to keep their side of the covenant, explaining the curses that fall upon them. The Prophets also demonstrate God's faithful actions and character on display, in doing so they also point Israel back to the blessings, showing the hope of God's future action on their behalf and calling for repentance in light of God's relationship with them. This emphasis is seen in both the historical narratives, which constantly evaluate the behaviour of the kings and the people in terms of the covenant, and in the books of prophecy, which often speak on behalf of God to bring charges of covenant breaking against Israel.

The Writings give guidance on life within the covenant: through wisdom, poetry, and narratives, the books show what living in covenant with God should look like. The narratives in this section embody this same emphasis; Chronicles, for example, frequently connects the successes of the kings of Judah with their faithfulness to God and their downfalls with their disobedience. This demonstrates God's faithfulness to His promises and His righteous character while showing the reader the best way to govern his or her life, according to the commandments of God (the explicit link between righteousness and blessing and wickedness and curse in this book strongly echoes the theology of The Proverbs).

Habakkuk, as we have seen, falls among the Prophets; as such, it fits well as part of a "Covenant History." In Habakkuk, we read of God raising the Babylonians to judge Judah. In Habakkuk we are given an unusual

---

[34] Drawing on the discussion in my books *The Gift of Reading – Part 1 & Part 2*, we could also say that each section has a distinguishing literary style. The Law has the largest quantity of literature written in didactic prose; the Prophets contain the majority of the Old Testament texts written in prophetic style; and the Writings contains the majority of texts composed in poetic style. Narrative texts are found in all three sections of the Old Testament.

[35] Van Pelt, *A Biblical-Theological Introduction to the Old Testament: The Gospel Promised*, 40.

perspective on this judgment. In the Major Prophets, God sends his prophets to the leaders of Judah and Israel to bring a covenant lawsuit against their flagrant sins against Him and to call them to repentance. The Major Prophets focus on these interactions; however, in Habakkuk the leadership of Judah are present but are not those to whom Habakkuk is sent.

The book of Habakkuk focuses on one prophet's intercession for his people, on his prayers for God to act and God's response. The Chaldeans are seen, in a shocking manner, not primarily as the tools of God's justice but as tools of God's salvation for the remnant of His people. We are, therefore, given a complementary yet radical perspective on God's work as a supplement to that recorded in the rest of the Prophets.

Furthermore, in the Major Prophets and many of the Minor Prophets, hope is found either in a call for repentance or the promise of God's future act to establish a New Covenant. Habakkuk's focus, in contrast, is much more immanent: he considers the hope for the righteous of Judah in this moment of crisis. His focus is individualistic: in this, he anticipates New Testament doctrine—though without explicitly introducing the Messiah and His centrality.

We can summarize Habakkuk's contribution to the Prophets as an individualistic look on the corporate crisis that is God's judgment of His covenant people. From the perspective of the righteous, the coming of Chaldea is to be seen as God's salvation. This righteous remnant of Judah are also shown that their salvation is not the result rigorous law keeping: their life before God is dependent on faith in Him. The rest of the prophets help us in our interpretation of Habakkuk by juxtaposing this picture with their emphases on judgment and the indictment of the wicked of Judah. There is also a great deal of intertextuality between Jeremiah, Isaiah, and Habakkuk that gives us insights into their shared picture of God's sovereign action among the nations.

The Twelve

Turning from the larger division of the Prophets, we next need to look at Habakkuk in the context of the Book of the Twelve (the Minor Prophets). Before considering the contribution this context makes to our interpretation, let us briefly consider what is meant by "the Book of the Twelve." It has long been recognized that the 12 Minor Prophets are closely linked, at the very least thematically united.³⁶

There has been much interest recently on this unity, with many papers and books being written on the subject. Many interpreters have argued that the books making up the Minor Prophets share not only a history of transmission (they were not just copied and transmitted together) but a thematic unity and plot that justifies considering them, in their present context in the Biblical canon, as a single book. That such unity exists has been demonstrated convincingly on both internal and external grounds.³⁷ To be sure, this position has its critics, but they have failed to give a sufficient reason why we should not read the Twelve together.³⁸

David L. Peterson argues that labeling the Twelve a "book" does not quite describe what we find there, "anthology" is more appropriate. An anthology brings together different works that are united by a theme but does

---

³⁶ An example is the existence of commentaries on the twelve since the early church, e.g. Theodore, *Commentary on the Twelve Prophets*.

³⁷ Some evidence adduced, along with thematic unity, include the consistent unity of the twelve in ancient manuscripts and the literary ties between the books—such as the close relationship between Amos 9 and Obadiah and the parallels between Joel 4:1, 18 and Amos 1:2, 9:13. These relationships are most evident in the order of the Masoretic Text, the priority of which the manuscript evidence supports (see Fuller). James D. Nogalski, "Book of the Twelve," in *The New Interpreter's Dictionary of the Bible: A-C*, vol. 1 (Nashville: Abingdon Press, 2006), esp. 489; Marvin A. Sweeney, "Sequence and Interpretation in the Book of the Twelve," in *Reading and Hearing the Book of the Twelve*, ed. James Nogalski and Marvin A. Sweeney, SBL Symposium Series no. 15 (Atlanta, Ga.: Society of Biblical Literature, 2000); Paul R. House, *The Unity of the Twelve*, ed. David J.A. Clines and Philip R. Davies, Bible and Literature 27 (Sheffield, England: The Almond Press, 1990); Russell Fuller, "The Form and Formation of the Book of the Twelve: The Evidence from the Judean Desert," in *Forming Prophetic Literature: Essays on Isaiah and the Twelve in Honor of John D.W. Watts*, ed. James W. Watts and Paul R. House, Journal for the Study of the Old Testament Supplement 235 (Sheffield, England: Sheffield Academic Press, 1996), 86–101.

Against the Jamnia hypothesis and the late formation of the Hebrew Canon, which would cast doubt on a unified reading in the NT, see Dunbar, "The Biblical Canon," 299–315.

³⁸ This does not necessarily mean, and it is probably not the case, that each book was originally written to be read together. But, either under the providential hand of God or by the hand of a redactor led by His Spirit, it so happens that these 12 books as we have them in our Canon are to be read as a single unit. Together they say something more than each one on its own.

not give them a meaningful order. A book, on the other hand, is made up of parts that work together in such a way that their relationship to one another, particularly their order, is significant for interpreting the work.. There is a greater level of unity in a book and it is most effective when read in a linear manner (in order), whereas an anthology says as much read out of order as when read in order. Neither description is quite appropriate for The Twelve, for each book is certainly self-contained yet there is a meaningful pattern in the composition of the Twelve. If we picture a sliding scale with an anthology on one hand and a book on the other, The Twelve is somewhere near the centre.

Paul R. House argues that a plot is unfolded across these twelve books.[39] This author thinks it is untenable to speak of a "plot" without any form of narrative structure or unifying narrator and that the categories which House employs are not legitimately applicable,[40] but we can learn something from his analysis. House's analysis demonstrates that the Twelve work together to unpack the three characteristic themes of the Prophets, namely, *indictment*, *judgment*, and *redemption*. House identifies in each of the Twelve a focus on one of these themes, and argues that the Twelve can be broken into several groups that focus on one of these themes. Countering House's argument, Ehud Ben Zvi argues that this analysis fails to account for the many overlapping themes in each book. But, in response to this criticism, it is important to observe that House does not deny this. House argues that each book contains the themes unpacked across the whole, but focuses on one of these; it is these central themes in each book that contributes to the message of The Twelve.

Considering The Twelve as a united work, we need to consider how The Twelve functions as the context for Habakkuk. Taken alongside those essays arguing for thematic threads uniting the Twelve,[41] House's exposition of

---

[39] House, *The Unity of the Twelve*, 114; Ehud Ben Zvi, "Twelve Prophetic Books or 'The Twelve': A Few Preliminary Considerations," in *Forming Prophetic Literature: Essays on Isaiah and the Twelve in Honor of John D.W. Watts*, ed. James W. Watts and Paul R. House, Journal for the Study of the Old Testament Supplement 235 (Sheffield, England: Sheffield Academic Press, 1996), 125–156; David L. Peterson, "A Book of the Twelve," in *Reading and Hearing the Book of the Twelve*, ed. James Nogalski and Marvin A. Sweeney, SBL Symposium Series no. 15 (Atlanta, Ga.: Society of Biblical Literature, 2000).

[40] Cf. Rutherford, *The Gift of Reading - Part 2*, chap. 4.

[41] Alongside House's *The Unity*, see James D. Nogalski, "The Day(s) of

major themes developed throughout the Twelve is helpful. What we have in the Twelve is a 12-part reflection upon the prophetic themes found in the Major Prophets. Every book is a microcosm of the whole and contributes through its main theme to the whole work. Like the covenant lawsuits found in the Major Prophets, Hosea-Micah presents an indictment against the sins of God's people and the nations around them. Nahum-Zephaniah then expounds God's response in judgment against Israel, Judah, and the nations. Finally, Haggai-Malachi picks up the theme of restoration found throughout the previous nine books, foretelling God's salvific action towards Israel and the nations.[42]

Following Nahum's presentation of the fate of any unrepentant nation, Habakkuk picks up the expectation that God will judge his covenant people.[43] We see in Habakkuk that God will not only bring terrible judgment upon Judah but will also bring the unrighteous nation He uses as His tool to justice. However, the focus remains on the covenant people. This greater context sheds light on our interpretation of Habakkuk in a few ways. The context of Habakkuk in the Book of the Twelve presupposes the gross sins of God's people expounded in the earlier books: they are guilty of spiritual adultery (Hosea), injustice and oppression (Amos),[44] and neglecting their duty as God's chosen instrument of mercy to the gentiles (Jonah, cf. Gen. 12:2-3). The reader of Habakkuk in its canonical context need not go far to find an explanation of the injustice decried in its early verses (esp. 1:4). Therefore, the greater canonical context supports the identification of those in verses 1-4 as leaders of Judah. In fact, this context should lead someone reading

---

YHWH in the Book of the Twelve," in *Thematic Threads in the Book of the Twelve*, ed. Paul L. Redditt and Aaron Schart (Berlin, Germany: Walter de Gruyter GmbH & Co., 2003), 192–213; Paul R. House, "The Character of God in the Book of the Twelve," in *Reading and Hearing the Book of the Twelve*, ed. James Nogalski and Marvin A. Sweeney, SBL Symposium Series no. 15 (Atlanta, Ga.: Society of Biblical Literature, 2000); Rolf Rendtorff, "How to Read the Book of the Twelve as a Theological Unity," in *Reading and Hearing the Book of the Twelve*, ed. James Nogalski and Marvin A. Sweeney, SBL symposium series no. 15 (Atlanta, Ga.: Society of Biblical Literature, 2000); James D. Nogalski, "Guest Editorial: Reading the Book of the Twelve Theologically," *Interpretation* 61, no. 2 (2007): 115.

[42] House, *The Unity of the Twelve*, 74–109.

[43] Ibid., 91.

[44] Ibid., 80–81. Specifically relevant here is the use of שֹׁד (destruction) and חָמָס (violence) in Amos 3:10 to refer to the leaders of Israel, cf. Hab 1:3.

Habakkuk in the context of the Twelve to immediately make this connection. Furthermore, the covenantal themes running throughout the Twelve give us some insight into what the phrase "the righteous one shall live" means (Hab 2:4, cf. Hos 6:2, 14:4-7; Amos 5:14-15). The language itself, especially taken with these covenantal themes, suggests that "live" is not just enjoying deliverance from oppression but the fullness of covenant life with God and the blessings a right covenant standing brings.[45] There are many more insights that reading Habakkuk within the Twelve reveal; many of the essays cited above discuss these. I will integrate the insights of such a canonical reading in the notes below, but there admittedly remains a lot of work to be done among Biblically-faithful Christians in this area.

The Larger Story

Having considered the textual horizons for interpreting Habakkuk, we must now turn to the Epochal Horizon. Among reformed theologians, it has been common to summarize human history, and the Biblical story interpreting it, as consisting of four main points: Creation, Fall, Redemption, and Consummation. Modifying this, I would suggest that a fivefold division is more appropriate: Creation, Fall, Redemption Initiated, Redemption Accomplished, Redemption Consummated.[46] The biblical storyline, often called redemptive-history, begins with Creation and Fall, but focuses mostly on the three stages of Redemption. Redemption can be described as the enacting of God's plan to save His creation from the curse and a people for His son through the coming of His kingdom in Jesus Christ, beginning with the patriarchs and Israel, coming to a climax in Christ, and reaching its full realization at Christ's return.[47] Though these points in the story are fairly

---

[45] Though I have not found a discussion of this in works on Habakkuk, Doug Moo takes notice of this. He writes, "The verb occurs sixteen times [in the Twelve], and, apart from places where it refers simply to 'living beings," most of the occurrences refer to 'true life,' 'life before God,' 'blessing' (Hos 6:2, 14:7; Amos 5:4, 6, 14; Zech 10:9 KJV, NASB…)." Douglas J. Moo, *Galatians*, Baker Exegetical Commentary on the New Testament (Grand Rapids: Baker Academic, 2013), 220.

[46] Brad Copp first suggested to me dividing Redemption into two stages, so as to emphasize the definitive position Christ's incarnation has in history.

[47] This of course could be unpacked further: who are His covenant people? Beginning with Abraham, Israel becomes His people and then the scope of redemption is expanded to all tribes, tongues, and nations with the coming of the

obvious, there is more debate over the way the Bible tells this story: is there a structure to Scripture's presentation of redemption, if so, what is it? I agree with the substance of the proposal given by Gentry and Wellum, to which they have given the name Progressive Covenantalism. Striking a *via media* between Covenant Theology and Dispensationalism, they describe the biblical storyline as God's kingdom coming through the biblical covenants.[48]

Unpacking this a bit, the story or metanarrative recounted in Scripture is structured around God's covenants, official relationships inaugurated by God with His creatures. In the beginning, God entered into a covenant with creation, with man as the representative over all of it.[49] This covenant is then re-affirmed with Noah. These covenants provide the overall framework of God's relationship with man, but beginning with Abraham, God enters into a more restrictive covenant relationship with a certain people whom He is redeeming. Building upon the promises made to Abraham, God enters into a covenant with all the descendants of Jacob at Sinai, giving the Law. In the Prophets, we read of God entering into a covenant with David and his descendants: they are to be His representatives ruling over His people Israel, but ultimately one of David's descendants is to rule over all the creation. All these covenants find their culmination in Jesus Christ through the New Covenant instituted in His blood. These covenants drive the storyline of Scripture forward, introducing key themes and promises that reach their climax in the coming of God's kingdom through Jesus.[50] Christ is at the

---

New Covenant in Christ's blood. The way the kingdom comes and its nature under the Old Covenant and the New Covenant deserves exploration, but this is beyond the scope of our purpose here.

[48] 594, passim. Cf. Dempster, "From Many Texts to One: The Formation of the Hebrew Bible."

[49] This covenant is debated, see further W. J. Dumbrell, *Covenant and Creation: A Theology of Old Testament Covenants* (Exeter, Devon; New South Wales: Paternoster; Lancer Books, 1984), 11–46; Gentry and Wellum, *Kingdom Through Covenant*, 147–221; Meredith G. Kline, "Kingdom Prologue," 1993, 10–14; Bruce K. Waltke and Charles Yu, *An Old Testament Theology: An Exegetical, Canonical, and Thematic Approach*, 1st ed. (Grand Rapids: Zondervan, 2007), 259–260; Paul R. Williamson, *Sealed with an Oath: Covenant in God's Unfolding Purpose*, New Studies in Biblical Theology 23 (Downers Grove: Apollos/InterVarsity Press, 2007), 44–58; P.R. Williamson, "Covenant," ed. T. Desmond Alexander and Brian S. Rosner, *New Dictionary of Biblical Theology* (Leicester; Downers Grove: Inter-Varsity Press, 2000).

[50] We may consider at this point how "dispensations" relate to God's covenants. Whereas "covenant" focuses on the relationship between God and

centre of the whole Bible: the kingdom of God finally arrives with Christ as its head and all the covenants find their end in Him (e.g. 2 Cor 1:20). His second coming will be the consummation of this creation and will signal the beginning of the new creation and the fulfillment of God's plan. All that I have been able to sketch here is a brief overview of the biblical storyline and its structure; the resources cited in this section contain a far more in depth look at this story line.[51] What we have here should suffice for our consideration of Habakkuk's role.

How then does Habakkuk fit into this redemptive-history: what role does it play? It is clear that Habakkuk falls into the epoch of this story in which we see God relating to and working out His redemption with His people through the covenant made at Sinai. We find this covenant and its expectations expounded in the Torah, the first five books of the Hebrew Bible. As we saw above, the Prophets provide God's interpretation of Israel's history in terms of its covenants and look forward to God's future work in a New Covenant. As it concerns the interpretation of history, Habakkuk with the other Prophets affirms God's sovereign work among the nations. Habakkuk shows that the coming of Chaldea is not an accidental occurrence of history, but the work of God's hand. Looking among the nations, it is God who did this deed: He is the one who raised them up (1:5-6).

As observed above, Habakkuk also gives a unique perspective on Chaldea's attack: yes, Chaldea was raised for justice and a rebuke (1:12), but it is also God's means of salvation for an oppressed remnant (1:5; 2:4; 3:2, 13, 17-19). Habakkuk, in addition, affirms that God will bring judgment upon Chaldea for their savagery: the violence they have wrought will come back upon their head (2:8, 17); their debt will be collected from their skin (2:7); they themselves will drink the cup in the Lord's hand (2:16).

---

another party, "dispensation" focuses on the way God governs and relates to the world on the basis of the relationship found in the covenants. Covenant and dispensation are not contradictory concepts, though the interpretations of each provided by Covenant Theology and Dispensationalism are. Within the position above, dispensations could be viewed as a complementary perspective on God's covenants, looking at them from the angle of God's government as opposed to the relationship and its obligations. See further, Craig A. Blaising and Darrell L. Bock, *Progressive Dispensationalism* (Grand Rapids: Bridgepoint Books, 2000), 16; Vern S. Poythress, *Understanding Dispensationalists*, 2nd ed. (Phillipsburg: Presbyterian and Reformed, 1994), 10; Gentry and Wellum, *Kingdom Through Covenant*, 39–80.

[51] Cf. J. Alexander Rutherford, *The Gift of Reading – Part 1: Reading the Bible in Submission to God* (Vancouver: Teleioteti, 2019).

The Major Prophets, in speaking of the desolation wrought by God, nevertheless interject hope, especially by looking to the institution of a New Covenant. In this, all of the Prophets look forward to the coming of the Messiah. Another contribution the Prophets make as a whole is to prepare the way for Jesus by laying bare the tension at the heart of God's covenants with man. Following the story of the Pentateuch, we are struck by the continual failure of God's covenant people: Adam, Noah, Abraham, and Israel each fail their obligations to be loyal and perfect covenant partners (Genesis 3, 9:21-28, 12:17). Yet God has promised to give Abraham's descendants the land of promise, to make his descendants as numerous as the sand of the seashore and to be their Covenant God. God has promised this, yet these blessings rest on the perfect obedience of Israel (Exodus 6, 15:25-26, 19:5-6; 23:23-33; Leviticus 26; Deut 3:26, 4:1-14, 25-26, 29-31, 40, 5:23-33, 8:19-20, etc.). As the Prophets show, this obedience is something that Israel is unable to provide. How then will God fulfill His promises to Abraham?

The Major Prophets provide a small clue: in Isaiah, Jeremiah, and Ezekiel the promise of Deuteronomy 30—that God will circumcise the hearts of His people so that they will believe—is reintroduced.[52] There will come a day when God will make a new covenant, a covenant where all His people are enabled to believe and will know Him (Jeremiah 31, Ezek 36:22-37:28, Isaiah 54). The Major Prophets look to a change in the very nature of the community of God's covenant people—in that day "all your children will be taught of God," "no longer shall each teach his neighbor and each his brother saying, 'Know the Lord,' for they shall all know me" (Isa 54:13, Jer 31:34). That is, every person will be a believer in the New Testament sense, in positive covenant relationship—no longer will the true people of God only be a remnant (as in 1 Kgs 19:18, Isa 10:22).

Habakkuk approaches the question of righteousness and covenant life under the Old Covenant directly, looking to faith not covenant obedience as the source of right covenant relationship with God. As we will see in the discussion of the New Testament's use of Habakkuk, the New Testament cites Habakkuk for this very reason: it is the only place after the Law was given where faith is said to be the means by which God's people will live before Him (before the Law, Gen 15:6ff). Habakkuk, in contrast with Major Prophets, does not directly look to the New Covenant; instead, he speaks of

---

[52] See the first chapter and appendix of my book *Prevenient Grace*. J. Alexander Rutherford, *Prevenient Grace: An Investigation into Arminianism* (Vancouver: Teleioteti, 2016).

the nature of the remnant, what makes them righteous and why they live before God while the rest of Israel faces judgment. Instead of speaking of the right living of the righteous, of their obedience, he speaks instead of their faith.[53] God through Habakkuk does not tell the readers of the book, "You shall therefore keep my statutes and my rules; if a person does them, he shall live by them: I am the LORD" (Lev 18:5). Instead, alluding to Genesis 15:6, Habakkuk writes, "but the righteous one shall live by faith."

Some Rabbis identified faith here as the fulfillment of God's statutes and rules,[54] but there is no indication of this in Scripture. These Rabbis saw the law being made easy, reduced to faith as the only requirement; yet when the New Covenant arrives, God's standard is only intensified, not reduced. No longer is it "You shall not murder" (Exod 20:13) but, "I say to you that everyone who is angry with his brother will be liable to judgment" (Matt 5:22). "You shall therefore be holy, for I am holy" becomes "You therefore must be perfect, as your heavenly Father is perfect" (Lev 11:45; Matt 5:48). If Habakkuk is not reducing the demands of the Law to faith, as the Rabbi's believed, then we must identify what God through Habakkuk is saying. I identified earlier a tension in Scripture between God's promises and Israel's unfaithfulness; by alluding to Genesis 15:6, Habakkuk revives the answer God had provided there to this tension. In doing so, he provides a key link in the theological chain stretching from Genesis 15 through Habakkuk to Romans and Galatians, resulting in the doctrine of justification through faith on account of the life, death, and resurrection of Jesus. As I defend in Appendix 8, Genesis 15 contains a promise from God that He will take upon Himself the punishment for Abraham's covenant failure and one day provide for the fulfillment of all the covenant demands, so that Abraham might receive them by faith. Habakkuk revives this hope: God's people even now— after the arrival of the Law—will still find life by faith not by perfect obedience, as did Abraham. With this key phrase in 2:4, Habakkuk introduces the emphasis on faith and individual covenant life and righteousness that will

---

[53] The word translated "faith" is usually translated "faithfulness" in the majority of the 48 other uses in the OT; the meaning "faith" will be discussed in the notes on 2:4.

[54] In *Makkoth* of the Talmud, the Rabbis identify a gradual reduction of the demands of the law: in Habakkuk, the full demands of the law are narrowed to faith. The New Testament, on the other hand, sees Jesus, not faith, as the fulfillment of the law (Rom. 10:1-13). Faith is not the new and only requirement for covenant obedience but the means by which we are credited with righteousness, righteousness from God. Rabbi Dr I. Epstein, ed., "Makkoth," in *Seder Nezikin*, trans. H. M. Lzarus, vol. 4, The Babylonian Talmud 13 (London, England: The Soncino Press, 1935), 169–173.

become characteristic of New Testament salvation. This is the central way that Habakkuk anticipates and looks to Jesus: by juxtaposing in his phraseology Leviticus 11:45 and Genesis 15:6, he points to the need for Christ's life, death, and resurrection to resolve the tension between promise and obedience.

Habakkuk in the New Testament

Significantly, of the four quotations taken from Habakkuk in the New Testament, three relate to this idea of living by faith. Our purpose here will be to consider briefly the use of Habakkuk in all four of these places and to ask how the New Testament's use of Habakkuk aids our interpretation. At this point, I intend only to outline the use and its significance for our interpretation; a fuller discussion will have to wait for the notes on each passage within Habakkuk.

Habakkuk 1:5 in Acts 13:41

The first quotation taken from Habakkuk in the New Testament is recorded by Luke in Acts 13:41. Luke writes of a speech made by Paul at Antioch in Pisidia. Given an opportunity to speak on the Sabbath in the local synagogue, Paul briefly expounds the history of Israel in order to proclaim the saviour Jesus Christ. Preaching this message of Salvation, Paul speaks of the death of Jesus at the hands of the rulers of the Jews in Jerusalem. Explaining it as the fulfillment of Scripture, Paul proclaims Jesus' resurrection and concludes by telling them that it is through this Jesus, not through the Law, that they could receive the forgiveness of sins and legal freedom. It is at the conclusion of this message that Paul goes on to quote Habakkuk 1:5:

> [40]Beware, therefore, lest what is said in the Prophets should come about:
> [41]"'Look, you scoffers,
>   be astounded and perish;
> for I am doing a work in your days,
>   a work that you will not believe, even if one tells it to you.'" (Acts 13:40-31)

Paul takes his quote from the Septuagint's translation of the all-important vision in Habakkuk, God's announcement of the coming judgment of Judah at the hands of the Chaldeans.⁵⁵ In Habakkuk, the faithless leaders of Judah are soon to be the objects of God's wrath on account of their godless actions. Paul is in a similar situation: he has proclaimed the message of Jesus Christ, God's saviour come in the flesh. If the Jews hearing his message reject it, they have rejected God and His plan to save along with all the Scriptures, which testify to Jesus. The consequence will be judgment. There will be final judgment when Christ returns, yes; but more immediately, there will be judgment on their land with the sacking of Jerusalem in AD 70 at the hands of the Romans.⁵⁶ The costs of unbelief are dire: Paul with this Old Testament warning takes a horrifying vision of Scripture and applies it to his time, underscoring the seriousness of Jesus and the consequences of rejecting Him—the same consequences that Judah faced when they were rejecting God.

Paul probably quotes Habakkuk, instead of another judgment text, because of the similarities between their messages. The message Habakkuk proclaimed was primarily one of salvation but, at the same time, it was a message of doom for those who rejected it. God raised Chaldea for judgment against the wicked Judahite leadership and for the salvation of those who had faith in Him. Jesus' ministry is in many ways similar, bringing salvation to those who believe but judgment to those who reject Him.⁵⁷ So Paul takes the double-sided proclamation of Habakkuk (in the form of the LXX's warning) and applies it to the Jews in His day. Just as God's salvation came with judgment in the days of Habakkuk, so now the wonderful good news of Jesus Christ is accompanied by the horrible threat of judgment on all scoffers who reject God's work in Him.

Paul's quote of Habakkuk in Acts 13 does not shed too much light on our understanding of the text of Habakkuk 1:5, but it does draw our attention to possible applications of the passage that we may not have otherwise seen. In this regard, Paul's use of Habakkuk 1:5 as a warning—despite its original focus on salvation—suggests that is it right to see in God's terrifying vision a veiled warning for the Jewish leaders of 1:1-4. Though God is answering Habakkuk's prayer, showing the righteous what He is about to do, this salvific

---

⁵⁵ For a discussion of the differences from the Hebrew text—mainly "Look, you scoffers" instead of the Hebrew "Look among the nations" and "be astounded and perish" instead of "be astonished and astounded"—see the notes below.

⁵⁶ Lenski also notes this immediate reference to AD 70. R. C. H. Lenski, *The Interpretation of the Acts of the Apostles* (Augsburg Publishing House, 1961), 545.

⁵⁷ See the notes on 1:5 for a further discussion of this text.

work is not universally good news. Like the Cross, God's salvation through Chaldea divides the sheep from the goats: it divides between the righteous and the wicked (Matt 10:34-39; Hab 1:13d-e, 2:2-4). Those who trust in God in light of His work receive it as salvation, but those rejecting it find their judgment therein.

This is consistent with the two reactions that God speaks of in Habakkuk 2:2-4. In response to the clearly written vision, some—those with bloated appetites—will run: they will respond negatively. Those who have faith, on the other hand, will wait and have life by their trust in their faithful God. Along with this insight into the message of Habakkuk, we also see more of how Habakkuk foreshadows and looks to Jesus. God's salvific act in Chaldea, as seen through the eyes of the righteous Habakkuk, anticipates the two sides of Jesus' ministry. Though speaking of the hope of the world, the Cross is itself a divisive message (Matt 10:34-39, 1 Cor 1:18-31). In Christ is salvation, and this is good news for those who believe. However, this same good news also brings judgment upon those who harden their heart. To hear of Jesus and reject Him is to be worse off than before. The Cross and the Resurrection are the pivotal moments in human history; like the critical vision in Habakkuk, those who believe find God to be their saviour, but those who reject Him face judgment (e.g. Matt 11:20-24).

Habakkuk 2:4 in Romans 1:17

The next quotation made from Habakkuk occurs in the central thematic statement of the book of Romans. In Romans 1:1-15, Paul introduces himself and some of the key themes of his letter. Before moving on to the main content, Paul introduces in Romans 1:16-17 the centrality of the Gospel for the Christian life—the idea he will expound throughout the rest of the letter. In proclaiming the Gospel as the very power for salvation inasmuch as it reveals God's historical saving act that both vindicated His righteous character and provided righteousness for the one who believes,[58] Paul underscores the centrality of faith for the Christian life. Faith is the means by which a believer receives this salvific righteousness from God. In verse 17, where he quotes Habakkuk, Paul writes,

---

[58] On this threefold interpretation of δικαιοσυνη θεου (*dikaiosunē theou*; the righteousness of God), see my paper J. Alexander Rutherford, "A Consideration of the Meaning of the Righteousness of God in Romans 1:17," 2016, https://teleioteti.ca/resources/papers/.

> For the righteousness of God is revealed [in the Gospel] from faith to faith, just as it is written, "But the righteous one shall live by faith."[59]

It is his last phrase, "from faith to faith," that Paul seeks to support with his use of Habakkuk.

In Romans, Paul is seeking the maturity of believers in Rome by imparting a gift of fellowship and exhortation (1:11-15). The end of this is to see the same fruit among them as he seeks among the rest of the gentiles, the obedient life that results from saving faith (1:5-6). At different stages of his ministry, this focus manifests in evangelism, seeking initial faith, or on instruction and admonition—seeking obedience from that faith. It is natural to suppose that both these emphases could and will be present at the same time, but in Romans the content and the fact that Paul is writing to an established church suggests the latter is his focus (cf. 1:5; 6, esp. vv. 16-17; 12:1-15:13; 15:18; 16:19, 26-27).

Paul's focus on the obedient life that results from faith emphasizes the centrality of faith as "the a-z" of the Christian life. Therefore, with many commentators, I understand "from faith to faith" to have the sense "entirely by faith."[60] Considering that God's righteousness is revealed in the Gospel entirely by faith and considering the centrality of the Gospel to the Christian life—as Paul will explain in the rest of the letter—it then follows that the entire Christian life is lived by faith. To support this central role of faith, Paul employs Habakkuk 2:4. As we will see in the body of this commentary, Habakkuk 2:4 is God's revelation of what makes one right in covenant with Him and, as a result, a recipient of His blessings (living before Him). In this verse, God gives faith in Him as the criterion that differentiates the wicked of Judah, who run in response to His vision (2:2, 4a), from the righteous, who wait in faith (2:3, 4b).

For Paul, Habakkuk's insistence on living by faith captures the heart of the Gospel in Christ: it is not by works that sins are atoned for nor is it by the law that one receives God's covenant blessings (His promises) and their ultimate fulfillment in eternal life with Christ (Romans 4-8). The forgiveness

---

[59] This is my translation.

[60] E.g. Schreiner describes it as "emphatic"; Moo, "the combination is rhetorical and is intended to emphasize that faith and 'nothing but faith'...." Thomas R. Schreiner, *Romans*, Baker Exegetical Commentary on the New Testament 6 (Grand Rapids: Baker Books, 1998), 72; Douglas J. Moo, *The Epistle to the Romans*, NICNT (Grand Rapids: Eerdmans, 1996), 76.

of sins, resulting in peace, and the fulfillment of the law, resulting in blessing, are ensured for the one who believes by the work of Christ (Romans 3-5).[61] For Paul, this centrality of faith finds its OT foundation here in Habakkuk 2:4.

How, then, does this shed light on our reading of Habakkuk? The implications of the use of Habakkuk here in Romans and later in Galatians are too numerous for us to do more than examine a few briefly. What we can do here is identify the three primary contributions Paul's quotation in Romans makes. First, it helps us in identifying in Habakkuk the centrality of righteousness and of the question "who is righteous?"; second, it indicates the importance of Habakkuk for the biblical teaching concerning faith, righteousness, and God's promise of blessing; third, it is an aid in identifying the meaning of אֱמוּנָתוֹ (*'ĕmûnātô*; his faith). These three contributions are shared by the quotation of Habakkuk 2:4 in Romans, Galatians, and Hebrews, so I will deal with one of these contributions in each individual discussion of the New Testament quotations.

To begin with Romans, our attention is drawn to the nature of the righteous. As I will explain in the commentary notes on 1:13 and 2:2-4, the question "who is righteous?" is central to understanding God's response to Habakkuk. Though many commentators miss this, a clue that should attune an interpreter of Habakkuk to this theme is the centrality of this distinction in 3 of the 4 NT quotes of Habakkuk. After taking notice of Paul and the author of Hebrew's uses of this verse, one's attention is then drawn in reading through Habakkuk to Habakkuk's false assumption that even the wicked of Judah are relatively more righteous than the wicked Chaldeans (1:13), a supposition God is quick to correct in 2:4 (cf. 2:5).

Habakkuk 2:4 in Galatians 3:11

Turning to Galatians, we find Paul again quoting Habakkuk 2:4. This time he places it in the context of the two verses to which Habakkuk 2:4 had already alluded. Many commentators have rightly noted that Habakkuk 2:4 alludes to Genesis 15:6, where Abraham's faith is said to be credited for righteousness. What is less commented on is the equally clear allusion to Leviticus 18:5: "You shall therefore keep my statutes and my rules; if a person does them, he shall live by them: I am the LORD." That one shall live by these regulations in context does not mean "to be alive" but "to enjoy the favor of God"—especially to be free from the covenant curses, to not experience God's wrath

---

[61] See Appendix 8.

(cf. Exod 20:11). This accords with the sense of "live" here in Habakkuk.

Paul employs both Genesis 15:6 and Leviticus 18:5, juxtaposing them in Galatians 3:11-12 as two paths to life. One yields only a curse (3:10-14), but the other yields life in Christ. In the context of Galatians 3, the focus resides on the blessings of the covenant already received in the Spirit (3:1-3) yet not at the expense of the eschatological focus of the blessings that we are right to infer from the whole of New Testament theology and Galatians 1:4.[62] Habakkuk and Leviticus do not employ the already-not-yet tension introduced by Christ, so the present and eschatological blessings are grouped together as present life ("shall live"). But in Christ we see the fulfillment of this promised life in part now and fully in the future, when He returns. Paul quotes Genesis 15:6 in this first part of Galatians 3, linking it with the same righteousness, and so life, mentioned in Habakkuk. What we see from Paul's use of Habakkuk, especially in the presence of these other two key texts, is the significance of Habakkuk 2:4 in the progressing revelation of God's redemptive plan culminating in Christ.

Above I wrote of a tension unfolding throughout the Old Testament, a tension between the assurance of God's promises and the disobedience of Israel. Genesis 15:6 and Leviticus 18:5 are at the two ends of this spectrum. In Genesis 15:6, Abraham is said to receive right standing with God for the enjoyment of His promises by faith. God promises these blessing not only to Abraham but to his offspring as well. Yet in Leviticus 18:5, Israel is told that these promises, which Abraham's offspring were to receive, are dependent not on faith but on obedience to God's regulations (cf. Deuteronomy 27). This tension, clear in Leviticus and Deuteronomy, is not absent from Genesis 12-17—the key chapters discussing Abraham's covenant with God—for the obedience Abraham needed to perform is emphasized in Genesis 17 and the chapters that follow.

When we arrive at the New Testament, we find the resolution of this tension in Jesus the Messiah, by whose substitutionary sacrifice those who believe receive peace—freedom from the wrath of God—and by whose obedience, as epitomized on the Cross (Romans 5:12-21), believers receive eternal life—the blessings of right Covenant standing with God. The quotation of Habakkuk in Galatians shows us Habakkuk's key role as a stepping-stone towards the resolution of this tension. In Habakkuk's day, Israel was still under the law, they were still bound by the covenant blessings

---

[62] Contra Schreiner, who focuses on eschatological at the expense of the present. Thomas R. Schreiner, *Galatians*, ed. Clinton E. Arnold, Zondervan Exegetical Commentary Series on the New Testament 9 (Grand Rapids: Zondervan, 2010), 207–209.

and curses of the Law, yet God offers life to them on the same basis as Abraham (cf. Gal 3:17). It is as if God in Habakkuk 2:4 were saying: "yes I have required obedience, but as with your ancestor Abraham, I will accept your faith as all that I need for now—how this resolves will have to wait about 630 years."

Habakkuk 2:4, at the end of the second section of the Hebrew Bible, resurrects the hope of Genesis 15, anticipating the focus of later books in the Twelve on the restoration of God's people. That is, the hope that God would intercede on behalf of a sinful people and would both fulfill their covenant obligations and take upon Himself their covenant curses so that they might live (Gen 15:8-21; Gal 3:10-14). The form that this resolution will take is obscure in the Old Testament—though Isaiah 53 and its context is another central text in this regard.[63] However, in light of the New Testament, especially Galatians 3, we can be confident that the promise of life by faith in Habakkuk 2:4 looks forward to the day when Christ would come as the fulfillment of the law and achieve what His sinful people could not.[64] This quote in Galatians, then, draws our attention to this key theme, a theme without which we might miss the central place that the work of Christ has in the hope of Habakkuk and the central place Habakkuk has in the Bible.

Habakkuk 2:3-4 in Hebrews 10:37-39

We have now come to the last text in which Habakkuk is quoted. In Hebrews, Habakkuk 2:4 is again quoted, though this time with verse 3 included. The form of the quote is interesting, the reasons for which we will consider in the notes. What we can say here is that the author of Hebrews has adapted Habakkuk 2:3-4 to his present application of the verses. Coming to the end of the book—at the conclusion of a significant warning addressed to those who are tempted to go back from the New Covenant in Christ to the Old Covenant of Judaism—the author of Hebrews quotes Habakkuk 2:3-4 in order to emphasize the necessity of holding fast the faith in light of Christ's return. In Habakkuk, these verses read as follows:

> ³for the vision is still for an appointed time,
>   it speaks to this end and does not lie.

---

[63] See, for example, J. Alec Motyer, "Stricken for the Trangression of My People," in *From Heaven He Came and Sought Her*, ed. David Gibson and Jonathan Gibson (Wheaton: Crossway Books, 2013).

[64] See Appendix 8.

> If it delays, wait for it,
>   for it will surely come: it will not tarry—
> ⁴behold, it is bloated: his appetite is not upright within him,
>   but the righteous one will live by his faith.

In Hebrews, the reference to the vision is replaced with a reference to the coming of Jesus and verse 4a and 4b are switched around, yielding this:

> and the coming one will come and will not delay;
> ³⁸but my righteous one shall live by faith,
>   and if he shrinks back,
>   my soul has no pleasure in him." (ESV)

Regarding the perplexing translation of Habakkuk 2:4a found in the LXX and maintained here in Hebrews 10:38c-d, we can say for now that it is a somewhat accurate paraphrase of the MT in its context. What the author of Hebrews has achieved with his adaptation of Habakkuk 2 is to emphasize "living by faith" instead of Habakkuk's emphasis on the man with the bloated appetite. This is important if we are to understand the author of Hebrews' intent, for though he is trying to warn his audience ("if he shrinks back, my soul has no pleasure in him") he seeks foremost to encourage them—they are indeed those who will persevere in faith—and so exhort them in endurance. This establishes a key transition from the warnings that have preceded this passage to the great "hall of faith" that follows in chapter 11, where many Old Testament figures are put forward as paragons of faith for the Hebrews to follow. We could paraphrase his use of Habakkuk in this way:

> Just as in Habakkuk's day, one lived before God in the face of coming judgment by his faith—but God would be displeased and judge those who shrank back, that is who showed themselves to be unbelieving—so also will God now reward you with life if you persevere in Christ. But if you shrink back at the dawn of His coming, you will face the displeasure and judgment of God.

The contribution that Hebrews makes to our reading of Habakkuk, shared with Romans 1:17 and Galatians 3:11, is the confirmation it gives to our interpretation of אֱמוּנָה (ĕmûnāh; faith) in Habakkuk 2:4. With many modern English translations, I have rendered this word as "faith" (ESV, NASB, NRSV, NIV84, contra NIV, NET). The more typical translation of this Hebrew word as it is found throughout the Old Testament is "faithfulness." Though there are many reasons for adopting the translation that I have, a significant one is the use of Habakkuk 2:4 in the New

Testament, especially here in Hebrews. For the author of Hebrews, the word "faith" is essential. Along with the rest of the New Testament, he regards this as the necessary response required of a believer under the New Covenant, yet his readers are showing signs of abandoning this faith and returning to the law of the Old Covenant. To correct this drift, he both warns them and exhorts them to believe, to have faith, and so inherit the promises God will give them (10:36, 39). He is confident that they will persevere in faith. It is Habakkuk's use of "faith" that primarily leads him to quote 2:4 here—though the juxtaposition with judgment is vital to his point. If Habakkuk meant something akin to obedience, as is sometimes supposed,[65] then the key transition the author of Hebrews intended would be ruined. The connection to the following chapter, with its unmistakable focus on faith—faith that looks to what God has promised though not yet seeing it (11:1-3)—is dependent on Habakkuk 2:4 meaning "faith." If this text in Habakkuk meant something else, Genesis 15:6 would be the only other Old Testament text that would clearly connect the promises with faith—yet the key ingredient of judgment would be missing. The author of Hebrews' use of Habakkuk rests directly on its careful contrast of two responses to God's vision, which he applies to the coming of Christ: a person either responds with a lack of trust—shrinking back—or trusts God completely.

What we have seen from these four uses of Habakkuk in the New Testament is the value a canonical reading has—giving us further insights into Habakkuk that help to make better sense of its argument and purpose in Scripture—and three direct exegetical and theological insights the New Testament's use of the Old Testament provide. All that remains for our introduction, before turning to Habakkuk and beginning our exposition, is to consider the style and text of Habakkuk.

Style and Text

Though not an absolute necessity for exegesis, being attuned to the style of an author is an incredible aid in reading a text—especially in the original languages. It is this, the style of Habakkuk, that I would like to consider last.

---

[65] Though it should be noted that "faithfulness" when translating אמונה (*'ĕmûnāh*, as "faithfulness" 34 of 49 instances in ESV) does not mean obedience in the Bible: it means that attitude of loyal fidelity that results in action. Cf. Moo, *Galatians*, 220.

The reader of Habakkuk in Hebrew is quickly struck by the beauty of his prophecy. A reason for this is the lyrical quality of Habakkuk's prophetic poetry: though most biblical prophecy is written in exalted prose, often becoming poetry, most prophecy is not as lyrical and psalm-like as the last two chapters of Habakkuk—chapter 3 explicitly being a prayer-psalm, marked in ways similar to the Psalms (3:1, 3, 9, 13, 19).[66] Habakkuk's prophecy is reminiscent of both Job and Song of Songs, echoing the former in its poetic dialogue involving God and the latter in avoiding explicit markers of character changes in the dialogue.

Each section of the dialogue employs vivid and terrible imagery from God and Habakkuk, heightening the tensions in Habakkuk's mind between God's revealed character and the realities of Judahite oppression and judgment through Chaldea. The pictures of Chaldea as the most fierce of wild animals (1:8), a malicious fisher (1:15), and an arrogant conquer (1:10-11) are awful. Even more terrifying is the language of YHWH coming in chapter 3: fiery devastation follows in His wake (3:5) and the elements join His campaign—rivers cleaving the earth (3:9), floods joining the battle (3:10), and even the lights of the sky freezing to make His terrible weapons shine as they strike (3:11). Incredible as Habakkuk's poetic art is, his employment of Scripture is more so. The book of Habakkuk is a masterful example of intertextuality: many of the verses in the book employ the imagery of or direct quotations from Deuteronomy 32, Judges 5, Isaiah, Jeremiah, and the Psalms.

We will consider many of these features below, but we will begin with the condition of the text of Habakkuk. Then we will turn to the book's Hebrew and the distinct features for which to pay attention in reading Habakkuk, looking at structural elements and word usage. We will consider the intertextuality of Habakkuk throughout the notes in the commentary proper.

The Text of Habakkuk

Closely related to the style of a written text is the condition of the text itself, for at times text critical decisions rest on the relative awkwardness of a specific reading in the context of the whole of the author's work. From reading the titles and contents of many articles published on the book of Habakkuk, and reading most contemporary commentaries, one might conclude that the text of Habakkuk is a mess: the Hebrew text (the Masoretic

---

[66] Delitzsch makes a similar observation.

Text, MT) would appear to be illegible and the versions (Syriac, LXX, Vulgate, etc.) to be in complete disagreement.⁶⁷ After declaring that the text of Habakkuk "is in fair shape," Ralph L. Smith suggests that the difficulties amount to some obscure passages, various *hapax legomenon* (words only appearing once in the Hebrew Old Testament), some supposed missing words, and an inexplicable one in 2:17.⁶⁸ His list is quite conservative compared to many works: the amount of proposed alterations to the text of 2:3-5 alone is substantial. However, to conclude from the articles and many commentaries that the text of Habakkuk is a mess would be a mistake.

Despite the doubts they express, the MT has weighty agreement with the other manuscript evidence we have—the differences being best explained as misunderstandings of, intentional stylistic or clarifying alterations to, or errors from copying a Hebrew text like the MT. O. Palmer Robertson notes that one-third of the variations between the MT and 1QpHab are just articles or conjunctions, and that with the versions' support of the MT over 1QpHab, "in all cases of doubt the safer criterion would be to follow the Masoretic reading."⁶⁹ Examining the manuscript evidence provided by BHQ's

---

⁶⁷ E.g. WIlliam P. Brown, *Obadiah through Malachi* (Louisville: Westminster John Knox, 1996); Bruce, "Habakkuk"; J. A. Emerton, "The Textual and Linguistic Problems of Habakkuk II. 4–5," *Journal of theological studies* XXVIII, no. 1 (1977): 1–18; William Creighton Graham, "A Note on Habakkuk 2:4-5," *The American Journal of Semitic Languages and Literatures* 42, no. 2 (1926): 128–129; Michael J Gruenthaner, "Chaldeans or Macedonians?: A Recent Theory on the Prophecy of Habakkuk (1)," *Biblica* 8, no. 2 (April 1927): 129–160; Janzen, "Habakkuk 2:2-4 in the Light of Recent Philological Advances"; Thomas Renz, "An Emendation of Hab 2:4a in the Light of Hab 1:5," *The Journal of Hebrew Scriptures* 13 (2013); James M Scott, "A New Approach to Habakkuk 2:4-5a," *Vetus Testamentum* 35, no. 3 (July 1985): 330–340; Ralph L. Smith, *Micah-Malachi*, Word Biblical Commentary 32 (Waco, Tex.: Word Books, Publisher, 1984); William Hayes Ward, "A Critical and Exegetical Commentary on Habakkuk," in *A Critical and Exegetical Commentary on Micah, Zephaniah, Nahum, Habakkuk, Obadiah and Joel* (Edinburgh: T. & T. Clark, 1965).

⁶⁸ Smith, *Micah-Malachi*, 96.

⁶⁹ The last quote is Robertson's paraphrase of Brownlee. Haak agrees regarding the consonantal text of the MT. In the BHQ introduction for the Minor Prophets, the editors indicate that only in two places has the 1QpHab text been preferred to the MT (1:7 [Sic, 1:17], 2:5), and here only with support from other witnesses. They comment further that Vulgate reflects a Hebrew text "closely similar to [the MT], with only minor stylistic variations." In the case of both texts where they follow the Qumran Pesher, I disagree with their conclusion: the

apparatus and commentary on Habakkuk, I did not find one case where the manuscript evidence decisively suggested a reading other than that preserved in the MT.[70]

Addressing Smith's list of difficulties, many have adequate solutions. First, *hapax* are not uncommon in poetic and prophetic texts—as Habakkuk exemplifies—and there is sufficient cognate and contextual evidence to arrive at the sense of each of these words. His inexplicable word in 2:17 can be best explained contextually, grammatically, and textually with the MT's reading (see the textual note in the commentary below). Furthermore, to suppose that words have dropped out in 1:5 or 2:4 is unnecessary: the texts can be explained as they are and there is insufficient textual evidence to support this claim (the difficulty of the MT's reading supports it being original).[71] An examination of most textual decisions that differ from the MT, in both journal articles and commentaries, reveal that in most—if not all—cases, the motivation is to make Habakkuk fit into a preconceived mold or resolve an unnecessary difficulty without sufficient—in many cases, without any— textual support. As my translation and notes will show, there are ways to resolve every supposed difficulty, ways that honor the context and grammar and do justice to the text critical evidence. The conclusion that makes best sense of the data we have is that the MT of Habakkuk can be trusted in the vocalization and consonantal text as a faithful copy of the original.

---

evidence for neither is overwhelming—the latter a bit stronger, but still not convincing. In both cases, the overall meaning would be the same; only the imagery would be altered. Robert D. Haak, *Habakkuk*, Supplements to the Vetus Testamentum XLIV (Leiden: E.J. Brill, 1992), 3–8; Robertson, *The Books of Nahum, Habakkuk, and Zephaniah*, 41; A. Schenker and et al., eds., *The Twelve Minor Prophets: Introduction and Commentaries on the Twelve Minor Prophets*, Biblia Hebraica Quinta 13 (Stuttgart: Deutsche Bibelgesellschaft, 2010), 6, 8.

[70] This is not to say that they did not suggest many emendations and alterations to the Masoretic text, only that I found none of their suggestions convincing on either internal (the evidence of book's context and transcriptional probability) or external (the manuscript evidence) grounds. A. Schenker and et al., eds., *The Twelve Minor Prophets*, Biblia Hebraica Quinta 13 (Stuttgart: Deutsche Bibelgesellschaft, 2010); Schenker and et al., *The Twelve Minor Prophets: Introduction and Commentaries on the Twelve Minor Prophets*.

[71] Floyd concurs that the MT text, at least in 2:4, has been made more problematic than it actually is by false assumptions. Floyd, *Minor Prophets. Part 2*, 122.

The Hebrew of Habakkuk's Poetry

Text critical discussions are quite dry, but we will now turn to the more interesting discussion of the Hebrew of Habakkuk. Being highly poetic, Habakkuk's Hebrew can be at times difficult—especially chapter 3—but recognizing the various features that accompany Hebrew poetry makes it an easier read. We will first look at the archaizing nature of poetry and its few effects on Habakkuk, then we will consider the syntactical features of Habakkuk's poetry—including accusative markers, articles, and grammatical person—and finish our examination of his style by considering poetic parallelism.

The first feature to consider here is archaizing language: in modern English poetry and hymns, there are instances where writers resort to outdated and archaic language for poetic value—instances of 'thee,' 'thou,' and 'thy' are obvious examples. This is more prominent where an author has been raised on King James English, whether through a Bible translation or a hymnal, or Shakespearean English. More than just archaic words, the archaizing of modern poetry extends to syntax as well: word order is jumbled up in ways that would not quite work in regular speech, and other rules are broken. These same features are found in Hebrew poetry, for the same reasons of poetic license and the influence of earlier, archaic language (such as is found in the Pentateuch).

These features in Habakkuk are not a major stumbling block, but are worth considering here. Richard Patterson considers these features only with regard to the third chapter, declaring that it is "of different Hebrew than the rest of the book."[72] As the examples below will show, these features of archaic and poetic Hebrew are found throughout the book, though heightened in the third chapter. First, considering the vocabulary and morphology Habakkuk employs, we find examples of an older 3rd masculine singular pronominal suffix in a few instances. Where the expected ending would be וֹ (ô), we find כֻּלֹּה (1:9, 15; kulōh; *they all, all of them*) and עֻזֹּה (3:4; 'uzzōh; *his strength*).[73] As for vocabulary, Habakkuk twice uses the more rare

---

[72] Patterson, *Nahum, Habakkuk, Zephaniah*, 122.

[73] Of the 35 instances of כֹּל (kōl; *all*) with the 3rd masc. sing. suffix, 18 have ה (ōh). Of these, all are found in the Prophets, 17 in the latter prophets (Isaiah-Malachi), with one occurrence in 2 Samuel 2:9. Patterson takes note of the ending on עֹז ('ōz; strength), and includes another reference in 3:11—yet this requires an

and poetic word for "god"—in 1:11, לֵאלֹהוֹ (lē'lōhô; *as his god*), and 3:3, אֱלוֹהַ ('ĕlôah; *God*). Some commentators have argued that Habakkuk employs the rarer, and debated, preterite conjugation frequently in the book—which, if it is indeed a feature of Biblical Hebrew, is employed most frequently (apart from vav) in poetry.[74] However, of all 12 prefix (yiqtōl) conjugation Hiphil verbs in Habakkuk, none shows the shortened reading expected of the preterite. Therefore, it is doubtful that any of these forms are preterites. The last archaizing feature I will note at this time is the probable use of a paragogic י (î) in 3:19.[75] In 3:19, the word בָּמוֹתַי (*bāmôtay, high places*), though appearing to have a 1 common singular suffix ("my high places"), may exhibit a more archaic form: Patterson notes that it is "doubtless a frozen form based on the old genitive case." This form occurs in two other poetic texts; in both of these cases, the apparent 1 common singular ending adds no meaning (it is "on high places," not "on my high places") (Psalm 18:33 [MT 34], 2 Sam. 22:34).[76]

The second feature we will consider is the various syntactical differences between Habakkuk's poetry and the more common prose, features that can cause some difficulties for someone just beginning to read poetry. Turning to poetry from the narratives making up much of the OT, a reader notices almost haphazard use of the definite article: the use of the article is already irregular, "loose,"[77] throughout Biblical Hebrew; this is true even more so of poetry and exalted prose.[78] The article would be expected with vocatives, which are by nature definite, yet it is absent in most cases where direct address

---

unnecessary emendation from the 3rd fem ending. Ibid., 122, 245.

[74] See Patterson, Andersen. Ibid., 122–123; Andersen, *Habakkuk*, 103. The preterite would be almost identical in appearance to the imperfect conjugation, except for in the Hiphil stem and hollow verbs—where it resembles the form of the jussive. Waltke and O'Conner write that it is impossible to know, beyond a reasonable doubt, whether the unbound (that is, apart from a conjunction) prefix conjugation can function as a preterite (501). IBHS 31.1.1, 33.1; Jouon§117c; William's Hebrew 176-177c.

[75] See Joüon § 93l-q, this is probably an example of the paragogic י for rhythmic value (cf. Ho. 10:11, Ps. 113:5, 6; 114:8; 123:1).

[76] Patterson, *Nahum, Habakkuk, Zephaniah*, 246.

[77] Joüon 137e.

[78] Cf. Joüon 137, IBHS 13

appears in Habakkuk, especially in chapter 2 (1:12 [x2], 2:9, 12, 19). There are other cases where a noun is clearly definite in context, yet the article has been omitted (e.g. 2:2-3; 3:11). Along with the absence of the article, the marker of the definite direct object, אֵת ('ēṯ), is often absent. Despite many transitive verbs receiving definite objects, Habakkuk only uses the DDO 3 times (1:4, 6; 2:14).[79]

Habakkuk's use and non-use of the article and DDO accord with the usage found other poetic sections of Hebrew; what is more peculiar is his tendency to alternate between 2nd and 3rd person while considering the same subject (2:9, 10, 15, 16).[80] This is especially prominent in the second chapter, though still present in the third. In the woe-taunt that the nations raise against the Chaldeans (2:6-19), Chaldea is frequently addressed in the third person and then directly addressed—e.g. in 2:6d and 7a, "'Woe to he who heaps up what is not his own…. Will your creditors not suddenly rise up?" In chapter 3, Habakkuk's prayer-psalm alternates between addressing God, describing His acts, and describing Habakkuk's response (here, there is a deliberate progression in the shift). In one case, this shift happens in the same series of lines: in 8a-b, "Is YHWH wroth with the rivers? Is your anger with the rivers, or your rage with the sea…?"[81]

Before turning to consider the structure and vocabulary of Habakkuk, it may also be helpful for some readers to consider the broader features of Hebrew poetry. Hebrew poetry employs many of the same literary features as English: there are metaphors (1:12), hyperbole, onomatopoeia (2:20),

---

[79] Many commentaries and translations would identify another use of the DDO in 3:13, yet it is best to read אֵת ('ēṯ) here as a preposition (*with*, beside). See the commentary on this passage. Watson describes some of these features of poetry. Wilfred G. E. Watson, "Poetry, Biblical Hebrew," ed. Geoffrey Khan, *Encyclopedia of Hebrew Language and Linguistics* (Leiden; Boston: Brill, 2013), 152–153.

[80] In chapter 3, the shifting of person indicates structural shifts (the transitions of stanzas and strophes). Though I disagree with his conclusions on the structure of chapter 3, Barré is correct to identify these shifts as literary feature guiding the identification of the structure of Habakkuk's prayer. Michael L. Barré, "Newly Discovered Literary Devices in the Prayer of Habakkuk," *The Catholic Biblical Quarterly* 75 (2013): 448.

[81] These two lines mark the shift between describing YHWH's approach and directly addressing Him. The middle of the prayer-psalm addresses God, and the last unit returns to third person and introduces first person accounts of the singer's reaction to God's work.

simile (2:5c-d), alliteration, assonance, and acrostics (Psalm 119)—among others. Rhyme is not as common as in English poetry, but word play and assonance are much more so. Word play and assonance are often achieved by using words of the same root (Hab 1:5) or words spelled similarly (1:6).[82] Words with similar meanings or very different meanings, yet similar spellings, are frequently employed for poetic value. Important to note is also the frequent use of ellipsis, the omission of a necessary word—verb or noun—to be supplied by the parallel lines.[83] Hebrew poetry, as well as prose, is also known for its terseness. "Terseness" describes the intentional minimalism of Hebrew poetry. Words are kept to a minimum: even if the result is ambiguous, Hebrew poets will use three words instead of ten.

Unlike English poetry, meter is not—as far as we can determine—key to the rhythm and nature of Hebrew poetry. Though is debated whether there is even meter in Hebrew Poetry, from the data it is best to say that meter is present but only as one of many tools used by the Hebrew poet to achieve a poetic rhythm that may best be described as a conceptual rhythm.[84] That is, the rhythm of Hebrew poetry is that of ideas and the interplay of lines that achieve the desired effect through the various perspectives used to communicate it.[85] When meter is employed, this sonic rhythm is achieved by patterns of syllables, accents, or words. In the first case, a series of sets of lines (a colon) may contain a pattern of syllables that is repeated in each colon or with a rhythmic variation. There may also be a pattern of accents per line

---

[82] Assonance may not be the proper word, for written Hebrew consists only of consonants and this is primarily what is emphasized in these poetic devices. That being said, I will continue to use assonance to refer to the poetic device of playing off similar sounds, whether consonantal or vocalic.

[83] Watson, "Poetry, Biblical Hebrew," 152; Andrew E. Hill and John H. Walton, *A Survey of the Old Testament*, 2nd ed. (Grand Rapids: Zondervan Publishing House, 2000), 383.

[84] Hill and Walton, *A Survey*, 387; David L. Petersen and Kent Harold Richards, *Interpreting Hebrew Poetry*, Guides to Biblical Scholarship (Minneapolis: Fortress, 1992), 37–39, 41; Watson, "Poetry, Biblical Hebrew," 152.

[85] This can be related to the approach of Hebrew narrative, which I once heard described as, in contrast to English storyline, more cyclical or holographic than linear or 2D. That is not to say that Hebrew narrative does not tell a linear story, but in telling a story, Hebrew narrative often revisits it form different perspectives, different angles: like a hologram, you are not give a flat, one dimensional view, but many different angles that tell you more than a single could (cf. Gen. 1 and 2; the four Gospels).

or the number of words in each line. Alliteration or assonance also contribute to this sonic rhythm.[86]

The substance of Hebrew poetry, that of which it consists, is series of parallel lines—each set known as a colon. A sort of rhythm is sometimes associated with the number of lines in a colon (*bicolon*, 2 lines; *tricolon*, 3 lines), but even here there is no uniformity: using varying numbers of lines is again a tool for achieving poetic rhythm, but not the whole of it.[87] The primary tool used to achieve conceptual rhythm in Hebrew poetry is the parallelism of ideas. Each series of lines balance in various ways an idea. Usually lines will parallel each other in their members as well, that is, they may not have the exact correspondence in the number of words but related verbs, nouns, and modifiers.[88]

On the older understanding of Hebrew Parallelism, the possible relationships between lines were considered "synonymous," "antithetical," or "synthetic." Much has been written in the last 40 years, though, to revise this system.[89] Understanding parallelism helps us to better appreciate Hebrew poetry. Parallelism employs, as the name suggests, parallel lines—poetic lines related grammatically, phonetically, semantically—to communicate in richer ways than prose. We could describe Hebrew Parallelism as the use of closely related lines for evocation—engaging the affections—and disambiguation. Disambiguation describes the way poets use parallel lines to resolve ambiguity resulting from the terseness and imagery of poetry, bringing another perspective in order to bring clarification.

Thus Hebrew poetry can be considered as analogous to a holograph: it is three dimensional not two dimensional language. The poet will present an idea and revisit in the following lines (sometimes an entire poem looks at the

---

[86] Hill and Walton, *A Survey*, 383.

[87] Petersen and Richards, *Interpreting Hebrew Poetry*, 41.

[88] Hill and Walton, *A Survey*, 383. David Tsumura has written on the vertical grammar of Hebrew parallelism, in which grammar unfolds across lines instead of sentences. He summarizes it as "*one sentence through two lines*," characterized by "*vertical grammar*, that is, a syntactic relation between two parallel lines." Emphasis in original. David Toshio Tsumura, "Vertical Grammar of Parallelism in Hebrew Poetry," *Journal of Biblical Literature* 128, no. 1 (2009): 169.

[89] E.g. James L. Kugel, *The Idea of Biblical Poetry: Parallelism and Its History* (New Haven: Yale University Press, 1981); Adele Berlin, *The Dynamics of Biblical Parallelism* (Bloomington: Indiana University Press, 1985); Robert Alter, *The Art of Biblical Poetry* (New York: Basic Books, 1985); J.P. Fokkelman, *Reading Biblical Poetry: An Introductory Guide*, trans. Ineke Smit, First edition. (Louisville: Westminster John Knox, 2001).

same idea from various perspectives): each line, then, gives a complementary perspective on the ideas the author wishes to communicate—it paints a three dimensional picture. This combination of ambiguity followed by disambiguation produces a sense of elation in us the readers as we move from confusion to realization of the meaning. There is a sense of discovery as a poem progresses. The use of multiple perspectives and compact language, as well as liberal use of metaphor, contributes to the rich emotional impact Hebrew poetry has.

Here are some examples from Habakkuk:

Example 1 (Hab 3:13):

¹³You come forth for the salvation of your people,
   for salvation with your anointed;

Example 2 (Hab 3:11):

The sun and the moon stand in their exalted abode,
   to make your arrows that fly gleam,
   to brighten your flashing spears.

These examples serve to illustrate some of the various ways in which parallelism is used in the Old Testament. In example one, the second line is used to explain how God is going to save His people; He will do so through His anointed, Chaldea. In example 2, the second and third line (11b & 11c) explain why the heavenly bodies are standing tall in the sky, in order to highlight the weapons God will use to achieve salvation for His people.[90]

With these essential pieces in place, our last consideration of the style of Habakkuk, and so the last part of this introduction, will be the literary structures Habakkuk employs to communicate and his use of vocabulary.

Habakkuk's use of Structure and Vocabulary

There is significant disagreement over the presence of groupings such as

---

[90] The previous discussion is adapted with permission from J. Alexander Rutherford, *The Gift of Reading – Part 1: Reading the Bible in Submission to God* (Vancouver, Teleioteti 2019), 131-141.

stanza and strophe in Biblical Hebrew; David Petersen concludes that for Hebrew poetry in general, these groupings do not exist.[91] He does not argue that there are no greater groupings beyond bicolons and tricolons, but that technically defined strophic or stanziac units do not exist. He prefers instead the more ambiguous "sense units." There is good sense in preferring the more ambiguous terminology, for there is no regularity in the groupings of colons he identifies as "discrete historical unit[s]," yet the technical terminology can be helpful if broadly defined. I will employ the terms "strophe" and "stanza" in a particular way throughout this commentary: I employ these terms to describe greater and lesser sense units, respectively, made up of groups of colons (the smallest sense unit of poetry, a grouping of lines). Strophe in my use would be roughly equivalent to a "verse" in contemporary lyrical poetry, the broadest division of a poem or song. Stanzas are the smaller units that make up a strophe. As it concerns Habakkuk, I have employed the term "strophe" to delineate the three major units of his prayer-psalm in chapter 3; each strophe is made up of 3 stanzas consisting of various numbers of colons and lines. In chapter 3, the use of a heading and conclusion bracket the whole prayer, and Habakkuk's use of "selah" indicates a division between strophes.[92] Chapter 2 also employs strophic and stanzaic breaks. As in chapter 3, there are three strophes in chapter 2, signaled by the refrain in 8c-d and 17c-d. The first and last strophe consist of one stanza each, but the middle strophe is longer, consisting of three stanzas. Each stanza represents one woe saying against the Chaldean. With this terminology in place, we can discuss the literary structures used by Habakkuk.

Beyond what we have already discussed, three other uses of structure (or parallelism beyond the level of a line) in Habakkuk are worth addressing.

---

[91] Petersen and Richards, *Interpreting Hebrew Poetry*, 60. Cf. discussion in 60-62.

[92] I have not encountered much discussion of *selah* as a discourse marker for Hebrew poetry, but from my own study, *selah* also functions as a discourse marker in Psalm 84. Though it is may be inaccurate from a grammatical point of view to label it as such, its function as a musical notation—indicating some sort of instrumental or vocal shift—would suggest to the singer and leader a shift within the psalm. In both Habakkuk 3 and Psalm 84, a division along these lines helps delineate the sense units.

Lugt considers *selah* to be a transitional marker in the Psalter, though one not as significant as I here consider it to be. Pieter van der Lugt, *Cantos and Strophes in Biblical Hebrew Poetry: With Special Reference to the First Book of the Psalter*, vol. I, Oudtestamentische studiën 53 (Leiden; Boston: Brill, 2006), 80.

The first is a significant chiasm in the woe taunt of chapter 2 (6d-19). Many commentaries discuss the odd nature of the fifth woe (2:18-19), but they fail to note that it is an inversion of the first woe. Taking the repeated saying in 8c-d and 17c-d as a refrain and not as part of any woe, the first and fifth woes are divided from the central three. Thus the whole taunt song is bracketed by the cola in which the word "woe" appears (6d-f, 19). Furthermore, the last part of the first stanza (7-8b) and the first part of the last stanza (18), are made of a tricolon with a bicolon. Each tricolon begins with a marked question (הֲ, *hă* [7a];[93] מַה־ *māh-*; *what?* [18a]), and is followed by an explanatory כִּי beginning a bicolon (*because* [8a], *for* [18d]). Evidence for a chiasm here is strengthened by the only other occurrence of an explicit question (that is, one with an interrogative particle) in the first word in the tricolon of verse 13, located in the middle stanza of the taunt song (12-14).[94] The central stanza, then, is bracketed by Stanzas 1 and 5, the refrain in verses 8 and 17, and Stanzas 2 and 4—these last two sharing a focus on the shameful actions of Chaldea and the resulting consequences. Furthermore, Stanzas 1, 3, and 5 all contain a tricolon beginning with a question. Stanza 3 is then the heart of the song, and it is a worthy heart: here, the Sovereignty of God is asserted and the purpose of raising and ending Chaldea's reign is identified as the filling of the earth with "the glory of YHWH," an idea echoed in 3:3c-5.

The next two structures worthy of notice are occurrences of complex parallelism, where the same group of lines interlock and can be viewed from numerous perspectives. I already mentioned the main structure of chapter 3, indicated by *selah* and various other features I will discuss in the notes, but there is another structure—a thematic structure—that coexists with it.[95] Adopting a slightly different division of the lines, ignoring the use of *selah* as a structural feature (cf. ESV and NIV), yields 4 thematically shaped strophes. The first strophe would contain verse 3-7, divided into stanzas at 3-4, 5-6b, and 6c-7. Here, the coming of YHWH in all His glory, the response of the creation, and then the response of the peoples are described. The next strophe in this structure is verses 8-12: here God is seen first as oppressing the forces of nature (8), but another perspective yields the truth that they are His allies in horrible warfare (9-11)—they are His weapons made ready (9).

---

[93] hă is untranslatable but the equivalent of the Spanish ¿, indicating the beginning of a question

[94] The question in 19c is unmarked and is sarcastic.

[95] Psalm 84, mentioned above, contains the same tension between a rhythmic and thematic structure, both equally insightful in understanding the poetry of the psalm.

Here, three stanzas are identifiable in 8-9b, 9c-10, 11-12. This strophe ends with Habakkuk describing God's threshing of the nations in indignation, echoing the question of God's anger against the rivers in verse 8. This last emphasis on the nations moves away from the emphasis on creation to the tools of God's onslaught, described in verses 13-15. Here in two stanzas, verse 13 and verses 14-15, Habakkuk describes God coming forth with his anointed tool to destroy the house of wickedness. The last strophe would be verses 16-19, divided into two stanzas, verse 16 and verses 17-19. Here Habakkuk's response and praise of God is described. Grouping the song both by its themes and by its structural markers gives differing though complementary insights into the song.

The last literary structure we will look is found in 2:2-4. As the indentation in my translation shows, the parallelism here is quite complex:

> So that one who reads it will run—
> ³for the vision is still for an appointed time,
> it speaks to this end and does not lie.
> If it delays, wait for it,
> for it will surely come; it will not tarry—
> ⁴behold, it is bloated: his appetite is not upright within him,
> but the righteous one will live by his faith.

These verses are all a bit complicated, so I will only note the parallelism here In these verses, there are three overlapping relationships employed by Habakkuk to achieve a poetic contrast between the wicked Judahite leadership and the righteous and a comparison of this same leadership with the Chaldeans. First, 2d with 4a-b forms a tricolon: 4a completes 2d for a contrast with 4b. The one who runs in 2d is identified as one with the bloated and crooked appetite by the use of הִנֵּה (*hinnēh*; behold) in verse 4a. This bloated runner is, then, contrasted with the one who lives by faith (4b). Second, His wicked response ("run") is contrasted with the righteous response, "wait," in verse 3. Verses 2d-3b forms a tricolon, contrasted with the bicolon in 3c-d. The subordinate lines in both these sets (3a-b, d) ground the two responses in the certainty of the vision's fulfillment. Third, these verses are the first part of an *a fortiori* (lesser to the greater) argument indicated by אַף־כִּי (*'af-kî*; how much more) in verse 5. Through this argument, God reveals that if he will judge the wicked Judah as revealed in his vision—those bloated and crooked in appetited—it is so much more certain that He will judge the bloated and arrogant Chaldean.

Our last consideration of Habakkuk's style, concluding our introduction, is Habakkuk's vocabulary. Habakkuk's vocabulary is rich, without a word wasted: every word he employs contributes to the rich imagery he paints and reveals careful consideration and a mastery of Hebrew vocabulary on his part.[96] Making life difficult for the interpreter, though, we find in Habakkuk multiple occurrences of *hapax legomenon* (1:9, 2:11, 3:4, 3:10, 3:14, 3:15) and rare words (1:4, 1:7, 1:8, 2:4, 2:15 , 3:1). The increased frequency of the *hapax* in chapter 3 underscores its poetic nature. Though these rarities provide challenges for interpretation, we are in a good place to propose reasonable meanings in every instance, understand the verses in their context, and so make good sense of the entire book. For this we must thank God, in His providence preserving what we need in the Biblical Canon, the book's own context, and extra-biblical materials that allow us to resolve these challenges.

Habakkuk uses his vocabulary throughout the book to stitch together its various sections.[97] He repeats key terms throughout the book to clue the reader to connections he is drawing. The most frequent key word used by Habakkuk is חָמָס (*ḥāmās*; violence). Used five times in the first 2 chapters, "violence" first describes the circumstances caused by the Judahite leadership (1:2, 3). The first connection this key word draws, in connection with שֹׁד (*šōd*, havoc), is to the wicked leaders already mentioned in the Twelve (Amos 3:10). Within Habakkuk itself, "violence" is one of several words that are used by Habakkuk to compare the behaviour of the wicked Judahites with the more wicked Babylonians, heightening the tension between Habakkuk's plight and God's response (1:2, 3; 1:9, 2:8, 2:17). Additionally, the word צַדִּיק (*ṣaddîq*; righteous) is used three times and the root אמן (*'mn*) twice, in their occurrences providing key anchors between the vision given (1:5-17) and God's instructions concerning it (2:2-4). אמן first describes the vision as one that would not be <u>believable</u> (1:6), then, in 2:4, it describes the response of the righteous to the vision as living "by his <u>faith</u>." So, the righteous one will live before God by believing in the unbelievable vision. צַדִּיק likewise provides a connection between the first chapter and the second, this time between Habakkuk's prayer, his first response, and God's answer. In 1:4, Habakkuk identifies some as righteous within Judah, others as wicked—the wicked leaders surround the oppressed righteous. Then, in 1:13, Habakkuk asks how God can allow "the wicked to swallow up those more <u>righteous</u> than they?" His original distinction has disappeared: in light of the horrors of Chaldea, the wicked and righteous among Judah have coalesced in Habakkuk's mind. God's response is then to identify what really makes one righteous: "<u>the

---

[96] We, of course, only have the Hebrew Bible as a judge of the range of Biblical Hebrew vocabulary, but according to this standard, this judgment holds true.

[97] Conveniently, key words used in this way are often called stitch words.

<u>righteous one</u> will live by his faith" (2:4). God's response is a correction of Habakkuk's misapprehension. God was not going to allow the wicked to swallow up those more righteous than they: the truly righteous would live by faith. Those to be swallowed up are the unrighteous, unbelieving, oppressive Jewish leadership.

The last important key word to notice is the root פעל (*p 'l*). Habakkuk employs this root three times in the book, providing a vital connection between the first and last chapters—the vision and Habakkuk's song concerning it. In 1:5, פעל occurs twice, as a noun and a verb: "I am <u>doing a deed</u> in your day." Habakkuk then uses it again in 3:2: "I fear, oh YHWH, this <u>deed</u> of yours." This connection identifies the content of Habakkuk's song not as a description of God's victory over Babylon, but God's use of Babylon to bring salvific judgment to Judah.

I have attempted in this introduction to draw attention to key features of the book of Habakkuk to aid our exposition. The features of Habakkuk's Hebrew and poetry will be helpful for those attempting to wrestle through the Hebrew text. The outline and theological survey will help all of us to understand Habakkuk within the whole of God's Word. It is now to the exposition of this text that we must turn: let us, then, prepare our hearts to hear from God's Word; with humble submission to Christ our Lord, let us prepare our minds for the task of interpreting His Scriptures; and with attentiveness to His Spirit, let us humbly submit our lives for His shaping.

> May the Lord grant us so to be engaged in the heavenly mysteries of his wisdom that we progress in true godliness, to his glory and our own edification.
> Amen.[98]

---

[98] John Calvin, *Daniel I: Chapters 1-6*, trans. T. H. L Parker, vol. 1, Calvin's Old Testament Commentaries 20 (Grand Rapids: Eerdmans, 1993), 14.

II. A TRANSLATION OF THE BOOK OF HABAKKUK

1 ¹The judgment oracle that Habakkuk the prophet saw:

Habakkuk's First Complaint

²How long, oh YHWH,[1] have I cried for help,
    but you do not listen?
I shout out to you "Violence!"
    but you do not save.
³Why do you let me see iniquity
    and look yourself upon wickedness?
Havoc and violence are before me,
    there are legal disputes,

---

[1] "YHWH" is transliterated from the Hebrew יהוה, God's name as revealed in Exod 3:14-15. Out of reverence, afraid of accidentally breaking the 3rd commandment and using God's name in vain, ancient scribes would read the Hebrew word "*Adonai*," meaning "lord," in the place of His name Yahweh (the probable pronunciation). This practice was continued by the Greek translation of the Old Testament (the Septuagint) and the New Testament. Among other titles, God, Lord, and Yahweh are the primary ways our God is referred to in the Bible. I will use them interchangeably.

In my translation, I use the transliteration "YHWH" to represent the Hebrew text, where this interplay between "Lord" and the name "Yahweh" is apparent.

and strife is suffered.
⁴Therefore the law is numb,
    and justice never goes forth,
For the wicked surround the righteous
    therefore justice goes forth crooked—

Yahweh's Response to Habakkuk's First Complaint

⁵"Look, all of you, among the nations and behold—
    and be astonished and astounded!
For a deed I am doing in your day;
    you would not believe it though it were told.
⁶For, behold, I am raising up the Chaldeans,
    that bitter and brash nation,

Who traverses the breadth of the earth
    to take possession of dwellings not his own.
⁷Terrifying and dreaded is he,
    from himself go forth his justice and majesty.

⁸Swifter than leopards are his horses;
    quicker than wolves of the evening,
    his horsemen leap forth.
His horsemen come from afar,
    they fly like an eagle
    hastening to eat.
⁹They all come for violence,
    the horde of their faces forward,
    and he gathers captives like sand.

¹⁰He makes a mockery of kings;
    dignitaries are a joke to him.
He laughs at every fortification
    and piles up a mound of earth and takes it.
¹¹He therefore moves on as the wind,
    crosses boundaries and is guilty,
    whose strength is his god."

Habakkuk's Second Complaint

¹²Are you not of old,
    oh YHWH, my God, my Holy One?
    We shall not die.

Oh YHWH, for justice you put him in place;
>oh Rock, to rebuke you appointed him.
¹³Your eyes are too pure to see evil;
>to look at wickedness you are not able!
Why do you look upon the treacherous,
>remain silent when the wicked swallows up those more righteous than he?

¹⁴You have made human beings like fish of the sea;
>like creeping creatures, no one rules over them.
¹⁵He brings all of them up with his fishhook,
>with his dragnet he drags them away.
He gathers them in his fishnet,
>thus he is glad and rejoices.
¹⁶And so he sacrifices to his dragnet,
>and burns incense to his fishnet.
For by these his portion is rich
>and his food corpulent.
¹⁷Will he, therefore, empty out his net?
>And continually slaying nations,
>will he not show mercy?

2 ¹At my post I will stand
>and station myself upon a fortification.
I will keep watch to see what he will say against me,
>and how I may respond to my rebuke.

Yahweh's Final Response

An Answer for Israel

²And YHWH answered me and said;

> "Write down the vision,
>> make it clear upon tablets,
> So that one who reads it will run—
>>> ³for the vision is still for an appointed time,
>>> it speaks to this end and does not lie.
>> If it delays, wait for it,
>>> for it will surely come; it will not tarry—
>> ⁴behold, it is bloated: his appetite is not upright within him,
>> but the righteous one will live by his faith.

An Answer for Babylon

⁵"How much more is wine betraying the arrogant man,
    he will not find rest.
Because he opens wide his appetite like Sheol,
    he is like death;
    he is never satisfied:
He gathers to himself all the nations,
    and collects for himself all the peoples.
⁶Will these not all raise a taunt against him—
    even a mocking poem, riddles concerning him—
and it will say:

    'Woe to he who heaps up what is not his own—
        for how long!—
        and who loads heavy debt upon himself!
    ⁷Will your creditors not suddenly rise up,
        those who make you tremble awaken?
        You will be pillage for them.
    ⁸Because you yourself plundered many nations,
        all the remnants of the peoples will plunder you.

    Because of the blood of man and the violence to the land,
        to towns and all their inhabitants.

    ⁹Woe to him who illicitly makes evil gain for his house,
        to place his nest up high,
        to deliver himself from the hand of catastrophe!
    ¹⁰You have planned a shameful deed for your house,
        to bring an end to many peoples;
        you are sinning against your own life.
    ¹¹Even stones from the wall will cry out,
        and rafters from the woodwork will answer them.

    ¹²Woe to him who builds a city on bloodshed
        and establishes a town in wickedness.
    ¹³Is it not, behold, from YHWH of hosts
        that peoples are labouring only for fire
        and nations are wearing themselves for nothing?
    ¹⁴For the earth will be filled
        with the knowledge of the glory of YHWH
        like the waters cover the sea.

> [15] Woe to him who gives drink to his neighbour,
>> you who mixes it with your wrath,
>> even to make them drunk,
>>> that you might look upon their nakedness.
> [16] You will be sated with dishonour instead of glory.
>> Now you yourself drink and have your uncircumcision exposed!
> The cup of YHWH's right hand is coming around to you,
>> and disgrace will come upon your glory.
> [17] For the violence done to Lebanon will overwhelm you,
>> and the devastation done to the beasts that terrified them.
>
> Because of the blood of man and the violence to the land,
>> to towns and all their inhabitants.
>
> [18] What benefit is an idol,
>> that its maker would hew it,
>> a cast image and a teacher of lies,
> For the maker trusts what he has made,
>> enough to craft speechless idols.
> [19] Woe to him who says to wood, "wake up!"
>> "awake!" to a dumb stone.
> Is it able to teach?
>> Behold, it is overlaid with gold and silver,
>> but there is no breath at all in it.
>
> [20] But YHWH is in His holy temple,
>> be silent before Him all the earth!

A Song of Habakkuk in Response to God's Answer to His Prayer

3 [1] A prayer of Habakkuk the prophet, according to the *Shigyonot*.

> [2] Oh YHWH, I have heard your report;
>> I fear, oh YHWH, this deed of yours.
> In the midst of years, give it life;
>> in the midst of years, make it known;
>> but in anger, remember to show mercy.
>
> [3] God comes in from Teman,
>> the holy one from mount Paran.

Selah

His majesty covers the heavens,
    and the earth is full of his renown.
⁴His brightness is like day;
    he has rays flashing from his hand;
    there is the concealing of his strength.
⁵Pestilence goes before him,
    and fiery devastation follows his steps.

⁶He stands and causes the earth to quake;
    he looks and causes the nations to jump.
The mountains of old are shattered,
    and the ancient hills cower;
    the ancient paths are his.
⁷I see the tents of Cushan under distress;
    the tent curtains of the land of Midian tremble.

⁸Is YHWH wroth with the rivers?
    Is your anger with the rivers,
    or your rage with the sea,
That you drive your horses along,
    your chariots of salvation?
⁹Your bow is wakened from its sheath,
    your rods sworn in with a word.

Selah

You split the earth with rivers;
    ¹⁰the mountains see you and writhe.
Downpours of water sweep through;
    the deep lifts up its voice,
    and raises its hands up high.

¹¹The sun and the moon stand in their exalted abode,
    to make your arrows that fly gleam,
    to brighten your flashing spears.
¹²With indignation you march through the earth;
    with your anger you thresh the nations.

¹³You come forth for the salvation of your people,
    for salvation with your anointed;
You smash the head of the house of the wicked,

laying it bare from the foundation to the neck.

Selah

¹⁴With his rods you pierce the head,
>his warriors storm in to scatter me,
>>their exultation as if to consume the oppressed in hiding places.

¹⁵You tread the sea with your horses,
>the great waters foam.

¹⁶I hear and my inward parts tremble;
>at the sound my lips quiver.

Rot enters into my bones,
>and I tremble where I stand,

While I wait for the day
>for distress to come up,
>for a people to attack us.

¹⁷Even when the fig tree does not bear fruit,
>>and there is no yield of the vine;
>the labour done for olives fails,
>>and the fields do not produce food;
>the flocks are cut from the fold,
>>and there are no cattle in the stalls,

¹⁸I will rejoice in YHWH,
>I will exult in the God of my salvation.

¹⁹The Lord YHWH is my strength;
>He sets my feet like a doe
>>and causes me to tread upon high places.

To the choirmaster, with my stringed instruments.

III. COMMENTARY

1. THE ORACLE OF HABAKKUK (1:1-2:20)

A. SUPERSCRIPTION (1:1)

1 ¹The judgment oracle that Habakkuk the prophet saw:ᵃ

Habakkuk shares with all but three of the Twelve (Jonah, Haggai, Zechariah) a superscription introducing the book. This superscription is quite minimal: it introduces the first section of the book (1:1-2:20), yet it tells us nothing about the intended recipients or circumstances (in contrast with Amos, Micah, Nahum, Zephaniah, and Malachi) and reveals nothing about the author except his name and role as prophet(similar to Obadiah).

Its function is to orient the reader to the contents of the book and coordinate with the other sectional markers (2:1, 2:20, 3:1, 3:19) to delineate the various pieces of Habakkuk. This first piece (1:1-2:20) is described as "The judgment oracle that Habakkuk the prophet saw." This, first, alerts us to the nature of what follows: it will introduce an oracle of God's judgment against a nation. Second, it prepares us to encounter a vision: that it was seen prepares the reader for a written account of a visional experience.

Not a man to waste words, Habakkuk leaves us to adduce the object of the oracle from the contents of the book. We should then expect that the information required to interpret the book in this regard will be quite evident. This is indeed the case. As we will see below, we are immediately attuned to the who, what, and why of Habakkuk.

ᵃ Isa 13:1, 15:1, 17:1, 19:1, etc.. Hos 1:1, Joel 1:1, Amos 1:1, Oba 1:1, Mic 1:1, Nah 1:1, Zeph 1:1, Mal 1:1.

1 ¹The judgment oracle that Habakkuk the prophet saw:

Exegesis of Verse 1¹

Verse 1. In addition to what has been said above, it should be observed that "[J]udgment oracle" translates the word מַשָּׂא (maśśāh); מַשָּׂה refers to a revelatory message of judgment (cf. Isa 13:1, 14:28; Ezek 12:10; Nah 1:1; Zech 12:1). Smith describes it as a "technical term to introduce prophetic oracles on foreign nations,"² yet many occurrences (e.g. here and in Isa 22:1) show that it is also applied to God's people. Therefore we may define it more carefully as a prophetic oracle against a nation.

We are also told that Habakkuk *saw* this oracle; הָזָה (hāzāh), translated "saw," can refer to perception in general, encompassing audio as much as visual perception, but frequently refers to visual perception. In the context of this highly pictorial book and considering the references to a "vision" in 2:1-3, "to see" is the appropriate sense here. We are then to view the first half of the book as a prophetic oracle of judgment that contains or is a vision. This oracle is first against Judah (1:5-2:4) and then against Chaldea (2:5-2:20).

"The Prophet"

What is a prophet? Though prophets are frequently mentioned in Scripture, we are never given a detailed job description. It is far above my pay grade to describe the Biblical role of a prophet, but one observation made from Habakkuk's prophetic role may give us insight into role of a prophet throughout the Bible. A great debate in theological circles concerns the continuity between the Old Testament prophets and those in the New Testament. Reformed theologians focus on the revelatory nature of the prophetic role, arguing that since Scripture has been completed, the prophetic role in the New Testament must be different than in the Old Testament. That is, because Old Testament prophets are responsible for receiving and delivering Divine revelation and such revelation has ceased, the prophetic role in the New Testament cannot be the revelatory role of the Old Testament prophets.

---

¹ Under "exegesis," I intend to explain the text before us: discuss the meaning of terms, obscure phrases, and draw attention to literary features.

² Smith, *Micah-Malachi*, 98.

It is true that the prophets in the Old Testament are particularly associated with revealing God's Word, they are God's spokesman: they give God's perspective on the world. Yet, their role is not exclusively the revelation of new words from God. All the prophetic material we have in the Old Testament is revelation from God, but the form it takes is often that of judgments or exhortations based on God's covenant already revealed. The historical books (Samuel, Kings) measure the kings by their faithfulness to God: Solomon is measured against the standards for a king already revealed in Deuteronomy 17:14-20. Jeremiah applies Deuteronomy 30 to his day, speaking of a New Covenant that still awaits fulfillment (Jer 31).

Habakkuk, in contrast, is a perfect example of the revelatory function of a prophet. In this book we have a vision revealed from God and a message of judgment against Chaldea (1:5-11, 2:5-19). However, most of the book is an interaction with these visions. Habakkuk guides the reader to the proper response through God's own revealed character (1:1-4, 1:12-17) and then leads them through a song embodying the response God has called for (ch. 3).

Habakkuk is nothing less than a spokesman for God, but he is also pastoral in the way he relates God's message. It would be wise then to broaden our understanding of the prophetic role. If my analysis of the role of the prophetic books in the Old Testament is correct (see the introduction), then we may view the Prophets as those commissioned to give a God's-eye view on the Covenant people and God's present and future actions towards them. This role leads to both encouragement (Jer 31) and warning (Isa 1). When we understand the prophetic role in this way, we can affirm continuity with the prophetic ministry in the New Testament, even before settling the revelation question.

B. HABAKKUK'S COMPLAINTS AND YAHWEH'S RESPONSES (1:2-2:20)

The largest section of Habakkuk consists of a four part dialogue between God and Habakkuk. Habakkuk is in mid-prayer, lamenting over Yahweh's apparent inaction, when Yahweh interrupts with the horrific answer to his prayer. Yahweh reveals in seven awful verses how He has not been silent: God has heard the cries of His people and has prepared a nation to be their salvation. However, the nation He has raised up appears worse than those against whom Habakkuk initially cried out.

Habakkuk, steeped in the Scriptures of his people—knowing the character of his covenant Lord—took it upon himself to probe what he saw as an inconsistency between God's actions and the character which he knew Yahweh possessed. It takes faith, trust in God's unwavering consistency—in His faithfulness and His utter goodness—to question the Creator of everything. Habakkuk would not dare do this lightly. But knowing the nature of His God, he rightly expected that Yahweh would vindicate His character. At first, God appeared silent in the face of horrible social evils; now He was apparently the agent behind worse evils. Habakkuk questioned how God can allow this (1:12-13) and, knowing that God will fulfill His purpose, sought out the fate of the horrible saviours God was raising up (1:14-17).

God responds, as Habakkuk knew He would. Yet His answer is not quite what Habakkuk expects. Habakkuk knows God's character and does not need to hear of God's track record. Yahweh does not give an explanation for the length of His apparent silence nor does He seek to justify His choice in tools: He answers Habakkuk's questions in such a way as to simultaneously put Habakkuk in his place—"Be silent before Him all the earth!" (2:20)—reveal the false categories upon which Habakkuk's judgment of the situation relied, and assure him that His justice would come around to the Babylonians.

i. Habakkuk's First Complaint (1:2-4)

²How long, oh YHWH, have I cried for help,
    but you do not listen?ᵃ
I shout out to you "Violence!"ᵇ
    but you do not save.ᶜ
³Why do you let me see iniquity
    and look yourself upon wickedness?ᵈ
Havoc and violence are before me,ᵉ
    there are legal disputes,ᶠ
    and strife is suffered.
⁴Therefore the law is numb,ᵍ
    and justice never goes forth,
For the wicked surround the righteousʰ
    therefore justice goes forth crookedⁱ—

With the introduction given, Habakkuk immediately plunges us into the action of the book, opening with a desperate plea to God. We learn that Habakkuk has prayed over and over again, crying out and pleading for help, yet God greets his desperate cries with silence. Habakkuk is surrounded by prolific social oppression, violent and chaotic sin, and legal corruption. So bad is the Jewish leadership that the Law itself has become "numb"—frozen—in their hands. Justice never goes forth, and what goes forth in the name of justice is crooked, bent so far from God's standard that it is unrecognizable. Habakkuk and those few who remain faithful, the righteous who still call on Yahweh as their God, are surrounded. They are drowning in a sea of wickedness. Why has God not acted? Why does He tolerate this

---

ᵃ Job 30:20

ᵇ Hab 1:3, 9; 2:8, 2:17; Job 19:7

ᶜ Hab 3:8, 3:13, 3:18

ᵈ Jer 9:4-6

ᵉ Amos 3:10, Ezek 45:9

ᶠ Cf. Deut 19:17-21 for the use of רִיב (*rîb*) in the sense of a legal dispute concerning criminal action, 25:1-2 in the sense of a civil lawsuit.

ᵍ Gen 45:26, Pss 77:3, 88:16, 38:9.

ʰ Hab 1:13

ⁱ Hab 1:7

among His people? Where is He among the horrors?

Exegesis of Verses 2-4

²How long, oh YHWH, have I cried for help,
    but you do not listen,
I shout out to you "Violence!"[i]
    but you do not save?
³Why do you let me see iniquity
    and look yourself upon wickedness?
Havoc and violence are before me,
    there are legal disputes,
    and strife is suffered.
⁴Therefore the law is numb,
    and justice never goes forth,
For the wicked surround the righteous
    and for that reason justice goes forth crooked.[ii]

Verse 2. From this very first line, we are immersed in Habakkuk's passionate prayer. We are confronted by a righteous prophet facing theological dissonance: YHWH is the covenant Lord of His people, yet He appears to be conspicuously absent in their moment of dire need. Habakkuk relates his repeated prayers to God and agonizes over the deafening silence that appears to be God's response. Yet as we will see in the following verse, God is there, and He has not been and is not silent.

    Most English translations render 2a (עַד־אָנָה יְהוָה שִׁוַּעְתִּי וְלֹא תִשְׁמָע) with an imperfective sense, such as the ESV's "O LORD, how long shall I cry for help, and you will not hear?" An analogy can be drawn with Exodus 16:28, in which the same phrase is used (עַד־אָנָה, *'ad-'ānâ*) with a perfect verb with the sense "How long will you continue." However, we must ask what best fits the context and try to make sense of the transition from the *qatal* tense-form in the 2a to the *yiqtol* in 2b. His transition between the two tense-forms suggests a transition from his history of prayers to his present act of praying. He has cried out for a long time and cries out yet again, but deafening silence remains constant. The impression given is Habakkuk's deep frustration over the present circumstances.[1]

---

[1] Patterson, *Nahum, Habakkuk, Zephaniah*, 141.

Echoed in Habakkuk's prayer are the similar words of Job, "Behold, I cry out 'Violence!' but I am not answered; I call for help, but there is no justice" (Job 19:7, ESV) and "I cry for help and you do not answer me; I stand, and you only look at me" (Job 30:20, ESV). Both characters share the same agonizing struggle of seeing despair and injustice without an answer from God. But, as we will see, Habakkuk like Job eventually finds rest in God and His inscrutability, even where answers are not present.

The result Habakkuk is seeking from his prayers is salvation: he asks God to rectify the wrongs around him. Though this is Habakkuk's initial request, we do not read of salvation again until the final chapter. Habakkuk's response to Yahweh instead focuses on judgment (1:12). But in the last chapter, Habakkuk's prayer uses the terminology of salvation once again (3:8, 13, 18). It seems that only after his dialogue with Yahweh does Habakkuk finally see Chaldea as God's answer to his prayer. Therefore, throughout the book we are witnessing Habakkuk wrestling with God's salvific intent through Chaldea.

Verse 3. Habakkuk now lays bare the situation by which he is surrounded. God is allowing Habakkuk to look on iniquity; He Himself is looking upon wickedness. Why would God do this? How can He do this?

Together, "iniquity" and "wickedness" communicate the thought of violent and sinful oppression. Iniquity (אָוֶן, *'āven*) has the sense here of sinful injustice, wickedness (עָמָל, *'āmāl*) that of oppressive harm. Together they diagnose Judah's problem as one of an oppressive, malevolent leadership: it is oppression from those who are commissioned to lead and protect.

The following tricolon describes this situation in more detail: social chaos and violence define Judah at this time. When the leadership fails to enforce justice, mayhem ensues among the people. שֹׁד (*šōḏ*; *havoc*) and חָמָס (*ḥāmās*; *violence*) occur together—in the reverse order—elsewhere a few times as a hendiadys with a similar force to the English "death and destruction."[2] The key difference is in the situation where the pairs are used: in English, "death and destruction" often describes military scenes, but חָמָס and שֹׁד in Hebrew are used rather to refer to self-inflected violent mayhem

---

[2] HALOT, 1418. A hendiadys refers to a construction where two words together convey a single idea.

among a nation (cf. Jer 6:7, 20:8; Ezek 45:9; Amos 3:10). The words have this force here.

In the last part of the tricolon, Habakkuk describes this social chaos as it unfolds in the legal sphere. "Legal disputes" and "strife" exemplify in the legal sphere but do not exhaust the chaos plaguing Judah.[3] These are essentially legal terms: Habakkuk describes miscarriages of justice. Conflicts abound and the legal system is inadequate to handle the conflicts, lawsuits, and injustices that are brought before them.[4] The picture is horrific, and God appears silent: where is Yahweh, the one who saved His people from the horrors of Egypt? Where is He now that His people are as bad as the Egyptians?

"Suffered" in 3e translates the Hebrew word נָשָׂא (*nāśā'*), which can have the sense "to endure" or "tolerate" something. Habakkuk seems to be playing on these two senses, suggesting that the people suffer legal strife while the courts tolerate the chaos, failing to act against it.

Verse 4. As suggested by "therefore," this verse is connected to verse 3 as a result of it: because of this prolific oppression and violence, the Torah has become numb. Law (תּוֹרָה, *tōrāh*) here refers not to a generic legal standard but to God's legal standard, the Torah revealed at Sinai and given by God for the governance of His people.[5] For some interpreters, this first line of the fourth verse determines how one reads the whole book.[6] I concede this to be true in as much as a proper understanding of verse 4 is part of the larger case for seeing wicked Judahites in these first three verses (see the Introduction), yet I am not convinced it is significant in the way argued by

---

[3] In poetry, lines containing a verbless clause or an imperfect may be followed by a line introduced with a vav-consecutive *yiqqtol* verb providing a specific example or further explanation of the event or state declared in the first line (e.g. Pss 29:5; 55:6, 18) . 3d-e describe unrest in the social sphere.

[4] Johnson, "The Paralysis of Torah in Habakkuk 1," 4; Theodore Hiebert, "The Book of Habakkuk," in *The New Interpreter's Bible*, ed. Leander E. Keck and et al., vol. VII (Nashville: Abingdon Press, 1996), 631.

[5] So most commentators: e.g. Baker, *Nahum, Habakkuk and Zephaniah*, 52; Goldingay and Scalise, *Minor Prophets II*, 54; Patterson, *Nahum, Habakkuk, Zephaniah*, 142.

[6] E.g. Johnson, "The Paralysis of Torah in Habakkuk 1"; Watts, "For I Am Not Ashamed."

these authors.

For Marshall D. Johnson, the paralysis is a failure of the Law's promise to come to fulfillment, though Habakkuk does not know why.[7] Rikki E. Watts argues that the numbness of the law is intrinsic: the Law is powerless to change the sinful people, to right the wrongs of Judahite society.[8] There is an inherent insufficiency to the Law. But, however true Watts' view may be theologically, the inherent insufficiency of the Law is not a central theme in Habakkuk.[9] That is, nothing here or later in the book suggests that the Law the target of the prophet's criticism. In this verse the law is described as "numb," or "paralyzed" (ESV; the NASB's "ignored" presents an interpretation of the metaphor). We must ask if this an internal or external condition: is Torah itself intrinsically numb and ineffective? or has the social unrest paralyzed Torah? פוג (*pûg*), translated "numb," has the sense "to be cold;" figuratively this describes in other places powerlessness or, in one instance, the deadening of the heart—a heart attack (Gen. 45:26). The word itself does not tell us whether the law is internally or externally numb. Watts and Gerald Janzen argue that the intransitive nature of פוג make the intrinsic reading the only possible one. However, this is mistaken. It should be noted that פוג is not intransitive (the subject does not perform an action) but stative (the subject is in or enters into a state of numbness). As a stative verb, פוג is consistent with a state that exists independent of an external force or that results from external intervention.[10] The Law's inability as a means to salvation—revealing sin but not combatting it—could be considered as inadequacy—powerlessness—yet this is not the focus of our context.[11] Considering the greater and immediate contexts, understanding this numbness as external, resulting from the failure of those entrusted with the Law, is the best interpretation.

---

[7] Johnson, "The Paralysis of Torah in Habakkuk 1," 262–265.

[8] Watts, "For I Am Not Ashamed," 5–6. Cf. J Gerald Janzen, "Eschatological Symbol and Existence in Habakkuk," *The Catholic Biblical Quarterly* 44, no. 3 (July 1982): 396–397.

[9] See further my comments on Hab 2:2.

[10] Cf. DCH, BDB. Contra Janzen, "Eschatological Symbol and Existence in Habakkuk," 397; Watts, "For I Am Not Ashamed," 5.

[11] We learn elsewhere, and see hints even in this book (Hab 2:4), that this was not the intended function of the Law (Gal 3).

First, what is in view is the Law as a legal standard, God's covenant regulation. In this regard, it is not a failure here or even in the New Testament when it is replaced. Paul argues that the Law has been fulfilled and ended in Christ (Rom 10:1-13),[12] indicating that its purpose has been achieved. This is why it has passed away for us under the New Covenant (Gal 3).

Second, Habakkuk has introduced Judah's present condition in terms of social oppression, violent chaos, and legal injustice; it is, "therefore," the case that the law is numb—a state further described in terms of justice never going forth. The law is numb because the leaders who are charged with enforcing it are themselves corrupt: like the blind leading the blind, they have no ability to help the righteous in the face of wickedness. The law is numb "and justice never goes forth." This latter clause explains the first: the numbness in the Law consists of the lack of judicial action, of godly justice failing to attain in the courts and among the leaders.

Our interpretation is confirmed in the next two lines. This numbness of the law and failure of the law is explained further: "for the wicked surround the righteous, therefore justice goes forth crooked." That the wicked surround the righteous is given particular emphasis, sandwiched between two lines describing the procession of justice and explaining them both. The net effect is that the Law's numbness can be described as the failure of justice: it never goes forth and what goes forth in the name of justice is bent out of shape. This is symptomatic of a society where the people who trust in YHWH, the righteous, are surrounded by the wicked.

Textual Notes

[i] **Verse 2c.** None of the versions recognize חָמָס (ḥāmās) as an exclamation, instead reading it as a participle from the verb of the same root. This results in the LXX's "…I cry out to you, being mistreated, and you will not save?" Similarly the Vulgate. The consonantal text could be read either way. But considering the context, it is best read as an exclamation, as the Masoretes have pointed it. Cf, Job

---

[12] Moo, *The Epistle to the Romans*; J. Alexander Rutherford, "Do Not Say in Your Heart: An Exposition of Romans 10:1-8" (Teleiotēti, 2016), accessed January 1, 2018, https://teleioteti.ca/resources/papers/.

19:7.

ⁱⁱ **Verse 4d.** מְעֻקָּל (*mᵉ'uqqāl*) is a *hapax legomenon*, but we have enough evidence to deduce that its sense here is "crooked." The same root is used elsewhere in the Hebrew Bible to refer to a twisting road (Judg 5:6, Ps 125:5) or a writhing snake (Isa 27:1). We then get the idea that justice here is crooked, bent out of shape: it is not straight, that is, in line with God's standard. See DCH and HALOT.

Exposition[1]

Habakkuk is distressed in his circumstances, and his response is to call out to God—how long? Why, oh Lord? That God will eventually answer Habakkuk is not in question, but the present silence is: "why is it that you haven't answered me," we hear Habakkuk asking, "why do you allow these things to go on before me and not act?" Later, in 1:12, he reveals his utter confidence in God—"we shall not die!"—yet he is here tormented by several theological questions. Why is God, the good and righteous God who entered into covenant with us, silent? Why has He, as of yet, failed to respond to His distressed people? Habakkuk does not, as many of us would today, rail against God, accusing Him of injustice, of being evil or neglectful. Instead, he agonizes over the apparent contradiction between the God he knows and the horrors he faces. If God could act now, why hasn't He? God does not reveal His purpose in withholding salvation, as He does not today tell us why Christ has not yet returned, but He tells Habakkuk that He will indeed save—He is in the process of saving now—and that Habakkuk is to trust Him.

This seems to be somewhat of a pattern in God's activity. For 400 years His people dwelt in Egypt before the Exodus; for over 400 years God was silent before He finally provided a savior (from Nehemiah to Jesus); and for 2000 years the return of Christ has been imminent, yet the world has gotten more and more chaotic and He has still not returned. We don't see the fullness God's plan, so we are left in suspense: we know God is going to act, but the time of His action is unpredictable. In the absence of His action, many of His people around the world can affirm with Habakkuk that they are surrounded by the wicked; they see violence and mayhem, the legal systems let them down, and they cry out violence! Some preachers tell us that God's number one concern is for our health, wealth, and safety, yet that was not the answer Habakkuk received. Knowing God's unfailing goodness, he

---

[1] Exposition is an arbitrary word in this regard, meaning merely "an explanation"; what I have labelled "exegesis" is likewise "an explanation." What I intend to do here, as exposition, is to draw out the meaning of the text in application to our day. So far, we have been concerned with description: in describing the text in English, we are engaging in translation and so considering the meaning of the text. Now we will focus more deliberately on extending this meaning from general translation to specific circumstances and trends within our culture.

was still confronted by long, agonizing, hopeless distress. He kept, time after time, doing the only thing he could: he cried out to God for salvation, yet God's answer proved even more distressing.

Today, we live between the climactic incarnation of Jesus Christ and the final act in the history of the old creation, His return. We suffer violence; we are sojourners in a foreign land.[2] Christians around the world suffer, yet Christ has yet to return. God has not given us His reason for delaying only the knowledge that He is at the doorstep but has yet to cross it. We were told to pray for His coming—event to hasten it (2 Pet 3:12)—yet we are still praying and waiting for final deliverance from sin and its consequences. We are not given an answer as to when Jesus will return, but we must not let the circumstances around us lead us to the conclusion that God does not care, that God is not at work.

God will not often come to our rescue, and if He does it may take a very long time; but in any case, we must not allow our present circumstances to delude us as to God's nature. For Habakkuk, he could look back on all that God had done in the Exodus and beyond for assurance of God's good character. For us, we look to the Cross. On the Cross, we see that God, after thousands of years of waiting, gave His answer to the most dire problems facing humanity: He provided salvation in Jesus Christ. On the Cross, He demonstrated for all times His righteousness, so we need not fear injustice on His part. On the Cross, He demonstrated for all times His loving goodness, so we need not fear abandonment. We may not see salvation or God's intervention for justice in our day, but we can look back and see it on the Cross. And because Jesus rose again, is alive and reigning, we can look to the future and know that one day our salvation will be complete and justice will be rendered against all the ungodliness and unrighteousness of men.

---

[2] Cf. Heb 11:8-16, 13:14; 1 Pet 1:1, 2:11.

ii. Yahweh's Response to Habakkuk's First Complaint (1:5-11)

⁵"Look, all of you, among the nations and behold—
    be astonished and astounded!ᵃ
For I am doing a deed in your day;ᵇ
    you would not believe it though it were told.ᶜ
⁶For, behold, I am raising up the Chaldeans,ᵈ
    that bitter and brash nation,

Who traverses the breadth of the earthᵉ
    to take possession of dwellings not his own.
⁷Terrifying and dreaded is he,
    from himself go forth his justice and majesty.ᶠ

⁸Swifter than leopards are his horses;
    quicker than wolves of the evening,
    his horsemen leap forth.
His horsemen come from afar,
    they fly like an eagle
    hastening to eat.ᵍ
⁹They all come for violence,
    the horde of their faces forward,
    and he gathers captives like sand.

¹⁰He makes a mockery of kings;
    dignitaries are a joke to him.

ᵃ Acts 13:41

ᵇ Hab 3:2, Ps 44:1-2

ᶜ Hab 3:2

ᵈ Amos 6:14, Jer 5:15, Exod 9:16.

ᵉ Rev 20:9

ᶠ Job 13:11

ᵍ Deut 28:49

> He laughs at every fortification
>   and piles up a mound of earth and takes it.
> ¹¹He therefore moves on as the wind;
>   crosses boundaries and is guilty,
>   whose strength is his god."ʰ

In the midst of Habakkuk's outcry—moments after Habakkuk complained that God does not answer—Yahweh breaks into Habakkuk's prayer. Yahweh shows Habakkuk that He has been and is currently at work, that Habakkuk's answer is on its way. What follows is a vision: Yahweh has commanded Habakkuk and the righteous to look among the nations, now He shows what they are to be looking at. His answer—His work of salvation, His tremendous deed—is the rise and looming invasion of Chaldea, a horrible godless nation!

Proclaiming the shocking deed, God describes the Chaldeans (i.e. the Babylonians) as a bitter and brash nation. This becomes the topic of the following exposition: the Chaldeans are first described in terms of their bitterness (6c-7), followed by their brashness (8-9). This bitter-brashness is then summarized in verses 10-11.

Exegesis of Verses 5-6b

> ⁵"Look, all of you, among the nations and behold—
>   be astonished and astounded!ⁱ
> For I am doing a deed in your day,
>   you would not believe it though it were told.
> ⁶For, behold, I am raising up the Chaldeans,
>   that bitter and brash nation,

Verse 5. Habakkuk provides us with no transition as he records God's interruption of his prayer. God breaks in to Habakkuk's complaint with a command to look upon His answer already in progress. Habakkuk here recounts with great irony his own experience. In the midst of a complaint about God's silence and inaction, he is interrupted by God's speech and informed that God has been at work the whole time. Further irony emerges as God's answer is framed in similar terms to the problem about which Habakkuk complains.

"Look" translates a plural imperative from רָאָה (*rā'āh*), so Habakkuk is

---

ʰ Deut 28:49; Hab 1:17, 2:18-19, 3:19.

not the only one being addressed ("all of you"). We may then ask, who is this vision addressed to? In 2:2-4, the written vision produces two different responses in the hearers; from this we can deduce that it is to be made known to wicked—those who "run"—and the righteous—who "wait" in faith. This is confirmed from the vision and the exposition of it throughout the book. Though the language God employs to describe His work is dark, there is nothing that explicitly identifies this as a word of judgment directed at the wicked (though the LXX does translate it in this way). From the greater context, we see that God's vision reveals the answer to Habakkuk's prayer: though difficult, the Chaldean invasion is a work of justice (1:12), it is to be responded to with trust in Yahweh (2:4), and is ultimately God's work of salvation (3:13-19).

I then propose that it is a vision rather like the message of Jesus: it offers salvation to those who respond in faith, the righteous, but judgment to those who respond with unbelief, the wicked (Matt 11:25-27, Mark 4:11-12, John 12:38-39). Habakkuk, as the model of the righteous believer, responds in the way God intends: he acknowledges God's work and praises him, confessing trust despite the awaited horrors. The vision is addressed to the whole of Judah, but is meant to be received as the promise of God's salvific action by those with ears to hear. Above I noted that the LXX translates this text as warning. In doing so it is not an entirely wrong translation, yet it is not an entirely adequate one either. The LXX translates the text in such a way that excludes the address to the righteous but captures the judgment against the wicked. It is then a restrictive—that is, it restricts the meaning of the passage—but not an erroneous translation.

The second line reiterates the command to "look," now נָבַט (*nābaṭ*), and commands the proper response with the repetition of the verb תָּמָהּ (*tāmāh*; be astonished) in two different stems. The two imperatives commanding Judah to look, רָאָה and נָבַט, connect YHWH's command with Habakkuk's prayer in verse 3.[1] There, he cried out "Why do you let me see [ראה] iniquity, why do you look upon [נָבַט] wickedness?" YHWH is then correcting his vision: Habakkuk has been looking upon the problem, but now he is to look upon YHWH's solution.

---

[1] So Patterson, *Nahum, Habakkuk, Zephaniah*, 149.

The repetition of תָּמָהּ achieves emphasis through poetic assonance, as I have tried to convey with "astounded" and "astonished"; the sense is, "be utterly astounded."[2] What God is about to show them is going to leave them dumbfounded! There is intentional ambiguity in the use of these terms, for they express both astonishment in general and terrorized shock. God has planned a deed to subvert their false conceptions, a deed that is utterly shocking to their expectations: this is what they are meant to see and believe. Yet, this deed, by its very nature, will also be a profound source of terror.

Habakkuk 1:5 in Acts 13:41

Here in verse 5 we find our first text quoted from Habakkuk in the NT. In the introduction, we already saw how Paul has employed Habakkuk in his speech at Antioch of Pisidia. With it, he underscores the pivotal nature of the coming of Jesus. There is no middle ground: if you do not believe, you will perish! I noted there that a textual difficulty remained to be explored. It is to this that we turn here.

With some minor changes (dropping επιβλεψατε [*epiblepsate*; look!] and θαυμάσια [*thaumasia*; wonders]), Paul quotes Hab 1:5 from the LXX. The major difference between the MT and LXX is the translation of גּוֹיִם (*gôyim*; nations) with οἱ καταφρονηταί (*hoi kataphronētai*; you scoffers!) and the addition of ἀφανίσθητε (*aphanisthēte*; perish!). Most commentators would here attempt to explain how the LXX and Paul, as he follows it, have arrived at this translation. I intend, however, only to explain why Paul has used the LXX's restrictive translation.

Paul elsewhere demonstrates a knowledge of the Hebrew text as we know it, conforming his quotes from Habakkuk 2:4 to it over against the LXX (Rom 1:17, Gal 3:11), yet he predominately uses the LXX. One of the reasons for this is the audience to whom he is writing. His ministry is directed towards the gentiles, who are Greek speaking, so it makes sense for him to use the translation of the OT they are familiar with. The situation would be similar if I had an opportunity to preach at a church that believes the KJV to be the only acceptable translation. Though it is not my preferred translation—having obvious

---

[2] So Goldingay and Scalise, *Minor Prophets II*, 57.

insufficiencies—in as much as it accurately conveys the meaning of the original text, I will use in order to avoid unnecessary battles.

Paul here employs the LXX for a similar reason; he is preaching in a synagogue but to the Jews of the diaspora, who are probably Greek speakers. The LXX is the text most readily available and, most importantly, it here correctly (though restrictively) conveys the sense of the Hebrew text. If we judge the LXX here as a general translation (see Appendix 5), it falls short. But if we consider it an application or specific translation, it is ideal for Paul's intended application of this text. In Hab 1:5, the Septuagint focuses on the judgment aspect of God's vision, ignoring the salvific side. Paul uses it because he is preaching that same aspect, though elsewhere he preaches Habakkuk with the salvific aspect in view (Rom 1:17).

In verse 5c, the conjunction כִּי (*kî*; for) is used to indicate that the next line expounds what is to be seen among the nations.[3] They are to see God's deed, His unbelievable work! "Doing a deed" translates a participle with a cognate accusative—both from פעל (*p 'l*; cf. 3:2)—emphasizing the action God is performing.[4] In context, the emphasis is intensive: God is on the move; He is acting; His work is unfolding, so pay attention! The deed is being done in the days of those addressed ("your" is plural): it is happening even now. The immediacy of God's action answers Habakkuk's questions concerning God's silence. God has not been silent, even now His work is coming to fruition.

God's deed is then described, in 5d, as one that would be unbelievable, even if it were told to them. This is not meant to be a prophecy of their response, for they are instructed to have faith in 2:4 ("faith" in 2:4 is from the same root as "believe" here: אמן, *'mn*), and Habakkuk responds with belief in chapter 3. Like the equivalent English idiom, that the vision is unbelievable describes it as astonishing, surprising, or utterly unexpected. They will be told, but even then they will struggle to accept that YHWH is doing this—that He could do such a thing! Yet, despite its unbelievable nature, this is indeed God's deed, and belief in the unbelievable is the very

---

[3] The plural of this word, גוי (*gôy*; nation), is used throughout the book only in reference to the victims of the Chaldeans (Hab 1:5, 17; 2:5, 2:8; 3:6, 3:12); this helps us identify Chaldea as God's anointed army in Habakkuk 3.

[4] Though there is no subject provided for the verbal participle, that YHWH is the one doing the deed is obvious from context.

thing He asks of His people. We will see later that Habakkuk connects his prayer in chapter 3 directly to the vision here by repetition of "deed" and allusions to "in your day" and "told."

Verse 6a-b. The next two lines give us further explanation, identifying this deed: YHWH is raising up the horrid Chaldeans. "For," כִּי *(kî)* again, provides the reason that God's deed is unbelievable. The combined force of God raising a pagan nation and the identity of that nation as the Chaldeans produces the unbelievable nature of God's work. "Chaldeans" was a general term at this time referring to the Neo-Babylonian empire, though it originally referred to a specific people group in Southern Mesopotamia that rose to power over Babylon.[5]

The nature of the vision suggests that the Chaldeans were already on the scene at the time of the vision. Babylon had a long history in the Ancient Near East, with Chaldea reaching ascendency in the later part of the 7th century BC. Depending on when Habakkuk prophesied, Habakkuk may very well have recognized and trembled at thought of them as God's tools. If his knowledge was not yet that clear, the rest of the vision would underscore the horrific nature of this people.

In my translation of 6a, I have retained the traditional and now archaic "behold" as the translation of the interjection הִנֵּה (*hinnēh*). "Behold" is not common in contemporary English, but captures well the sense of הִנֵּה here. הִנֵּה functions in many different ways, one of these is what we could call a directive interjection. It is used to command the reader or listener's attention toward something within the text or narrative: in the latter instance, it may introduce an unexpected scene or event; in the former, it may draw attention to a word or clause.[6] In verse 6a, a first common singular suffix is attached (הִנְנִי, *hinnî*; behold me!), providing the subject for the following participle. This draws attention to the action and especially God as its subject: behold what I am doing, I am raising the Chaldeans. "Raising up" describes God act to establish the Chaldeans, bringing them on to the world scene and giving

---

[5] I will use "Babylon" and "Chaldea" interchangeably throughout this commentary.

[6] I am told that Brazilian Portuguese still retains, in formal speech and writing, a word similar to *hinnēh*. "*Eis que*" functions to draw attention to a following word or clause.

them power to fulfill his purpose (cf. Exod 9:16).

The following line forms a lose parallel, describing "Chaldea." The description given here, "bitter and brash," introduce the rest of the vision. In the following lines, Chaldea is first described in terms of their bitterness (6c-7) and then brashness (8-9). The word I have translated "bitter," מַר (*mar*) has a similar range to the English "bitter"; here, the sense is not "bitter about being wronged," but the bitterness of a hard personality, characterized with coldness and hostility.[7]

"Brash" translates a Niphal participle from מָהַר (*māhar*). The Qal means to move quickly, to hasten; the Niphal is only used 4 times. In Isaiah 32:4, it refers to someone who is brash, making decisions too quickly and not taking the time to gain knowledge and understanding; his brashness will be remedied under the reign of the righteous king. The Niphal of this verb then means "to be quick," often in a metaphorical sense (also Isa 35:4). Here, in the context of the bitter Chaldeans and their rampaging, it refers to their brashness, their unthinking violence and rampaging. The consonantal similarity shared by הַמַּר (*hammar*) and הַנִּמְהָר (*hannimhār*) suggest that Habakkuk uses these particular words for the poetic assonance.

---

[7] HALOT suggests "grim," BDB "fierce." Cf. 1 Sam. 22:2, Ps. 64:3.

Textual Notes

[i] **Verse 5b.** The LXX translates this text quite differently, inserting "and perish" and translating "among the nations" with "you scoffers." Despite Paul's use of the LXX, explained above, the MT is to be maintained. Three reasons can be given in support of the MT, apart from its general reliability over against the LXX.

First, the manuscript evidence supports it, with a significant qualitative majority in its favour. Second, the translation of the Old Greek and the Syriac can be explained as an assimilation to 1:13 and 2:5. Third, though the context of Habakkuk justifies the LXX's translation as a restrictive application of the text, the context favours an emphasis on Yahweh's unbelievable work of salvation among the nations, addressed not primarily to the unbeliever but the believing remnant.

Exegesis of Verses 6c-7

Who traverses the breadth of the earth
>to take possession of dwellings not his own.
⁷Terrifying and dreaded is he,
>from himself go forth his justice and majesty.

Verses 6c-d. These two lines and verse 7 form the first of three groups of lines that describe the Chaldeans; all three groups are related to the description in 6a-b as "bitter and brash." This first group describes them in terms of hardness, their grim determination and disregard for others. As noted earlier in a footnote, Habakkuk refers to Chaldea with the masculine singular pronoun throughout the book, probably with reference to its king (cf. 3:13-14).

The two lines here describe the Chaldeans as conquers, a nation that expands itself throughout all the known world, evicting the defeated from their homes and countries and taking their lands for themselves. This behavior, disregard for others and ravaging of foreign nations, becomes the central indictment against Chaldea in chapter 2. There, these nations lift up a song declaring Chaldea's demise, a demise precipitated by their unlawful gain of profit, their shameful deeds, their plundering of nations, and the blood they shed in doing so.

The picture in these lines is of a nation hardened in greed, cold towards the plight of fellow man, and ever pressing onward for more power. This is some of what it means for the Chaldean to be bitter.

Verse 7. The description of Chaldea's bitterness in the first two lines is completed in verse 7, where their bitterness is described in terms of the fear they incite and their self-made rule. Robertson describes Chaldea in this verse as "autonomous": they care not for a higher justice, bowing to no rules, nor do they care for those whom they oppress.[1] Judah put out twisted justice, but Chaldea is the source of their own "justice."[2] But we know that apart from God this cannot be true justice. Their powerful presence, the splendor of their opulence and power, is not derived from submission to a God greater

---

[1] Robertson, *The Books of Nahum, Habakkuk, and Zephaniah*, 152.

[2] "When the Babylonians are about, there is no doubt that *misphat* ["justice"] ... "goes out," or gets exercised. But it is "their law," "their authority," which is just as perverted as the one exercised in Judah." Goldingay and Scalise, *Minor Prophets II*, 58.

than themselves; instead, it is conjured by their own vain might (or at least they think it is, cf. 1:5). All this to say, they are hardened, cruel, cold, and selfish. This is God's tool. The nations and Judah are rightly astounded by God's deed and terrified by His instrument of salvation.

The pairing of יָצָא (*yāṣā'*, goes forth) and מִשְׁפָּט (*mišpāṭ*, justice) here in verse 7, "from himself go forth his justice …," calls to mind the same pair used twice in verse 4, "and justice never goes forth … therefore justice goes forth crooked." Yahweh in this way uses the language of Habakkuk's complaint to describe Chaldea, His answer to the problem raised in verses 1:2-4. Some commentators draw on this and other examples of parallels between the party against which Habakkuk complained (1:1-4) and the party about which Yahweh speaks (1:5-11, 2:2-20) to argue that 1:1-4 does not speak about Judah but Chaldea.[3] In the introduction, I argued that it makes the most sense of the book to follow the traditional interpretation and identify the Chaldeans revealed in 1:5-11 as a different party from the Judahites Habakkuk complains about in 1:1-4.[4] As we saw above, the fact that a significant problem in 1:1-4 is the numbness of the Torah strongly points to Judah and not a gentile nation as the problem.[5] The language parallels between 1:1-4 and 1:5-11 are not, therefore, intended to identify the two parties but to indicate their similarity. This will continue throughout the book, suggesting that the wicked of Judah are not so different from the pagan gentiles. This will be a significant theme throughout the book.

---

[3] Floyd, *Minor Prophets. Part 2*, 82, 95–96; Cleaver-Bartholomew, "An Alternative Reading of Hab 1 and 2," 45–59; Sweeney, "Structure, Genre, and Intent in the Book of Habakkuk," 63–83.

[4] See pages 6-11, under the heading "The Parties Involved in Habakkuk."

[5] This could, of course, speak of Israel, but the prominence of Chaldea and not Assyria points to Judah.

Exegesis of Verses 8-9

⁸Swifter than leopards are his horses;
   quicker[i] than wolves of the evening,
   his horsemen leap forth.[ii]
His horsemen come from afar,
   they fly like an eagle
   hastening to eat.
⁹They all come for violence,
   the horde[iii] of their faces forward,[iv]
   and he gathers captives like sand.

Verse 8a-c. The MT's "wolves of the evening" has been rejected by some translators in favor of a re-vocalization or consonantal emendation—"wolves of Arabia" (LXX) or "wolves in the desert" (NET). This is unnecessary, however, for the context is less concerned with the identity of a specific wolf species than the ferocity of their habits; as leopards are swift, and eagles plummet to grasp their prey, these wolves hunt in the twilight hours of the evening. The connotations of expert and fiercely swift night hunting contributes to the overall ferocity of the Chaldean imaged in these lines.

Verse 8d-f. There is a slight progression from the proceeding lines to this bicolon: in 8a-c, the Chaldeans leap forth with stunning ferocity; now they are mid charge.

Verse 9. As the textual notes indicate, the second line of this verse is difficult. Yet, despite the difficulties we have ascertaining the exact meaning of the words translated "horde" and "point forward," the sense of the verse as a whole is clear enough. The Chaldeans come forth united in the determination to wreck violence on all the nations before them.

In this verse Yahweh again uses a key term from Habakkuk's initial prayer to surface the similarities between the Chaldeans and the wicked of Judah: as Habakkuk was surrounded by "havoc and *violence* [חָמָס, *ḥāmās*]" (1:2), so now the Chaldeans come forth bent on performing further acts of "violence" (חָמָס, *ḥāmās*).

Here in verse 9, the singular "his" becomes briefly "them," turning from the nation as represented by its king to the Chaldeans as a numerous people. The interchange between "him" and "them" continues throughout the book.

"Sand" is a common biblical picture for a vast quantity (e.g. Josh 11:40); it is ironic that the people promised to be numerous like the sand of the seashore are destined become part of the vast "sand" of the Babylonian captives (cf. Gen 22:17). Yet, as we learn elsewhere, it is through this very captivity that a remnant of faithful Israel will be preserved so that God's promises to Abraham may be fulfilled (e.g. Deut 30:1-14; Jer 29:1-23, 30:1-33:26). This hope may be implicit in Habakkuk, as God instructs the righteous of Judah to view the invasion as a salvific act and to wait for it (Hab 2:2-4).

כֻּלֹּה (*kullōh*), the first word of verse 9, may not be familiar form to the reader. It is only כֹּל (*kōl*), "all," with an alternate 3ms suffix (ה, *ōh*, instead of ו, *ô*; cf. 1:15, 3:4). As observed in the introduction, this is an older form of the 3ms pronominal suffix.

Textual Notes

ⁱ **Verse 8B.** "quicker" is literally "sharper," חַדּוּ (*ḥaddû*; "they are quick," from חדד). חדד is used in the Qal stem only here. In the other stems, the term is used literally or metaphorically (cf. Prov 27:17) for the sharpening of a sword. "Sharper" in English is, however, not an adequate translation because it communicates keenness instead of speed and ferocity. The context suggests that speed is the primary sense of the word here, so "quicker." In the context, speed contributes to a greater sense of ferocity, leading to the translation of the ESV ("fiercer"). Cf. F. F. Bruce, "Habakkuk," in *The Minor Prophets: An Exegetical and Expository Commentary*, ed. Thomas Edward McComiskey (Grand Rapids: Baker Book House, 1992), 849; C.F. Keil and F. Delitzsch, *Commentary on the Old Testament in Ten Volumes: Minor Prophets; Two Volumes in One*, trans. James Martin, Reprint., vol. 10.2 (Grand Rapids: Eerdmans, 1978), 60.

ⁱⁱ **Verse 8C.** "leap forth" translates the verb פּוּשׁ (*pûš*), a rare word in the Hebrew Bible. In Malachi 4:2, this word is translated "You shall go out leaping like calves from the stall." The preceding context suggests a sense of joyfulness in this act, thus DCH's "skip about." However, the following verse speaks of "[treading] down the wicked, for they will be ashes under the soles of your feet," which may suggest a more militant image—though this is, at first glance, hard to reconcile with the subject being "calves." The second use of this verb, however, may shed light on this imagery. The standard translation of the other use of this word, in Jeremiah, suggests rather the careless frolicking of those who have wrought horrible sacrilege yet care not, thus an act of arrogance: "Though you rejoice, though you exult, O plunderers of my heritage, though you frolic like a heifer in the pasture, and neigh like stallions" (Jeremiah 50:11, ESV). However, the Hebrew text reads much more like Malachi: "for you leap like a calf threshing, and shout like a mighty animal" (my translation). In light of these two texts, פּוּשׁ (*pûš*) probably does not mean "frolic"

or "skip about" but kick the ground/leap with a surge of strength such as happens as a young bull leaps from its stall to stamp out grain. Applied to horses of war, this is thus an image of them kicking off to begin their charge.

[iii] **Verse 9B.** מְגַמָּה (*megammâ*; "horde") is a hapax legomenon. "Horde" or "all" is the typical English rendering (NASB, NIV; ESV, NET). Context may suggest totality or unity, a sense that may be supported by the Arabic cognate *jamma* meaning "be/become abundant." See Richard Duane Patterson, *Nahum, Habakkuk, Zephaniah*, The Wycliffe Exegetical Commentary (Chicago: Moody Press, 1991), 151–152; Wilhelm Gesenius, *Gesenius' Hebrew and Chaldee Lexicon to the Old Testament Scriptures*, trans. Samuel Prideaux Tregelles (Bellingham, WA: Logos Bible Software, 2003), 448.

[iv] **Verse 9B.** The final word of this line is also difficult; קָדִימָה (*qādîmâ*) usually means "eastward," "towards the east." The Qumran Pesher Habakkuk drops the final ה (*h*), yielding "[like] the east wind." The MT is, however, the more difficult reading and should be retained. "Towards the east" is odd, for the Babylonians would originate from the East. It may be that "eastward" signifying a turning around to mop up the remnants of their conquest, but this seems to be reading too much into the term and does not suite the context. Cf. O. Palmer Robertson, The Books of Nahum, Habakkuk, and Zephaniah, NICOT (Grand Rapids: W.B. Eerdmans, 1990), 154. Thus, it is probably best to focus less on their eastward direction and more on the unity and resolve indicated by "the horde of their faces is directed toward the east," that is, gathered together in the same direction. Thus, "their faces forward" seems to adequately capture the sense of the line.

Exegesis of Verses 10-11

> ¹⁰He makes a mockery of kings;
>   dignitaries are a joke to him:
> He laughs at every fortification
>   and piles up a mound of earth and takes it.
> ¹¹He therefore moves on as the wind,
>   crosses boundaries and is guilty,ⁱ
>   whose strength is his god."

Verse 10. "Dignitaries are a joke to him" is literally, "dignitaries are laughter"; English fortuitously has a similar idiom in "they are a joke," so I have translated it accordingly.

In the context of military conquest, especially directed towards a "fortification" (מִבְצָר, *mibṣār*), "and piles up a mound of earth and takes it" suggests the building of a siege ramp in order to break down the walls of a fortified city.¹ The Assyrian king Sennacherib's boast about his conquest over Judah is illustrative in this regard: "As to Hezekiah, the Jew, he did not submit to my yoke, I laid siege to 46 of his strong cities, walled forts and to the countless small villages in their vicinity, and conquered (them) by means of well-stamped (earth-) ramps, and battering-rams brought (thus) near (to the walls) (combined with) the attack by foot soldiers, (using) mines, breeches as well as sapper work."²

Verse 11. "Therefore" (אָז, *'az*), which opens the first line in Hebrew, indicates that the behaviour described in verse 11 logically follows from that of verse 10. Though the connection is not immediately evident, it would seem the same arrogance that expresses itself in Chaldea's mocking scorn towards those they conquer drives them to continue sweeping across the land, bringing them into guilt.

In verse 11b, God plays with the ambiguity of עָבַר (*'ābar*; to transgress, pass over), connecting it first with the movement of the wind in 11a and the guilt raised in the second half of 11b. It is their moving on like the wind that brings them across the boundaries ordained by God, entering into transgression and so guilt.

---

¹ So Patterson, *Nahum, Habakkuk, Zephaniah*, 153.

² James Bennett Pritchard, ed., *The Ancient Near Eastern Texts Relating to the Old Testament*, 3rd ed. with Supplement. (Princeton: Princeton University Press, 1969), 288.

Verse 11c forms an interesting end to Yahweh's vision. Some lines have indicated that Chaldea, though they serve God's purpose, are deeply wicked (7b). In 11b, the author identifies their behaviour as sinful—garnering guilt—but here the source of their guilt is finally identified: they hold up their strength as their god. That is, though God raised them up (5-6), they believe their success derives from themselves and so direct their worship accordingly (cf. Dan 4:19-33). Considering that Yahweh is a God of glory, concerned with bringing the glories of His name throughout the earth (cf. 2:14), this verse is ominous for Babylon.

Idol worship is weighty transgression: to exchange the glory of God and worship the creature instead of the Creator will surely earn God's wrath (e.g. Isa 21:9, Jer 50:35-38, Rom 1:17-2). Indeed, this theme punctuates the book, concluding the 2 major sections that follow this (cf. Hab 1:15-16; 2:18-1) and receiving it's response in Habakkuk's confession of faith in 3:18-19. The Chaldeans worship their own strength, but the faithful of Judah recognize the true source of strength, Yahweh their God.

English translations are torn between rendering verse 11 as a bicolon (ESV, NET, NIV) or tricolon (NASB). I have rendered it as a tricolon because this seems to best capture the poetic flow of the verse and its sense. 11b appears to be a Janus line,[3] looking back at 11a ("moves on" חָלַף [ḥālap], "crosses boundaries" עָבַר ['ābar]) and forward to 11c ("and is guilty," "whose strength is his god"). The transition from the *wayyiqtol* of עבר in the first part of 11b to a vav conjunction with the *qatal* of אָשֵׁם suggests that these verbs are a pair.

---

[3] "Janus" as an adjective refers to a something that looks both ways, towards what precedes and what follows. Thus, a Janus verse connects to the preceding and following paragraph (e.g. Eph 5:21), and a Janus line in parallelism equally partakes of the preceding and following lines in a colon. The term comes from the Latin god Janus, who had two faces, one facing backwards and one forwards.

Textual Notes

ii **Verse 11b.** Several commentators attempt to emend אשם (*'šm;* be guilty) in various ways. 1QpHab reads ואשם (*v'šm*) as וישׂם (*vyšm*), resulting in the translation "crosses boundaries and *devastates.*" Robert Haak follows the Qumran text, arguing with Driver and Brownlee that ישׂם (*yšm*) is equivalent to אשם and should be treated as a homonym with the more common אשם (be guilty). This would yield the meaning "make desolate" in both the MT and the Qumran Pesher. Robert D. Haak, *Habakkuk*, Supplements to the Vetus Testamentum XLIV (Leiden: E.J. Brill, 1992), 45–46; W.H. Brownlee, *The Text of Habakkuk in the Ancient Commentary from Qumran*, Journal of Biblical literature: Monograph series (Society of Biblical Literature and Exegesis, 1959), 23.

However, all the examples given to prove that אשם is identical to ישׂם are better read as the common verb אָשֵׁם (*'āšēm*), "to be guilty" (Isa 24:6, Hos 14:1, Ps 34:22). Indeed, following the MT reading in Habakkuk 1:11 makes remarkable sense of the context. אשם (to sin/be guilty) overlaps in meaning with עבר (*'br*, to pass over/transgress), which itself overlaps with חלף (*ḥlp*, to move on). The Masoretic reading (אָשֵׁם, to be guilty) is followed by most of the versions (the various Greek texts, Syriac, and Targum), though the Vulgate reads *et corruet* ("and it destroys"). In addition, it is possible that the Qumran text does not offer a different meaning but only an orthographic variation of the MT. However, even if the author of 1QpHab wrote ישׂם as an orthographic variation of אשם, the reading presented by the Qumran text is undoubtedly the source of the Vulgate's *et corruet*. In this way, we have early evidence of ישׂם meaning "to devastate." Therefore, the writer of 1QpHab could have had a copy of Habakkuk with either ישׂם or אשם, in the later case writing an orthographic variation. In either case, the manuscript before him could have meant "be guilty" or "to devastate." So 1QpHab is not necessarily in favour of "to devastate" or "to be guilty." Cf. A. Schenker and et al., eds., *The Twelve Minor Prophets: Introduction and Commentaries on the Twelve Minor Prophets*, Biblia Hebraica Quinta 13 (Stuttgart: Deutsche Bibelgesellschaft, 2010), 116.

Thus, the reading אשם, taken as an instance of the common verb meaning "to be guilty," explains all the manuscript evidence and makes the best sense of the context. Cf. DCH; Keil and Delitzsch, *Commentary on the Old Testament in Ten Volumes: Minor Prophets; Two Volumes in One*, 10.2:62–63; Patterson, *Nahum, Habakkuk, Zephaniah*, 153.

Exposition

Yahweh's answer for Habakkuk is not what he expected, and God knows this. Verses 5-6b lay heavy emphasis on this point: it is unbelievable! Be astonished; be astounded! Instead of relieving the tension between God's revealed character and the present circumstances, the beginning of this vision only heightens it. Yahweh has not been silent, yet what He is doing appears worse than Habakkuk's current experience. Habakkuk expressed in prayer his struggles with the present evil, with how God could endure to look upon the abuse of His people and allow the righteous to be surrounded by the wicked, allow them to witness the social chaos surrounding them. Instead of absolving Himself of these complaints, God heightens them: instead of the wicked Judahite leadership, His people will face the wicked Chaldeans.

Imagine if God's response to our prayers against the moral evils of our society, against abortion and abuses of authority, was to bring a horrible foreign nation upon us. 80 years ago, the equivalent would have been an invasion by Nazi Germany. It is not hard to imagine the horror this would invoke. Yet in Habakkuk's day, God intends this attack as salvation for His people: this is to be welcomed not rejected. Yahweh expects His people to believe the unbelievable: they are to trust God despite the incomprehensibility of His actions.

In chapter 2 we are told that the Chaldeans will face judgment in the end, and that the wickedness of God's people must be judged, but Habakkuk never gives us an explanation for how God can be the instigator behind the coming army, who exult "as if to consume the oppressed in hiding places" (3:14). We can surmise from the whole testimony of the Bible various answers that vindicate God's character, but we are not given a certain answer—and one may never be given. Habakkuk is left to trust the one thing he knows for certain, God's revealed character. He trembles, his bones fail him (3:16), yet he boldly declares, "I myself will rejoice in YHWH, I will exult in the God of my salvation" (3:18).

We have yet in our generation, here in North America, to face horrors the like of which Judah faced, horrors like those Europe faced at the hands of the Nazis—or Christians worldwide have faced at the hands of Islam and Communism more recently. But our time may come; surely God has no reason to protect the godless nations of North America. If we are faced with the inexpressible horrors of inexplicable evil: what will be our response? If God's answer to our prayers turns out to be nuclear devastation, how will we respond? Such are the questions Habakkuk is faced with in this vision and which God would have us ponder as we read Habakkuk. Will we believe the unbelievable, that God is good despite what we see—that He could do something against our greatest moral intuitions?

That God introduces the Chaldeans as a nation *He* is raising up establishes a theme throughout Habakkuk that has great relevance for our understanding of God. Habakkuk here, and throughout, has much to say about God's sovereignty, His rule and control over all the nations of the earth. Sovereignty is a word that is not comfortable for the West, a civilization that has not known kings for hundreds of years, where the only authoritarian rulers are tyrants. Elsewhere in the world, that one is sovereign, in control, does not necessarily have the same negative connotations that it has for us.[1] Yet, whether we intuitively perceive control and those who wield it positively, negatively, or neutrally, we must be willing to consider God's control as He would define and explain it.

In Habakkuk, we are not shown a God who sits back and lets the earth run itself nor a God who lets evil have its way and tweaks it this way or that for His own purposes. So far in Habakkuk, God has claimed to be at work, to be up to something. He is doing something on a grand scale: He Himself has established the authority and power of a horrible nation (1:5-6), and He is wielding them like a sword to deliver his justice and salvation (1:12, 3:13). Moreover, they are associated with Him, they are *His* army. Habakkuk describes the Chaldean invasion like this: God "comes in from Teman… Pestilence goes before him, and fiery devastation follows his steps" (3:3, 5). God comes forth for the salvation of his people "with his anointed," the Chaldean, whose rods for punishment will pierce the head of the wicked and whose warriors "storm in to scatter me, their exultation as if to consume the oppressed in hiding places" (3:13, 14). Yahweh gives them power, uses them for His purposes, yet He has no obligation to sustain them. He gives them His cup to intoxicate the nations with their wrath, yet He will turn this cup back upon them (2:15-16). God gave them life, and He will take it. All of this is done for justice against the wicked (1:12, 2:12-14) and salvation for His righteous (1:2, 3:13, 18-19). In Habakkuk we are given a picture of a God utterly in control, who bends the nations to His will yet without ever

---

[1] Timothy Keller recounts an interesting story from a missionary, where God's sovereignty became a door for the Gospel. In preaching to Korean prostitutes, this missionary found that preaching God's love, so effective in North America, failed yet preaching God's sovereignty and predestination succeeded. Timothy Keller, *Center Church: Doing Balanced, Gospel-Centered Ministry in Your City* (Grand Rapids: Zondervan, 2012), 125–126.

nullifying their responsibility.

This last point is tremendously important for the way we understand God's relationship to human beings, especially in the debate over predestination and election. Many authors uncritically assume that the Bible teaches what philosophers call "incompatibilist" or "libertarian" freedom; that is, that humans are responsible for their actions if and only if there is no cause for it—if they could choose something other than they did (hence another title, "freedom of alternate choice").[2] Though this debate is far beyond the scope of our exposition of Habakkuk, I bring it up because Habakkuk here and throughout assumes the contrary position to what these authors have assumed, called "compatibilism." Habakkuk teaches that God can be in control, that He can cause something to happen, ordain it, and yet it can also be true both that He Himself is unstained by the actions of His tools and that they remain responsible.

Regarding the former, we learn that God can "raise up" a nation, ordain it for a good purpose (1:12; 3:13) achieved by evil means (2:6-11) for the purpose of His glory (2:12-14; 3:3), and remain the Holy God (1:12-13), a rock for His people (1:12; 3:18-19). God acts in the world, and—without giving us an explanation—God's use of wicked tools leaves them responsible (2:16) and He untarnished (1:12).

Regarding the latter, that Chaldea is God's anointed, His tool for salvation and justice (1:12; 3:13), does not absolve them from their guilt (2:5-20). So Habakkuk simultaneously maintains God's complete sovereignty, God's pure holiness, and the moral responsibility of human beings even when it is God who has brought their evil actions to pass.

The Bible does not give us easy answers here, but it does give us parameters within which we must formulate our theological views. Any theological account of God's sovereignty and human freedom must maintain both God's unfettered freedom—His rule and control—and full human moral responsibility. I have defended elsewhere a form of compatibilism that I still believe does justice to the Biblical teachings,[3] and John Frame has

---

[2] For a more lengthy definition of this position and arguments against it, see my book *Prevenient Grace: An Investigation into Arminianism* (Vancouver: Teleioteti, 2016).

[3] Ibid.

suggested a metaphor to describe God's sovereignty that likewise accounts for the Biblical teaching.[4] However, at the end of the day, whether our answers hold true or are disregarded at a later date, we must confess with Paul the unfathomable nature of God's work and bow our heads in humble awe and worship of Yahweh, who is at work for His purposes and our good even among the most horrifying circumstances (Rom 8:28):

> [33] Oh, the depth of the riches and wisdom and knowledge of God! How unsearchable are his judgments and how inscrutable his ways!
> [34] "For who has known the mind of the Lord,
>   or who has been his counselor?"
> [35] "Or who has given a gift to him
>   that he might be repaid?" (Rom 11:33-35)

---

[4] John M. Frame, *The Doctrine of God*, A Theology of Lordship (Phillipsburg: P&R Publishing, 2002), 156–159.

iii. Habakkuk's Second Complaint (1:12-2:1)

¹²Are you not of old,ᵃ
    oh YHWH, my God, my Holy One?
    We shall not die.
Oh YHWH, for justice you put him in place;
    oh Rock,ᵇ to rebuke you appointed him.
¹³Your eyes are too pure to see evil;
    to look at wickedness you are not able!
Why do you look upon the treacherous,ᶜ
    remain silent when the wicked swallows upᵈ those more righteous than he?

¹⁴You have made human beings like the fish of the sea;
    like creeping creatures, no one rules over them.
¹⁵He brings all of them up with his fishhook,ᵉ
    with his drag net he drags them away.
He gathers them in his fishnet,
    thus he is glad and rejoices.
¹⁶And so he sacrifices to his dragnet,
    and burns incense to his fishnet.
For by these his portion is rich
    and his food corpulent.
¹⁷Will he, therefore, empty out his net?
    And continually slaying nations,
    will he not show mercy?

2 ¹At my post I will stand,

ᵃ Pss 74:12; 77:6, 12; 143:5

ᵇ Deut 32:4; Sam 22:2, 3, 32, 47; Isa 30:29; Pss 18:3, 19:15.

ᶜ Jer 12:1

ᵈ Ps 35:22

ᵉ Jer 16:16, Amos 4:2

and station myself upon a fortification;ᶠ
I will keep watch to see what he will say against me,
    and how I may respond to my rebuke.ᵍ

So far, we have read Habakkuk's distressed cry to God for salvation (1:1-4) and then the horrific vision God gives Habakkuk revealing His present work (1:5-11). In 1:12-21, we read Habakkuk's response to the vision. He begins with a statement of faith in Yahweh—"we will not die!" (1:12)—but is quick to press God for answers. He wants an answer for what appears to be inconsistency between God's actions and His self-revelation.

Habakkuk acknowledges that God is at work for judgment against Judah but questions how He can look upon such faithless traitors as the Babylonians—these godless idolaters and wicked men. He knows his own people are bad, but how can God use those even worse than Judah to be His tool of judgment? Is this not against His very character? Is He not too pure to involve Himself in the sinful affairs of humanity?

After describing the actions of the Chaldeans as he perceives them, Habakkuk declares his intent to wait for God's answer. He has put out a challenge. How is God going to defend himself? Here Habakkuk moves beyond humble questioning and edges into presumption ("I will look to see how I may respond to my rebuke").

Exegesis of Verses 12-13

¹²Are you not of old,
    oh YHWH, my God, my Holy One?
    We shall not die.ⁱ
Oh YHWH, for justice you put him in place;
    oh Rock, to rebuke you appointed him.
¹³Your eyes are too pure to see evil;
    to look at wickedness you are not able!
Why do you look upon the treacherous,
    remain silent when the wicked swallows up those more righteous than he?

Verse 12. After receiving the vision in verses 5-11, of the coming Chaldean invasion, Habakkuk responds in a rather curious manner—or so it seems at

---

ᶠ Isa 21:8; Jer 6:17; Ezek 3:16-27, 33:7-9; Hos 9:8.

ᵍ Job 31:14, 35

first. Most translations and many commentators understand קֶדֶם (*qedem*) in the first line as "are you not of everlasting" (ESV, NASB, NIV), however the NET approaches our translation here with "you have been active from ancient times." An ontological statement—that God is an everlasting or eternal being—would not make much sense in our context, but there is a better way to understand קֶדֶם. קֶדֶם often refers not to a time before creation (eternity) but to ancient times (e.g. Pss 74:12; 77:6, 12; 143:5). Habakkuk is, then, not considering God's eternal nature but His past activity: it is because God is the God of ancient times—the God of Abraham, Isaac, Jacob, Moses, and David—that Habakkuk can have confidence.

Reading the text in this way sheds light on the connection between Habakkuk's rhetorical question in 12a-b and his statement in 12c, "We shall not die!" Because God is the God of Israel's history, the Covenant Lord of His people, Habakkuk has assurance that Yahweh's purpose will not be the end of His righteous people. Habakkuk can be assured of his survival not because God is old but because He is the God of old. He is the God who has always acted and will continue to act for His people. Martin Lloyd-Jones has put it well: "What is the significance of those words: 'My God, mine Holy one, we shall not die'? He is recalling that God is the God of the Covenant.... God had given His word and He would never break it."[1]

Verse 12a-c expresses great confidence in Yahweh, the covenant God of Israel; this confidence appears to continue in the following to lines. By calling God "rock," Habakkuk considers God as an adamant, faithful defender of His people (consider the way this language is used in Deut 32:4, a passage alluded to throughout Habakkuk). However, 12d-e betrays a subtle misunderstanding of God's purpose through Chaldea. Habakkuk originally prayed for salvation (1:1-4): he was asking for God to intervene and save His righteous people. Though Habakkuk is confident in the survival of God's righteous people, he views the Chaldean invasion not as a salvific act that will save Judah but an act of Judgment through which they would barely survive (cf. vv. 13-17). It, therefore, betrays a shocking transformation when Habakkuk's resignation in 1:13—"Oh YHWH, you put them in place for justice; oh Rock, you appointed them to rebuke"—becomes in 3:13 and 3:18 "You come forth for the *salvation* of your people, for *salvation* with your anointed" and "I will exult in the God of my *salvation*." There is a profound shift in the way Habakkuk views the Chaldean invasion from chapter 1 to

---

[1] D. Martin Lloyd-Jones, *From Fear to Faith: Studies in the Book of Habakkuk* (London: Inter-Varsity Press, 1970), 31. Cf. Armerding, "Habakkuk," 618.

chapter 3. We will see that 2:2-4 is the pivotal section that effects this change.

Verse 13. It is important to observe that two key verbs from this first section reappear in this verse. נבט (*nbṭ*, to look) and ראה (*r'h*, to see) have already appeared together in 1:3 (*let me see... look yourself upon*) and 1:5 ("*look, all of you*"); Habakkuk now revisits his claim in verse 3, that God "looks upon" evildoers. God not only looks upon evil doers but even directed His people to behold them in verse 5. "How is this compatible," Habakkuk cries out to God, "with your Holy character?" The confidence expressed in verse 12 is confronted with the realities of God's actions; Habakkuk's "Holy One" appears to be contaminating Himself with things unholy! After recounting God's holy character, his moral inability to endure even the sight of evil, Habakkuk then asks the probing question, "why?" Why would God do this? Why would He make an already unbearable situation even worse?

Habakkuk sees the vision of the Chaldean invasion and instead of salvation, he sees the perpetuation of the very injustice against which he first cried out. As God has permitted the wicked Judahites to endure, so now with the wicked Chaldeans! "This is just too much," cries Habakkuk, "it is one thing to endure your faithless and sinful people, a whole other one to endure such a godless nation as Chaldea!" With this claim, Habakkuk makes a profound theological error. He suggests that the wicked Judahites are not so wicked when compared to the Chaldeans, to the wicked who "swallow up those more righteous than they." In his despair over the vision, Habakkuk forgets the very reason why he first prayed: the wicked Jews were oppressing the righteous Jews. But the Chaldean invasion reduced all of Judah to the category of "more righteous." Habakkuk's "why" question and this misstep will receive their answer in 2:2-4.

"Treacherous" here has a religious sense: בגד (*bgd*, to act treacherously) can refer to unfaithfulness towards human allegiances or towards God. Here the latter sense is intended: the Chaldeans have obligations to God as all other nations do, yet they are faithless men and women who transgress God's orders (cf. 1:11). A subtle contrast is thus raised against the treacherous Jews who numb God's Law (1:4) and the treacherous Chaldeans who are a law to

The Holiness of God

Habakkuk, in verses 12-13, draws our attention to a central way the Bible describes God. He is Holy. Throughout the Bible, the theme of holiness is repeated: Israel is a holy nation, the Temple is a holy place, and Christians like Israel are a holy people. Yet behind and above all these

themselves (1:7).

holy things is Yahweh, the Holy one of Israel. All holiness attributed to created things derives from God's holiness. That God is holy means that He is separated from all His creatures by His complete and consistent dedication to manifesting the fullness of His character—to display His glory—in all He does.[i] That is, we can discern from Scripture that God's ultimate purpose in creating and redeeming is to magnify His glory, that is, to make His magnificent nature clear to His creatures, to reveal Himself in all His splendor (consider Hab 2:14, John 17:24, Rom 9:22-24). That God is Holy means that all His interactions are intended to share the glorious beauty and joy He enjoys in Himself with others. This is good news for the Christian, for we learn that God Himself is joyful, that this sharing of Himself is the ultimate source of joy for His creation (consider Ps 16:11, Ps 84, Matt 5:2-12; 1 Tim 1:11).Out of this commitment flows all of God's actions.[ii]

In contrast with this, the entire created order is twisted by sin away from this purpose for which God created the world. Man, who was supposed to worship the Creator, instead worships God's creation (cf. Rom 1:18-23). Men and women in this way are *unholy*: they are not devoted to God's purposes—indeed, they are set in complete opposition to them (cf. Rom 8:5-8). Humans, locations, and objects become Holy by consecration: God rededicates them to His purposes. This is the way the Bible most often speaks of "holiness," but theologians often use the term "holiness" to refer more broadly to the way God is different from His creatures.

Yahweh is different from us in His unfailing devotion to upholding His glory in all He does, but He is also profoundly different in the very nature of His being. In this sense of the word, Yahweh's holiness encompasses all of who He is considered in terms of His difference from His creation. That Yahweh is holy means that there is no one like Him (1 Sam 2:2). All of who God is different from His creation. God is not, like the Greek "gods," an upgraded version of creation; He is not merely a more powerful version of us. God is bigger and better in our similarities, this is true, yet He is the source of all these similarities. God is the reference point for goodness, love, kindness, etc.: we only know what is good, what is kind, what is love because of God. These only have meaning in reference to God, the ultimate measure of all that is good and the ultimate antithesis of all that is bad. In this God is *qualitatively* different, not just *quanitatively*: God is the original, we are the copy.

God's perfections are eternal, our reflections are merely derivative. That God is holy means that He is the Creator in distinction from the creation. In this way, Scripture teaches two categories of existence: there is God and not-God. God is distinct, separate from His creation. Visualizing this, we could follow Cornelius Van Til in picturing two circles that do not touch, one is labelled "Creator" and the other "creature." In this theological sense of the word, holiness means that the distinction between these circles, between the Creator and the creature, is never blurred. Even in the Incarnation, Christ never stopped being the infinitely Holy Creator while taking on the creation. This may be something we cannot comprehend.

Usually in theology, holiness refers to such a distinction in nature, but it may also refer to the distinction in purpose we first saw. Distinction in purpose is the primary way that holiness is used in the Bible. The words we translated "holy," "saint," "sanctified," and refer to "consecration," being dedicated for a specific use. God is Holy in this way: He is utterly committed to His purposes and unfailing seeks them.

---

[i] On the meaning of Holiness as separation for a purpose, see *The Gift of Reading – Part 1* (Vancouver; Teleioteti, 2019).

[ii] John Piper in my estimation has done more than anyone in recent years to draw our attention to this truth. However, he uses the term "holy" in the more broad theological sense noted below. See especially his book, *Desiring God*.

Textual Notes

[i] **Verse 12.** Some translations have for verse 12 "you will not die" (HCSB, NIV, cf. NET) in the place of "we shall not die" (cf. ESV, NASB). The difference

is not textual but traditional. That is, no extant text reads "you will not die" but Rabbinic tradition tells us that this is one of the so-called *tiqqune sopherim*, or "emendations of the scribes." Though the nature of the *tiqqune sopherim* is debated, it is commonly held that these are instances where changes or emendations were made to the original text in order to resolve a problem the original introduced (such as suggesting God could die). This is by no means certain, however, and several authors have argued that the text the Rabbi's claim to be original, "you will not die," is at best a "false correction." Cf. McCarthy and Barthelemy cited and discussed in A. Schenker and et al., eds., *The Twelve Minor Prophets: Introduction and Commentaries on the Twelve Minor Prophets*, Biblia Hebraica Quinta 13 (Stuttgart: Deutsche Bibelgesellschaft, 2010), 116–117.

    The MT's "we shall not die" makes the best sense of the context, as argued above, and it would be irresponsible to follow the rabbinic tradition without any textual evidence. For these reasons, I believe the MT preserves the original reading. Carl E. Armerding, "Habakkuk," in *The Expositor's Bible Commentary: With the New International Version; Daniel and the Minor Prophets*, ed. Frank E. Gaebelein, vol. 7 (Grand Rapids: Zondervan, 1985), 622; Richard Duane Patterson, *Nahum, Habakkuk, Zephaniah*, The Wycliffe Exegetical Commentary (Chicago: Moody Press, 1991), 156–157; O. Palmer Robertson, *The Books of Nahum, Habakkuk, and Zephaniah*, NICOT (Grand Rapids: W.B. Eerdmans, 1990), 157.

Exegesis of Verses 14-17

¹⁴You have made human beings like the fish of the sea;
   like creeping creatures, no one rules over them.
¹⁵The Chaldean brings all of them up with his fishhook,
   with his dragnet he drags them away.
He gathers them in his fishnet,
   thus he is glad and rejoices.
¹⁶And so he sacrifices to his dragnet,
   and burns incense to his fishnet.
For by these his portion is rich
   and his food corpulent.
¹⁷Will he, therefore, empty out his net?[i]
   And continually slaying nations,[ii]
   will he not show mercy?

Verse 14-16. At first, verse 14 almost has a proverbial ring to it; yet it is clear from context that this statement, that God has made "humankind like fish… like creeping creatures," pertains to the specific situation of the Judahites at this time.[1] The image appears to be twofold. First, in light of the fishing imagery in verse 15-16, "fish" and "creeping creature" picture humanity like fish and either small sea creatures or insects (רֶמֶשׂ, *remeś*) which are caught in nets (cf. 1:8c, "They gather captives like sand"). Second, the use of דָּג (*dāg*, fish) and רמשׂ ("swarming" or "creeping creature") together harkens back to Genesis. In Genesis 1:26 and 28, the "fish of the sea" and "every creeping thing [רֶמֶשׂ, *remeś*]" or "living thing that moves [רמשׂ, *rmś*]" are the first and last creatures over which God gives man dominion. There is thus an ironic reversal as humanity is brought low, made like the creatures

---

[1] Richard Whitekettle has made an interesting argument that "fish" and "creeping creatures" represent the righteous and wicked caught up without discrimination in the Chaldean invasion. This might make sense of the context (though 1:13 suggests that Habakkuk has collapsed all Judah into the category of "righteous") yet Whitekettle's argument is not persuasive. His reasoning involves many stretches: he focuses on the taxonomical relationships of words and phrases rather than their meaning in context, and he relies on modern taxonomical categories (דָּג = fish = scales and fins) without enough Biblical support. Richard Whitekettle, "Like a Fish and Shrimp out of Water: Identifying the Dāg and Remeś Animals of Habakkuk 1:14," *Bulletin for Biblical Research* 24, no. 4 (2014): 491–503.

over which they were to rule.²

This first verse raises for us a question: does 14 describe the same situation as verses 15-16, humanity in light of the Chaldean invasion,³ or the situation preceding their invasion. Most commentators seem to assume the former position, but the context indicates the latter. That is, God making "humanity like the fish of the sea" does not refer to His actions through Chaldea but the state of Judah at this time; with corrupt leadership and social chaos, it is helpless and ripe for capture (cf. 1:1-4). This is made clear in several ways: 1) the Chaldeans are able to draw the Judahites up in nets because they are already like fish and creeping things; being caught up would not make them like this. 2) The problem Habakkuk complained about in 1:1-4 was a lack of law, justice, and societal order, the very problem that would emerge if God had made it like they had "no ruler." And 3) There is a progression from what God has done, made men like fish, and what Chaldea is about to do.

That God has not only prepared Chaldean as invaders but has also made the land ripe for invasion ("*You* have made") increases the irony in Chaldea praising their own weapons for their victory instead of God (1:16, cf. 1:11).

It is interesting—and important—that Habakkuk resumes in verses 15-16 the same theme of idolatry with which God ended the vision in 1:5-11. In verse 11, God describes the Chaldeans as those who transgress the bounds He set for them and who consider their strength to be their god. Here, Habakkuk describes the Chaldeans rejoicing over their plunder (15c-d) and then making sacrifices to their weapons (16a-b). Once again, they have ignored Yahweh—who has empowered them (1:6a) and prepared the nations before them (1:14)—and worshiped themselves. As in verse 11, this note of idolatry prepares us for the judgment of Babylon pronounced in 2:5-20 and contrasts with the righteous believer in 3:16, who declares that "The Lord YHWH is my strength." We are thus prepared already to answer the question Habakkuk will raise in verse 17.

---

² James D. Nogalski, *The Book of the Twelve: Micah-Malachi*, Smyth & Helwys Bible Commentary (Macon, Ga: Smyth & Helwys Publishing, 2011), 644; O. Palmer Robertson, *The Books of Nahum, Habakkuk, and Zephaniah*, NICOT (Grand Rapids: W.B. Eerdmans, 1990), 162.

³ So John Calvin, *Commentaries on the Twelve Minor Prophtes; Habakkuk, Zephaniah, Haggai, Zechariah, Malachi*, trans. John Owen, vol. 4, Calvin's Commentaries XV (Grand Rapids: Baker, 1996), 48.

Several features and terms in these verses may need to be clarified here. כֻּלֹּה (*kullōh*) is כֹּל (*kōl*), "all," with an alternate 3ms suffix (ה, *ōh*, instead of ו, *ô*) (cf. 1:9, 3:4). As observed in the introduction and above, this is an older form. "Rich" (שָׁמֵן, *šāmēn*) and "corpulent" (בָּרִיא, *bārî'*) used to describe the Chaldean's loot in verse 16 are both words for "fat"; fatness is a common Semitic idiom for luxuriousness, richness, or abundance. The distinction between "dragnet" (מִכְמֶרֶת, *mikmōret*) and "fishnet" (חֵרֶם, *herem*) is not very clear, yet Armerding is probably right in identifying the first term as a siene net, a weighted net used for gathering fish, and the second for a fishing net thrown from the shore.[4] This distinction is supported by the two terms the LXX uses in its translation (αμφιβλήστρον, *amphiblēstron,* casting net; σαγήνη, *sagēnē,* seine). However, an exact identification of the tools intended is impossible and unnecessary to understand the text.

Verse 17. Verse 17 is the second of two important questions Habakkuk asks in his response to Yahweh (1:12-2:1). In verse 13, he asked why God doesn't stop the wicked: "Why do you look upon the treacherous, remain silent as the wicked swallows up those more righteous than he?" Now, assuming that God is indeed refraining from action, Habakkuk asks if he will act, if He will eventually stop the wicked Chaldeans from rampaging. Both these questions will receive a response from God in Habakkuk 2. In 2:1-4, God will show the error of Habakkuk's question asked in verse 13, subtly answering it. Then in 2:5-20, God through the nations will declare the imminent end of Chaldea.

"Therefore," in 17a, indicates that Habakkuk's question evolves from his previous complaint. In light of Chaldea's vicious rampage, he asks, will you do anything? Though it is possible 17a is intended to be iterative, "keep on emptying his net" (ESV, cf. NET, NIV), a simple statement about the future is probably intended (cf. NASB). That is, Habakkuk is most likely asking, "will Chaldea go on after us and slaughter more nations, or will you finally put an end to them?" The difference may be negligible, but it seems to me that the Hebrew text and my translation above suggest Habakkuk is hoping for or expecting an imminent judgment on Chaldea. That is, he knows God's character, that He will have to stop them some time. Habakkuk's question is not if God will judge Chaldea but how long will He continue to bear with their sin.

The syntax of this verse is complicated, but it is clear Habakkuk is stressing that the Chaldeans continue to show no mercy. This again highlights

---

[4] Armerding, "Habakkuk," 619–620.

the tension between the character of God, who shows mercy (Ex 33:16), and the tools whom He has raised up. The question left by Habakkuk is, therefore, when and how will God vindicate His character? Again, by looking for to the time when God will judge Chaldea as the resolution of the theological tensions he faces, Habakkuk loses sight of the very reason he first cried out, the unrighteousness of the wicked Judahites. By looking to God's judgment of the Chaldeans for resolution, Habakkuk misses that their invasion is an act of God holy justice against the wicked *and* His salvific will for the righteous. However, it is not in the judgment of the Chaldeans but in their invasion that God's character is vindicated. This is the lesson Habakkuk will learn in chapter 2. However, before he receives God's response, Habakkuk has one last thing to say.

Textual Notes

[i] **Verse 17a.** Some commentators make much of the Qumran reading חֶרֶב (*ḥereb*, sword) in the place of the MT's חֵרֶם (*ḥerem*, net). The Syriac, LXX, and Vulgate all follow the MT with "net"; one Greek manuscript and the *Naḥal Ḥever* minor prophet scroll support "sword." There are several reasons to prefer the MT's reading. 1) The image of drawing the sword does not fit well with the progression of Habakkuk's thought, but the thought of emptying a net is ideal. 2) Despite the previous point, חֵרֶם is actually the *lectio difficilior,* the most difficult reading, for ריק חרב (*ryq ḥereb*) is a frequent idiom (e.g. Lev 26:33, Ezk 5:5, Ps 35:3). A scribe would be more likely to correct to or accidently reproduce חֶרֶב than attempt to or accidently change it to חֵרֶם. 3) The manuscript evidence also, in my opinion, favours the MT. Though the Qumran text is indeed quite early, as is *Naḥal Ḥever*, the MT is a very reliable tradition and is supported by the early Greek translation and the latter Syriac and Vulgate translations. However, the difference is not significant for understanding Habakkuk's response. Carl E. Armerding, "Habakkuk," in *The Expositor's Bible Commentary: With the New International Version; Daniel and the Minor Prophets,* ed. Frank E. Gaebelein, vol. 7 (Grand Rapids: Zondervan, 1985), 622; Richard Duane Patterson, *Nahum, Habakkuk, Zephaniah,* The Wycliffe Exegetical Commentary (Chicago: Moody Press, 1991), 166–167.

[ii] **Verse 17b.** Qumran does not have the vav before תָמִיד (*tāmîd*, continually). F.F. Bruce suggests that the MT may have resulted from dittography with the preceding 3ms suffix on חֵרֶם (*ḥerem*, net). The Syriac translation and several Targum manuscripts support the Qumran. The editors of the BHQ consider this syntactical change a response to the more difficult syntax of the MT, making the MT the *lectio difficilior.* A. Schenker and et al., eds., *The Twelve Minor Prophets: Introduction and Commentaries on the Twelve Minor Prophets,* Biblia Hebraica Quinta 13

(Stuttgart: Deutsche Bibelgesellschaft, 2010), 118; Patterson, *Nahum, Habakkuk, Zephaniah*, 167. In addition to being the *lectio difficilior*, the MT reading also creates a rhythm suiting Habakkuk's style while continuing to lay stress on the tension between God's character and the Chaldeans: will He who is merciful (Ex 33:19) continue to tolerate the merciless? Thus, the MT is to be preferred because it is syntactically more difficult and well suited to the context.

Exegesis of Chapter 2, Verse 1

2 ¹At my post I will stand,
>and station myself upon a fortification.
>
>I will keep watch to see what he will say against me,
>and how I may respond to my rebuke.

Verse 1. Habakkuk has expressed faith in God—"we will not die" (1:12)—yet he has also raised many questions. Why does God do this? How can He do this? When will He finally bring justice? Habakkuk is troubled yet thus far his tone has been faith-filled and humble; he is turning to God in his despair. This tone changes here. In the first verse of Habakkuk 2, as he concludes his response, his tone edges into presumption—"I will keep watch to see what he will say against me, and how I may respond to my rebuke."

We again hear echoes of Job here; as Job cried out for an opportunity to take up his case with YHWH (31:14, 35), Habakkuk has attempted to plead his case and expects a dialogue to ensue. He expects to receive a *rebuke* (תּוֹכַחַת, *tôkaḥat*), as God has raised up the Chaldeans to *rebuke* (יכח, *ykḥ*) Judah (1:12).¹ This may suggest that his view of God is skewed at the moment: no longer is He the God who delights to deliver and bless His people, instead He is a God eager to rebuke. Patterson considers this rebuke a positive thing: Habakkuk would expect that God is rebuking him for his own good.² Though this is consistent with the biblical teaching about God's correction (Prov 27:5, 29:15), this is inconsistent with Habakkuk's skewed perception in 1:12-2:1. Habakkuk confuses God's horrifying act of salvation as a heavy-handed act of discipline; he is confused over the nature of the vision God has given him. Within this skewed perception, a negative reading of "rebuke" is more likely.

It is more clear, however, that Habakkuk knows he has earned a stern rebuke: he has questioned the character of Yahweh, the glorious king of the universe. God will surely vindicate Himself. In this, Habakkuk again shows his faith, however badly expressed; he knows who Yahweh is and knows to expect that He will vindicate His character, that God will ensure His glory abounds and that His name will not enter disrepute. Robertson's words are

---

¹ Patterson, *Nahum, Habakkuk, Zephaniah*, 162.

² Ibid., 161.

fitting:

> Habakkuk is quite aware of the audacity of his most recent remarks. He has challenged the propriety of the purpose of the Lord himself. It is understandable therefore that he braces himself for a straightforward rebuke from the Lord.[3]

"How I may respond to my rebuke" is literally "what will I return upon [עַל, *'al*] the rebuke of me?" In English idiom, "how I may respond" appropriately communicates Habakkuk's sense. עַל could mean "against" but probably has here the sense of אֶל (*'el*), "to." These prepositions are often interchangeable, especially in the prophetic literature. "The rebuke of me" is most likely an objective genitive, indicating God's rebuke of Habakkuk. Habakkuk is considering what he will say when God rebukes him, when God speaks "against me." the preposition בְּ (*bᵉ*) following a verb of speaking often indicates the agent through whom one speaks (e.g. "he spoke *by* his servants," 2 Kgs 24:2) or the occurrence of a conversation (e.g. "I speak *with* him," Num 12:6), but it can also indicate libel or rebuke, speaking *against* someone (e.g. Num 12:8, 21:7; Jer 31:20). Because he is expecting a rebuke in the next line, Habakkuk is expecting God to say something "against me."

Like many of the Prophets, Habakkuk adopts the stance of a watchman, looking for a word from the Lord (e.g. Isa 21:6-8; Jer 6:17; Ezek 3:16-21, 33:7-9; Hos 9:8). He sets himself upon the wall and looks out, watches intently. Judging from the change of tone between Habakkuk's response in 1:12-2:1 and his prayer in 3:1-19, the answer he sees was not quite what he expected.

---

[3] Robertson, *The Books of Nahum, Habakkuk, and Zephaniah*, 165.

Exposition

The Prophets, the Hebrew Bible's second section, is not known for portraying saintly figures. The books that make up the Prophets are more interested in showing what people did to earn God's judgment and His faithfulness than giving us examples of faithful behavior. Despite this, we can often learn from the men and women whose stories are recorded in the Prophets. Habakkuk is not portrayed as perfect in the book of Habakkuk—in 2:1 at least, his tone moves beyond faithful questioning into presumption—nevertheless, there is much we can learn from Habakkuk's response in 1:12-2:1.

Habakkuk is faced with the problem of unresolved tension. There is conflict between what he knows from God's revelation and what he experiences every day. God is Judah's covenant Lord and deliverer, yet Judah is immersed in violent chaos. God is holy and pure, yet He has raised up and made a wicked and impure people His tools. Habakkuk has questions—as we all would—yet his response to God is grounded from beginning to end in faith. Though Habakkuk is confused and horrified, he brings his questions before God from a posture of faith. In verse 12, he acknowledges that God is the God he had heard about from childhood—the God of the Patriarchs, Moses, Joshua, and David. Because of who God is, Habakkuk is able to say, "we shall not die" (1:12).

It is because Habakkuk knows and believes the Scriptures that he wrestles with the Chaldean invasion: he knows who God is, so why is God now doing something that seems so out of Character (1:13)? It is because Habakkuk believes God's past revelation that he now struggles with his present action. There must be a reconciliation, he only struggles to find it. Even in 1:14-17, as Habakkuk describes the Chaldean's behavior and asks if it will continue, he draws upon the charge of idolatry revealed in 1:11 and seems to assume in his question that Chaldea will face judgment at some point. That is, he has faith that God will act against idolatrous rebels, that he will bring judgment upon them, yet he wonders when it will happen.

We will see in chapter 3 that Habakkuk turns from his questioning to awe-filled faith and praise, a transformation that would be impossible if Habakkuk did not begin with a posture of faith. If Habakkuk did not begin with faith, with trust in God, then he would have long ago let go of God's past revelation in exchange for his present experience. Without faith, God's present silence would have been definitive in Habakkuk's eyes. Yet because he believed in God and trusted His revelation, Habakkuk knew there must be more than what he was seeing. He pressed on despite his experience to discover the true nature of God's work and to worship Him for it. In this way, Habakkuk gives us an example of how to deal with unresolved tensions in our lives and theology; we must begin with humble faith.

Like Habakkuk, Christians are a people confronted by tensions, points of apparent conflict between our beliefs and our experience. As an Old Testament believer, many of the tensions Habakkuk would have faced were resolved with the incarnation of Jesus Christ, yet other tensions endure even for us today. How God can superintend all human activity and remain holy and pure is difficult, as is the truth that humans remain free despite God's control over history. The Bible helps us with these questions; it gives us hints at their resolution but never presents the full picture, as we will see in Habakkuk 2. Another tension Christians face is the imminent return of our Lord. Jesus has been on the verge of returning for 1900 years; the book of Revelation ends with Jesus's words, "Surely, I am coming soon" and John's response, "Amen. Come, Lord Jesus!" Jesus is coming—is at the very door (Matt 24:33, Jam 5:8-9)—and has been for almost 2000 years. This is a tension we experience, living in light of Christ's imminent return with the experience of His delay. We know that a day is a like 1000 years to the Lord (2 Pet 3:8-10), so this is not entirely unexpected. The tension nevertheless remains. When such conflicts arise, Habakkuk proves to be a sure guide for us.

Our approach to such conflicts, whether we choose to live with them or attempt to find an intellectually satisfying answer for them, must begin with humble faith. Without humble faith that trusts God, that believes He is greater than we are and knows better than we do, we might just think Jesus was wrong about His return or that the Biblical authors' were mistaken to call God good or sovereign in light of all the evil we experience. The faith we see from Habakkuk is the courage to live by faith and not by sight, to trust our creator and sustainer, Lord and king, over ourselves—even when others think we are fools for doing so. Beginning with faith, we can wrestle with the so-called "problem of evil" or the question of free will and love and follow God whether or not we find a satisfying answer. Beginning with faith, we can live in light of Christ's return despite His apparent delay, knowing that God "is not slow to fulfill his promise as some count slowness, but is patient toward [us], not wishing that any should perish, but that all should reach repentance" (2 Pet 3:9). As we face tensions in our lives, Habakkuk provides a fitting role model as a believer who moves from faith into deeper faith despite the inexplicable work of God in the world. In this we are right to imitate him.

iv. Yahweh's Final Response (2:2-2:20)

Thus far we have considered Habakkuk chapter 1 and the first verse of chapter 2. In those verses we were introduced to the problem of The Book of Habakkuk, the tension between what Habakkuk sought and God's answer. We have read the vision of the Chaldean invasion and heard Habakkuk's response.

Moving into the rest of chapter 2, we arrive at the heart of the book. We read in this chapter how God resolves Habakkuk's questions, producing the amazing response of praise in chapter 3. In his response, Habakkuk asked of God two questions (1:13c-e, 17). First, how could a righteous God judge one nation with a more wicked nation? It seems unfair! Second, when would God bring justice to this wicked nation? God's final answer to Habakkuk is shaped as a response to these two questions. God's answer begins in 2:2-4, addressing Habakkuk's first question. Though only 3 verses long, this is often (and rightfully) considered the heart of the book.

1. A Reply for the People: the Question of Righteousness (2:2-4)

²And YHWH answered me and said;

> "Write down the vision,
> > make it clear[a] upon tablets,[b]
> So that one who reads it will run—
> > > ³for the vision is still for an appointed time,[c]
> > > it speaks to this end and does not lie.[d]
> > If it delays, wait for it,
> > > for it will surely come; it will not tarry—
> > ⁴behold, it is bloated: his appetite is not upright within him,
> > but the righteous one will live by his faith.[e]

God begins His response to Habakkuk by addressing the nation of Judah. Habakkuk has asked how God can allow a wicked nation to swallow up those more righteous than itself (1:13). Yahweh in these verses will indirectly answer this question; in these verses He identifies what it truly means to be righteous.[1]

God obliterates in Habakkuk's mind the distinction between unrighteous Jews and unrighteous Gentiles. This point has already been made subtly by using the same language to refer to the wicked Jews and Chaldeans (in 2:4-5 this comparison is most clear), but it is made explicit here by the comparison of two figures. The first is bloated and wicked in his appetites, or desires. The second is the truly righteous one, the one who believes. These

---

[a] Deut 27:8

[b] Isa 30:8. The plural of לוּחַ (*lûaḥ*, tablet) is most often used for the stone tablets of the ten commandments (Exodus, Deuteronomy, 2 Chron 5:10).

[c] Dan 3:35

[d] Prov 6:19; 12:17; 14:5, 14:25; 19:5, 9

[e] Isa 26:2; Rom 1:17; Gal 3:11; Heb 10:37-38. The words צָדִיק (righteous) and אֱמוּנָה (faith, faithfulness) appear together with the root ישׁר (be upright) once elsewhere, in Deut 32:4. Cf. 1 Kgs 3:6, Ps 58:2.

[1] Bomgaars similarly identifies a relationship between Habakkuk's question and this text. Dennis Leroy Bomgaars, "Habakkuk: Some Introductory and Literary Issues" (Master's Thesis, Reformed Theological Seminary, 1984).

are presented as two possible responses to the vision. One is the response of someone perverted in their desires and the other of someone who is a righteous believer. The first responds negatively—he runs!—the second waits, has faith.

Yahweh's response beginning in verse 2 is not quite what Habakkuk expected. Instead of a rebuke, he receives instructions. Has God ignored his questions, dismissed his troubles without a word? Though it may appear that way, God's response to Habakkuk reveals the false assumptions Habakkuk made, namely, that the wicked of Judah are more righteous than the wicked Chaldeans.

As I have contended throughout this commentary, the vision Habakkuk is instructed to write down is the coming Chaldean invasion, revealed in 1:5-11. God instructs him to proliferate this vision, to make all of Judah aware of what is to come. Two responses will be given when the vision is read. The first response is to run. That is, when most Judahites read the vision concerning the Babylonian invasion, they will attempt to flee—at the very least they will panic. Though this may seem like the appropriate reaction, God demands something different from those who trust in him. They are to "wait for it" (v. 2). The vision is sure to come, even if it seems to delay, it will arrive at the right time; yet this should not be a cause for fright among those who trust God. As we saw in chapter 1, Habakkuk cried out for salvation and God showed him the coming Chaldean attack. Because it is salvation, Habakkuk and the faithful of Judah are to wait for it, indeed to trust God that this is salvation—to trust God in the face of the very thing he declared unbelievable (1:5). Those who run reveal themselves to be unrighteous, gorged with sinful appetites and desires. Those who wait show themselves to be righteous and so find life before God.

This is heart of the message of Habakkuk. Life with God, covenant life enjoying God and His covenant forever, is not on the basis of ethnicity (being Jewish) nor works (obeying the Law). Life comes by believing the unbelievable. Life comes by trusting God despite His unbelievable actions (cf. 1:5). The righteous are those who have faith, and only those who have faith will have life before God.

Exegesis of Verses 2-4

²And YHWH answered me and said;
"Write down the vision,
    make it clear upon tablets,
So that one who reads it will run—

> ³for the vision is still for an appointed time,
>   it speaks[i] to this end and does not lie.
> If it delays, wait for it,
>   for it will surely come; it will not tarry—
> ⁴behold, his appetite is bloated:[ii] it is not upright within him,
>   but the righteous one will live by his faith.

Verse 2. Yahweh uses interesting language in his command to Habakkuk; write down the vision, *make it clear* (באר, *bʾr*) *upon tablets* (לוחות, *lûḥôt*). As I argued in the introduction of this commentary, the "vision" (חָזוֹן, *ḥāzôn*) is God's words in 1:5-11. What is interesting is the two words he uses to describe the writing of this vision. As commentators have observed before me, these words are most commonly associated with the Sinai covenant.² In the plural, לוּחַ (*lûaḥ*) most often refers to the tablets upon which the ten commandments were written (e.g. Exod 31:18). באר is a rare word (3x), appearing elsewhere only in Deuteronomy. In Deuteronomy 1:5, Moses *expounds* the law, but in Deuteronomy 27:8 he is commanded to write (כתב, *ktb*) the words of God *clearly* (באר). These two words only occur together in Deuteronomy 27:8 and here in Habakkuk 2:2. We are thus reminded of Sinai when we read verse 2. Some have surmised from these allusions that God is initiating a covenant renewal in these verses.³ However, this is by no means evident and does not fit the present context well. That is, though באר (*bʾr*) is used for a covenant renewal ceremony, this ceremony looks nothing like what we read here (cf. Deut 27, Josh 8:3-35).

In both of covenant renewal accounts (Deut 27, Josh 8:3-35), a copy of

---

² Cf. Rikki E. Watts, "'For I Am Not Ashamed of the Gospel': Romans 1:16-17 and Habakkuk 2:4," in *Romans and the People of God*, ed. Sven K. Soderlund and N.T. Wright (Grand Rapids: Eerdmans, 1999), 7–8.

³ O. Palmer Robertson, *The Books of Nahum, Habakkuk, and Zephaniah*, NICOT (Grand Rapids: W.B. Eerdmans, 1990), 168; O Palmer Robertson, "'The Justified (by Faith) Shall Live by His Steadfast Trust': Habakkuk 2:4," *Presbyterion* 9, no. 1–2 (1983): 52–71; Watts, "For I Am Not Ashamed," 8. It is interesting that Hab 2:4 shares three significant words in common with Deut 32:4, an allusion that is sometimes used to support the arguments for a covenant renewal. Granting an allusion, I do not see how this supports their argument. Instead, the reader is reminded of the character of Yahweh as they read this text, specifically, God's character in the context of judgment.

the law of Moses is written on stones, then the blessings and the curses of the covenant are recounted. In contrast, nothing in our context indicates that the blessings and curses are to be read nor is anything said about writing a copy of the law.[4] Furthermore, nothing in Habakkuk has suggested a covenant renewal is in order. Instead, the book speaks of the covenant curses coming upon those who disobeyed the covenant, much like Deuteronomy 32—a song alluded to throughout this book—anticipates. Therefore, I think there is a better explanation of these allusions.

As with the song recounted in Deuteronomy 32 (cf. Deut 31:19), the recounting of the blessings and curses and the inscription of the law on large stones in Deuteronomy 27 and Joshua 8:30-35 appear to be witnesses to Israel of the covenant and the consequences of obedience or disobedience. I think that this aspect of Deuteronomy 27 is the reason for the allusions Yahweh makes here in Habakkuk 2:2. By alluding to the covenant renewal ceremony, in which the Law is recounted, and the tablets on which the Law was written, the vision of the Chaldean invasion is connected firmly with the covenant curses that invoked it.

The vision, written on tablets like the ten commandments, written clearly like the stones of covenant renewal, shows to those who read it the consequences of their transgression of the covenant. That the allusions here are intended to invoke the witness function of the covenant may be supported by a similar text in Isaiah, where God instructs Isaiah to write an oracle on a tablet (לוּחַ, *lûaḥ*) to be a witness against the rebellious people (Isa 30:8). This finds support in the allusion God makes in 2:4 to Deuteronomy 32:4. The words צַדִּיק (*ṣadîq*, righteous) and אֱמוּנָה (*'ĕmûnāh*; faith, faithfulness) with the root ישׁר (*yšr*, be upright) occur together only in these two passages. The affect of the allusion is to juxtapose the sinfulness of the wicked Judahites with the character of God revealed when he comes to judge His sinful people, which is the context of Deuteronomy 32:4. It has a very

---

[4] There is a rabbinic interpretation that says Habakkuk here narrows the demands of the Law from Sinai's hundreds of commandments to one, namely faith. Rabbi Dr I. Epstein, ed., "Makkoth," in *Seder Nezikin*, trans. H. M. Lzarus, vol. 4, The Babylonian Talmud 13 (London, England: The Soncino Press, 1935), 173. This assumes that Hab 2:4 is the "vision," an assumption that is not supported by the text (see my argument in the introduction). Furthermore, nothing in context suggest that Habakkuk is revising or repeating the Law. Lastly, the New Testament does not suggest that the demands of the Law are narrowed—indeed Jesus emphasizes its demands (Matt 5)—but that Jesus fulfilled the whole Law and we receive the benefits of this work through faith.

similar function therefore to the allusion to Deuteronomy 27.

Turning to the fourth line of verse 2, we see that the result of Habakkuk publishing the vision serves as an answer the question he raised in 1:13. Major translations differ on how to render 2:2, such as "so the one who announces it may read it easily" (NET) or "so he may run who reads it" (ESV). The NET is understanding the word "run" (רוּץ, *rûṣ*) to mean "run ones eyes over it" and so "read it easily," a sense that רוּץ does not have in the Hebrew Bible. The ESV and NASB suggest by the helping word "may," indicating potentiality, that clear writing enables one reading the vision to run (the NIV is similar). That is, running is not the result of reading the vision but an action made possible by the clear writing. The text, however, is not suggesting that "run" is a good thing. It is, indeed, hard to make sense of this translation.

How does clear writing make one run? The suggestions of commentators are unlikely, namely that a herald is enabled to read it while running[5] or—by inverting the Hebrew syntax—that even one who runs by the tablet will be able to read it.[6] The latter interpretation ignores the syntax,[7] but the former has its own problems. First, there is no other example in the Hebrew Bible where קָרָא (*qārā*, to call out or read) refers to a herald. It is probable that קָרָא does not refer to reading in one's head, a phenomenon that appears almost a thousand years later; however, there are many instances where, though out loud, the reading is private (Deut 17:18-19, 2 Kgs 5:7,

---

[5] E.g. M.A. Sweeney, *The Twelve Prophets*, ed. David W. Cotter, vol. 2, Berit Olam (Collegeville, Minn.: The Liturgical Press, 2000), 471; Robertson, *The Books of Nahum, Habakkuk, and Zephaniah*, 170; Richard Duane Patterson, *Nahum, Habakkuk, Zephaniah*, The Wycliffe Exegetical Commentary (Chicago: Moody Press, 1991), 171; Henderson, *The Twelve Minor Prophets*, 301.

[6] Such an interpretation makes the verb "run" an substantival participle, "runner," and the participle a verb, "read." For example, Matthew-Henry has "he who runs may read." Matthew Henry, *Matthew Henry's Commentary on the Whole Bible: Complete and Unabridged in One Volume* (Peabody, Mass.: Hendrickson, 1994), 1359. Cf. John Calvin, *Commentaries on the Twelve Minor Prophtes; Habakkuk, Zephaniah, Haggai, Zechariah, Malachi*, trans. John Owen, vol. 4, Calvin's Commentaries XV (Grand Rapids: Baker, 1996), 64.

[7] John Marshall Holt makes the same observation. John Marshall Holt, "So He May Run Who Reads It," *Journal of Biblical Literature* 83, no. 3 (September 1964): 299.

19:14, 22:16, Isa 37:14) and no instance where the announcement of a herald is read or proclaimed (the participle is used 25 times, never for a herald).[8] Second, it hard to imagine a herald running with "tablets"—most likely made of stone. Third, it is unclear why clear writing would enable the herald to run, unless he is reading while running. For a message of the size and seriousness of the vision (1:5-11), this hardly seems likely. However, most argue that the herald is running because of the importance of the vision, an act for which clear writing seems to be of no help.[9] "Tablets" is also plural, possibly because of the length of the message[10] or because multiple tablets were to be set up in a public place.[11] In either scenario, the interpretation of a herald reading clearly does not fit.

In contrast, by translating "will," I emphasize the certainty of the result achieved, making it a causal connection (reading it causes him to run) and not a volition connection (clear writing enables him to run). רוץ ($rûṣ$) usually means "run" in a general sense, though sometimes "run" means flee (Judg 7:21) or even do evil (Isa 59:7). Running in both of these cases involves a negative response, running because of bad circumstances or acting wantonly for evil. Taking "run" in the sense of a negative reaction is rather enigmatic, but it is explained further in verse 4. Consider who might have reason to flee or act badly in response to a vision of the Chaldean invasion. If it is intended to be salvation, as I have argued, then the righteous of Judah should not flee but welcome God's act on their behalf. In other words, they should wait in faith for it (cf. 2:3-4). However, for the wicked of Judah, the natural response would be to run, to turn away from the coming judgment. We will see in verse 4 why this is important.[12]

---

[8] See DCH, HALOT.

[9] E.g. James D. Nogalski, *The Book of the Twelve: Micah-Malachi*, Smyth & Helwys Bible Commentary (Macon, Ga: Smyth & Helwys Publishing, 2011), 667.

[10] Paul Kleinert, "The Book of Habakkuk," in *The Minor Prophets: Exegetically, Theologically, and Homiletically Expounded*, ed. Johann Peter Lange and Philip Schaff, trans. Charles Elliott (New York: Scribner, 1874), 22.

[11] John H. Walton, Victor Harold Matthews, and Mark W. Chavalas, *The IVP Bible Background Commentary: Old Testament* (Downers Grove, Ill: InterVarsity Press, 2000), 792. Cf. 1 Macc. 14:25-39, Patterson, *Nahum, Habakkuk, Zephaniah*, 171.

[12] For a similar approach to "so that the one who reads it will run," see Robert D. Haak, *Habakkuk*, Supplements to the Vetus Testamentum XLIV (Leiden: E.J. Brill, 1992), 56.

Verse 3. "For" (כִּי, *ki*) subordinates verse 3 to verse 2, explaining it. Why would someone run? Because the vision is certain and true, and so it will not disappoint. I have rendered it as a parenthetical comment because verse 4 is intimately connected to verse 2, identifying "the one who runs." Verse 3 is, however, highly important. The figure in verse 2 is not Habakkuk and his response, "he will run," contrasts with the command given in verse 3: even if it tarries, "wait for it." There is a contrast, then, between verse 2 and 3: one figure runs, one waits. This is similar to the contrast in verse 4: one figure is bloated and not right; the other is righteous and believes.

"The Vision" or "the Messiah" in Verse 3?

In the LXX, the Greek translation of the Old Testament, verse 3 has a masculine pronoun where one would expect a feminine pronoun referring to the vision. This leads some interpreters to a messianic interpretation of the LXX:[i]

> Because there is still a vision for the time,
>   and **he** will appear at an end, and not in vain; (LES)

In the MT, the pronoun refers to the vision, but the vision cannot be the antecedent here, for the word for vision is feminine in Greek (ορασις, orasis). However, a messianic reading is not evident. There is, first, nothing in the context that would lead one to a messianic reading of the masculine pronoun. Second, there are more plausible explanations. One possibility is an appeal to the LXX translators' tendency for line-by-line translation, leaving it to the reader to sort out the text. But I think Patterson has proposed a better solution.[ii] If one reads LXX without trying to conform it to the MT, the most apparent antecedent is not the Messiah but καιρον (the time, season): the time to which the vision bears witness is not going to delay.[iii] This is approach is taken by the NETS,

> For there is still a vision for an appointed time,
>   and it will rise up at the end and not in vain.

Now, it is true that Hebrews applies this text to the return of Christ, yet there is no need to suppose that he thought that is what the text originally referred to, as I discuss in the introduction and below.[iv]

---

[i] Robertson, *The Books of Nahum, Habakkuk, and Zephaniah*, 172–173.

ⁱⁱ For the LXX tendency, see Watts, "For I Am Not Ashamed," 10.

ⁱⁱⁱ Patterson, *Nahum, Habakkuk, Zephaniah*, 175. Kraus also agrees, and notes that the LXX's interpretation interestingly gets support from 1 QpHab 7:13. Wolfgang Kraus, "Hab 2:3- in the Hebrew, Septuagint, and New Testament," in *Septuagint and Reception: Essays Prepared for the Association for the Study of the Septuagint in South Africa*, ed. Johann Cook, Supplements to the Vetus Testamentum v. 127 (Leiden ; Boston: Brill, 2009), 104, 107–109.

ⁱᵛ Contra F. F. Bruce, *The Epistle to the Hebrews*, NICNT (Grand Rapids: Eerdmans, 1964), 271–275.

Verse 4. There are several important issues that are raised concerning this verse. The first is the identity of the one with the bloated appetite. ("Appetite" translates נֶפֶשׁ, *nepeš*, which often refers to "life" but here refers to one's desires or appetites.) I implied above that the one who is bloated is a recipient of the vision, and thus a Judahite. This needs some defense. Though some identify the one with a bloated appetite as the Chaldean (cf. v. 5), I think that it is more fitting to identify this as the wicked of Judah. I offer several reasons for doing so.

First, though similar language is used for both the figure in verse 4 and Chaldea in verse 5, this does not mean they are identical. As I have observed previously, similar language is used for both parties in Habakkuk 1 (e.g. 1:2, 1:9; 1:4, 1:7; 1:4, 1:13).

Second, verse 5 clearly refers to the Chaldeans (5:e-f), but verse 4 certainly refers to a party of Judahites. It is significant that the person in verse 4 is contrasted with those who have faith, hardly a clear comparison to make between the Chaldeans and the Judahites.

Third, if verse 4 does not refer to a Judahite party, then the object of Habakkuk's initial complaint in 1:1-4 is completely forgotten after his initial prayer.

Finally, the most significant piece of evidence is the suffix on "appetite" in verse 4. The Hebrew text reads "*his* appetite" (נַפְשׁוֹ, *napšō*), begging us to ask to whom does "his" refer. The only possible antecedent in our chapter is "the one who reads" in verse 2, a masculine singular participle (קוֹרֵא, *qōrē*'). A Chaldean would not read the vision, and certainly would not run at the thought of a Chaldean invasion. The only persons in the book who would have reason to run when they read of the Chaldean invasion are the wicked Judahites, those against whom Habakkuk first cried out (1:1-4) and for whom the invasion is judgment (1:12).

Thus, as Habakkuk identifies two groups within Judah in 1:1-4, the *wicked* who surround the *righteous*, so God distinguishes two responses to the Chaldean vision. One response is to wait in faith for it, seeing it as the salvation Habakkuk asked for (1:2, 3:18). The other response is to run in panic, recognizing it as judgment. It is significant that God intentionally distinguishes the wicked and righteous *within Judah* here whereas Habakkuk in 1:14 gathered them together as the "more righteous" in contrast with the "wicked" Chaldeans. In this way, God answers Habakkuk's first question. How can God swallow up the (relatively) righteous with a wicked nation? That is not His intention. Judah is not righteous; most of it is wicked. And the righteous are not the objects of His judgment; they are those He intends to save.

Now, someone may object that this interpretation causes a historical problem, for the wicked of Judah did not run from the Chaldeans (at least not initially, cf. Jer 39:4-10) but ignored the prophetic oracles and even rebelled against Chaldea at one point. This need not be a problem, however, for "run" indicates a negative response in contrast to the positive response of "waiting." It is not a promise that they will literally run but that they will not respond appropriately to the vision. Habakkuk does not detail what their response was, but from the rest of the Old Testament, especially Jeremiah and Kings, we read that the response of the wicked Judahites was obstinate rebellion ignoring the prophecies (e.g. Jer 26:1-15).

The next issue is the meaning of the second line, especially what the word אֱמוּנָה (*'ĕmûnāh*; which I have translated "faith") means, what "by his faith" modifies, and what it means that the righteous will "live." As any student of Hebrew will observe, "faith" is an odd translation for אֱמוּנָה, which usually rendered "faithfulness." However, faith is the traditional rendering of אֱמוּנָה in this verse (cf. Vulgate, *fide*; KJV, faith). Several recent translations and many commentators have followed the more usual sense of אֱמוּנָה, translating it as "faithfulness" (NET, NIV). There are, however, at least three good reasons for the translation "faith."[13]

---

[13] Cf. C.F. Keil and F. Delitzsch, *Commentary on the Old Testament in Ten Volumes: Minor Prophets; Two Volumes in One*, trans. James Martin, Reprint., vol. 10.2 (Grand Rapids: Eerdmans, 1978), 73–74. The scholarship is full of many other reasons given to translate "faith," though their arguments are not necessarily compatible with one another or with my own arguments. E.g. E Ray Clendenen, "Salvation by Faith or by Faithfulness in the Book of Habakkuk?," *Bulletin for Biblical Research* 24, no. 4 (2014): 505–513; Edmund F Perry, "Meaning of 'emuna in

1) The limits of Hebrew vocabulary suggests that if one wanted to say "faith," אֱמוּנָה would be the ideal word. For one, there is no Hebrew noun for "faith."[14] However, there is a verb meaning believe or have faith, אמן (cf. Hab 1:5). This would be the ideal word root from which to draw the noun "faith," especially if one intended to allude to texts involving the verb, such as Genesis 15:6 and Habakkuk 1:5. Furthermore, the noun pattern of אֱמוּנָה is a frequent pattern for abstract nouns; as such it would be ideal for "faith."[15] It may seem odd to use the same word for "faithfulness," meaning the quality of being trustworthy or a dependable object for faith, yet the Greek language shows that this is by no means unreasonable, for πιστις (pistis) means both "faith" and "faithfulness." It seems reasonable to conclude that if one intended to say "faith," אֱמוּנָה (*'ĕmûnāh*) would be the ideal noun for doing so. Further support for this can be derived from latter Jewish writings: it is argued by some that the Qumran Pesher commentary on Habakkuk intends "faith," for אמונה is followed by the preposition ב, usually used for an object of faith ("faith in", see 1QpH Col. VIII 1-3).[16] Though the Targum interprets

---

the Old Testament," *Journal of Bible and Religion* 21, no. 4 (October 1953): 252–256; Robertson, "'The Justified (by Faith) Shall Live by His Steadfast Trust.'"

Patterson and others argue that אֱמוּנָה mixes in this instance "active and passive" senses of the root אמן. Whether or not "active" and "passive" is an accurate description of "faith" and "faithfulness," I do agree that אֱמוּנָה can have either sense. However, I do not find his reasoning persuasive nor his conclusion that both senses are found here: "faith" is much more evident. Patterson, *Nahum, Habakkuk, Zephaniah*, 219–222.

[14] James Barr, *The Semantics of Biblical Language* (Oxford: Oxford University Press, 1961), 173. He also hints that, in his opinion, there may be good sense in understanding אֱמוּנָה here as "faith" (173 n. 1).

[15] Bruce K. Waltke and Michael Patrick O'Connor, *An Introduction to Hebrew Syntax* (Winona Lake, Ind.: Eisenbrauns, 1990), 89–90, 104.

[16] William Hugh Brownlee, ed., *The Midrash Pesher of Habakkuk*, Monograph series - Society of Biblical Literature ; no. 24 (Missoula, Mont.: Scholars Press, 1979), 125–129; Alice Ogden Bellis, "Habakkuk 2:4b: Intertextuality and Hermeneutics," in *Jews, Christians, and the Theology of the Hebrew Scriptures*, ed. Alice Ogden Bellis and Joel S. Kaminsky, SBL Symposium Series no. 8 (Atlanta, Ga.: Society of Biblical Literature, 2000), 373–375; N.T. Wright, *The New Testament and the People of God*, Christian Origins and the Question of God 1 (Minneapolis: Fortress, 1992), 336.

אֱמוּנָה as speaking of the truth of the vision, the rabbinic discussion of this text assumes that אֱמוּנָה means "faith."[17] If it is accepted that אֱמוּנָה may mean "faith," a case could be made that Psalm 119:30a also means "faith."[18] So far, I have argued that אֱמוּנָה *can* mean "faith," indeed that it is the ideal Hebrew noun for "faith." There are two more reasons for the translation "faith," both indicate that "faith" is not only possible but the ideal translation.

2) The context of Habakkuk indicates that אמונה means "faith." We have already seen that the key question at this point is the difference between the wicked and the righteous. The wicked are bloated in their desires and "run" when they hear the vision (2:4). The righteous, on the other hand, "wait" for the vision (2:3). The only reason they would wait is if they understand—and believe—that the Chaldean invasion is their salvation. In fact, God describes the vision as unbelievable (1:5), yet by waiting they show that they have believed the unbelievable—that God is using a wicked nation to save the righteous.

Furthermore, in chapter 3 (Habakkuk's prayer in response to the vision) the key theme is trust or faith: he believes the deed so much that he identifies Chaldea as God's tool for salvation (3:3, 13-14), ask for this deed to come true (3:2, cf. 1:5), and declare it to be salvation—despite its horrors (3:13, 16, 18-19). This shows that "faith" makes far more sense of the book than the more common translation of אֱמוּנָה (*'ĕmûnāh*), that a person will live by his faithfulness (NET, NIV), especially when it is observed that אֱמוּנָה usually does not refer to right behaviour as in English but trustworthiness or

---

[17] Kevin J. Cathcart and Robert P. Gordon, trans., *The Targum of the Minor Prophets*, The Aramaic Bible 14 (Wilmington, Del.: Michael Glazier, Inc., 1989), 150–151; Epstein, "Makkoth," 169, 173.

[18] The context is full of the language of faith or trust, as the Psalmist prays for life and favour from God. He sets the commands before him (30b), "clings" to God's testimonies (31), and will run in the way of them (32). Essentially, he trusts on God for help, believes and trusts in the commandments. Thus, the Psalmist may very well intend to say "I have chosen the way of faith." אֱמוּנָה is used several times in this Psalm, yet it usually refers to Yahweh and his actions (75, 90, 138). It only refers to the law in v. 86. When referring to the Law, the psalmist prefers to use אֱמֶת (*'ĕmet*, truth; 43, 86, 142, 151, 160). In v. 66, the Psalmist proclaims that he "believes in your commandments," giving precedence for interpreting "faith" or "belief" earlier.

reliability.

3) The three quotations of Habakkuk 2:4 in the New Testament all intend "faith." A quote from Habakkuk 2:4 plays a central part in three key New Testament texts; in each instance, the author makes clear that he intends "faith"—indeed, faithfulness would be inappropriate in the context.[19] The first of these is the central thesis statement of the book of Romans; in 1:16-17, Paul writes,

> For I am not ashamed of the gospel, for it is the power of God for salvation to everyone who believes, to the Jew first and also to the Greek. [17]For in it the righteousness of God is revealed [beginning and ending in faith], as it is written, "the righteous shall live by faith." (ESV, following mg. reading)

For Paul, the Gospel revolves around the revelation of what God has done for His people through Jesus Christ and is the very power for salvation. As Protestants have traditionally taught, the key idea in the first part of Romans (1:18-4:25) is that God has made righteousness—right standing before Him—available to Jew and Gentile alike through faith. "Faith" or "belief" stands out beside righteousness as a key term in the letter, defended by Paul as the means by which one is saved (e.g. "believe," 3:22; 4:3, 5, 11, 17, 18, 24: "faith," 3:22, 25, 26, 27, 28, 30, 31; 4:5, 9, 11, 12, 13, 14, 16, 19, 20).[20] In the immediate context, verse 16 makes it clear that Paul is talking about those "who believe." At this key moment in the beginning of his letter, Paul uses Habakkuk to underscore his point that the Christian life is completely by faith.[21] His point rests entirely on Habakkuk meaning "faith" and not

---

[19] For a fuller treatment of these passages, see the section *Habakkuk in the New Testament* in the Introduction.

[20] The translation of πιστις (*pistis*, faith or faithfulness) followed by the genitive Ἰησου (*Iesou*, Jesus) or Χριστου (*Christou*, Christ) is heavily debated; however, from my own study I have found that the traditional reading, "faith in Jesus Christ," is by far the most persuasive. See Douglas J. Moo, *The Epistle to the Romans*, NICNT (Grand Rapids: Eerdmans, 1996), s.v. 3:22; Thomas R. Schreiner, *Romans*, Baker Exegetical Commentary on the New Testament 6 (Grand Rapids: Baker Books, 1998), s.v. 3:22.

[21] In appendix 3 I have included a paper I wrote on the way Paul is using Habakkuk. Though I disagree with his interpretation of Habakkuk, Moo comes to

"faithfulness."

The same can be said for Galatians 3:11, where Paul contrasts justification by the law and justification by faith. His proof text that justification comes by faith—and has always come by faith—is Habakkuk 2:4. In the context of his letter, especially the contrast between fulfillment of the law and believing (cf. 3:22), Paul is certainly interpreting Habakkuk to mean "faith."[22]

The same conclusion can be drawn from Hebrews 10:37-38, which uses Habakkuk 2:4 to warn the Hebrews to preserve in faith, trusting God for His promises. These verses turn the flow of the letter towards faith, the subject of the famous "hall of faith" in Hebrews 11, in which the author argues that faith is an firm confidence in God's future promises that is manifest in lives of the biblical heroes.

In each case, the New Testament authors understand Habakkuk 2:4 to mean "faith" not "faithfulness." We have seen that this is the legitimate understanding of the Hebrew text and not only Greek translations. We can then be confident that Habakkuk 2:4 should be translated "live by his faith" and not "live by his faithfulness."

The phrasing of this conclusion raises two more questions concerning verse 4b: what does Habakkuk mean by "live" and what does "by his faith" modify? At first it may seem obvious that "the righteous one *will live*" means exactly that, that he will not die. And at one level, this may very well be what Yahweh intends, for the invasion is meant to be salvation and those who obeyed God's prophets would have gone off into exile instead of staying and dying (Jer 21:1-10, 24:1-10). Even if this is intended, it is not the primary sense of "live" here. Often, in both the Old and New Testaments, "life" has a specific significance. The familiar phrase from John, *eternal life*, refers to life in this sense—life with the qualities of fellowship with God (e.g. John 3:36, 17:3). In the Old Testament, we could call this fuller sense of "life" the

---

a similar conclusion about Paul's use of Hab. 2:4 here. Moo, *The Epistle to the Romans*.

[22] Thomas R. Schreiner, *Galatians*, ed. Clinton E. Arnold, Zondervan Exegetical Commentary Series on the New Testament 9 (Grand Rapids: Zondervan, 2010); Douglas J. Moo, *Galatians*, Baker Exegetical Commentary on the New Testament (Grand Rapids: Baker Academic, 2013).

blessed life.²³ That is, "life" often has the significance of right covenant relationship with God and the benefits that result therefrom.

This is the sense intended in Leviticus 18:5, "You shall therefore keep my statutes and my rules; if a person does them, he shall live by them." Live does not mean merely physical life but the enjoyment of God's blessings, recounted most fully in Deuteronomy 28:1-14 and summarised in 31:15-20 as the choice of life as opposed to death. It is significant that this is the predominant sense of "life" in the book of the Twelve. Hosea 6:2 is particularly clear in this regard, talking about God restoring Israel after they repent: "After two days he will *revive us* [i.e. make us alive]; on the third day he will raise us up, that we may *live* before him" (cf. Hos 14:4-7, Amos 5:14-15, and Zech 10:9).²⁴

Understanding life in this way creates a subtle tension between Habakkuk 2:4 and Leviticus 18:5, a tension picked up in the New Testament (Rom 1:17, 10:5-9; Gal 3:10-12). It appears that God is here alluding to this text in Leviticus as well as Genesis 15:6; "And [Abraham] believed the LORD, and he counted it to him as righteousness."²⁵ Genesis 15:6 is also a key text used in the New Testament alongside Habakkuk 2:4 and Leviticus 18:5 (Rom 4:3, Gal 3:6). Habakkuk 2:4 alludes to Genesis 15:6 and Leviticus 18:5, setting the two texts in juxtaposition, offering two different paths to life. In essence, this concise phrase anticipates Paul's argument in Galatians 3, where he argues that salvation has always been through faith, for the Law was unable to grant the life it promised. This leads us to our second question, what does "by his faith" modify?

That is, should we translated 2:4b as "the one who is righteous by faith

---

²³ Cf. David S. Dockery, "The Use of Hab. 2:4 in Rom. 1:17: Some Hermeneutical and Theological Considerations," *Wesleyan Theological Journal* (October 1, 1987): 26; Francis Brown et al., *The Brown-Driver-Briggs Hebrew and English Lexicon* (Peabody: Hendrickson, 1996), 311.

²⁴ Doug Moo writes, "The verb occurs sixteen times [in the Twelve], and , apart from places where it refers simply to 'living beings," most of the occurrences refer to 'true life,' 'life before God,' 'blessing' (Hosea 6:2, 14:7; Amos 5:4, 6, 14; Zech. 10:9 KJV, NASB...)." Moo, *Galatians*, 220.

²⁵ Only here and in Hab 2:4 does the root אמן with the sense "believe" and צדק appear together. In other texts, God is identified as "faithful" and "righteous" and some of his servants, such as David (1 Kgs 3:6) are said to walk in "truth" and "righteousness."

shall live" or "the righteous one shall live by his faith." New Testament commentators have argued that Paul reads the text in the former way.[26] This is a difficult issue, for the context is dealing with the exact question "who are the righteous?" However, the prepositional phrase reads more easily with the verb and I think the parallelism focuses on the actions of the wicked and the righteous (that *he will run... it is bloated; his appetite is not upright within him*" / "the righteous shall live *by his faith*").[27] This is the usual approach of commentators on the Hebrew text.[28]

However, I think Rikk Watts, an NT scholar, is on the right path when he writes "Interpretations which force the reader to relate ἐκ πίστεως [from faith] with either ὁ δίκαιος [the righteous one] or ζήσεται [will live] rarely appreciate the reciprocity inherent both in the MT and in the versions of Hab 2:4."[29] That is, it is hard to pin down which part of the sentence the phrase refers to, for in a sense "to live by faith" is to be "righteous by faith." We have already seen that God is alluding in this text to Genesis 15:6, in which faith brings righteousness, and Leviticus 18:5, in which law keeping brings life. These two are connected because righteousness is the condition for life: to receive life from God one has to be righteous—in right standing before God—either by law keeping (Lev 18:5) or faith (Gen 15:6). To say that the righteous "lives by faith" is to imply that he is righteous by that same faith. Likewise, to says that the righteous by faith shall live is to say that he lives by the faith that has made him righteous. This is an important point to make, yet I think this is the implicit logic behind the text, not the syntax. Syntactically, it makes the best sense of the context to connect the preposition with "will live": "the righteous one will live by his faith."

The LXX Translation of 2:2-4

The attentive reader may have noticed that the Septuagint translation of 2:4 is substantially different than the Hebrew text. Translations of the LXX suggest that 2:2 is also slightly different, "so that the reader might pursue them" (NETS). In the sixth appendix of this commentary, I make the argument that the

---

[26] E.g. Moo, *The Epistle to the Romans*, 76–77.Moo 76-77.

[27] Though faith is a noun, it is a verbal noun that implies the action "believing" and is parallel with "wait" in verse 3.

[28] E.g. Patterson, *Nahum, Habakkuk, Zephaniah*, 221.

[29] Watts, "For I Am Not Ashamed," 20 n.90.

Septuagint should be translated as equivalent to the Hebrew text in this verse ("that the one who reads it will run"). The same cannot be said of verse 4:

If it draws back,
    my soul is not pleased in it.
But the just shall live by my faith [or faithfulness, mg.]. (NETS)

(At least one Greek manuscript has "his faith/faithfulness," yet the original translation appears to be "my faith/faithfulness." It is valuable to observe that, despite the LXX's translation "my faith," all the NT quotations of Habakkuk 2:4 have "faith," equivalent in context to "his faith.")

Though some might make a big deal about these differences, I am not convinced the differences are so significant. First, the manuscript evidence supports the MT reading as original. Second, though I am no expert in Septuagint studies and so will not attempt to reconstruct *how* they got this translation (e.g. through paraphrase, reading of a different Hebrew text, or misunderstanding), I think that the meaning is not significantly different.

Like the Hebrew text, the subject of "draws back" may be rendered as a masculine pronoun, "he," referring to the reader of verse 2 (ὁ ἀναγινωσκων, *ho anaginōskōn*). Though implicit in the Hebrew of verse 4, the indictment of the reader in both texts is that he responds negatively, by running (2:2, MT & LXX) and drawing back (2:4, LXX). It is implicit in the Hebrew that this person is wicked and thus the object of God's judgment, a truth brought out by the Septuagint's "my soul is not pleased in [him]."

The biggest difference is found in verse 4c, where the faith of the righteous becomes God's faithfulness. We may say two things about this reading. First, the manuscript and internal evidence supports the Hebrew as original, as does the New Testament (Rom. 1:17, Gal 3:11, Heb 10:38-39). And the Greek still retains the sense of contrast in the Hebrew, between the "one who draws back" and "the just."

We should not, therefore, make a great deal out of the differences between the Septuagint and the Hebrew text found in the MT.

Textual Notes

[i] **Verse 3.** "speaks" translates פוח (*pvḥ*), a contentious word—cf. "it *hastens*" (ESV, NASB). The first issue is whether or not there are two roots פוח. HALOT and DCH both give two entries for these consonants, the first meaning "blow" and the second "testify." It is, however, unlikely that these represent two different roots. "Blow" and "testify" (as an act of speech) are related closely enough to be considered two different meanings within the semantic range of the verb פוּחַ (*pûaḥ*). Moreover, in the several uses of פוּחַ translated "testify," the word probably means "speak" with the context indicating that this speaking is specifically an act of testimony (Ps 10:5; Prov 6:19; 12:17; 14:5, 25; 19:5, 9). Thus, the verb seems to mean "to blow," in some context breathing out words—speaking—and others describing breathing or the blowing of the wind (Ezek 21:36, Ps 12:6, Song 4:16).

The second issue is the exact connotations of פוּחַ. The ESV and NASB derive from the sense "blow" the idea of panting, extending from this the action that leads to panting—the vision hastened. This is a stretch in my opinion, I see no evidence to justify a leap from "blow" to "hasten." It is more justified to understand פוּחַ as "speaks." In the Proverbs, פוּחַ is often used with the noun כָּזָב (*kāzāb*, lie), as it is here. In those contexts, a witness *speaks* truth not lies (Prov 6:19; 12:17; 14:5, 25; 19:5, 9). A similar idea is present here, thus supporting my translation. Francis I. Andersen, ed., *Habakkuk: A New Translation with Introduction and Commentary*, 1st ed., Anchor Bible 25 (New York: Doubleday, 2001), 206–207.

[ii] **Verse 4.** This is the only occurrence of the pual of עפל (*'pl*, to be swollen), so this word has caused great consternation among exegetes. If we take it as it stands, as this author has, then we have a description of "his appetite" as swollen. We can surmise this meaning from the other occurrences of this root in Scripture. The noun עֹפֶל (*'ōpel*) refers to a mound or a hill. In 1 Samuel 5-6, there are multiple occurrences of a noun עפל, referring to some sort of dangerous swelling (tumor, hemorrhoid, boil) (also Deut 28:27). If the one occurrence of the Hiphil is from this same root, it suggests impudence or arrogance, an overestimation of oneself—maybe a bloated self-opinion (Num 14:44). (BDB and HALOT suggest an alternate root for this occurrence.) That עפל means something like "to be swollen" also finds support from Arabic cognates: the Arabic words *'afalun* (noun) and *'afila* (denominative verb) refer to a tumor

From this data, we may surmise that the root indicates something like swelling. The pual is then a stative denominative form, to be swollen/have a tumor. In context, the appetite is swollen, bloated. Cf. Ebenezer Henderson, *The Twelve Minor Prophets* (Grand Rapids: Baker, 1980), 302; Thomas Renz, "An Emendation of Hab 2:4a in the Light of Hab 1:5," *The Journal of Hebrew Scriptures* 13 (2013): 2–3.

Exposition

Of the thousands of verses in the Old Testament, only a few are quoted in the New Testament—despite the many quotes and allusions to the Old Testament in it. Of those few that are found in the New Testament, not many are quoted several times. Habakkuk 2:4 is quoted three times in the New Testament. This ought to give us a clue as to its importance. According to Paul, justification by faith alone is not a new teaching; it is firmly grounded in the Old Testament. One of his favorite, if not the favorite, text for demonstrating this is Habakkuk 2:4 (Rom 1:17, Gal 3:11). Habakkuk, along with Genesis 15:6, most clearly teaches that believers are made right before God and have life by their faith.

For Habakkuk, the focus is on faith and what exactly that looks like. For Paul, the focus is on the sufficiency and results brought by faith—namely, it is sufficient for the entire Christian life (Rom 1:16-17) and gains for the Christian eternal life (Gal 3:11). The author of Hebrews is closest to the intent of Habakkuk with his use of the verse, for the quotation of Habakkuk 2:4 shifts the focus of the book to the nature of faith as evidenced in the lives of the Biblical heroes, described in Hebrews 11. Therefore, in addition to showing that faith alone gains the blessings of God—namely, eternal life— the specific focus of the book of Habakkuk has much to teach us about the nature of our faith in Jesus Christ.

God here, in these three verses, asks for a radical response of faith from those who are terrified. God has promised a horrific and unbelievable Chaldean invasion to save his righteous people. They are to believe God, trust Him, for this very thing. Habakkuk is therefore confronted, despite his questions, with a choice. Will he doubt and abandon his faith in the God of his ancestors or will he trust God even when it hurts, when he cannot make sense of God's actions. God identifies this as the very foundation of a relationship with Him—belief, even in the face of the unbelievable. Yahweh grants Habakkuk some answers, but He does not resolve every difficulty. Even if Habakkuk does not have all the answers, will he trust God? In chapter 3, we see that he does. In doing so, he sets a model for all believers.

God does not give Habakkuk all the answers he may desire, but He gives him the promise that He is acting for salvation. This promise is firmly grounded in God's character revealed in the rest of the Old Testament, especially in His past faithfulness to His people (cf. 1:12). The question that faces us when we put our faith in Jesus Christ is the same. Will we trust God, that He is who He says He is, that He is our authority? Will we believe that He has the right to act in ways we don't understand? When Jesus delays for 2000 years and counting, will we trust that He is faithful? When pain comes, when those close to us get sick and die, will we trust that God is good?

Every day God does things that make no sense to us. Yet part of faith He has called us to is the confession that He is Lord (cf. Rom 10:9). Minimally, this means trusting Him as our authority, the very standard of true and false, good and bad. The choice to believe or reject Jesus Christ is the same as the choice the Judahites faced in light of Habakkuk's vision. They could either rebel against God, rejecting salvation through Chaldea and facing judgment, or believe His unbelievable act; we can either rebel against God, rejecting Jesus and facing judgment, or believe that He is our salvation and hope in Him.

For the Christian, the response must be to believe. Our answer must be yes: we will trust in God even when it is uncomfortable and even deadly. On this confession of faith, trusting God through every circumstance, rests our salvation. We must believe in our hearts that God sent Jesus, that He died and that He rose again. And we must submit to God, confessing with our mouths Jesus as Lord (Rom 10:5-13). Both of these aspects of faith are found in God's words here in Habakkuk 2:4. Habakkuk must trust God, that what He has said is true, and must hold fast in submission to Him. Will we do likewise?

2. A Reply for Babylon: They Will Receive My Cup (2:5-2:19)

⁵"How much more is wine betraying the arrogant man,
>   he will not find rest.
Because he opens wide his appetite like Sheol,ᵃ
>   he is like death;
>   he is never satisfied:
he gathers to himself all the nations,
>   and collects for himself all the peoples.
⁶Will these not all raise a taunt against him—ᵇ
>   even a mocking poem, riddles concerning him—
>   and it will say:

>   'Woe to him who heaps up what is not his own—ᶜ
>   for how long!—
>   and who loads heavy debt upon himself!
>   ⁷Will your creditors not suddenly rise up,
>   those who make you tremble awaken?
>   You will be pillage for them.
>   ⁸Because you yourself plundered many nations,
>   all the remnants of the peoples will plunder you.

>   Because of the blood of man and the violence to the land,
>   to towns and all their inhabitants.

>   ⁹Woe to him who illicitly makes evil gain for his house,
>   to place his nest up high,ᵈ
>   to deliver himself from the hand of catastrophe!
>   ¹⁰You have planned a shameful deed for your house,ᵉ

ᵃ Isa 5:14

ᵇ Isa 14:4.

ᶜ Hab 1:6

ᵈ Jer 49:16

ᵉ Hab 3:13

> to bring an end to many peoples;
> you are sinning against your own life.ᶠ
> ¹¹Even stones from the wall will cry out,
> and rafters from the woodwork will answer them.
>
> ¹²Woe to him who builds a city on bloodshed
> and establishes a town in wickedness.ᵍ
> ¹³Is it not, behold, from YHWH of hosts
> that peoples are labouring only for fire
> and nations are wearing themselves for nothing?ʰ
> ¹⁴For the earth will be filled
> with the knowledge of the glory of YHWH
> like the waters cover the sea.ⁱ
>
> ¹⁵Woe to him who gives drink to his neighbour,
> you who mixes it with your wrath,ʲ
> even to make them drunk,
> that you might look upon their nakedness.ᵏ
> ¹⁶You will be sated with dishonour instead of glory.
> Now you yourself drink and have your uncircumcision exposed!
> The cup of YHWH's right hand is coming around to you,ˡ
> and disgrace will come upon your glory.
> ¹⁷For the violence done to Lebanon will overwhelm you,
> and the devastation done to the beasts that terrified them.ᵐ
>
> Because of the blood of man and the violence to the land,

ᶠ Prov 20:2

ᵍ Mic 3:10

ʰ Jer 51:58

ⁱ Num 14:21, Isa 11:9.

ʲ Jer 25:27-28; 51:7; Rev 18:6.

ᵏ Gen 9:22

ˡ Jer 25:15, 27-28; Lam 4:21. Matt 20:22; 26:39; Mark 10:38; 14:36; Luke 22:42; John 18:11; Rev 14:10; 16:19.

ᵐ Isa 14:8

to towns and all their inhabitants.

¹⁸What benefit is an idol,
> that its maker would hew it,
> a cast image and a teacher of lies,
For the maker trusts what he has made,
> enough to craft speechless idols.ⁿ
¹⁹Woe to him who says to wood, "wake up!"
> "awake!" to a dumb stone.
Is it able to teach?
> Behold, it is overlaid with gold and silver,
> but there is no breath at all in it.º

²⁰But, YHWH is in is holy temple,ᵖ
> be silent before Him all the earth!

The previous section, Habakkuk 2:2-4, is the heart of the book of Habakkuk. We have now passed this central text, but God is not yet finished: He has one last thing to say to Habakkuk. Two sections ago, we saw Habakkuk asking two questions of God (1:12-2:1): How can He tolerate those who are evil, especially as they ravage the righteous (1:13)? and will God allow the wicked to continue their deeds forever (1:17)? The first question was answered in 2:2-4 by a re-orientation of Habakkuk's understanding of righteousness. God was not using the wicked to judge the righteous; He was using the utterly wicked to judge the utterly wicked. Only those who had faith in Him were righteous. In 2:5-20, God turns to answer the second question. Would Chaldea go on forever? Habakkuk 2:5 begins with a lesser-to-the-greater argument. God has already declared that the sinful, wicked Judahite leadership will be destroyed for their sin; how much more, then, will the idolatrous Chaldeans reap the harvest of their wicked deeds?[1]

ⁿ Isa 2:8

º Dan 5:23

ᵖ 2 Sam 22:7, Ps 11:4

[1] Lesser-to-the-greater arguments are frequent in Scripture. In such an argument, the author argues *if A* (representing anything, such as a person or event, that is so much less valuable or evil than B*)*, *how much more B* (which is so much greater/worse). If **B** is so evil and God deals with the minor evil **A**, wont He surely

God's answer to Habakkuk's question takes the form of a lengthy song sung by those Chaldea has conquered. It speaks of Chaldea's eventual demise and reveals that their rise and fall was planned by God so that His glory may cover the earth (2:12-14). We read that God will bring an end to injustice; He will destroy Chaldea for their deeds.

In verse 20, God ends Habakkuk's questioning and the song of the nations. God has revealed His salvific purpose to Habakkuk and answered many of his questions. Now Habakkuk needs to learn that God is God and he is not: "YHWH is in His holy temple, be silent before Him all the earth!"

This whole section is structured in three strophes, separated by the refrain "because of the blood of man and the violence to the land, to towns and all their inhabitants" (8c-d, 17c-d). The first and last strophe are made of a single stanza; the middle strophe is made up of 3 stanzas. Each stanza of this 5 stanza poem is marked by the use of הוֹי (*hōy*, woe!; vv. 6, 9, 12, 15, 19). The whole poem is structured as a Chiasm (I provide the reasons for identifying this as a chiasm on page 49 of the introduction). The centre is strophe 3 (2:12-14). This central strophe demonstrates the reason why God has raised Chaldea and is using them to judge Judah and why He will ultimately bring them to a end. Ultimately, the glory of human empires will fall, their works will float away like smoke, but the glory of God will be magnified and His renown known across the earth. The whole earth will be filled with His glory.

Exegesis of Verse 5-6c

⁵"How much more is wine[i] betraying the arrogant man:
    he will not find rest.[ii]
Because he opens wide his appetite like Sheol,
    he is like death;
    he is never satisfied:
he gathers to himself all the nations,
    and collects for himself all the peoples.
⁶Will these not all raise a taunt against him—

---

deal with **B**? For example, we could argue in this way: if the government punishes the minor crime of shoplifting, how much more will they punish someone for stealing a vehicle?

even a mocking poem, riddles concerning him—
and it will say:

Verse 5. Most translation have translated the opening words of verse 5, אַף כִּי (*'ap kî*, "how much more"), for emphasis ("indeed," NET, NIV) or emphatic progression ("moreover," ESV; "furthermore," NASB). However, these two words in combination often have a particular rhetorical function in Hebrew, to indicate the apodosis of a lesser-to-the-greater argument.[2] That is, in an argument "If A (e.g. shoplifters are punished), how much more B (e.g. a car thief will be punished)," אַף כִּי indicates "how much more."[3] In the context of the previous section, where the wicked of Judah are distinguished from the righteous as objects of judgment, this argument begins the answer to Habakkuk's second question. He asked in chapter 1 first, "how could God judge a righteous people with a wicked one?" and second, "would God bring an end to the wicked nation?" In 2:2-4, God has answered the first question, in effect saying that He is not judging a righteous nation; He is bringing judgment on a wicked, bloated people. Then He continues in 2:5: if I will judge the wicked of my people, "How much more is wine betraying the arrogant man: he will not find rest." That is, how much more will the drunken excess of Babylon reap God's judgment.

The repetition of ו in lines d and e, with the pronoun הוּא in 5d, suggests a tricolon, as I have presented the lines.

---

[2] On my count, it indicates either lesser to the greater ("how much more") or greater to the lesser ("how much less") about 22 out of 25 times they are used together (e.g. Prov 15:11, 19:7; Ezk 14:20). (They occur together also in Gen 3:1, yet here they seem to have independent force.)

[3] 9 out of roughly 22 times אַף כִּי functions in this way, the protasis (if clause) is introduced with הֵן or הִנֵּה (*hēn, hinēh*; behold!). Sweeney connects הִנֵּה in verse 4 with אַף כִּי in this verse, suggesting that together show that 5 reinforces the previous statement, illustrating it. This coincides with this identification of the proud one in verse 4 with Babylon, the subject of verse 5. I fail to see how this is consistent with the usual use of אַף כִּי in a lesser-to-the-greater, which implies two distinct events or objects being referred to (if this happens, how much more this; e.g. Deut 31:27, Prov 11:31). I have suggested that הִנֵּה is being used to connect verses 2 & 4 after the parenthetical clause; I think this is better explanation of the relationship between the two sections than connecting it with אַף כִּי (it could conceivably be connecting to both vv. 2 & 5, which would not detract from my interpretation). Cf. DCH; M.A. Sweeney, *The Twelve Prophets*, ed. David W. Cotter, vol. 2, Berit Olam (Collegeville, Minn.: The Liturgical Press, 2000), 472–473.

Verse 6. In this verse, the poem or song in the following lines is introduced. It is described as a מָשָׁל (*masal*, "taunt"), a מְלִיצָה (*mᵉlisah*, "mocking poem"), and as חִידוֹת (*hidot*, "riddles"). מָשָׁל is a broad term for poetic and allusive communication; that is, it describes texts or speech with the characteristics of Hebrew poetry, ambiguity and metaphor with parallelism and rhythm (see introduction). It is often used to refer to a proverb (Deut 28:37; 1 Sam 10:12, 24:14; 1 Kgs 5:12; Prov 1:1, passim) or prophecy (Num 23:7, 18; 24:3, 15, 20, 21, 23). It is very similar to חִידָה, which refers to speech or texts characterized by their ambiguity, to sayings that require thought to unravel—thus, a "riddle." On several occasion, other than here, מָשָׁ has a specifically negative sense, referring to a taunt poem (Isa 14:4, Mic 2:4) or meaning "byword" (Deut 28:37, Jer 23:9, Pss 44:15, 69:12). In our context, it is clear that מָשָׁל is being used negatively, indicating a poem or song of ridicule or taunt. מְלִיצָה indicates an allusive saying like חִידָה in Proverbs 1:6 and Sirach 47:17 but appears to come from the root ליץ which means to scoff or scorn, so it seems to mean an allusive saying intended for ridicule. Thus, the broad term מָשָׁל is explained further by two specific terms, "a mocking poem" and "riddles."

Most translations render 6c as "and say" (ESV, NASB, NET), indicating that "all of these" from 6a are the subject speaking here. Yet the text deliberately shifts from a plural in 6a to a singular in 6c, suggesting that the verbal subject has changed. It is better to understand the song itself as the subject in this line: "it [the mocking poem] will say." אָמַר is used on occasion in biblical literature with a text as its subject (e.g. 15:1; 1 Kgs 12:16, 22; Ezek 3:16, 29:17). A specific parallel is 1 Samuel 24:14.

Textual Notes

ⁱ **Verse 5a.** In the place of the MT's הײן (*hayyayin*, the wine), the Dead Sea Scrolls has הון (*hvn*), usually pointed as הוֹן (*hōn*, wealth). The LXX translates this word as a participle, usually "the conceited one" but in at least one manuscript "the drunken one." Accordingly, scholars have suggested that the Qumran text should be pointed not as wealth but as הַוָּן (*havvān*), "proud man/presumptuous one." For several reasons, I consider the Masoretic text the strongest reading.

First, against the scholars proposition, 1QpHab clearly understands הון as "wealth" (cf. line 10-11). Second, the proposed word never appears in the Old Testament and is derived from a root that only appears once, in the Hiphil meaning "regard as easy" (Deut 1:41). Though it might explain the LXX translation, it has no textual support in its favour.

Second, given the strength of the Masoretic textual tradition, including here in Habakkuk, we should begin by giving it the benefit of the doubt. It is strengthened by the support of the Vulgate and Targum (Syriac omits the line). From this stance, we can understand the departures of the LXX and 1QpHab. To say that wine is betraying the Chaldean anticipates the later portion of the song (2:15-17) and fits well in context. The Chaldeans are getting "drunk" on conquest and plunder, but the very source of their pride and power is betraying them, for God will judge their behaviour. 1QpHab has taken what is metaphorical and rendered it more literally: their "wine" is the wealth they plunder from the nations. We can see how an intentional change might be made from the metaphorical to the literal, but the closeness of the appearance of these forms could also have led to a graphical error (from היין to הון). The LXX has been freer in its translation, rendering a participle instead of a noun, "the *one who is presumptuous* and a despiser" even though in the MT the word translated "despiser" is the participle (in 1QpHab it is a finite verb, but results in the same sense). It may be that "drunken" is the original or maybe that they did not understand what was intended by "wine is betraying" and translated according to sense—a relatively common practice. Whatever the case was, the MT fits perfectly into the context, can explain the other meanings, and—when it is given the benefit of the doubt—there is no compelling reason to follow an alternative reading. Cf. F. F. Bruce, "Habakkuk," in *The Minor Prophets: An Exegetical and Expository Commentary*, ed. Thomas Edward McComiskey (Grand Rapids: Baker Book House, 1992); C.F. Keil and F. Delitzsch, *Commentary on the Old Testament in Ten Volumes: Minor Prophets; Two Volumes in One*, trans. James Martin, Reprint., vol. 10.2, 10 vols. (Grand Rapids: Eerdmans, 1978); Richard Duane Patterson, *Nahum, Habakkuk, Zephaniah*, The Wycliffe Exegetical Commentary (Chicago: Moody Press, 1991); A. Schenker and et al., eds., *The Twelve Minor Prophets: Introduction and Commentaries on the Twelve Minor Prophets*, Biblia Hebraica Quinta 13 (Stuttgart: Deutsche Bibelgesellschaft, 2010).

ii **Verse 5b.** The Hebrew word translated "finds rest" is נוה (*nvh*). It is rare, only occurring once elsewhere. There, in Psalm 68:13, it is a participle that appears to mean "(female) dweller, inhabitant" (DCH). This sense corresponds well with the nouns derived from this root. נָוֶה (*nāveh*) refers to a habitation, a dwelling place, and נָוָה (*nāvāh*) to a pasture, where sheep find sustenance and rest (Zeph 2:6, Joel 2:22, Ps 23:2). The verb seems to mean to have (Ps 68:13) or find (Hab 2:5) a dwelling. In our context, it refers not so much to having a physical dwelling as to the effect of having a dwelling, stopping activity—resting. Thus, the Chaldean is drunken and boastful, never finding a place to stop and dwell—never ceasing.

Exegesis of Verse 6d-8

'Woe to him who heaps up what is not his own—
>for how long!—
>and who loads heavy debt upon himself!
7Will your creditors not suddenly rise up,
>those who make you tremble awaken?
>You will be pillage for them.
8Because you yourself plundered many nations,
>all the remnants of the peoples will plunder you.

Because of the blood of man and the violence to the land,
>to towns and all their inhabitants.

Verse 6d-f. The second part of verse 6 begins the song of judgment against Chaldea. It opens with the first of five "woes" (הוֹי, *hōy*) that appear in each of the following stanzas. הוֹי is a strong interjection, such as "Oh!" or "Hey!," calling for the reader or listener's attention. In prophetic contexts, it will often take on an explicitly negative tone, a measure of warning, that is accurately conveyed by the English "woe" (e.g. Amos 6:1, Mic 2:1, Nah 3:1).

"What is not his own," לֹא־לוֹ (*lō'-lô*), is repeated from Hab 1:6, where God's initial description of the Chaldean invasion is given. In this way, this song of judgment begins to draw on the language used by Habakkuk and God earlier in the book to describe the Chaldean invasion; this charge against them is framed in God and Habakkuk's own words. "For how long!" is literally "until when" (עַד־מָתַי, *'ad-matay*); it echoes Habakkuk's similar question in 1:17. Here it is an indictment of their foolishness: "how long did you think this could go on?"

Verse 7-8b. "Suddenly" (פֶּתַע, *peta'*) suggests that Chaldeans ruin will come without warning, a sudden unexpected end. The suddenness results from Chaldea self-imposed blindness, their ignorance of the consequences of their behaviour. The double repetition of the verb שָׁלַל (*šālal;* to plunder) is reminiscent of Jeremiah 50:10, "Chaldea shall be *plundered*; all who *plunder* her shall be sated, declares the Lord." Both passages share the same tone, that Chaldea will meet its end and be plundered as they plundered others (cf. Jer. 50:11).

Verse 8c-d. These verses are repeated again before the last stanza of the song, in 17c-d. These lines thus form a refrain that distinguishes the two outer strophes from the center one.[1] "Violence," חָמָס (*ḥāmās*), appears three times in chapter 1. It characterizes the chaotic state of Judah (1:2, 3) and the destructive behaviour of the Chaldeans (1:9). They come forth for violence, yet because (מִן, *min*) of the violence they wreck, they will receive judgment.

Exegesis of Verse 9-11

⁹Woe to him who illicitly makes evil gain for his house,
  to place his nest up high,
  to deliver himself from the hand of catastrophe!
¹⁰You have planned a shameful deed for your house,
  to bring an end to many peoples;
  you are sinning against your own life.
¹¹Even stones from the wall will cry out,
  and rafters[i] from the woodwork will answer them.

Verse 9. "Illicitly makes gain" translates the phrase בֹּצֵעַ בֶּצַע (*bōṣēaʻ beṣaʻ*, the one illicitly gaining illicit gain*)*. "Evil" translates another word, רָע (*rāʻ*), so the text is very emphatic about the immoral nature of Chaldea's actions. Jeremiah 49:16 uses a similar image as 9b for the arrogance of Edom before they are toppled by God. "From the hand of catastrophe" is very literal but fits well in English idiom

Verse 10. "You are sinning against your own life" is translated in various ways by major translations: "you have forfeited your life" (ESV), "So you are sinning against yourself" (NASB), "you will self-destruct" (NET). The phrase in Hebrew is וְחוֹטֵא נַפְשֶׁךָ (*vᵉḥōṭēʼ napšekā*). The initial וְ (*vᵉ*; "and," untranslated) probably indicates a line break here. The difficulty is translating the exact sense of the participle חוֹטֵא (*ḥōṭēʼ*), "sinning," and the noun נַפְשֶׁךָ (*napšekā*, your life/self/soul). The ESV and NET are focusing on the result of sin, "guilt," with the object "yourself" resulting in the idea, "you are incurring guilt upon yourself and therefore forfeiting your life." They translated differently to bring out varying nuances of this sense. The combination could mean "sinning against your life" or perhaps "incurring guilt against your life," but rarely is חטא used with an object in this way (maybe Prov. 20:2). Furthermore, "incurring guilt against your life" really has the sense, "causing your life/self to be guilty." This would be more appropriate

---

[1] Cf. Bruce, "Habakkuk," 865; Sweeney, *The Twelve Prophets*, 2:475.

for a Hiphil stem, though it is unattested there (the Hiphil means "to declare guilty" or "cause to sin"). If "incurring guilt against your life" is probably not the meaning of the phrase, then we are left with "sinning against your life."

This seems to fit well in context. Line A gives the charge that the Chaldeans have devised something shameful, line B then describes this shameful deed. Thus, the focus in context is not so much on result, "you have become guilty," but on the act taken, "you have sinned." With the addition of נֶפֶשׁ (*nepeš*) as the object of the act of sinning, these lines emphasize that the theme of the whole song, that Chaldea will reap the rewards of their reckless rampage.[1] Now, נֶפֶשׁ often is used as a reflexive pronoun, resulting in the translation "yourself" (e.g. NASB). However, given that line B specifies the sin of the Chaldeans as bringing "an end to many people," it is a fitting parallel that their sin is actually against their own *life*: it is a fatal error.

Verse 11. These lines are a fitting end to this stanza. כִּי (*kî*) as it is used here does not mean "for" (cf. ESV) but "even" or "surely." That is, 11a is not explaining why or giving the reason for the shameful deed and self-sin in verse 10; instead, these lines return to the testimony of the conquered nations, which is the theme of the whole song. Continuing the metaphor of a house (cf. 9-10), we see in these lines some of the very materials that were used to build the house—the conquered nations and their plunder (vv. 7-8)—are now crying out and the rest are responding and joining the chorus. Together they cry for justice, and God will hear them.

Textual Notes

[i] **Verse 11b.** כָּפִיס (*kāpîs*) only appears once in the Hebrew Bible, here. In parallel with "stone of the wall" it suggests that it is a piece of עֵץ (*'ēṣ*, wood). It seems that עֵץ is referring to the wooden portion of the home, "woodwork," and כָּפִיס to a specific piece of this woodwork—generally, a timber. The use of the word in 1QH appears to confirm this (6:26, 6:36). Cf. 1QpHab 10:1.

---

[1] This actually fits well with Prov 20:2 as well. In context, the emphasis is less on the result—that the fool has forfeited his life—but more the nature of the action he has taken; you have sinned against yourself/life. This fits well with the theology of foolishness in Proverbs.

Exegesis of Verse 12-14

> ¹²Woe to him who builds a city on bloodshed
>   and establishes a town in wickedness.
> ¹³Is it not, behold, from YHWH of hosts
>   that peoples are labouring only for fire
>   and nations are wearing themselves for nothing?
> ¹⁴For the earth will be filled
>   with the knowledge of the glory of YHWH
>   like the waters cover the sea.

Verse 13. With this verse, the taunt song begins to change its tone, moving from the inevitable end of the Chaldeans to the source and purpose of that end. Yahweh of Hosts, the one who first raised up the Chaldeans (Hab 1:5) is now identified as the one who will render the labour of the Babylonians futile.

13b-c are found also in Jeremiah 51:58, amidst another passage proclaiming the downfall of the Babylonians. There is a slight difference, "only for fire" and "for nothing" switch places. בְּדַי often means "enough of" or "sufficiency," but here is it has the sense "(for) only fire" and "(for) only emptiness." That is, what they have laboured for is not the sufficient plunder they sought but all the nothingness they could desire. Everything they sought will go up in flames or disappear like vapour. This is as much God's doing as their ascension to power.

Verse 14. Verse 14 explains this: the Babylonians sought to exalt themselves to a position of glory, a position only God could occupy. All their vain efforts only served to demonstrate the truth: God alone is worthy of glory and all the nations are only parts of the symphony that sings his praises.

"The earth will be filled / with the knowledge of the glory of Yahweh" is actually a verbal phrase. Literally, "the earth will be filled to know the glory of Yahweh." Most frequently, the infinitive would indicate the purpose or result of the verb, or it would function as a compliment (e.g. seek *to know*), however here it indicates the content of the verb "to be full." It is thus functioning like an English gerund; "the earth will be filled with the knowing of the glory of God."[1] Though unexpected, this is not unheard of and is the

---

[1] Cf. Keil and Delitzsch, *Commentary on the Old Testament in Ten Volumes: Minor*

best way to read the phrase in Hebrew, especially in light of the two parallel passages (Num 14:21, Isa 11:9).[2]

As the exile of Israel was intended to, and succeeded in, magnifying the name of Yahweh (Exod 9:16, Josh 2:8-14), so the ascension and collapse of the Babylonian empire would contribute to the spreading of the knowledge of the glory of Yahweh. In Numbers 14:21 and Isaiah 11:9, similar language is used for the certain outcome of all of God's actions; eventually, in the last day, all the earth will be drenched with God's glory. "For" in Habakkuk 2:14 thus indicates that the end of Babylon is orchestrated by God to ensure this outcome, the magnification of His glory throughout the creation.

This stanza, reaching its crescendo in this verse, lies at the very centre of this song in Habakkuk 2. It can thus be seen as the theological centre to which the rest of the song points. The rise and fall of Babylon has this one purpose, to magnify the glory of God through the demonstration of His justice, both in the judgment of His sinful people and in His judgment of the sinful tools He uses to enact that judgment.

Prophets; Two Volumes in One, 10.2:86–87.

[2] In his paper on the broken construct chain, David Noel Freedman appears to assume this is a construct noun, דַּעַת (*dā'at*, the construct form is identical to the Qal infinitive). However, the לְ (*lᵉ*) prefix is indicative of an infinitive construct and would serve no purpose if attached to a noun here. Furthermore, the אֶת (*'et*) that follows only makes sense as the marker of the DDO, which is most commonly used to indicate the object of a verb. Given the rarity of the "broken construct chain"—if any of the examples are legitimate (I have rejected his other proposed example in Habakkuk, 3:13)—it is far better to read this as a verbal phrase. Commentators and translators usually just render it as a noun. David Noel Freedman, "The Broken Construct Chain," in *Pottery, Poetry, and Prophecy: Studies in Early Hebrew Poetry* (Winona Lake, Ind.: Eisenbrauns, 1980), 339–342.

Exegesis of Verse 15-17

¹⁵Woe to him who gives drink to his neighbour,
    you who mixes[i] it with your wrath,
  even to make them drunk,
    that you might look upon their nakedness.
¹⁶You will be sated with dishonour instead of glory.
    Now yourself drink and have your uncircumcision exposed!
The cup of YHWH's right hand is coming around to you,
    and disgrace will come upon your glory.
¹⁷For the violence done to Lebanon will overwhelm you,
    and the devastation done to the beasts that terrified them.[ii]

Because of the blood of man and the violence to the land,
    to towns and all their inhabitants

Verse 15. A glance at various contemporary translations will reveal that there is some disagreement over the translation of this text. However, these disagreements are not so much over what the text says but how to resolve the supposed problem provided by the word מספח. As the textual notes indicate, I have followed the approach taken throughout this commentary to follow the Hebrew text unless there is good textual evidence otherwise and to rely on the Hebrew text to identify the meaning of rare words. Doing so yields great sense for this verse.

This stanza employs the metaphor of a cup of wrath that is found throughout the Old and New Testaments. At first, it is the Chaldean who gives the cup of his wrath to drink, however he will reap what he has sown and drink from the cup of God's wrath. Revelation 18:6 seems to be specifically alluding to this: "Pay [Babylon] back as she herself has paid back others, and repay her double for her deeds; mix a double portion for her in the cup she mixed."

Line B explains the first line, the drink given to the Chaldeans neighbour is mixed with wrath. This may suggest duplicity but not necessarily. Line C then gives the reason for Chaldea's action, that he might make the nations drunk and expose them to shame. An allusion to Genesis 9:22 seems to be present here, which emphasizes the theme of shame and dishonour that is present throughout this stanza.

"Even" in line C translates אף (*'ap*); though some translations render this word as "and," it is not merely a coordinating or additive conjunction. It indicates escalation or emphatic addition, "moreover," "furthermore." It can also function to give specification or explanation, as it is here.

Verse 16. Verse 16 is well crafted chiasmus in Hebrew (an **a – b – b – a** pattern), as I have tried to represent in the translation. The outer two lines focus on the exchange of glory for dishonour and the inner two lines explain this in terms of a reversal of the Chaldean's circumstances. In verse 15, the Chaldeans gave a drink mixed with wrath to their neighbours in order to hold them up to shame; now God would put the Chaldeans to shame by giving them the cup of His wrath.

"Nakedness" in verse 15 here takes on theological connotations: the "uncircumcision" of the Chaldeans is to be exposed, demonstrating that they are outside of God's covenant.

Verse 17. Language from chapter 1 appears again here; "violence" and "destruction" described the social chaos caused by the wicked Judahite leadership in 1:3, now it describes the wreckage caused by Chaldea on "Lebanon" and the "beasts." Again, Chaldea will get a taste of their own medicine; they will receive the very destruction they rained on the nations.

The use of "Lebanon," known for its forests, and "beasts," suggests a natural metaphor for Chaldea's destruction of the nations. As workers might clear a forest and hunt animals, so Chaldea ravaged the nations and in turn will be ravaged.[1] This would then be similar metaphor to that of Habakkuk 1:15-16, where the ravages of Chaldea are likened unto a fisherman gathering fish in his net.

Lines C & D are repeated from verse 8; they indicate a transition from the centre strophe of the song to the last strophe (vv. 18-20).

Textual Notes

[i] **Verse 15b.** מְסַפֵּחַ (*mᵉsappēaḥ*, the one mixing) occurs only here in the Piel stem. In the Qal, it appears once meaning "to join/attach to" (1 Sam 2:36); in the Niphal, meaning, "join oneself" (Isa 14:1); in the Pual, meaning "huddle together" (Job 30:7); and in the Hithpael, meaning attach oneself (1 Sam 26:19, cf. DSS CD

---

[1] Keil takes these words literally: Chaldea not only ravaged mankind but nature as well. In my opinion, the figurative meaning makes more sense. Keil and Delitzsch, *Commentary on the Old Testament in Ten Volumes: Minor Prophets; Two Volumes in One*, 10.2:89–90.

4:11). A pretty consistent pattern in the meaning of the word is evident in these uses; the Niphal and Hithpael employ a reflexive sense of "join"—join oneself to—and the Pual an intransitive sense (huddle or join together). From context and the other uses of the word, the sense "bring together" seems clear for the Piel of ספה. In context, with the imagery of giving a drink, drunkenness, and wrath, "mix" seems to be the best translation.

The manuscript evidence and versions support this same consonantal text, so efforts to emend the text should be rejected; they have no textual evidence. The ESV and NIV suggest a new root for this verb meaning "to pour out," but once again there is no evidence in the Hebrew Bible for this reading. The Masoretic text in this instance makes great sense and identifying this verb as an instance of the root meaning "to join" makes great sense of the context. Cf. C.F. Keil and F. Delitzsch, *Commentary on the Old Testament in Ten Volumes: Minor Prophets; Two Volumes in One*, trans. James Martin, Reprint., vol. 10.2 (Grand Rapids: Eerdmans, 1978), 87.

Some commentators and translations have "give drink... from the bowl of your wrath." They have emended the verb and revocalized it to read "from a bowl" instead of the verb "mixing" (e.g. NET, Bruce). However, there is no textual evidence for this emendation and the Hebrew text makes the best sense in context. F. F. Bruce, "Habakkuk," in *The Minor Prophets: An Exegetical and Expository Commentary*, ed. Thomas Edward McComiskey (Grand Rapids: Baker Book House, 1992), 871.

[ii] **Verse 17b.** Several translations and commentators are not satisfied with the Hebrew text here, instead opting to follow several of the versions in reading "will terrify you" instead of "by which you terrified them." The Syriac, Greek, *Naḥal Ḥever*, and Targum texts support the second person suffix (will terrify you). The Masoretic Text and the Vulgate have the feminine suffix (them). The 1QpHab text has יחתה, which the BHQ commentary and DSS editors identify as a corruption from הכתה. This would be equivalent to the Greek and Syriac texts ("will terrify you"). Alternatively, it could represent a singular 3rd feminine pronominally suffix used to refer to the plural בְּהֵמוֹת collectively. Since this is attested elsewhere in Scripture (using a singular to refer to a plural; Waltke and O'Connor give Jer 36:23 as an example), I think this is a better explanation of the 1QpHab text than an error. Thus, the Pesher text cannot be used to support the Greek reading. Therefore, there is no Hebrew text representing the Greek reading, "will terrify you." Furthermore, the MT text is not impossible—it makes sense—and yet is more difficult than the reading of the Greek and Syriac texts, for the previous line has a second person pronominal suffix—"will overwhelm you." For these reasons, I think the Masoretic Text is the superior reading in this case. Cf. A. Schenker and et al., eds., *The Twelve Minor Prophets: Introduction and Commentaries on the Twelve Minor Prophets*, Biblia Hebraica Quinta 13 (Stuttgart: Deutsche Bibelgesellschaft, 2010), 121.

Exegesis of Verse 18-20

¹⁸What benefit is an idol,
  that its maker would hew it,
  a cast image and a teacher of lies,
for the maker trusts what he has made,
  enough to craft speechless idols.
¹⁹Woe to him who says to wood, "wake up!"
  "Awake!" to a dumb stone.
Is it able to teach?
  Behold, it is overlaid with gold and silver,
  but there is no breath at all in it.

²⁰But YHWH is in is holy temple,
  be silent before Him all the earth!

Verse 18. The taunt song concludes in these verses with biting mockery directed at the idolatrous Babylonians. Like the previous two sections of Habakkuk, Yahweh's speech ends on the topic of idolatry (cf. 1:10-11, 14-17). All three of these first sections deride the Chaldeans for trusting in idols for strength; this theme will be concluded in Habakkuk 3, when the people of God identify God as their source of strength (3:17-19).

18e begins with an infinitive לַעֲשׂוֹת (*la'asot*), "to make." Syntactically, this is a result clause: he trusts in what he has made, so that he crafts a speechless idol. However, within the irony of this stanza and the logic of lines D & E, God seems to mean more than merely "so that" but "so much so that he...."

Line E ends with the phrase אֱלִילִים אִלְּמִים (*'ĕlîlîm 'illᵉmîm*), as the transliteration shows, the phrase employs alliteration. The word for "idols" is always negative in the Bible, meaning something like nothing or valueless. Thus, an informal equivalent of this phrase could be achieved in English with the translation, "dumb dummies" or "voiceless voids."

Verse 19. "Is it able to teach?" is הוּא יוֹרֶה (*hû' yôreh*), literally "is it a teacher?" It is a janus line, concluding the previous bicolon and forming the first line of the final tricolon.

Unlike the previous 4 stanzas, this one has the "woe" in the last part of the stanza (either the second last colon or the beginning of a pentacolon). Robertson is probably correct when he writes, "likely Habakkuk alters the order of the oracle simply as a literary device to provide variety and climax in his expression."[1]

Verse 20. In one sense, this verse is the conclusion of the taunt song beginning in 2:5-6c, however it has a greater function in the book of Habakkuk. As the conclusion of the taunt song, it calls for the nations to cease their restless cries for justice and trust the holy God to do what is right. It calls the Babylonians to cease their idolatry and boasting. Finally, it calls Habakkuk to cease his line of questioning (cf. 2:1) and trust in God. Like Isaiah's vision of the throne room, the holy temple in which God dwells is probably not the earthly Jerusalem but the heavenly throne room (Isa 6:1-7; Mic 1:2; Ps 11:4), though there may be some overlap between these two.

"Be silent" is an onomatopoeia in Hebrew, הַס (*has*), like the English "hush."

---

[1] O. Palmer Robertson, *The Books of Nahum, Habakkuk, and Zephaniah*, NICOT (Grand Rapids: W.B. Eerdmans, 1990), 207.

Exposition

I think for most Christians in the Western world, concern for ultimate justice is not high on our list of priorities—let alone our hopes. It is true that many in North American society are passionate about social justice, caring for the poor and down-trodden, yet that is not the justice I am speaking of—or which Habakkuk seeks. For many of us, the words that come to mind when we think of the conquest of Canaan, the Babylonian and Assyrian invasions of Israel, the crucifixion of Jesus Christ, or the sacking of Jerusalem in AD 70 are words like "horrific," "devastating," "unjust," "genocidal," "brutal," "massacre," "inhumane," etc. This is not entirely wrong, for as we have just read, the Babylonian invasion of Judah was brutal and horrific. The Roman sacking of Jerusalem was probably worse. Crucifixion, though directed against an individual, is horrific and brutal in a similar fashion. Even the conquest of Canaan, commissioned as it was by God Himself, involved the slaughter of men, women, and children—those created in the image of God. In some sense, it is right to respond with horror to these events; however, that must not be our only response. If we remain in a state of horror, we will miss God's good purpose in each of these events.

Beyond horror and brutally, each of these events shares something in common; the conquest of Canaan, Chaldean invasion, sacking of Jerusalem, and crucifixion of Christ were all acts of God's judgment (Gen 15:16; Hab 1:5-6, 12; Luke 19:44; Rom 3:24, Gal 3:10). Considered as such, we can also add Hell into the mix, the final act of God's judgment (Matt 26:31-46). It is only because human sin is so great—such a serious problem—that such brutal judgment is necessary. In fact, according to Jesus, the same fate awaits us all if we do not repent (Luke 13:5)! We all deserve God's judgment in this life and in the life to come, yet with great patience He waits, allowing everyone a chance to repent and cast themselves on His mercy (Rom 2:4, 3:25; 2 Pet 3:9).

Because justice in this ultimate sense of dealing with wrongdoing is so low on our priorities, we react with horror when God acts to bring justice on earth, to deal with human sin. Part of the problem is that we really do not see sin like God does. A careful meditation on God's acts of judgment will—if we begin with the faith that God understands justice better than we do—begin to show us the true weight of human sin. That sin would lead God to command the slaughter of men, women, and children created in His image shows us the seriousness of sin.

Though we struggle to grasp God's view of justice concerning all human sin—concerning every act of rebellion against Him—I think we grasp it a little bit when it comes to particularly heinous or personal sin. When a murderer gets away with his acts or a rapist is never captured, we know there has been a colossal injustice. When a terrorist attacks and kills many people, we desire that they receive what they deserve, justice in return for their deeds. When someone robs us, we want not only restitution of what was taken but also retribution: we want them to be punished for their deed (cf. Exod 22:1, 4). In cases of personal sin, when someone harms us, we do not want that sin to be forgotten and buried, for then it may seem like the hurt or wrong is meaningless. That is ultimately the purpose of justice, to demonstrate just how wrong injustice truly is.

For God to arbitrarily forgive sin, to declare rebellion and wickedness a non-issue would be to say that it does not matter at all, that it has no weight. This is something God cannot do, for every sin of men and women is an act of rebellion against God. It is repudiation of His character and goodness and a claim that we are superior in judgment and power to our Creator. As we have just seen, God's purpose in this world is to display His glory for all to see and enjoy; to set aside sin without justice is to abandon that purpose and give glory to His creation—to affirm their power, authority, and judgment in the place of His.

Flipping that around, for God to give justice, to pay retribution upon sin and rebellion, is for Him to demonstrate His glory. It is to show that He is God and we are not; it demonstrates that He is good and we are not. Furthermore, it is to say that human sin actually matters, that it has weight to it; judgment shows that sin is no insignificant issue. When God pays back human sin with His perfect justice, it is His declaration that all the damage we have wrought upon one another is a serious matter, that the verbal abuse we received was a serious issue, that the rape and murder of those created in the image of God is worthy of the attention and judgment of God, and that the slaughter of our children through abortions does not go unnoticed. Justice is the ultimate vindication of what we all know about some sin, its complete evilness, and the revelation of the complete evilness of every sin— even those we dismiss as 21st century people. Beyond that, it is the display of God's character and the affirmation that He is indeed God and Lord and we are not.

Judgment Reveals the Character of God

This has two implications. First, judgment reveals something profound about God, His goodness and God-ness. And knowing this, how just judgment is inextricably tied to who God is, magnifies the wonder of the postponement of judgment. When God has great forbearance, withholding judgment, we can now see that He is not simply refraining from acting. He is allowing His creation to actually think they are gods; He is allowing His name to be trampled in the mud and His glory—the very reason the creation exists—to be denied. Why would He do such a thing? As we see in 2 Peter and Romans, God withholds judgment that all might have a chance to repent (Rom 2:4, 3:25; 2 Pet 3:9). But even more so, He has withheld wrath for so long to orchestrate the ultimate display of His Character, for His justice and mercy to be displayed simultaneously (Rom 3:25).

God has allowed human sin to exist in the first place and withheld wrath so that His Son might come into the creation and die on a cross. In this He shows just how just and gracious He is; so much so that He would give Himself to uphold His goodness and simultaneously show mercy. He now withholds wrath for the final day, for Hell, so that when all accounts are balanced in final judgment and His wrath is finally poured out for an eternity, His redeemed people and those who have rebelled against Him would behold for all eternity the breadth of His mercy (Rom 9:22-24). That is, the horrors of Hell have this ultimate purpose, to demonstrate the horrors of the cross and the magnitude of God's mercy demonstrated there.

We will not know what it truly meant for Jesus to drink the full cup of the wrath of God until we understand the weight of human sin, demonstrated by the eternal horrors of Hell. Every minute of eternity will only heighten our understanding of what it truly cost for God to die on the Cross for our sake and how serious our rebellion actually was, how much the forbearance of God for thousands of years actually cost. This, I believe, is why judgment is so intrinsic to God's plan of redemption, why it is so necessary for the magnification of His glory. Judgment is so central because it is by these displays of God's justice on earth and the final display in Hell that we will understand the breadth of His mercy.

Judgment Is a Foundation for Hope

Yet this is not the only implication meditating on God's justice has for us. Second, God's judgment climaxing on the Cross and concluding in Hell is a source of great hope and the ground of our acts of forgiveness. Consider this song here in Habakkuk 2; the nations look to Yahweh for justice and have confidence that He will act. This answers Habakkuk's initial question, will Chaldea pay for its crimes? (Hab 1:17). Though Habakkuk receives an immediate answer, that they will indeed pay, we often do not receive such an answer for the injustices we perceive. At the height of World War II, the question would have been, will Hitler pay for the atrocities he has committed? In the years that followed, would Stalin face punishment for the mass slaughter he committed? How about Pol Pot? All these men have died, yet is that sufficient justice for the millions they killed? Or consider the millions of children that have been massacred in the Western world; will those who have orchestrated easy access and justification for such murder face justice for their crimes? In Canada, there are many unsolved cases of missing and murdered indigenous women; will the perpetrators of these crimes face justice? If our hope were in this life alone, the sad truth would be that justice is not served; these crimes would go unanswered.

However, the book of Habakkuk is a testimony to the fact that God cares about justice and is concerned about the atrocities His creatures commit. He does not let horrors go without answer. And as Habakkuk and the nations that Chaldea ravaged hoped in God's just retribution, we can also find hope in God's good character expressed in justice. As He brought justice to the Chaldeans, so also will He bring justice to the abuses that have gone unanswered in this life. This is the promise of the Cross and Hell: the Cross is God's answer to sin for those who will be redeemed; Hell is God's answer to sin for those who continue in their rebellion and reject His mercy. In one place or the other, on the Cross or in final judgment, all the sins of mankind will be accounted for. This is the ultimate assurance to us that the sins perpetrated around and against us do matter to God; He cares about the lives of men, women, and children murdered and maimed by His rebellious creatures. The Cross and Hell are our assurance that God takes sin seriously and that He does not turn a blind eye to sin.

This truth, that sin matters but God will deal with it is the firm ground for forgiving others. God's just judgment is His promise that though we forgive those wrongs done against us and forget them by not holding a record of wrong, God will not forget. We do not have to keep an account of the wrongs done against us nor do we need to seek vengeance against those who have hurt us. Indeed, we cannot, for this would be to exalt ourselves to the place of God.

Because God is faithful to address the problem of sin, we need not take justice into our own hands. We can surrender the weight of trying to keep everyone accountable for their wrongdoing and instead be radically kind and forgiving. This releases us of a great burden, to avenge wrongdoing at every opportunity and to mourn when this is not done. Instead, God will avenge every wrong. We know that by forgiving those who have sinned against us, we are not saying that these sins do not matter. Indeed, to forgive is to acknowledge that a serious offence has happened. We are free to forgive knowing that God will demonstrate the seriousness of the sin and deal out appropriate justice, something we are incapable of doing. One way or another, all sin will be addressed; whether on the Cross of Jesus Christ or in Hell, no sin will be forgotten. In this way we can love and serve those who hurt us, forgiving them for the hurts they have caused us, for vengeance is God's and He will repay. This takes great faith, trusting God that He is faithful to deal with sin so that we do not have to.

> Beloved, never avenge yourselves, but leave it to the wrath of God, for it is written, "Vengeance is mine, I will repay, says the Lord." To the contrary, "if your enemy is hungry, feed him; if he is thirsty, give him something to drink; for by so doing you will heap burning coals on his head." Do not be overcome by evil, but overcome evil with good. (Rom 12:19-21)

C. CONCLUSION: LET ALL THE EARTH BE SILENT (2:20)

[20]But YHWH is in is holy temple,
  be silent before Him all the earth.

Habakkuk 2:20 not only brings the taunt song to an end; it also brings an end to Habakkuk's protest that God does not listen (1:1-4) and his questions concerning God's actions (1:12-2:1). The rebuke Habakkuk expected in 2:1 has finally come; "be silent, trust in your Holy God" is God's final response. Habakkuk has received an answer to both his questions and has seen a vision of God's plan of salvation. What remains at the end of the first part of the book of Habakkuk is the question, how will Habakkuk and those who read His prophecy respond?

God has shown him an unbelievable vision (1:5), yet He has also demanded that Habakkuk respond with faith, waiting for the vision's fulfillment (2:2-4). God will save His people, yet it will be through an invasion by the bloodthirsty Chaldeans. God will also judge Chaldea, yet this will only come after they have wrought His judgment. The righteous are distinguished from the wicked by their faith, and they will receive the salvation of God. Will Habakkuk and the righteous of Israel respond in this way?

Exposition

Habakkuk 2:20 is a humbling verse; like Job 38-41 and Romans 9:19-24, here God silences the questions of the creature with the authority of the Creator. It is not that God has not given answers; He has. Yet there remains much unsaid. God does not feel the need to divulge all of His secret ways. In the end He calls on the creature to submit to his Creator. When God speaks "silence!" there is no room left for human questioning. Though God has given man great intellectually ability and a breadth of revelation to answer many questions, there comes a point where all the question humans ask resolve in submission, reliance on one whose authority is greater.

In many ways this is what it means to be a creature, by definition a product of a greater power. Moreover, this is the result of being under the lordship of God. All human beings, believing and unbelieving a like, are subjects of God their king. As subjects, they are under His rule and subject to His Law. He is not an arbitrary ruler; all He does is perfectly wise, just, and good. Yet there is no guarantee that His creatures will see His rule as just, wise, and good. At many points we must submit ourselves to Yahweh and confess that His thoughts are greater than ours, as are His ways (Isaiah 55:6-11). Ultimately, though He has revealed many things, the secret things belong to the Lord (Deut 29:29). There will always be a point where God says, "Be silent!" "Where were you…?" "Who are you, O man, to answer back to God?" (Hab 2:20, Job 38:4, Rom 9:20). We then have a choice: do we acknowledge that God is greater than us and is trustworthy? Will we trust Him? Or will we usurp His throne and claim that we are more knowledgeable than He is? Our answer to this question identifies our place in His kingdom: are we humble servants or haughty rebels? Do we serve Christ or Satan? To whose kingdom will we submit?

That God is Lord demands a lot from us, that we give up moral and intellectual autonomy at the very least. However, it is also incredibly freeing. Who among us, if we are honest, is capable of being lord of this universe? Who of us is capable of delineating right and wrong, determining truth and falsehood? Were we there when Yahweh laid the foundations of the earth, that we might correct Him? Were we there when He laid out His plan for the creation, that we might question its wisdom? How can we question the one who gave us the ability to question, whose faithfulness enables our thinking, whose wisdom engineered our ability to know, and whose knowledge is the measure of our truth? We are in no place to do so, which means that we are freed from the obligation to do so. We do not have to answer every question, for we know the one who has all the answers. We do not need to wallow in skepticism, for the one who knows all things has made truth known us. We do not need to wander aimlessly in life, for God has revealed our purpose— "to glorify God and to enjoy Him forever."[1] We do not need to look for ourselves for moral guidance, God has revealed His will.

This relieves us of an unbearable burden. Modern academia tells us we cannot have certainty and that probable knowledge only results from vast

---

[1] The testimony of Scripture as summarized in the Westminster Shorter Catechism; the answer to Q1.

learning. On the contrary, we can be certain about many things because God has made them known. Contemporary philosophy tells us that communication is impossible and morality is relative. Yet we can trust our ability to interpret and be interpreted because God has created language for this very purpose, clear communication. And we can know right from wrong and delight in what is right because God has made His will clearly known in Scripture. Therefore, these words, "Let all the earth be silent" are words of great comfort. "Cease from your turmoil," God beckons us, "cease from your doubts and fears." Instead, find rest in the arms of the Creator, the one who loved us, revealed Himself to us, and sent His Son to redeem us. This God sits in His holy temple and we can trust the judge of the earth to do what is right.[2]

---

[2] I unpack the freedom God's authority grants us in the realm of knowing and truth in my book, *The Gift of Knowing: A Biblical Perspective on Knowing and Truth* (Vancouver, Teleioteti 2019)

2. HABAKKUK'S PRAYER OF FAITH IN RESPONSE TO THE ORACLE (3:1-19)

A. SUPERSCRIPTION (3:1)

3 ¹A prayer of Habakkuk the prophet, according to the *Shigyonot*.ª

As the first part of Habakkuk began with a superscription (1:1), so this second part begins with one. Instead of a "judgment oracle," we are introduced to a "prayer" (תְּפִלָּה, *tᵉpillāh*). We often think of prayers in terms of a petition, asking God for something; however, "prayer" has a broader meaning in the Bible. A prayer may refer to many forms of communication with God, including praise, petition, and lament. Considering the content of this prayer song, we could identify this psalm as a confession of praise. In it, the one praying proclaims faith in the work that God is doing—even petitioning for it—and offers praise to Him, all of this despite the difficult nature of God's deed. Habakkuk's prayer has themes of petition (3:2) and lament (3:16), but awe filled praise seems to be the primary tone struck in the prayer, reaching its climax in verses 18-19c.[1] The phrase "according to" along with the concluding remarks in 19d indicate that this prayer is a song to be sung.

Exegesis of Verse 1

¹A prayer of Habakkuk the prophet, according to the *Shigyonot*.ⁱ

Verse 1. The phrase "according to..." is characteristic of the Psalms. It is used for musical direction, potentially to indicate the melody to which the

---

ª Ps 7:1 (MT), Hab 1:1; Ps 6:1 (MT), 8:1 (MT), 9:1 (MT), etc.

[1] Heath A. Thomas similarly observes that praise is a significant theme in the prayer. *Habakkuk*, The Two Horizons Old Testament Commentary (Grand Rapids: Eerdmans, 2018), 143.

song is to be sung.² Though *shigyonot* may simply be a reference to melody, it may also indicate that this prayer has something in common with Psalm 7, which is identified as this type of song (v. 1, MT: "a *shiggayon* of David, which he sang to YHWH," my translation). There are significant commonalities between Habakkuk 3 and Psalm 7; both contain petition for the Lord to rise up in judgment and praise for the Lord's judgement. This may indicate that *Shigyonot* indicates not only melody but a type of song that shares these themes. The plural here would then mean, "according to [the melody of] the Shiggayon-type songs."

Textual Notes

[i] **Verse 1.** *Shigyonot* is a transliteration of the Hebrew word שִׁגְיֹנוֹת (*šigyōnôt*). It only occurs here (in the plural) and in the title of Psalm 7 (verse 1 in the MT), though there it is singular. It is unclear what the term actually refers to, though as mentioned above, the "according to" formula suggests it is refers to a melody or a song with a melody to which this one is to be sung. In the later case, "*shigyonot*" may be a group of songs that share the same melody.

---

[2] Cf. Carl E. Armerding, "Habakkuk," in *The Expositor's Bible Commentary: With the New International Version; Daniel and the Minor Prophets*, ed. Frank E. Gaebelein, vol. 7 (Grand Rapids: Zondervan, 1985), 637; Keil and Delitzsch, *Commentary on the Old Testament in Ten Volumes: Minor Prophets; Two Volumes in One*, 10.2:93.

B. HABAKKUK'S PRAYER OF FAITH IN RESPONSE TO THE ORACLE FROM GOD (3:2-19C)

A lot of ground has been traversed before this prayer. In the judgment oracle (1:1-2:20), God revealed His plan for salvation through judgment and asked of His people one thing as they face the coming Chaldean invasion. He commands them to believe the unbelievable (1:5, 2:4). Contrary to Habakkuk's initial response (1:12-13), we have seen that God intended this invasion to be the answer to Habakkuk's prayer for salvation. Habakkuk asked of God two question; Yahweh answered them (2:2-20), though he rebuked Habakkuk's impetuousness and invoked His status as the Holy God in Heaven (2:20). Whether or not Habakkuk received the answer he wanted to hear, 2:20 signals a change in the book. The conversation is over. God asked of Habakkuk the unthinkable—to believe the unbelievable. Now Habakkuk, and all who would call themselves the righteous—God's people—had to respond. Two choices faced the Judahites who heard Habakkuk's vision: they could ignore God's purpose in the invasion and "run," rejecting God's purpose in it, or they could "wait," trust His unbelievable deed (2:2-4). With God's definitive answer given, Habakkuk does the only thing left for a servant of the Lord to do. Habakkuk does not grudgingly concede God's justice—as if he were to say, "okay Lord, I hate what you are doing, but I will not pester you in prayer about it anymore"— no, he whole heartedly embraces God's good purpose, and though he is utterly terrified, he writes a song for those like him who will trust Yahweh. Habakkuk's prayer vividly portrays the Babylonians storming into Judah as God's army: God Himself comes forth with His anointed tool. The natural elements join in the battle, and Habakkuk leads the righteous in expressing unwavering faith in their saving God (3:17-19).

The prayer in Habakkuk chapter 3 forms a fitting climax to the book. It is a carefully composed song that ties God's salvific act through Chaldea to Israel's grand history. It must have been utterly shocking at first for those who sung this song to attribute to the Chaldean invasion the same language that described God's mighty acts to save them from Egypt (the Exodus), to bring them into the Promised Land (the Conquest), and to save them from their enemies in the land. The song is made up of four strophes—an introduction followed by three main strophes. The three main strophes are themselves composed of three stanzas. Each strophe presents a different perspective on the Chaldean invasion. Shockingly, God is presented as leading the Chaldean invasion. The second strophe describes the invasion from a distance, using 3rd person pronouns; the third strophe describes God's arrival, using 2nd person pronouns; and the fourth strophe describes Habakkuk's, and by extension the righteous Judahites', response to the invasion. In addition, the final colon of the first strophe (3:3a-b) and the third stanza of the second and third strophe (3:6-7, 3:13) begin a transition to the strophe that follows.

i. Strophe 1: Bring Your Deed to Life (3:2-3B)

²Oh YHWH, I have heard your report;[a]
   I fear, oh YHWH, this deed[b] of yours.
In the midst of years,[c] give it life;
   in the midst of years, make it known;[d]
   but in anger, remember to show mercy.

³God[e] comes in from Teman,[f]
   the holy one from mount Paran.[g]

Selah[h]

The first strophe of Habakkuk's prayer is the shortest, but it has the vital function of establishing the context for what follows. Habakkuk confesses his fear (cf. 3:16-19), yet steps out in faith to ask God to fulfill the salvation He promised. These verse orient the prayer that follows to the Chaldean invasion by repeating the פעל (*p'l*, "deed") root from Habakkuk 1:5; by bringing together the notes of fear and faith that were found in the first part (Hab 1:12-17, 2:2-4); and by the petition for mercy in the midst of wrath, a petition that is only fitting if the objects of wrath are God's people. These are some of the reasons I have rendered the content of the prayer beginning in verse 3 in the present tense: Habakkuk is describing the Chaldean invasion which God has revealed to him and his response to it, not a past event.[1]

---

[a] Hab 1:5

[b] Hab 1:5

[c] Ps 102:24

[d] Hab 2:14

[e] אֱלוֹהַּ (*ĕlôah*), used in Deut 32:15; 2 Sam 22:32; Isa 44:8; Ps 18:32, 18:47, 50:22, etc.; throughout Job; Neh 9:17.

[f] Jer 49:7

[g] Deut 33:2

[h] Throughout the Psalms, e.g. Pss 3:2, 4, 8; 7:5; 9:16, 20; 84:4, 8.

[1] In contrast, many commentators and translators interpret this song as a

Exegesis of Verses 2-3B

²Oh YHWH, I have heard your report;
   I fear, oh YHWH, this deed of yours.
In the midst of years, give it life;
   in the midst of years, make it known;
   but in anger, remember to show mercy.

³God comes in from Teman,
   the holy one from mount Paran.

Selah ⁱ

Verse 2. The report Habakkuk has heard is the vision in 1:5-11, the "deed" Yahweh has orchestrated (1:5). This explains why Habakkuk fears it, for this "deed" is the Chaldean invasion of Judah. "Heard your report" is semantically parallel to "told" in Habakkuk 1:5, strengthening this connection.

Despite his fear, Habakkuk then prays that God would do this work. His positive perception of the invasion demonstrates that he has believed God's unbelievable deed and acknowledges that it is the answer to his prayer for salvation (1:1-4, 1:5-6, 2:2-4, 3:16-19).

"In the midst of years" is a phrase not used elsewhere in the Bible, the closest parallel being "in the midst of my days" (Psalm 102:25 MT, v. 24 English; cf. Jer 17:11). However, in Psalm 102 "middle" is חֲצִי (*ḥăṣî*; half, middle); here here it is בְּקֶרֶב (*bᵉqereb*, in the midst/middle of). In Psalm 102, "midst of my days" means "in the middle of my life as opposed the end," "imminently as opposed to far off at the end." This seems to be the sense here in Habakkuk: "in the midst of years" seems to mean "soon" rather than "later." So he prays, "soon Lord, make your salvation happen!"¹

---

reflection on God's past actions. E.g. ESV, NIV, Armerding, Patterson. Cf. NASB, NET, Robertson. Armerding, "Habakkuk," 634–635; Richard Duane Patterson, *Nahum, Habakkuk, Zephaniah*, The Wycliffe Exegetical Commentary (Chicago: Moody Press, 1991), 230–234; Robertson, *The Books of Nahum, Habakkuk, and Zephaniah*, 219–220.

¹ Cf. NET, C.F. Keil and F. Delitzsch, *Commentary on the Old Testament in Ten Volumes: Minor Prophets; Two Volumes in One*, trans. James Martin, Reprint., vol. 10.2 (Grand Rapids: Eerdmans, 1978), 95.

Alternatively, "in the midst of years" may mean something like "in history," that is, make happen in time and space what to this date has only been promised. The impact is the same for either interpretation: Habakkuk is asking that God would accomplish this deed sooner rather than later.

"Give it life," חַיֵּהוּ (*hayyê*) could also mean "revive" (cf. ESV, NASB, NET), suggesting that Habakkuk is calling for God to perform once again His past deeds. This reading would fit very well if the song was a reflection on God's past deeds; in that case, this introductory prayer would then connect the reflection to Habakkuk's present circumstances. However, if the song is a prayer concerning the imminent invasion of Chaldea, as I have argued, then חַיֵּהוּ (*hayyê*) may mean "give it life!" that is, "make it happen!"[2] "Make it known" echoes the central theme of Habakkuk 2:5-20, God's glory made known throughout the earth when God judges Chaldea (2:14).

Verse 3a-b. As noted above, these lines begin a transition to the following strophe. "Teman" and "Mount Paran" both refer to the south, to Edom, and reflect the historic path by which Yahweh led Israel into the promised land (Deut 33:2).[3] This provides theological not geographical orientation for the Chaldean invasion, identifying it with the Conquest. That is, historically the Chaldeans would have invaded from the North, but the South has theological significance as the route by which God brought Israel to the land and judged the Canaanites. This begins a series of identifications between God's present act through Chaldea and His past acts of salvation. "The holy one from Mount Paran" also echoes Deuteronomy 33:2.

Selah is a musical term the meaning of which we are not certain. However, it certainly indicates a musical shift in the song. I have observed in my own studies of the Psalms, particularly Psalm 84, that this shift often correlates with a shift from one section of a Psalm to another. Breaking Habakkuk 3 into strophes where *selah* is found makes great sense of the song.

---

[2] John Goldingay and Pamela J Scalise, *Minor Prophets II* (Peabody: Hendrickson, 2009), 80; Keil and Delitzsch, *Commentary on the Old Testament in Ten Volumes: Minor Prophets; Two Volumes in One*, 10.2:94.

[3] F. F. Bruce, "Habakkuk," in *The Minor Prophets: An Exegetical and Expository Commentary*, ed. Thomas Edward McComiskey (Grand Rapids: Baker Book House, 1992), 882; Patterson, *Nahum, Habakkuk, Zephaniah*, 230–231; O. Palmer Robertson, *The Books of Nahum, Habakkuk, and Zephaniah*, NICOT (Grand Rapids: W.B. Eerdmans, 1990), 222.

Textual Notes

[i] **Verse 3b.** סֶלָה (*selāh*) Various suggestions have been offered as to the meaning of סֶלָה, but its original meaning is ultimately lost for contemporary interpreters. However, we can come to some understanding of its function by studying how it is used. I have found that it often indicates a transition from one section of a psalm to another; this is consistent with the traditional understanding of the word as musical interlude (cf. LXX, Kidner). Pieter van der Lugt also considers *selah* to be a transitional marker in the Psalter, though one not as significant as I consider it to be. Derek Kidner, *Tyndale Old Testament Commentaries : The Proverbs* (Downers Grove, Ill.: InterVarsity Press, 1983), 36–37; Pieter van der Lugt, *Cantos and Strophes in Biblical Hebrew Poetry: With Special Reference to the First Book of the Psalter*, vol. I, Oudtestamentische studiën 53 (Leiden; Boston: Brill, 2006), 80; Richard Duane Patterson, *Nahum, Habakkuk, Zephaniah*, The Wycliffe Exegetical Commentary (Chicago: Moody Press, 1991), 234; P.C. Craigie, *Psalms 1-50, Volume 19: Second Edition*, ed. M. Tate et al., Electronic., Word Biblical Commentary (Grand Rapids: Zondervan, 2018).

Exposition

How often do we look past our fears and doubts and cling to faith in our God? I doubt many of us often simultaneously acknowledge trembling fear and pray for the very thing feared. Yet that is exactly how Habakkuk opens this song. Yahweh's answers have not assuaged his fears; they have not removed his initial terror. But they have reminded Habakkuk that God is trustworthy. So Habakkuk and all the faithful who follow him in singing this song declare from the outset their reaction to God's good news. It is a fearful thing to face an invasion by the Chaldean army. However, they express the unbelievable faith to which God has called them: they pray for God to accomplish the very thing they fear.

God often says things in His Word or does things that make us reel, that cause us to doubt or tremble. If we had perfect faith, this would not be our response—we would have complete peace over everything God says and does. Yet none of us has perfect faith; we all doubt and we all can identify things in the Bible—if we read it enough—that make us uncomfortable. When we fall short of the ideal, when we still doubt or are repulsed by something God has taught, we are called to nevertheless turn to God. It remains our obligation to pray, "Your kingdom come, your will be done," even if in our sin we do not quite want that. The challenge of the book of Habakkuk is to believe the unbelievable, to push past doubt and fear and seek God's will, to do His will, especially when it makes us uncomfortable. Habakkuk and the righteous of Judah sought God's salvation even when they knew it would be devastating and uncomfortable.

This is the nature of saving faith, to seek God's will even when we disagree, to submit our imperfect wills and ideas to God's perfect will, to humbly ask for His will to be done even when we are terrified about the consequences of Him answering that prayer.

ii. Strophe 2: God Comes Forth (3:3c-9b)

His majesty covers the heavens,
    and the earth is full of his renown.[a]
⁴His brightness is like day;[b]
    he has rays flashing from his hand;
    there is the concealing of his strength.
⁵Pestilence goes before him,
    and fiery devastation follows his steps.

⁶He stands and causes the earth to quake;[c]
    he looks and causes the nations to jump.
The mountains of old are shattered,
    and the ancient hills cower;[d]
    the ancient paths are his.
⁷I see the tents of Cushan under distress;
    the tent curtains of the land of Midian tremble.[e]

⁸Is YHWH wroth with the rivers?
    Is your anger with the rivers,
    or your rage with the sea,
That you drive your horses along,
    your chariots of salvation?[f]
⁹Your bow is wakened from its sheath,
    your rods sworn in with a word.[g]

Selah

The last lines of the first Stanza 1 portrayed God as once again marching

---

[a] Hab 2:14

[b] Ezek 1:27, Ps 148:13-14

[c] Judg 5:4-5, 2 Sam 22:8, Isa 5:25, Ps 114:7. For the following verses, cf. Ps 77:17-21

[d] Cf. Ps 114:3-4

[e] Deut 2:25

[f] Deut 33:26, Isa 66:15

[g] Jer 47:6-7, Ezek 21:23.

from the south towards the promised land, this time at the head of the Chaldean army. As the Lord enters the land of Judea, we are given the perspective of a far off observer. Habakkuk pictures God's salvific invasion in cosmic terms; the earth itself and its waters respond to God's invasion, quaking and then shattering before Him. The earth itself mirrors the fear of the Judahites and the nations before God's invasion. In the midst of such description, we continue to see the correct perception expressed by Habakkuk and the faithful; God comes forth wreaking destruction, yet He comes forth with "chariots of salvation." Through terrifying judgment, God intends salvation.

Exegesis of Stanza 1: God Comes in Glorious Power (3c-5)

His majesty covers the heavens,
> and the earth is full of his renown.
⁴His brightness is like day,
> he has rays[i] flashing from his hand;
> there is the concealing of his strength.[ii]
⁵Pestilence goes before him,
> and fiery devastation[iii] follows his steps.

Verse 3c-d. Yahweh has come forth and His mighty character is clearly seen. "Majesty" translates הוֹד (*hôd*); הוֹד is similar to כָּבוֹד (*kābôd*, glory) in that it describes something as visible or evident, yet whereas כבד connotes awe and greatness, הוֹד often connotes royal or kingly presence (Ps 21:6, 45:4, Dn 11:21, 1 Cor 29:25).[1] It may suggest then the glory of a sovereign, evident power. God's sovereign power over His creation is clear in His actions.

"Renown" translates תְּהִלָּה (*tᵉhillah*); תְּהִלָּה usually means "praise," however it can refer to the subjective recognition of "glory," which is the objective manifestation of a magnificent character. It seems to have this sense of subjective recognition here, so "renown" or "fame" are appropriate translations. Thus, 3c-d is closely related to 2:14, where the ultimate end of God's work through Chaldea—both to raise them up and judge them—is seen to be the revelation of His glory across the earth. Even now, in the Chaldean invasion, this work begins; God's glory is recognized.

---

[1] Cf. Carl E. Armerding, "Habakkuk," in *The Expositor's Bible Commentary: With the New International Version; Daniel and the Minor Prophets*, ed. Frank E. Gaebelein, vol. 7 (Grand Rapids: Zondervan, 1985), 640.

Verse 4-5. In verse 4 Habakkuk continues to reflect upon God's glorious power on display. Lines b and c are a little difficult. In the context of glorious displays, it seems that קַרְנַיִם (*qarnayim*) bears its secondary sense "rays." Why exactly it is in the dual is not clear, though it probably carries over from the more common use of the word in the dual, for "horns."[2] For a similar transference of the dual form from anatomical to secondary meaning, in this case a metaphor, see Josh 8:20 (יָדַיִם, *yādayim*; lit. two hands). There is probably a play on words here, for קֶרֶן is often used metaphorically for power or strength (cf. 4c); thus, God's power is evident in the display of His glory.[3] By focusing the display of God's power in "His hand," the revelation of God's glory is focused on His mighty actions—in this case, the Chaldean invasion.

It is interesting that 4c reverses the idea found throughout this first stanza. "Majesty," "renown," "brightness," and "rays," all suggest revelation, God's character made evident. However, in 4c we read that in this light display, God's power is concealed. I take this to mean that even as His mighty deeds display His glory, all that power is only a fragment of His true strength; God's true might remains concealed behind even this mighty revelation of His power.

In the verse 4, Yahweh's power is said to be in His hand; verse 5 turns to His feet and recounts the devastation that results from the power. Pestilence, a wicked plague, goes before Him and fiery destruction is all that remains when He is done.

Textual Notes

[i] **Verse 4b.** קֶרֶן (qeren) most often refers to a literal protrusion, such as on the altar (Exod 27:2) or an animal horn (e.g. Gen 22:13). In another instance, it refers to a hill (Isa 5:1). In the context of light and glory, it is possible that it means

---

[2] Cf. Bruce K. Waltke and Michael Patrick O'Connor, *An Introduction to Hebrew Syntax* (Winona Lake, Ind.: Eisenbrauns, 1990), 117. There are several instances where the dual does not clearly refer to two protrusions: Ps 75:11, 1 Kgs 22:11, 2 Chron 18:10.

[3] David W. Baker, *Nahum, Habakkuk and Zephaniah: An Introduction and Commentary*, Tyndale Old Testament Commentaries 27 (Nottingham; Downers Grove: Inter-Varsity Press; IVP Academic, 2009), 71.

a protrusion of light, a light ray. This may be why the verb קרן is used in Exod 34 to refer to the shining of Moses's face (vv. 29, 30, 35). The various instances where קֶרֶן or another anatomical dual is used for a non-anatomical plural or singular justify translating "rays" instead of "twin rays" or "two rays."

ⁱⁱ **Verse 4c.** עֻזֹה (*'uzōh*) has an archaic form of the 3ʳᵈ masculine singular pronominal suffix, ה instead of ו.

ⁱⁱⁱ **Verse 5b.** רֶשֶׁף (*rešep*) is often translated "plague" or "pestilence" because of its is use in parallel with דֶּבֶר (*deber*, plague/pestilence) and קֶטֶב (*qeṭeb*, pestilence). However, in the 7 times it is used, it refers to a thunderbolt (Ps 78:48) and arrow (Ps 76:4) and at others times a flame (Song 8:6, Job 5:7). Other than the Song of Songs use, it always refers to destruction often with connotations of fire. Something that causes fiery destruction (Deut 32:24; Pss 78:48; 76:4; Job 5:7, Song 8:6) or its result, "fiery devastation" (Hab 3:5), seems to be appropriate. Cf. HALOT.

Exegesis of Stanza 2: The World Responds to His Coming (6-7)

⁶He stands and causes the earth to quake;ⁱ
  he looks and causes the nations to jump.ⁱⁱ
The mountains of old are shattered,
  and the ancient hills cower;
  the ancient paths are his.
⁷I see the tents of Cushan under distress;
  the tent curtains of the land of Midian tremble.

Verse 6. The first stanza describes the revelation of God's glory and demonstration of His power through the Chaldean invasion. Now, Habakkuk describes the world's response to God's actions. The emphasis on "old/ancient," draws the reader back to God's past actions. One again Yahweh treads the paths He once walked; as He led Israel as a conquering nation into the promised land, so now He leads Chaldea. The "mountains of old" and "ancient hills" may also emphasize that nations which have endured for a long time—such as the kingdom of Judah—are now being toppled.[1]

Verse 7. Our interpretation of "ancient paths" as a reference to God's past actions is confirmed in this verse. Midian and Cushan are both references to the book of Judges, where Cushan-Rishathaim of Mesopotamia and the Midianites were subdued by Israel (cf. Judg 3:8, 6:1-7:25).[2] For "distress" as a translation of אָוֶן (*'āven*), usually iniquity, see Numbers 23:21, Jeremiah 4:14, Psalm 90:10, Job 5:6, Proverbs 12:21 and 22:8.

---

[1] John Goldingay and Pamela J Scalise, *Minor Prophets II* (Peabody: Hendrickson, 2009), 83, 88.

[2] O. Palmer Robertson, *The Books of Nahum, Habakkuk, and Zephaniah*, NICOT (Grand Rapids: W.B. Eerdmans, 1990), 228–229; Patterson, *Nahum, Habakkuk, Zephaniah*, 237.

Textual Notes

[i] **Verse 6a.** The translation "quake" assumes that וַיְמֹדֶד is a polel form of the verb מִיד (*myd*) or מוד (*mvd*). Several translations relate this lexical form to a different verb, מדד (*mdd*), resulting the translations "survey" or "measure" (NASB, ESV). However, for several reasons, commentators and linguistics have argued that this is a hapax legomenon from an unused root (i.e. no corresponding noun or adjective) מוד. In favour of this interpretation is the occurrence of the Polel form, most commonly used with biconsonantal forms; geminate verbs such as מדד will usually follow the normal Piel pattern. In fact, מדד is found in the Piel 5 times and the sense "to measure" is hard to make sense of in this context. So there is good reason to think that this is a hapax of the verb מוד. If this is the case, we can adduce the meaning from context and support it in several ways.

In parallel with line b, "he looks and a causes the nations to jump," the usual translation "causes the earth to shake" or "quake" makes great sense. This is how the LXX understood this verse. The Arabic word *myd* has the same meaning, "to be moved mightily." Cf. HALOT. It may also be the case that מוד is a by-form of the far more frequent מוט (*mvṭ*) or נוד (*nvd*), which have the same meaning. The morphology and context give us sufficient justification for arguing that the form in question is from the verb מוד meaning in the *Polel*, "to cause to quake." Cf. C.F. Keil and F. Delitzsch, *Commentary on the Old Testament in Ten Volumes: Minor Prophets; Two Volumes in One*, trans. James Martin, Reprint., vol. 10.2 (Grand Rapids: Eerdmans, 1978), 101; Richard Duane Patterson, *Nahum, Habakkuk, Zephaniah*, The Wycliffe Exegetical Commentary (Chicago: Moody Press, 1991), 236.

[ii] **Verse 6b.** "Jump" translates the verb נתר, which occurs 4 times in the MT, though one instance is often emended. In Lev 11:21 and a parallel text in the Dead Sea Scrolls, 11QT 48:5, it clearly means "hop" or "leap." This meaning also makes sense in Job 37:1. The MT of 2 Sam 22:33 also has this verb, though most translations emend it to match the parallel text in Psalm 18. Following the Hebrew text, 2 Sam 22:33 would read, "This God is my strong fortress, He causes my way to leap in blamelessness." The meaning here is not clear, however the idea of leaping seems to fit well with the following line. Whatever we make of 2 Sam 22:33, Lev 11:21 and Job 37:1 along with 11QT 48:5 warrant the translation "jump" here.

Exegesis of Stanza 3: God is Ready for War (8-9b)

⁸Is YHWH wroth with the rivers?
    Is your anger with the rivers,
        or your rage with the sea,
That you drive your horses along,
    your chariots of salvation?
⁹Your bow is wakened from its sheath,
    your rods sworn in[i] with a word.

Selah

Verse 8. As the first second stanza pictured the earth being ravaged by the Chaldean invasion, so now the waters seem to be the object of God's judgment. The invasion is absolutely brutal, yet the brutality that raises questions in theses line is nothing other than the manifestation of God's salvation. As we see elsewhere in Scripture, Salvation is often—if not always—accompanied by judgment. However, Habakkuk recognizes that though brutal and devastating, the Chaldean army are "your chariots of salvation." In these verses Habakkuk transitions from the 3rd person address that has characterized this first strophe to the 2nd person address that will dominate the second strophe.

Verse 9. "Wakened from its sheath" is literally "wakened into nakedness" (עֶרְיָה תֵעוֹר, *'eryāh tē'ôr*). This interpretation takes עֶרְיָה as an adverbial accusative. Some commentators propose that עוּר ('vr) should be taken as a hapax from the same root as עֶרְיָה, meaning "to be stripped bare." However, the verbal cognate from this root is the III-He verb ערה (*'rh*) and the frequent verb עוּר "to be awakened" makes great sense here. In either case, God is preparing for battle, removing His bow from its case and commissioning His "rods."

    Line b of this verse is one of the more difficult lines in Habakkuk, yielding several different translations (cf. ESV, NASB, NET). The ESV's "arrows" makes a fitting parallel with "bow" in the previous line, yet out of 252 occurrences of מַטֶּה (*mateh*) in the Bible, it does not mean "arrow" anywhere else. "Rods" actually makes great sense in context. In Isaiah and elsewhere מַטֶּה and its close synonym שֵׁבֶט (*šebeṭ*) connote rod's used for discipline (Isa 9:3; 10:5, 24; 14:5; Ezek 7:10, 11; Mic 6:9). This sense fits the word's use here and later in Habakkuk 3:14. Thus, God is preparing His rod or staff for judgment.

The most difficult problem in this line is translating שְׁבֻעוֹת, "sworn in." As argued below, this word is from the root שׁבע and is either a noun literally meaning "oaths," leading to the *ad sensum* translation "sworn in," or more likely a qal passive participle meaning "to be commissioned with an oath." In this case, אֹמֶר (*'omer*) is an adverbial accusative of manner, "with a word."

Textual Notes

ⁱ **Verse 9b.** "Sworn in" translates שְׁבֻעוֹת (*šᵉbuʿôt*). At first glance, this could be a feminine plural noun from שְׁבוּעָה, an oath. As plural noun, we would need to supply a verb resulting in a translation such as, "your rods are put under oath with a word." However, the form could also be read as a Qal passive participle from שׁבע, which means "to swear an oath" in the Niphil stem. The passive participle in the Qal occurs once elsewhere in Ezekiel 21:23. If we take שְׁבֻעוֹת as a Qal passive participle, it would mean something like "to be put under oath." This would make great sense in our context, resulting in the same translations offered for the noun, "your rods are put under oath with a word." For the Ezekiel passage, the verb is translated and interpreted as if it were a Niphal participle, "they have sworn solemn oaths." However, it would make as much sense of the context to translate it as we have here; "They have been put under solemn oaths." This would yield the following for Ezekiel 21:23 [MT 28], "And it will seem to them a false divination, to them they were under solemn oaths, but he will bring to remembrance their iniquity that they should be taken." C.F. Keil and F. Delitzsch, *Commentary on the Old Testament in Ten Volumes: Minor Prophets; Two Volumes in One*, trans. James Martin, Reprint., vol. 10.2 (Grand Rapids: Eerdmans, 1978), 104–106.

This explains the MT text we have without recourse to revocalization as several commentators and some translations prefer, cf. ESV and NIV, Richard Duane Patterson, *Nahum, Habakkuk, Zephaniah*, The Wycliffe Exegetical Commentary (Chicago: Moody Press, 1991), 241–242.

Exposition

In North America, God is described almost exclusively in terms of His love, kindness, and generosity. Of course, these are not bad things: God is indeed loving, kind, and generous. These characteristics are all central to what God the Father has done through the Son in the Gospel. Yet our picture of God is deficient if this is *all* we think about Him. In a world full of violence and terrorism, it is easy to identify in God those things that make us comfortable and reassure us. It is easy to set aside, even for a moment, those aspects of His character that make us uncomfortable. If we do this, though, we run the risk of drastically misunderstanding the God we worship. We risk watering down His testimony concerning Himself and of ignoring much of the Bible. We especially risk misunderstanding the end of the age that we await, the return of Christ.

Old Testament theologians and exegetes often describe the language we are reading here in Habakkuk 3 as the "Divine Warrior" motif or theme. This is language that describes God as a warrior, as a conqueror, king, and saviour waging war for His people. This language is not exclusive to Habakkuk; indeed, it permeates the entire Bible. When Yahweh brings His people out from Egypt, His actions are described in terms of warfare He waged against Pharaoh and his so-called gods (e.g. Exodus 15). When Israel conquered Canaan, God unleashed His power through the elements—hail and the heavenly bodies—to defeat their enemies and bring them victory (Joshua 10). This language is also used all over the book of Psalms (e.g. Psalm 18). Throughout Church history, in an effort to distance themselves from such imagery, rogue teachers have suggested that this language describes a different god than that of the New Testament. Others have suggested that God has changed His ways since Jesus's incarnation—that this language is no longer adequate to describe our God. Both of these views are horridly deficient and destructive to the unified picture that the Bible paints of Yahweh. God is not one way in the Old Testament, angry and wrathful, but another in the New Testament, peaceful and loving. God was as merciful and gracious during the Old Testament as He is now during the New Testament age (cf. Rom 3:25). He is as just now as He was during the Old Testament times.

Furthermore, the New Testament is not free from this "Divine Warrior" language. Jesus was gentle and gracious, receiving children and eating with tax collectors and repentant sinners. Yet He also pronounced judgment upon the Jerusalem temple by flipping tables and driving out merchants with a whip (Mark 11:15-19, John 2:14-17). This judgment was fulfilled by the complete destruction of the temple in AD 70. Describing His return, Jesus in Matthew 25 told His disciples that He would sit in judgment upon His throne and would divide those among all humanity who have trusted and served Him from those who have not. Those who did not follow Him would be cursed to depart "into the eternal fire prepared for the devil and his angels… into eternal punishment" (25:41, 46). In Revelation, Jesus is described as a King riding a white horse. When He returns in judgment, "From his mouth comes a sharp sword with which to strike down the nations, and he will rule them with a rod of iron. He will tread the winepress of the fury of the wrath of God the Almighty" (19:15).

This theme of the Divine Warrior is therefore a significant revelation of our God: He is today, as He was then and will be forevermore, a triumphant warrior and king. "What is the significance of this?" we may ask. How does this aspect of God affect our lives today?

First, a right understanding of the wrath of God will magnify our understanding of Jesus's sacrifice on the Cross. Every instance we see of God's wrath is an anticipation of final judgment, when God will call all humanity to account for their wicked and rebellious deeds. God is great in patience, withholding judgment for that day described in Matthew 25. Yet from time to time, He acts now in judgment, bringing that future judgment into the present age. He obliterated Babylon (Jeremiah 50-51), consumed Sodom and Gomorrah with fire (Gen 19:23-29), and struck down Ananias and Sapphira for lying to the Holy Spirit (Acts 5:1-11). All of these events foreshadow the judgment that awaits the sins of humanity. In one sense, the Cross is the greatest of these. On the Cross, when Jesus died, God poured out the fullness of His wrath—that final judgment—upon His son in the place of those who would believe in Him (Rom 3:21-27; Eph 5:2, 25; Heb 9:11-28; Rev 5:9-10, 13:8, 20:11-15). In another sense, final judgment will be reminder of what Jesus did on the Cross for those who believe in Him. When we witness God's wrath against sin in final judgment, we will finally understand the weight Jesus bore on our behalf (cf. Rom 9:22-24). Therefore, all these instances of wrath, of judgment, also testify to the horror of what Jesus experienced on our behalf when He bore the judgment we rightfully deserved.

Second, a right understanding of God as warrior helps us live with confidence in this age as we fulfill the mission He has given us, to go into all nations, baptizing, making disciples, and teaching (Matt 28:18-20). Part of the difficulty of applying the Old Testament to the lives of New Testament believers is understanding what has changed between God's people under the Old Covenant and God's people under the New Covenant in Christ. Here is one place where we can see the significance of this change. Under the Old

Covenant, God's people were a nation, a people with a land and an earthly king. They were a people whose enemies were flesh and blood, who needed to be fought with swords and spears.

We, under the New Covenant, are not such a people: we are sojourners and exiles in foreign nations. We are in but not of this world. Christ's kingdom is at the moment a heavenly one, breaking into this world through the changing of hearts by the Holy Spirit and the Gospel not through political revolution and war. Paul at times refers to his fellow ministers of the Gospel as soldiers (Phil 2:25; Phlm 2; 2 Tim 2:3) and tells the Ephesians that they are, indeed, at war. The war they fight, though, is not the flesh and blood battles fought by Israel. It is a war "against the rulers, against the authorities, against the cosmic powers over this present darkness, against the spiritual forces of evil in the heavenly places" (Eph 6:5). He describes his ministry not as warfare against flesh and blood but against ideas, warfare waged by submitting every thought to obey Christ (2 Cor 10:1-6). This warfare is of a different sort than Israel's, yet it is still waged by the power of God (Eph 5:10-20).

Our confidence that we will have victory over the spiritual forces at work in this world, over every lofty opinion raised against Christ, and over the sinful deeds at work in our flesh is the power of God at work in us. The same God who strode through the earth making the mountains tremble—who smote the armies of Pharaoh with the sea, who brought fire and stone from the sky upon His enemies—is the God who is at work in us so that we can work and will to do His good pleasure (Phil 2:12). Yahweh, who fought Israel's wars long ago and now wages a different war within and through us, is our hope for endurance until the coming of Christ and for accomplishing the mission of bringing the Gospel to all people.

iii. Strophe 3: Yahweh Arrives (3:9c-13)

You split the earth with rivers;
    ¹⁰the mountains see you and writhe.[a]
Downpours of water sweep through;
    the deep lifts up its voice,[b]
    and raises its hands up high.

¹¹The sun and the moon stand in their exalted abode,[c]
    to make your arrows that fly gleam,
    to brighten your flashing spears.
¹²With indignation you march through the earth;[d]
    with your anger you thresh the nations.

¹³You come forth for the salvation of your people,
    for salvation with your anointed;[e]
You smash the head of the house of the wicked,
    laying it bare from the foundation to the neck.

Selah

The final stanza of the first strophe (3c-9b) shifted from 3rd person address to the 2nd person; this continues in this strophe. Habakkuk directly addresses God's actions and portrays the Chaldean invasion in the terms of God's most significant salvific and judgmental acts. There have been echoes of the Exodus throughout this book, potentially in 3:3c-9b; references to Israel's trek towards the promised land (3:3b); and allusions to God's victories through the judges (3:6-7). Now Habakkuk draws on allusions to the Flood account and the conquest narratives. In the first stanza, the flood waters are pictured as tools once again in God's hands. In the second stanza, the sun and moon are used by God as they were in the time of Joshua (Josh 10:12-13). In the previous strophe, the elements are presented as responding in

---

[a] Exod 19:18; Judg 5:5

[b] Ps 93:3

[c] Josh 10:12-13; Isa 63:15

[d] Hab 1:6c

[e] Jer 27:6; 43:10; Isa 45:1

terror to God's arrival; now they are tools in His mighty hands.

All of this must have been profoundly shocking to the Judahites singing this song: the Babylonian invasion is presented in terms of the major events in their history. Most shocking would have been the statement in verse 13b that Nebuchadnezzar, the leader of the Chaldeans, was not only God's tool of salvation but His anointed tool, the same word from which we get the words "messiah" or "christ".

Exegesis of Stanza 1: The Waters Join Your Assault (9c-10d)

You split the earth with rivers;
    ¹⁰the mountains see you and writhe.
Downpours of water sweep through;
    the deep lifts up its voice,
    and raises its hands up high.

Verse 9c-10. In this stanza, the water's above the earth and the deep below join in God's assault. This echoes the Genesis flood account, where the "deep," תְהוֹם ($t^e hôm$), burst forth from the ground (Gen 7:11) and rains pour out (Gen 7:12).

"Lifts up its voice" and "raises its hands up high" in context signify the waters joining in God's actions, presenting with personification the bursting forth of the deep in Genesis 7:11.

Exegesis of Stanza 2: The Luminaries Strengthen Your Weapons (11-12)

¹¹The sun and the moon stand in their exalted abode,
    to make your arrows that fly gleam,
    to brighten your flashing spears.
¹²With indignation you march through the earth;
    with your anger you thresh the nations.

Verse 11. The first line is a clear allusion to the events of Josh 10, when Joshua called for the sun and the moon to stop and lengthen the day and Yahweh "heeded the voice of a man," fighting for Israel (Josh 10:12-14). "Exalted abode," זְבֻל (zᵉbul), occurs 5 times in the Bible and always has connotations of a exalted or grand dwelling (1 Kgs 8:13, Isa 63:15, Ps 49:15, 2 Chron 6:2). The relationship between 11b-c and 11a as well as the significance הָלַךְ (hālak, go) is interpreted in several ways among commentators and translations.

The ESV is representative of one approach, "The sun and moon stood still in their place, at the light of your arrows as they sped." The NIV takes the same approach, interpreting "stand" as the response, presumably in terror, of the sun and moon to God's onslaught.¹ The NASB and NET take a different approach, interpreting "The sun and moon" as the subjects of הָלַךְ in 11b, yielding the translation "They went away at the light of Your arrows" (NASB). Both approaches see the Sun and Moon responding negatively to God's onslaught. I think neither of these approach fits the context. In the passage from Joshua to which Habakkuk alludes, the elements are not the object of God's attack but the instruments He uses to fight for Israel. Such an interpretation would fit with the previous stanza, where the waters join in God's assault. For this reason, הָלַךְ should be translated with "your arrows" as its subject, forming an attributive phrase, "your arrows [that] fly" (cf. NIV). The two occurrences of the preposition lamed in 11b and 11c should be taken as indicators of purpose, literally "*as* light for your arrows that fly" and "*as* brilliance for the lightning of your spears." This can be rendered verbally as I have above. Thus, the sun and moon take their stand in the heavens illuminating the destructive force of God's weapons.

Verse 12. גּוֹיִם (goyim, nations) occurs several times throughout the book of

---

¹ Cf. Keil and Delitzsch, *Commentary on the Old Testament in Ten Volumes: Minor Prophets; Two Volumes in One*, 10.2:106–109; Patterson, *Nahum, Habakkuk, Zephaniah*, 246.

Habakkuk; the plural always refers to the objects of the Chaldean's assault (2:5, 8; 3:6; cf. 1:17). Its occurrence here as the object of God's "threshing" strengthens our contention that this song recounts the Chaldean invasion with God at its head.

Exegesis of Stanza 3: You Come for Salvation with His Anointed (13)

¹³You come forth for the salvation of your people,
   for salvation with your anointed;
You smash the head of the house of the wicked,
   laying it bare from the foundation to the neck.

Selah

Verse 13. I have followed the Vulgate, King James Version, Calvin, and others in my rendering of verse 13b; contemporary translations and commentators translate 13b as they do 13a, "for the salvation of your anointed" (13b). There are several problems with this interpretation. First, it is not clear who the "anointed" is in this scenario, so they are forced to come up with ingenious and unlikely solutions (such that it refers to Moses[1] or the whole people of God, neither of which are called God's anointed).[2] Second, it ignores the deliberate syntactical shift Habakkuk makes, from a construct chain in 13a to a prepositional phrase in 13b. Those who see 13a and 13b as equivalent have to follow the LXX by interpreting את as the marker of the definite direct object. This is extremely unlikely, for "salvation" is not a verbal form, as evidenced by its use in the construct in 13a.[3] Syntactically, the preferable option is to interpret את as a preposition meaning "with." This

---

[1] Patterson, *Nahum, Habakkuk, Zephaniah*, 252; Carl E. Armerding, "Habakkuk," in *The Expositor's Bible Commentary: With the New International Version; Daniel and the Minor Prophets*, ed. Frank E. Gaebelein, vol. 7 (Grand Rapids: Zondervan, 1985), 644.

[2] Cf. David W. Baker, *Nahum, Habakkuk and Zephaniah: An Introduction and Commentary*, Tyndale Old Testament Commentaries 27 (Nottingham; Downers Grove: Inter-Varsity Press; IVP Academic, 2009), 74.
Keil and Calvin interpret it with reference, ultimately, to Jesus. Keil and Delitzsch, *Commentary on the Old Testament in Ten Volumes: Minor Prophets; Two Volumes in One*, 10.2:108–109; John Calvin, *Commentaries on the Twelve Minor Prophtes; Habakkuk, Zephaniah, Haggai, Zechariah, Malachi*, trans. John Owen, vol. 4, Calvin's Commentaries XV (Grand Rapids: Baker, 1996), 162–163.

[3] Freedman's argument that this is a "broken construct chain" is unsubstantiated, as I suggested above (2:14). David Noel Freedman, "The Broken Construct Chain," in *Pottery, Poetry, and Prophecy: Studies in Early Hebrew Poetry* (Winona Lake, Ind.: Eisenbrauns, 1980), 339–342.

also makes the best sense of the context.

If God is going forth for salvation "with [His] anointed," we must ask who the anointed is. It should be clear from my argument so far that God's anointed in this context is Nebuchadnezzar, the king of Babylon. This fits with the flow of the argument and God's claim to have raised up Babylon for this purpose (Hab 1:5). Robertson draws on Isaiah 45:1 and suggests that Cyrus is God's anointed here, yet that does not fit the context: this song focuses on the vision Habakkuk has received (Hab 1:5-11) and not the judgment of Chaldea expounded in 2:5-20.[4] However, God's words in Isaiah 45:1 justify the possibility that God would call a foreign ruler His anointed. Interpreting "your anointed" as Nebuchadnezzar also makes the interpretation of the following verse simpler than is often acknowledged. Most significantly, this identification ties the argument of the book of Habakkuk together nicely. Habakkuk first cried out for salvation, but God responded with a vision of the Chaldean invasion. I have argued that this vision is God's answer to that prayer, that Chaldea is God's act of salvation. This is the point of Habakkuk 2:2-4. As I have argued, chapter 3 is best read as a faith-filled response to the vision of the Chaldean invasion. Thus, for Habakkuk to say that God comes forth for the salvation of His people (13a) with His anointed one Nebuchadnezzar (13b) is to summarize the horrifying truth at the heart of the book: God will achieve the salvation of the righteous Judahites through the invasion of the wicked Chaldeans.

Lines c-d employ a mixed metaphor, employing imagery from construction (house - foundation) and anatomy (head - neck). The idea is clear enough, Yahweh will completely destroy "the head of the house of the wicked." The wicked here refers to the wicked Judahites, the objects of Habakkuk's original complaint (1:4). Yahweh will crush their leader and end their oppression. Habakkuk has therefore adopted God's perspective and abandoned his original complaint (1:13).

---

[4] O. Palmer Robertson, *The Books of Nahum, Habakkuk, and Zephaniah*, NICOT (Grand Rapids: W.B. Eerdmans, 1990), 237–238.

Exposition

Our exposition of Habakkuk has covered a lot of ground and unearthed weighty theological questions. The climactic confession in this strophe, that Chaldea is God's anointed, may be the weightiest, bringing us to the heart of man's relation to God. To accomplish salvation, a good end, God employs terrible means, the Chaldeans. However, God is not implicated in or stained by their evil; indeed, He will hold them accountable for their bloodthirst. The tension here between God's holiness and His wicked instruments, between God's sovereignty and human responsibility, is something we in the Western world struggle with deeply. Habakkuk's anguish over these issues demonstrates that we are not alone. Ultimately, the song in Habakkuk chapter 3 raises the question, "How can God be attributed with an action and be praised for it while the Chaldeans are condemned for the same act?"

I want to offer three different perspectives by which we as Christians can submit to God and trust Him when confronted with such a question. We need to understand, first, what theologians have called the Creator-creature distinction; second, the universal sinfulness of man (Total Depravity); and third, the end for which Yahweh created the world—what is ultimately good. These are themselves huge topics, so all I hope to do is give a brief overview.

What is man? Many today might define humanity in relationship to other creatures—we are "animals," "mammals"—or by our function and capabilities—we are intelligent, can communicate complex ideas (have language), and live in relationships. However, no such description arrives at the biblical definition of humankind. The Bible defines human beings by their relationship to God first and only then to creation as an outworking of that first relationship. In the beginning, God formed man from the dust (Gen 2:7), therefore man is fundamentally a creature (cf. Rom 9:20). In comparison to God, humans are also miniscule in every way: "O LORD, what is man that you regard, him, or the son of man that you think of him? Man is like a breath; his days are like a passing shadow" (Ps 144:3-4). We are fundamentally *creatures*, but we are creatures distinct from all others because God made us in His image and likeness (Gen 2:26-27); because we are created for relationship with Him, to be His people (e.g. Tit 2:14); and because God Himself became a man (John 1:5, 14-18; Gal 4:4-5). For this reason, humanity was given the job of representing God, of having dominion over the earth (Gen 1:26-27; Ps 8:3-9).

We, as creatures, relate to God as our Creator. That is, we are not His equals. We are not on the same level as He is: we do not possess the same rights, powers, or knowledge. If we are creatures, then all our thinking must be done as such. We must think about all things in the world as creations of God and must relate to God as those created by him. Being His creatures means that we are His—all the earth is His (Exod 19:5; Ps 24:1)—and so He is able to act towards us as His creations in ways that would be wrong for us creatures to act. He has rights we do not have. In addition, God has also entered into a covenant with us all, making us His servants or subjects. As our covenant Lord—our king—and our Creator, He has authority over us. As the Creator, He also has knowledge we do not have; this means that, as a trustworthy witness (He is true and His words are truth; 2 Sam 7:28, John 17:17), we must trust Him over against our own finite judgments.

This "Creator-creature distinction" has profound implications for our life and thinking. As it regards the question we are asking—the difference between God and Chaldea—Paul would caution us against thinking too much of ourselves: "who are you, O man, to answer back to God? Will what is molded say to its molder, 'Why have you made me like this?' Has the potter no right over the clay?" (Rom 9:20-21). Habakkuk affirms this: "YHWH is in His holy temple, be silent before Him all the earth" (2:20). Furthermore, because He knows all things and is trustworthy, we can trust His declaration that His actions are compatible with His revealed character even if we do not quite see how. Finally, we must acknowledge that God has rights Chaldea does not have. It is well within God's powers as God to take human life, but for man to do so is an insult towards God Himself (a sin: Gen 9:5-6, Exod 20:13).

God has the right to take human life, but when He does so we call it "judgment." God acts in judgment when He acts to hold men and women accountable for their sins in this life. This is important, for the Bible teaches that all humans are guilty of sin. Ultimately, we are identified with Adam under the covenant he transgressed and so are guilty with him of sin (Rom 5:12-21, 1 Cor 15:21-22). But we are all also guilty of continuing to sin in our thoughts and actions: "the intention of man's heart is evil from his youth"; "the wrath of God is revealed from heaven against all ungodliness and all the unrighteousness of men"; "none is righteous, no, not one"; "no one does good, not even one"; "all have sinned and fall short of the glory of God" (Gen 8:21; Rom 1:18, 3:10, 12, 23). A continual theme throughout the Bible is that humans hate God so much that it takes a supernatural work of God in the heart for a person to even believe (Deut 30:6; John 6:44; Rom 8:7-8).

If all humans are sinful, then it follows that we are all deserving of judgment—of God's wrath! God has the right, in fact the obligation, to take our lives as punishment for our rebellion against Him. We must then ask, "why has He not?" In Romans 3:25, Paul writes that God has displayed great patience passing over former sins—reserving judgment for a later day—until the incarnation of Jesus. God has displayed mercy towards sinners by not giving them the wrath they deserve. Instead, He poured it out upon Jesus on behalf of all who would believe in Him and will wait until the final judgment to render judgment on all not found in the book of life (Rev 13:8; 20:11-15).

Occasionally though, God brings that future judgment into the present. He acts now in judgment, anticipating the final day of judgment. The very fact that we have breath is, therefore, an act of God's mercy. It is only by His patient grace and mercy that we have not already died for our sins! The judgment God wrought through Chaldea would be the norm if it was not for this mercy. Regarding the present issue (how God is just but Chaldea is guilty for the same action), we must acknowledge that all humans are deserving of God's judgment, so God cannot be held guilty for acting in judgment whenever He so wishes. Chaldea, on the other hand, is not in this same position. They themselves are worthy of judgment, and they compound their guilt by committing idolatry (1:17) and using the powers given to them by God to shame their enemies and to pursue false security (Hab 2:9-11, 15-17). Scripture is clear the humans are responsible creatures: their sinful disposition is not an excuse but a reason for further condemnation (Matt 7:15-20). The Chaldeans, though a tool of judgment and salvation in God's hands, chose in their sinfulness to wreck mayhem instead of God's perfect justice. By doing this, they brought upon themselves further condemnation.

This brings us to our last consideration: what is "good"? That is, if Chaldea is sinful but God is righteous in this act of salvation-judgment, what standard are we using to judge? Any moral judgment we make (e.g. stealing is wrong!) assumes a standard of reference: a crime in the Canadian legal system is judged by the various laws governing the land. (Considering a different sphere, height is measured in centimeters; the standard of reference is some sort of ruler.) What standard do we use to judge God's actions, or Chaldea's actions? Do we use the laws of America, of Canada—maybe Saudi-Arabia? Though the laws of these nations have commonalities, they are different in significant ways: some things are considered wrong in one place but right in another. The penalties for wrongdoing are also different. If we were to use one over the other, how would we determine which one is right? To do so we need a higher standard.

What about God? By what standard could we judge His actions? If He is the Creator and Scripture testifies that we have no right to judge our Maker, then the standard by which His actions are measured must not be part of creation. The ancient philosopher Plato once addressed this question in a dialogue called *Euthyphro* and got stuck here. He knew that moral law could not be a created thing, for then God [the gods for him] could will rape to be wrong one day but right another—chaos would ensue! Yet, if God did not create the law and yet was judged by the law (judged to be right or wrong, just or unjust, good or bad), then the law was greater than God. The law would in fact be God. Plato never resolved this in his dialogue: he was intent on showing only that the "gods" were not what they were claimed to be.

However, we do not have to give up when faced with the "Euthyphro dilemma," this problem. Christianity offers us a way out, and thus an answer to our pressing question of Chaldea and God. Scripture makes it clear that the law is not an arbitrary creation—rape is legitimately sinful and deserving of judgment—yet neither is it above God. What Plato failed to do was conceive of the possibility of a *personal* standard. That is, a God who thinks, who acts, and who can be *faithful* and *consistent*. Because our God is *faithful*, He is His own standard of right and wrong, and His character becomes our standard of right and wrong. That is, God does not do something good because it is good; He does something good because *He* is good. Everything He does is good, but that does not lead to the chaos Plato envisioned, for God is *consistent* or *faithful*. What is good to Him one day is good to Him every day; He is unchanging, the same yesterday, today, and forever (Heb 13:8).

Therefore, if God is the standard of right and wrong, we have no right to accuse Him of wrongdoing, for He is incapable of doing wrong. This necessitates a profound shift in our thinking. If God is the ultimate standard of right and wrong, of what is good, and He is independent of creation (He is the Creator), if He existed before humanity, then good and bad have as their ultimate reference point *God* and not *humanity*. What is good is not necessarily what is good for man but what is good for God. This is a terrifying thought at first, for it is deeply unsettling and offensive to the way we usually think. Yet, "Has the potter no right over the clay, to make out of the same lump one vessel for honorable use and another for dishonorable use?" (Rom 9:21). Many theologians have concluded from studying the entire Bible that the end for which God created everything, what is ultimately good, is His glory—the display of His character (e.g. Exod 9:16).

What is good is then what gives God glory, and this is what Habakkuk identifies as Chaldea's purpose: "Is it not, behold, from YHWH of hosts that peoples are labouring only for fire and nations are wearing themselves for nothing? 14For the earth will be filled with the knowledge of the glory of YHWH like the waters cover the sea" (Hab 2:13-14, cf. 3:3). Yet this is not at the expense of humanity, in fact we are created by God to find our greatest joy and happiness in the enjoyment of Him (e.g. Psalms 16, 84). God's pursuit of His own glory meshes beautifully with His creation of man: for God to pursue His own glory is to bring the greatest joy and fulfillment to His human creations. Explaining God's purpose in choosing to save some and leave others in sin to face judgment, Paul concludes his argument in Romans 9 with a profound question:

> "What if God, desiring to show his wrath and make known his power, has endured with patience vessels of wrath prepared for destruction, in order to make known the riches of his glory for vessels of mercy, which he has prepared beforehand for glory—even us whom he has

called, not from the Jews only but also from the Gentiles" (Rom 9:22-24).

This has been a long aside, but I believe time spent here is well worth the effort: Habakkuk had to wrestle through these issues and the result was praise; can we come to the same end? In sum, we have seen that God has rights as the Creator that we as creatures do not have. God's rights include the freedom to show mercy to whom He will show mercy and to demonstrate His wrath and judgment against all of His sinful creatures. Chaldea did not have these rights and chose in their sinfulness to fulfill their God-given purpose in such a way as to reap only further condemnation. God did all this so that His people—Habakkuk, Judah, and us today—may know Him more. He did this so that we may come to love and enjoy the fullness of His complex being, thereby experiencing the fullness of joy He destined for those who love Him. There is profound mystery here, but with Paul I can only say,

> Oh, the depth of the riches and wisdom and knowledge of God! How unsearchable are his judgments and how inscrutable his ways!
>
> "For who has known the mind of the Lord,
>   or who has been his counselor?"
> "Or who has given a gift to him
>   that he might be repaid?"
>
> For from him and through him and to him are all things. To him be the glory forever. Amen. (Rom 11:33-36)

iv. Strophe 4: Habakkuk's Response of Faith (3:14-19d)

¹⁴With his rods you pierce the head,
>   his warriors storm in to scatter me,
>   their exultation as if to consume the oppressed in hiding places.
¹⁵You tread the sea with your horses,
>   the great waters foam.ᵃ

¹⁶I hear and my inward parts tremble;
>   at the sound my lips quiver.
Rot enters into my bones,
>   and I tremble where I stand,
While I wait for the day
>   for distress to come up,
>   for a people to attack us.

¹⁷Even when the fig tree does not bear fruit,
>   and there is no yield of the vine;
>   the labour done for olives fails,
>   and the fields do not produce food;
>   the flocks are cut from the fold,
>   and there are no cattle in the stalls,
¹⁸I will rejoice in YHWH,
>   I will exult in the God of my salvation.ᵇ
¹⁹The Lord YHWH is my strength;
>   He sets my feet like a doe
>   and causes me to tread upon high places.ᶜ

In verse 13, Habakkuk's song began to transition to this final stanza with its focus on God's salvific intent. In verse 14, the song transitions from the 2nd person pronouns that characterized the third strophe (3:9c-13) to the 1st person pronouns that characterize the fourth and final strophe (3:14-19b). This strophe brings the book to a climax, evidencing both the trembling fear that Habakkuk has expressed (1:12-17, 3:2) and the faith to which God has called him (2:2-4). Habakkuk makes clear his distress; he has looked among

---

ᵃ 2 Sam 22:17; Isa 17:13; Jer 51:13, 55; Ezek 26:19

ᵇ Pss 9:14, 13:5, 21:1, 35:9.

ᶜ Ps 18:33, 2 Sam 22:34.

the nations and is "astonished and astounded" (1:5). Yet despite his horror, he confesses faith in God no matter what may result. Yahweh who raised up the Chaldeans (1:5) and now rides forth at the head of their armies (3:2-3b) is nevertheless "the God of my salvation" (3:19b).

Exegesis of Stanza 1: With the Anointed One's Weapons You Strike Me (14-15)

> ¹⁴With his rods you pierce the head,
> his warriors[i] storm in to scatter me,
> their exultation as if to consume the oppressed in hiding places.
> ¹⁵You tread the sea with your horses,
> the great waters foam.[ii]

Verse 14. Our first question when approaching verse 14 should be, "who does 'his' refer to." The approach taken by the major translations with which we have been interacting is broadly the same; "his" refers to the "head of the house of the wicked" in the previous verse, resulting in a reflexive translation: "You pierced with his own arrows the heads of his warriors" (ESV); "With his own spear you pierced his head" (NIV). However, this idea of reflexive destruction is absent from the rest of the song; indeed, the previous verse has God going forth with His anointed and crushing "the head of the house of the wicked" (3:13). It would be odd, therefore, for Habakkuk to write now that the head has actually self-destructed itself.

Instead, "his" refers to "your anointed" in the previous verse. "The head" refers to "the head of the house of the wicked" in 3:13. This fits with verse 9, where God's preparation of the Chaldean invasion is related as "your rods sworn in with a word." Thus, with the rods of Chaldea God "pierces" the wicked Judahites.

14c repeats the general theme of chapter 2, Chaldea is God's tool yet they are themselves wicked. They exult in the vicious work with which they have been entrusted, but Habakkuk has the assurance that they will be brought to justice.

Verse 15. "With your horses" translates סוּסֶיךָ as an adverbial accusative of manner. Many commentators see an allusion to Psalm 77:19 (MT 20) here, yet that verse speaks of Yahweh walking through the Red Sea with His people during the Exodus. Neither the language nor the ideas present in these verses suggest such an allusion. "Great waters" or "many waters," as the ESV often translates it (here "mighty waters"), is used in the prophets for the waters by which the nations make themselves rich (Isa 23:3, Jer 51:13) and some times for the rebellious or distressed voices of the nations (Isa 17:13, Jer 51:55). For this reason, its seems that "the great waters foam" refers to the great upheaval and destruction the nations experienced at the hands of the Chaldeans.

Textual Notes

[i] **Verse 14b.** "warriors" translates פְּרָזָו, which occurs only here in the Hebrew Bible. "Warriors" fits the context very well and is supported by the Vulgate's *bellatorum* (those who make war) and LXX's δυναστῶν (*dunastōn*, warriors). The noun פְּרָזוֹן is probably from the same root; though often translated "peasants" in Judges 5:7 and 11, "warriors" makes far more sense (cf. NET). Cf. DCH, HALOT, C.F. Keil and F. Delitzsch, *Commentary on the Old Testament in Ten Volumes: Minor Prophets; Two Volumes in One*, trans. James Martin, Reprint., vol. 10.2 (Grand Rapids: Eerdmans, 1978), 110–111; Richard Duane Patterson, *Nahum, Habakkuk, Zephaniah*, The Wycliffe Exegetical Commentary (Chicago: Moody Press, 1991), 253.

[ii] **Verse 15b.** "foam" translates חֹמֶר (*ḥōmer*). This assumes that it is from the root חמר, which is used 4 times in the Hebrew Bible, with the sense of foaming or fermentation (Pss 46:4; 75:9; Lam 1:20, 2:11). In Psalm 46:4, it is explicitly water that foams. In some manuscripts of Isa 27:2 the same vowel pattern (חומר) is used for wine, probably with reference to its fermentation. Thus, it seems reasonable that Hab 3:15 also represents a noun from this same root, meaning "foaming," as the LXX translated it. This makes great sense of the context; God tramples the sea and the waters foam. The ESV and NASB translate it "surge," presumably viewing it as an instance of חֹמֶר meaning "heap" (Exod 8:14 [v. 10 MT]). However, in the passage were "heap" is the clear meaning, it is the bodies of frogs that are heaped up. In favour of foam is the clear association with water and liquid found in Ps 46:4, 75:9, and Isaiah 27:2, as well as the context. Unless one presupposes a reference to the crossing of the read sea, the waters "heaping" does not clearly fit this context.

Exegesis of Stanza 2: Though Terrified, I Will Wait For Him (16)

¹⁶I hear and my inward parts tremble;
    at the sound my lips quiver.
Rot enters into my bones,
    and I tremble where I stand,
while I wait for the day
    for distress to come up,
    for a people to attack us.ⁱ

Verse 16. "While" translates אֲשֶׁר (*'ăser*) adverbially (cf. Josh 14:10, Ps 139:15). "For" translates the 3 occurrences of the preposition *lamed* in lines E-G. I think each of these prepositional phrases is subordinated to "wait": לְיוֹם (*lᵉyôm*), "for the day" (16e); צָרָה לַעֲלוֹת (*ṣārāh la'ălôt*), "for distress to arise" (16f); לְעַם יְגוּדֶנּוּ (*lᵉ'am yᵉgûdennû*), "for a people to attack us" (16g). The two prepositional phrases (16e, 16g) and the verbal phrase (16f) refer to the same thing, the Chaldean invasion. The ESV, NET, and NIV interpret "the day of trouble" as God's judgment of Chaldea; yet a we have seen, this is not the subject of this song. In its context, the song Habakkuk sings is one of faith, waiting for the God to save His people *through* Chaldea. It is far more fitting for Habakkuk to wait in fear for God's horrifying salvation than for him to await the demise of God's chosen tools. Interpreted this way, this verse closely parallels the opening of the song (3:2).

"Wait," נוח (*nûaḥ*), is literally "settle down" or "rest." It does not focus on the expectation of the thing awaited but on the attitude of the one waiting, waiting without anxiety. For this reason, the ESV and NASB translate it "wait quietly" and the NIV "wait patiently." It thus combines the faith and waiting that God calls for from His people in Habakkuk 2:3-4; Habakkuk waits patiently and without protest, trusting that this invasion is God's salvation.

Textual Notes

ⁱ **Verse 16g.** "Attack" translates the verb גוד (*gûd*), from the same root as גְּדוּד (*gᵉdud*, group of soldiers, marauders), thus it may refer more specifically to an organized attack (Gen 39:19). Cf. DCH, HALOT.

Exegesis of Stanza 3: When All Fails, I Will Rejoice in Yahweh (17-19c)

> ¹⁷Even when the fig tree does not bear fruit,
>   and there is no yield of the vine;
> the labour done for olives fails,
>   and the fields do not produce food;
> the flocks are cut[i] from the fold,[ii]
>   and there are no cattle in the stalls,[iii]
> ¹⁸I will rejoice in YHWH,
>   I will exult in the God of my salvation.
> ¹⁹The Lord YHWH is my strength;
>   He sets my feet like a doe
>   and causes me to tread upon high places.[iv]

Verse 17. Verse 17 provides the protasis of a conditional clause, introduced by כִּי (*kî*); the apodosis begins in verse 18 (וַאֲנִי, *va'ănî*; [then] I). "When" is the appropriate translation for the protasis because there is no uncertainty in the condition. "Even" is contextually governed; many translations render כִּי with "though," for there is a clear concessive relationship between 17 and 18, "even though…, I will…." In my translation I have attempted to retain the force of the condition ("when") while emphasizing the concessive nature of the relationship between the protasis and apodosis ("even").

Nogalski observes that the portrayal of the invasion as utter agricultural destruction is reminiscent of many verses throughout the Twelve, especially the destruction left by the locust in Joel (cf. Hos. 2:5, 8, 12 [MT 7, 10, 14]; Joel 1:5, 7, 12, 10, 17; 2:12-14, 20; Hag 1:11; 2:17-19; Zech 1:2-6, 8-15; 8:9-12).[1]

Verse 18. Though the invasion will be brutal, even when conditions are inhospitable, Habakkuk will give praise to Yahweh. Not only will he praise Him, he will do so in full acknowledgment that the God who has raised up and rides forth at the head of the Chaldean army is "the God of my salvation." Habakkuk acknowledges as he did in verse 13 that God's terrible deed is the answer to his prayer in 1:1-4.

Verse 19. This verse is quoted with minor variation from 2 Samuel 22:34 (Psalm 18:33 [34 MT]), in which David identifies Yahweh as his true source

---

[1] James D. Nogalski, *The Book of the Twelve: Micah-Malachi*, Smyth & Helwys Bible Commentary (Macon, Ga: Smyth & Helwys Publishing, 2011), 687.

of strength. This conclusion is a fitting response to the theme manifest in the final verses of the three sections of the book: 1:11, 1:15-16, and 2:18-19 all focus on the idolatry of the Chaldeans, who think their tools and idols give them strength. In God's own words, Chaldea's "strength is his god" (1:11). However, Habakkuk concludes his song and the book with the declaration that true strength is found in Yahweh; He gives strength to His people. Like a doe navigating the treacherous heights, so God will guide His people through the danger and devastation of the Chaldean invasion. Habakkuk's confidence does not rest in ideal circumstances—indeed, the circumstances terrify him—but in the faithfulness of God, the Holy God of old and the rock upon whom Habakkuk could depend (1:12-13).

Textual Notes

[i] **Verse 17e.** "fold" translates מִכְלָה; this is the only occurrence of this form. It appears to mean "sheepfold," as the Vulgate translates it (*ovile*). It is related to מִכְלָא (Pss 50:9, 78:70), either as a biform or a contracted feminine form (מִכְלָאָה). DCH, HALOT, Patterson, *Nahum, Habakkuk, Zephaniah*, 260; Keil and Delitzsch, *Commentary on the Old Testament in Ten Volumes: Minor Prophets; Two Volumes in One*, 10.2:114.

[ii] **Verse 17e.** In the Qal, גזר usually has an active meaning "to cut off, separate" (Ps 136:13; 1 Kgs 3:25; 2 Kgs 6:4). Here, it is literally "[When] he cuts the flock off from the fold." This is appropriately rendered a passive, for there is no specific subject for verb; this is a common construction in Hebrew.

[iii] **Verse 17f.** "Stall" translates רֶפֶת, which only occurs here in the Hebrew Bible. In context, it must be some sort of shelter for cattle, hence the translation. The root *rft* in Arabic means "an enclosure for small livestock," which provides supporting evidence. HALOT, DCH.

[iv] **Verse 19c.** "High places" is בָּמוֹתַי (*bāmôtay*), literally "my high places." However, the yod is most likely a remnant of an older form and not a pronominal suffix ("my"). It occurs in this form in all three parallel passages (2 Sam 22:34, Hab 3:19, Ps 18:33 [MT 34]). The ESV is inconsistent in translating "on the heights" in Samuel 22:34 but "on my high places" in Habakkuk 3:19. Patterson, *Nahum, Habakkuk, Zephaniah*, 264.

Exposition

Throughout the book of Habakkuk, a subtle contrast is developed. God's sovereignty permeates the book, yet Chaldea and the righteous of Judah express two different responses to it. Chaldea is a nation God has blessed; He raised them to exalted heights, yet they considered their success to be a product of their own strength. Indeed, they worshipped their strength and turned from the true God to idols, to the weapons and plunder of their warfare (Hab 1:11, 17; 2:18-19).

In contrast, Habakkuk, as the representative of the righteous people of God, knows the source of his strength. God is his rock, the God who has been faithful for generations (1:12). When Habakkuk has no strength, when he trembles in fear, he nevertheless knows that he will be sustained during the coming Chaldean onslaught. In contrast to the Chaldeans whose strength was their god, Habakkuk proclaims "The Lord YHWH is my strength." The very God who raised up the Chaldeans was able to sustain and save His people amidst—indeed, through—the Chaldean invasion.

Habakkuk was faced with unbelievable circumstances, yet faith meant trusting God for strength. Faith meant rejoicing in and trusting God when He did unthinkable deeds. The faith called for in the book of Habakkuk is radical; it will be preposterous to many. The faith God calls for then and now is not a faith rooted in comfort—the sort of faith that trusts God when there is money in the bank account and food in our fridge. It is a faith that trusts God when we have no place to lay our head, when we are hiding from those who seek to devour us. When bombs are dropping, when investments fold and health fails, this faith does not flee but turns to God. And in God the faithful find their true source of strength. They find a strong tower in whom God's people find refuge (Nah 1:7, Ps 46:1), a firm foundation when the waves are crashing in (Hab 1:11, Matt 7:24-27), and a good shepherd when we have gone astray (John 10:7-18).

When circumstances are dire, in whom do we trust? When circumstances are great, whom do we praise? Do we trust in and praise ourselves or God? Habakkuk points us to God as the source of prosperity and despair, the originator of earthly kingdoms and the devastator of nations. Yet the same God who originates disaster and provides abundance has sworn to be with and take care of His people. In Habakkuk's time, God promised salvation through judgment. In our day, God has provided us salvation through judgment and has promised to provide for all the needs of His people (Matt 6:33). The same God who raises tyrants can deliver through them; the same God who topples governments can sustain us amidst the chaos. No matter the circumstances, one truth remains:

> ¹⁹The Lord YHWH is my strength;
>   He sets my feet like a doe
>   and causes me to tread upon high places.

The question that faces us when crisis strikes is not the goodness of God but nature of our faith. Will we believe the unbelievable, or will run from God and face His judgment? That was the choice that faced the Judahites in Habakkuk's day, and it is the choice that faces us today. In whom does our strength lie? In whom will we trust?

C. CONCLUSION: MUSICAL INSTRUCTIONS (3:19D)

To the choirmaster, with my stringed instruments.[a]

This concluding verse brings the final chapter of Habakkuk to an end with musical instructions. "To the choirmaster," or musical director, indicates that the song was composed—or at least recorded—for corporate use. It thus represents the faith to which all the righteous of Judah were called to express (2:3-4).

Exegesis of Verse 19d

To the choirmaster, with my stringed instruments.

Many commentators suggest that "my stringed instruments" represents an older Hebrew morphological form and so the pronominal suffix should be ignored, resulting in translations such as "with stringed instruments" (ESV, NET). We saw such a form in the previous line; in 2 Samuel 22 and Psalm 18, the pronominal suffix does not make much sense, so we concluded that it was a frozen form left over from an older stage of the language. However, we have no such parallel for this line. Every time נְגִינָה (nᵉginah, "stringed instruments") is used with a 1ˢᵗ person pronominal suffix, it has a personal meaning (Isa 38:20, Ps 77:6 [MT 7]). Furthermore, an almost identical line appears in the titles of several Psalms without the suffix (Ps 4:1; 6:1; 54:1; 55:1; 67:1; 76:1). This indicates that Habakkuk is not quoting from an earlier source that used an older form, as may be the case in previous line, but is intentionally changing a standard form of notation.

With the *bet* preposition (בְּ), נְגִינָה is usually understood to mean "with

---

[a] Isa 38:20; Psalm 4 and 61; Ps 77:7.

the accompaniment of stringed instruments."[1] This has lead some commentators to draw the conclusion that Habakkuk is a Levite with the role of playing music in public worship; thus, this song was written to be played on Habakkuk's instruments.[2] To me this seems a leap based on a slight evidence, and such an exclusive interpretation (this is to be played by me on my instruments) hardly fits the universal intent of the song. It is more appropriate in context to view this as a personal signature. The other two cases of נְגִינָה with the suffix personalize the reference, it is "my song." Habakkuk seems to be saying, "[Composed] for the Choirmaster on my stringed instruments."[3] Thus, the song is composed for public worship and originally set to stringed instruments by Habakkuk himself. Such a personal note in conclusion emphasizes the highly personal nature of this song; this is Habakkuk's response of faith, intended as a model for the personal response of faith God demands of His righteous people.

---

[1] DCH, HALOT.

[2] Keil and Delitzsch, *Commentary on the Old Testament in Ten Volumes: Minor Prophets; Two Volumes in One*, 10.2:116.

[3] The interpretation "composed upon" instead of "accompanied with" fits with all the Psalm references and would result in the same practical result.

Exposition

In his letter to the Corinthians, Paul exhorts his readers "be imitators of me, as I am of Christ" (1 Cor 11:1). Habakkuk, by personally signing this song, invites the Judahites to do the same. "Follow me as I trust in God," he beckons. This is the invitation of Habakkuk for us today. Will we follow Christ as Habakkuk did—limited in his knowledge as he was? Will we follow Paul and the rest of the apostles in their radical commitment to Christ. Let us not be ignorant as to what this means: the commitment called for by Jesus and His apostles, the trust demonstrated so powerfully by Habakkuk in this song, is costly. This commitment is nothing else than the surrender of autonomy, self-determination, pleasure, comfort, and even life itself.

It is true that none of this was ours in the first place—earthly life is fleeting and our desperate attempt to pursue self-determination and autonomy will come to an end when Christ returns—however, that does not lessen the cost. Jesus calls us to nothing less than death, to take up our cross—that horrid tool of shame and execution—and follow Him. The cost is steep, yet the reward is nevertheless far greater. As Jesus told His disciples, "if anyone would come after me, let him deny himself and take up his cross daily and follow me. For whoever would save his life will lose it, but whoever loses his life for my sake will save it. For what does it profit a man if he gains the whole world and loses or forfeits himself?" (Luke 9:23-25). Jim Elliot, a martyred missionary, captured this with his well known quote, "he is no fool who gives what he cannot keep to gain that which he cannot lose."

Jesus' demand on our life is absolute, to love Him with all of our heart, soul, mind, and strength (Mark 12:30). Habakkuk in this concluding song gives us an example of this, as he trusts in God with all of His heart while simultaneously quivering at the thought of God's terrible deed. God was in the midst of doing the unbelievable, yet the only fitting response for the people of God was to believe it, to trust God that His terrible deed was their salvation. Habakkuk models for the people of God the faith to which God calls His people and he invites us to imitate him in this regard. We are left at the conclusion of the book with a profound challenge: will we follow Christ even when He demands our all? Despite the cost, we are nevertheless left with profound assurance,

"¹⁹The Lord YHWH is my strength;

> He sets my feet like a doe
> and causes me to tread upon high places."

As we follow Habakkuk and God's people throughout the centuries in faith, we have the assurance that we are not alone. We do so in the company of God's saints—His people past, present, and future—and with the strength of God Himself. We are not fools for having such faith, and the rewards of knowing and enjoying God forever will far outweigh anything we may lose in this life.

IV. APPENDICES – FURTHER THEOLOGICAL AND EXEGETICAL MEDITATIONS

INTRODUCTION TO THE APPENDICES

To supplement the main content of the commentary, I have provided the following appendices, adapted from various essays and books chapters I have written over the years..

The first four appendices shed light on the hermeneutical approach of this commentary, which is unpacked at length in my book *The Gift of Reading – Part 1 & Part 2* (Vancouver; Teleioteti, 2019). Appendices 1 and 2 consider the function of context in interpretation, specifically how the immediate and canonical context of a book shape meaning. Appendix 3 considers the unhelpful use of context, how historical background is often abused and how it can be rightfully used. Appendix 4 concludes this section with a consideration of emendations and the meaning of rare words.

The second four appendices address issues of translations and interpretation. Appendix 5 is taken from my book *The Gift of Reading – Part 1: Reading the Bible in Submission to God* and presents my philosophy of Bible translation. Appendix 6 argues that the Septuagint of Habakkuk 2:2 should be translated in the same way as the Hebrew text, over against many contemporary translations. This provides early support for the interpretation taken in this commentary. Appendix 7 considers at length how Paul uses Habakkuk 2:4 in Romans 1:7, providing some canonical context for our interpretation. Finally, appendix 8 considers the relationship between imputation and the Old Testament, specifically arguing that Genesis 15:6 sets the Biblical theological trajectory that explains the imputation of Christ's righteousness in the New Testament. Though this essay only touches upon it, Habakkuk plays a key role in this trajectory, connecting the righteousness of all God's people to faith. Before each essay, I will introduce the context of its writing and its contribution to this commentary.

APPENDIX 1 – ON CONTEXT

This essay was originally written for my website, teleioteti.ca, to flush out some of my ideas concerning meaning. I continued the work I began here in an excursus of my ThM thesis on the books of Samuel,[1] reproduced in the following appendix. In the introduction to this commentary, I place great emphasis on the role of canon in interpreting a book. This article explains some of how I understand the relationship between context and meaning.

Context is essential to understanding all communication, yet why is this the case? In this article, I contend that context both limits and reveals textural meaning so that texts can be used. Texts of every sort are "multivalent"; they have a wealth of *meaning potential*. A text is meant to say *something* but could be used in an infinite number of ways; it has numerous potential applications,[2]

---

[1] James Rutherford, "God's Kingdom through His Priest-King: An Analysis of the Book of Samuel in Light of the Davidic Covenant" (ThM Thesis, Regent College, 2018).

[2] I am using meaning and application interchangeably to refer to the use that is made of a text. What a text "says" is the text understood in its context. We apply it, in this sense, when we make use of the text, when we communicate what is says in another language (translation); when we apply it to a specific situation (traditional application); when we explain it (exposition); and when we reduce it to a philosophical proposition. None of these "applications" replaces the original text— none say what the original says—instead they apply the text to a number of various situations, giving "meaning." רוץ in a speech of warning *means* in English, "run!" It *means* as an English proposition, "There is a reason for the addressee to run in situation A." It *means* in grammatical parsing: Qal imperative 3MS from the root רוץ. For the addressee it *means*, "I should run!" The various valid "meanings" of these symbols could be expounded at length, yet it is evident that some of these are

numerous meanings. A commandment, such as "You shall not kill," can be used to create legislation, to command behaviour, describe God's character, state a moral principle ("killing is wrong"), or to govern one's choices. Texts are thus multivalent in the sense of "use." The meaning of words, considered on their own, is also multivalent. Each word could "say" many different things.

That texts are multivalent in this sense can be wonderful! The multivalence of Biblical texts is the reason they apply to cultures and situations far beyond those in which they were originally written. However, misunderstood, a text's multivalence can lead to its abuse or neglect. If a text has infinite meaning potential, for example, it is practically meaningless. That is, all its meaning is derived from the reader and not the text itself. For example, the three symbols "רוץ" on their own are meaningless; what good would it do to have a document with only "רוץ" written on it? For the person who does not read Hebrew, it could mean anything they want it to—for nothing constrains their reading. For the person who reads Hebrew, it could mean any number of things (to run, flee; one running, fleeing; etc...). Without an appropriate restraint on meaning potential, a text can be used for any purpose or no purpose at all. For any word or text to have meaning it needs *context*, a larger unit of text in addition to the language with which to understand combinations of symbols (such as רוץ).

Context constrains the meaning of a text, reduces infinite meaning potential to finite meaning potential. This is how texts *mean*: they use symbols to make words in specific morphological forms and give them meaning by putting them into combinations. For a language to have meaning it needs context. Context constrains the meaning of words and syntactical combinations, producing a text with a finite meaning potential. It is by constraining meaning that context gives meaning.

Where there is context, and therefore meaning, there are valid and invalid interpretations of a text.[3] For example, careful attention to the context

---

more appropriate for different situations. For an English speaker studying the text to learn Hebrew grammar, what it means in English and its grammatical meaning are most appropriate. In the moment of its original utterance, or when it was written, the most appropriate meaning is that for the addressee.

[3] It should be observed that not all context is explicit. For example, one liners and short quotes presuppose—if they are to have meaning—a shared context of meaning, such as a similar experience (experience of the same T.V. show) or a worldview in which the words used have the same meaning for the speaker and the listener.

of the Ten Commandments, especially the word I rendered "kill" above, reveals that the meaning "killing is wrong" is actually an invalid meaning of the commandment (deriving the proposition "killing is wrong" is an invalid application, or use, of the text). The Hebrews word refers more specifically to "murder."

Because there can be valid and invalid meanings of a text and these are given by the context, context is essential for understanding and using a text. Context, the surrounding texts and thought in which a text is found, hedges the meaning potential of a text.

Context tells the reader what is being said by restricting the meaning potential a text would otherwise have. Context also excludes potential uses of a text and guides the reader to those that are most appropriate.[4] Context can also illuminate for a reader meaning potential that is originally obscure, such as revealing a shade of meaning for a word or structure previously unknown or alerting one to a detail that went previously unnoticed.

Consider the following. The four symbols "h-e-a-t" could be one of two words, each with a wealth of meaning potential (1. to cook, warm up, prepare; 2. the attribute hotness or a manifestation of hotness). The sentence, "Tim enfolded an empanada in tin foil in order to heat it up" limits the potential "heat" has substantially. It is now clear what these four symbols (h-e-a-t) mean here. However, though what is being said is clear enough, how it could be used ("application") is vague: who is Tim, and why does it matter that he heated his empanada in tin foil? The uses at this moment are near infinite: any Tim may be the subject of the action and his action could have infinite applications. Adding further context, however, will restrict the uses we could make of this sentence significantly and also illumine the appropriate uses (I concede that the following is preposterous):

> A doctor is treating a victim with substantial burns over his upper body. Readying the admission form, he reads the description of the incident that led to this hospital visit as recorded by Tim's mother.

---

[4] The idea of *appropriateness* qualifies what we mean by *valid* interpretations. It is possible to have a valid interpretation that is not appropriate. For example, it is valid to use the text "you shall no murder" to formulate the proposition, "'murder' is the fourth word in the command 'you shall not murder.'" This is true, yet it is irrelevant to the author's purpose in giving the command: it is a trivial use of the text, a inconsequential and so—in a sense—a interpretation that is not appropriate (irrelevant). Appropriateness is not a measure of the validity of an application, but its worth. (If validity describes the legitimacy of an application, appropriateness describes its usefulness.)

Apparently, during his lunch break, "after coming home, Tim enfolded an empanada in tin foil in order to heat it up; he then put it in the microwave for 10 minutes!! Shortly thereafter, Tim opened the microwave to investigate his food and flames and sparks burst forth, covering the poor boy!"

This sheds much light on the word "heat," and on the sentence as a whole. We now know how it can be used and how we should not use it. We can imagine another scenario where "heat up" actually means that the action in a basketball game is intensifying. For one who is unfamiliar with this idiomatic use of "heat," the context of a sports game will reveal what was, up to this point, unknown meaning potential.

Therefore, the primary function of context is limiting: it restricts meaning (as in the case of Tim and the empanada). A secondary function is illuminating: it reveals meaning (as in the case of a sports game). Reading within appropriately defined contextual boundaries will achieve both purposes. It would be fruitful for us to explore how a specific context may limit the material enclosed within. How does the context of Habakkuk, for example, limit and illuminate our reading?

Case Study in Context: Habakkuk

Scripture: Habakkuk is part of God's authoritative self-revelation. It thus pertains to Yahweh and His redemptive activities, and it possesses the divine-word attributes (inspiration, inerrancy, authority, usefulness, etc.).

Old Testament: Habakkuk is part of the Old Testament and thus concerns the Old Covenant and the Old Covenant people Israel. It also anticipates Jesus (Luke 20:44).

The Prophets: Habakkuk is not a collection of aphorisms but a progressive piece of literature directed at making God's interpretation of history and His required response known to His people. Habakkuk depends on the Torah and specifically functions as a indictment based on this Law and as a call for faithfulness to this covenant. Habakkuk will also interweave the themes of indictment, judgment, and salvation together, as the rest of the prophets do.

The Latter Prophets: Habakkuk is not a primarily narrative but a prophetic oracle.

The Twelve: Habakkuk delivers a complete prophetic pronouncement only in conjunction with its 11 other chapters, which unpack different aspects of indictment-judgment-salvation. Habakkuk is concerned with the covenant unfaithfulness of Israel and Judah and is intended to call them back to the

Torah with an eye to God's future redemptive action.

Layers of biblical context:

We can see from the example of Habakkuk some initial ways its various contexts shape our reading. We could of course go much deeper, but instead we will conclude this article with a conclusion of the various layers of context that shape our reading of Biblical texts.

The Context of the whole Bible:

<u>Synchronic context</u>: how does a text relate to the whole of Scripture?
<u>Diachronic context</u>: how does a text relate to the metanarrative related in Scripture (redemptive history)?
<u>Structural Contexts</u>: how does a book relate to other books of the Bible?
- **Structural Corpi**: how are books grouped together according to the structure of the Bible? Structural context helps us discern the thematic and functional role a text plays: a book in the Prophets functions prophetically and focuses on the themes of indictment, judgment, and redemption.
- **Structural Juxtaposition**: the presence of texts in sequential proximity emphasizes different features (cf. Malachi/Psalms, Chronicles/Matthew).
- **Corpi of Similitude**: In the NT epistles, non-structural corpi are formed by authorial attribution. Where such an attribution is present, this context provides a necessary sphere for grammatical/lexical comparison (e.g. the Pauline letters, Luke and Acts, the letters and Gospel of John).
- Such non-structural corpi, however, should not be set against the greater claims of Scripture to its unity and should not be used to rule out interpretive appeals to other books of the NT (such as using John to explain Paul). Though human authors share unique perspectives on God's work and have distinctive styles, the unity of Scripture ensures that these perspectives and the way they are expressed are compatible and—indeed—illuminating for the others.

The context of a distinct work:

- **A Distinct Work, or Book:** A distinct work is a unified whole designed in its final canonical placement to be read as whole and is only fully understood as such. A distinct work is often equivalent to the "books" of our English Bibles, though this is not always the case. 1-2 Samuel, 1-2 Kings, and 1-2 Chronicles are each a distinct work. They are stylistically, structurally, and internally bound together and historically treated as single books (the same is probably true of Ezra and Nehemiah). Luke and Acts, though historically united, are not a distinct work, for they are canonically separated and able to be understood separately. Their shared author and addressee, however, qualify both books together as a corpus (as discussed above).

- The Book of the Twelve is a more difficult case. Historically and in many ways internally, it seems to be a distinct work. Yet each book also appears to be self-contained. At this moment it is hard to definitely call it a distinct work, yet the weight of historical and internal evidence strongly leans this way.
- **Pericope:** Pericopes are large sections of a *distinct work*, either a section of a letter or an act of a narrative (in scholarship on the Gospels, Pericope is often used for a scene).
- **Paragraph:** A Paragraph is a smaller division of a *distinct work*, a paragraph in a letter, strophe in a poem, or scene in a narrative. A paragraph is a complete strophe, full scene, or syntactically self-contained group of more than one sentence.
- **Sentence**: a single clause or set of clauses that is completed with final punctuation, forming a independent whole. Therefore, either a independent clause ("Bob sat") or an independent clause with any number of dependent clauses ("Bob sat because of his weariness").

APPENDIX 2 – CANONICAL CONTEXT AND MEANING[1]

This appendix was originally published as a excursus in my thesis on the books of Samuel. In it, I defend a statement made in the final chapter of the thesis. Essentially, I argue that canonical context is essential to understanding the book of Samuel as we have received it. I argue something similar in the introduction to this commentary, so this appendix is a defense of those statements as well. This appendix advances and refines the argument of the previous appendix.

---

1) Though it is true that Samuel began its life as an independent book, its incorporation into Scripture makes it only a piece in a greater literary whole, 2) a whole that both incorporates the meaning of Samuel into itself and draws it into a greater story that expands the significance of the events recorded in Samuel.

It is fair to assume that Samuel originated before the collection and closing of the Old Testament canon, but the first claim, that it has become part of a larger literary whole, may be debated. This claim is obviously true from a descriptive perspective, but the above assumes this is true also from a prescriptive perspective—that its greater context *should* influence its interpretation. From a biblical perspective, the New Testament considers the

---

[1] This appendix is adapted with permission from my thesis on 1 & 2 Samuel, published as Rutherford, "God's Kingdom."

Old Testament in terms of a collective whole (e.g. Luke 24:44), and its pieces likewise as wholes (e.g. Acts 15:15-18, 26:22, 28:23; 2 Cor 3:12-18).[2] Without biblical warrant for ignoring this unity, the Christian committed to following the Bible's own lead in interpreting it ought to read it as a unity. In addition to what may be called "structural unity," much has been written on the unified metanarrative provided by the Old Testament.[3] In terms of the shape and story of the Old Testament, there is thus good warrant for viewing it as a literary unity and interpreting as such.[4]

---

[2] Cf. Roger T. Beckwith, *The Old Testament Canon of the New Testament Church and Its Background in Early Judaism* (Grand Rapids: Eerdmans, 1986); David G. Dunbar, "The Biblical Canon," in *Hermeneutics, Authority, and Canon*, ed. D. A. Carson and John D. Woodbridge (Grand Rapids: Academie Books, 1986); Stephen G. Dempster, "From Many Texts to One: The Formation of the Hebrew Bible," in *The World of the Aramaeans*, ed. P. M. Michèle Daviau et al., Journal for the Study of the Old Testament 324–326 (Sheffield: Sheffield Academic Press, 2001); Stephen G. Dempster, "An 'Extraordinary Fact': Torah and Temple and the Contours of the Hebrew Canon Part 1," *Tyndale Bulletin* 48, no. 1 (1997): 23–56; Stephen G. Dempster, "An 'Extraordinary Fact': Torah and Temple and the Contours of the Hebrew Canon Part 2," *Tyndale Bulletin* 48, no. 2 (1997): 191–218; Stephen G. Dempster, "Canons on the Right and Canons on the Left: Finding a Resolution in the Canon Debate," *Journal of the Evangelical Theological Society* 52, no. 1 (March 2009): 47–77; E. Earle Ellis, *The Old Testament in Early Christianity: Canon and Interpretation in the Light of Modern Research*, Wissenschaftliche Untersuchungen zum Neuen Testament 54 (Tübingen: J.C.B. Mohr, 1991); Goswell, "The Order of the Books in the Hebrew Bible"; Timothy H. Lim, *The Formation of the Jewish Canon*, Anchor Yale Bible reference library (New Haven: Yale University Press, 2013); Sailhamer, *Introduction to Old Testament Theology*.

[3] Cf. Dempster, *Dominion and Dynasty*; Gentry and Wellum, *Kingdom through Covenant*, 27–34, 91; Graeme Goldsworthy, *According to Plan: The Unfolding Revelation of God in the Bible* (Leicester: Inter-Varsity Press, 1991); Graeme Goldsworthy, *Christ-Centered Biblical Theology: Hermeneutical Foundations and Principles* (Downers Grove: IVP Academic, 2012); Kline, *The Structure of Biblical Authority*; Sailhamer, *Introduction to Old Testament Theology*; Waltke and Yu, *An Old Testament Theology*, 49–63; Van Pelt, "Introduction."

[4] Cf, Gentry and Wellum, *Kingdom through Covenant*, 89–108; Graeme Goldsworthy, *Gospel-Centered Hermeneutics: Foundations and Principles of Evangelical Biblical Interpretation* (Downers Grove: InterVarsity Press, 2006); Kline, *The Structure of Biblical Authority*; Van Pelt, "Introduction"; Van Pelt, "Structure of the Christian Bible"; Van Pelt, "Seams in the Canonical and Covenantal Structure"; Van Pelt, "Order and Structure of the Books in the Writings."

The second claim is an attempt to articulate just how the macro-context (the canonical context) of Samuel affects our interpretation of it. Our answer to this question will presuppose an understanding of what it means for a biblical text to have "meaning." On Evangelical Christian epistemological presuppositions, namely that the Living God has made Himself known in human language in order that He might be followed and worshipped (e.g. 2 Tim 3:16), an inquiry into what is meant by "meaning" must be descriptive, beginning with the assumption that texts have communicated meaning in the past and do so today in the same way.[5]

For many evangelicals in recent years, the meaning of a biblical text is its single propositional content.[6] John Frame has rightfully criticized this theory of biblical meaning:

> What we must categorically reject, however, is some mysterious, intermediary thing called 'the meaning' that stands *between* the text and its application. Instead of increasing the objectivity of our knowledge, such an intermediary is a subjective construct that inevitably clouds

---

[5] Cf. Vern Sheridan Poythress, *In the Beginning Was the Word: Language: A God-Centered Approach* (Wheaton: Crossway Books, 2009), 37–38. This presupposition assumes that humans are capable of communication and that the fact of and the particular content of biblical revelation has epistemological implications, on which see John M. Frame, *The Doctrine of the Knowledge of God*, A Theology of Lordship (Phillipsburg: P&R Publishing, 1987); John M. Frame, *Cornelius Van Til: An Analysis of His Thought* (Phillipsburg: P&R Publishing, 1995).

That this implies a descriptive task follows in this manner: if God has revealed Himself and His statutes in order that His people might be fully equipped for the good works He has commanded of them (2 Tim 3:16), and God is competent to achieve that which He undertakes, His revelation is able to be understood by those for whom it is intended. It is of course common sense that texts mean and have meant, but this has come under assault by deconstructionist philosophies and so needs to be articulated.

[6] Cf. Walter C. Kaiser, "The Single Intent of Scripture," in *The Right Doctrine from the Wrong Texts?: Essays on the Use of the Old Testament in the New*, ed. G. K. Beale (Grand Rapids: Baker Books, 1994); Norman L. Geisler, "Appendix B: Explaining Hermeneutics: A Commentary on the Chicago Statement on Biblical Hermeneutics Articles of Affirmation and Denial," in *Hermeneutics, Inerrancy, and the Bible*, ed. Earl D. Radmacher and Robert D. Preus (Grand Rapids: Zondervan, 1984), 163–190; Earl D. Radmacher and Robert D. Preus, eds., "Appendix A: The Chicago Statement on Biblical Hermeneutics," in *Hermeneutics, Inerrancy, and the Bible* (Grand Rapids: Zondervan, 1984).

our understanding of the text itself.[7]

He argues that to posit as the anchor of objective meaning not the text but a proposition derived from the text, one has already distanced himself from any objective basis by dealing from then on with a subjective construct (a proposition). He suggests that in practical use, we use meaning in a way indistinguishable from application.[8] Therefore, meaning naturally refers not to the propositional "sense" behind the text but all the legitimate uses we make of a text, uses that (when valid) demonstrate our understanding.[9] As an example, someone has only understood, or grasped the meaning of, "you shall not murder" when one can explicate the appropriate situation in which

---

[7] Frame, *Doctrine of Knowledge*, 98.

[8] Not being too much of a stickler for terminology, Frame offers as an alternative to identifying meaning with application the possibility of identifying meaning with the text and application with its uses. Ibid.

[9] Vern Poythress's account of meaning, which has some similarities to Frame's, reveals the fundamentally confused nature of the propositional or single-sense view of meaning. Poythress argues for a position that is both similar to yet more sophisticated than the usual single-sense view: he contends that the "sense" of a text is the objective anchor of application which can be paraphrased or communicated in different languages. It is this objective basis that leads us to conclude when we compare a paraphrase with the original that "they say the same thing." Yet he concedes that such a paraphrase represents a loss: it can never communicate the fullness of the original text. Yet, if meaning is this objective sense and the sense is appropriately embodied in both the paraphrase and the original, what is lost? The answer is that we lose some of the potential applications of the original. Thus, we are faced with a loss of meaning: the paraphrase is not as usable or rich as the original.

We can make more sense of this situation if we adopt Frame's view. We recognize in an accurate paraphrase continuity with the original, this text has been applied appropriately to a new context; in the case of a paraphrase, someone has explained part of the original. Yet as an application, the paraphrase is a restriction of the original; it cannot be used in as many ways as the original. In fact, it is impossible to recapture the full range of a text's appropriate applications by recommunicating a text in any other manner—that is, without reproducing the text in its full context. Thus, it is the text as restricted by its context (see below) that is the objective anchor of meaning, defined as legitimate uses of the text. Vern Sheridan Poythress, *God Centered Biblical Interpretation* (Phillipsburg, N.J.: P&R Publishing, 1999), 69–92; Poythress, *In the Beginning Was the Word*, 163–185.

this command applies: he only understands it when he can use it.[10]

Instead of the single-proposition view of meaning, we can build on Frame's conclusion and posit that meaning is not a singular objective universal idea that can be instantiated in new contexts and languages but the sum-total of the possible legitimate uses one could make of a text. That is, the "objective" aspect of a text is the text itself, delimited by its context, and not a mysterious proposition that lies behind it.[11] On this understanding, we could define meaning as *every justified use of a text as determined by its literary and linguistic context*.[12] A meaning would be justified if it makes a valid use that is

---

[10] Frame, *Doctrine of Knowledge*, 66–67.

[11] Ibid., 93–98. See my fuller discussion of this point in J. Alexander Rutherford, "Towards an Evangelical Hermeneutic: A Critique of the Chicago Statement on Hermeneutics (1982)" (Teleioteti, December 2016), accessed January 23, 2018, https://teleioteti.ca/resources/technical-papers/. We could argue, in addition, that there is no reason to believe God's thought about a text is a proposition; it would cohere more with our experience of texts (we read texts and use them) to think that God knows perfectly the text in its context and all the real and potential implications that derive from the text. There is no reason to believe that behind the text there lies a singular proposition, either in the mind of an author (I can assure you none of what I am saying can be fully summarized in a proposition) or in the mind of God.

[12] "Literary" refers to the textual body (book, anthology, etc.) in which a text is to be read and "linguistic" to the rules and nature of the language in which it was composed. Where does this leave history? I have intentionally downplayed history to limit the scope of this thesis; however, as it regards the text—not situations to which the text will be applied—historiography (encompassing social history) and archaeology could be understood as parts of the linguistic context. That is, they help us to better understand the language of the text and the texts field of reference (referential meaning). However, caution must be taken in both regards.

Consider reference: though texts have what we could call "implied referents"—that is, referents that are described within the textual body—textual reference also extends beyond bounds of a text to the actual objects, persons, and events it recounts. A similar relationship exists between implied and historical referents as with implied and historical authors. Though an implied referent corresponds in the case of historical narrative to a historical referent, it is an intentional representation of the latter. Therefore, one must be careful about reading extra-textual knowledge of the historical referent into the implied referent. Cf. D. A. Carson, *Exegetical Fallacies* (Grand Rapids: Baker Books, 1996), 63–64; Moisés Silva, *Biblical Words and Their Meaning: An Introduction to Lexical Semantics*, rev. and expanded ed. (Grand Rapids: Zondervan, 1994).

appropriate to the function of the text and fitting for its field of reference.[13] A use is valid if it is part of the text's meaning potential as delimited by context; it is appropriate if it corresponds to the function of the text, so that it would be inappropriate to use a text intended to lead one in right behaviour to counsel wrong behaviour (because God says murder is wrong, go murder!); and it is fitting if the use does not equivocate on the relationships between the text and referents (thus, to use a text about Israel's exodus from Egypt to make historical conclusions about the going forth of an unrelated people group from an unrelated location named Egypt would not be *fitting*). Validity, appropriateness, and fittingness in these senses are co-inherent and thus different perspectives by which the whole meaning potential of a text could be viewed, each depending upon the others and determined by a text's context.[14]

Linguistic understanding—specifically vocabulary and grammar—can be considered similarly. There exists a historical Hebrew language that has a close relationship with the historic languages of Ugarit, Syria, Aram, Egypt, and other peoples. Yet, the language of the Bible (and, indeed, the language of each author) is an implied language. That is, no author has a full understanding of his or her own language, therefore we must reckon in interpretation not with the historical language to which they were related but the implied language that they used. Consider, for example, the apostle John: he uses grammar in Rev 1:8 that does not reflect appropriate Greek usage (ἀπὸ ὁ). The 'error' is part of the implied language of John but not the historical language of Koine Greek.

That God has exhaustive knowledge of each valid use of a text means that there is a true boundary to all textual meaning; it is not potentially infinite from a divine perspective. Poythress observes that at some point, a consideration of application "must somewhere along the way appeal directly to God's knowledge, authority, and presence." Vern Sheridan Poythress, "Divine Meaning of Scripture," in *The Right Doctrine from the Wrong Texts?: Essays on the Use of the Old Testament in the New*, ed. G. K. Beale (Grand Rapids: Baker Books, 1994), 87–88.

[13] "Validity," "appropriateness," and "fittingness," are similar to Poythress's three perspectives on textual meaning—sense, application, and import. Poythress, *God Centered Biblical Interpretation*, 72–74. They differ in that, with Frame, I identify sense with the original text itself and not something that could be equally expressed by a paraphrase. Therefore, I extend "application" to cover re-expression of the text, such as paraphrase or translation. Cf. Frame, *Doctrine of Knowledge*, 93–98; Poythress, *God Centered Biblical Interpretation*, 72.

[14] That each of these is a co-inherent perspective on the meaning of a text means that the entire meaning potential of a text could be described from each of these perspectives. If a list of every valid use was provided, it would imply every

Appendix 2 – Canonical Context and Meaning

Each text, therefore—whether it is a symbol, word, syntagm, sentence, etc.—has finite meaning potential (or a semantic range) that is delimited by the relevant contexts (textual, linguistic, cultural, etc.). If a context is expanded, there is a change to the meaning potential of a text. I have elsewhere attempted to articulate this relationship between context and the meaning potential of a text in this way:

> Context constrains the meaning of a text, reduces infinite meaning potential to finite meaning potential. This is how texts *mean*: they use symbols to make words in specific morphological forms and give them meaning by putting them into combinations. For a language to have meaning it needs context. Context constrains the meaning of words and syntactical combinations, producing a text with a finite meaning potential. It is by constraining meaning that context gives meaning …. Context also excludes potential uses of a text and guides the reader to those that are most appropriate.[15] Context can also illuminate for a reader meaning potential that is originally obscure, such as revealing a shade of meaning for a word or structure previously unknown or

---

appropriate and fitting use. The same is true of an exhaustive list of appropriate or fitting uses. On the use of "perspective" in this sense, see Frame, *Doctrine of Knowledge*, 89–90, 191–193; John M. Frame, *Perspectives on the Word of God: An Introduction to Christian Ethics* (Eugene, Or.: Wipf and Stock, 1999); John M. Frame, *The Doctrine of the Christian Life*, A Theology of Lordship 4 (Phillipsburg: P&R Publishing, 2008), 33–37.

From a human perspective, which does not simultaneously grasp the whole range of validity-appropriateness-fittingness, it could be said that meaning is found at the nexus of validity, appropriateness, and fittingness; yet from a divine perspective, these are co-inherent, and thus their nexus excludes no valid, appropriate, or fitting uses of a text.

[15] A footnote here in the original reads: "The idea of *appropriateness* qualifies what we mean by *valid* interpretations. It is possible to have a valid interpretation that is not appropriate. For example, it is valid to use the text 'you shall not murder' to formulate the proposition, '"murder" is the fourth word in the command "you shall not murder."' This is true, yet it is irrelevant to the author's purpose in giving the command: it is a trivial use of the text, an inconsequential and so—in a sense—an interpretation that is not appropriate (irrelevant). Appropriateness is not a measure of the validity of an application, but its worth. (If validity describes the legitimacy of an application, appropriateness describes its usefulness.)" Here, the question of fittingness, or appropriate reference, is not considered.

alerting one to a detail that went previously unnoticed.¹⁶

According to the single-proposition view of meaning, meaning is in the text and discovered through the context. Therefore, only the latter function of context is applicable: canonical context is only capable of illuminating the meaning already in a text. In contrast, on the meaning potential view of meaning, a consideration of the canonical context expands the meaning potential of a text.¹⁷ No longer are the appearances of gentiles among David's mighty men or the redemption from Egypt (2 Sam 7:23) merely descriptive of historical events or the self-understanding of Samuel's characters; they become rich with the meaning of the redemptive historical story they reflect (e.g. Gen 12:1-3; Exod 15). It is this later view of meaning presupposed above.

---

¹⁶ J. Alexander Rutherford, "An Investigation into the Role of Context in Interpretation," *Teleioteti*, January 16, 2018, accessed January 24, 2018, https://teleioteti.ca/2018/01/16/investigation-role-context-interpretation/.

¹⁷ Meaning-potential is a justified use of the text, as determined by the criteria of validity, fittingness, and appropriateness. When a new context is added, the text remains the same, but the field of reference, function, linguistic understanding will be affected. Some referents for "redemption" from "Egypt," for example, are removed from the realm of possibility (what may be "fitting" is narrowed). Yet, the justified uses of a text are increased. Without context to provide the fitting referent of "redemption" and "Egypt," a use that assumes the referent is the Exodus of Israel achieved by God is possible but not fitting, and so not justified. But with the addition of context that makes clear the referent, many possible uses are excluded, but this possible use is justified.

APPENDIX 3 – ON THE USE AND ABUSE OF HISTORICAL BACKGROUND

Originally written as an article on Teleioteti.ca, this essay was adapted as the final chapter of my book *The Gift of Reading – Part 2: A Biblical Perspective on Hermeneutics*. This appendix is a reprint of that chapter; it explains the problem with the usual use made of extra-biblical evidence and outlines what I think are the appropriate uses to be made of this data. This view of extra-biblical data is presupposed in the above commentary.

Now these things happened to them as an example, but they were written down for our instruction, on whom the end of the ages has come. – 1 Corinthians 10:11

Much of modern Biblical interpretation revolves around the study of the Ancient Near Eastern and 1st century Roman world in which the Biblical texts were written. In the study of the Old Testament, much time is given to the study of the Hebrew Language within its context as an ancient Semitic language; there is also lots of attention given to the literary milieu in which it was written—to the Babylonian, Ugaritic, Egyptian, Assyrian, etc. texts from a similar time period. In the study of the New Testament, much attention is given to the Greek literature of the late 1st century BC and the 1st Century AD in order to better understand Koine Greek, the dialect in which the New Testament was written. Furthermore, much attention is given to literature of Second Temple Judaism and of the Roman world at this time in order to better understand the worldviews of the Biblical authors, their audiences, and the circumstances which the Biblical letters were meant to address. If the argument of the books in this series *(The Gift of Knowing; The Gift of Reading Part 1 & 2)* has been cogent so far, then this approach to the Bible needs to be radically revised.

First, the intention and thought-world of the author are not the basis for meaning; the text interpreted in its Biblical context is the basis for meaning. Second, the audience for which Scripture was written was not the original audiences of each Biblical text, an audience that might approach the text with 1st century or ANE assumptions; instead, we—Christian throughout the ages, those "on whom the end of the age has come" (1 Cor 10:11)—are its intended audience. Third, the worldview of the authors who wrote Scripture, of its original audience, and of us today are not radically different from one another—as the worldviews of the ANE, of the 1st century Roman Empire, and of any 21st century culture are. To the contrary, we all share the worldview revealed by the Bible and delivered to us through the community of faith that has shaped us. We are all subject to the reforming work of Scripture and bear to greater and lesser degrees its worldview, over against the worldviews that characterize the kingdom of Satan—with its assumptions of the autonomy of persons and opposition to God. We cannot, therefore, assume that an understanding of the ancient world and its languages will have the impact on our studies that it *is* thought to have. However, we cannot throw out this evidence either. We know from the history of interpreting the Bible that this evidence—the evidence of extra-Biblical literature and archeology—has helped us grow in our understanding of the Bible. What we need is not a wholesale rejection of extra-biblical resources but a proper understanding of their place, an understanding that appropriately relates them to the Bible as it declares itself to be—authoritative, self-interpreting, and universally relevant. For the rest of this chapter, I want to briefly outline what role I think such evidence should take in our study of the Bible.

To re-phrase the problem of using of extra-biblical evidence in Biblical interpretation and to frame our discussion for the rest of this chapter, consider the following statement and its implications: *when a historical parallel is used to explain a text, the evidence necessary to establish a link between a piece of extra-biblical data and the text needs to be sufficient to make the point independently.*[1] That is, if the extra-biblical data is said to say something the text itself does not say, this is called imposition or eisegesis—reading into the text something that is not there. Meaning is no longer found in the text, it is found in the author's mind, in his thought processes that led to the text he wrote. However, as I have argued above, this is an inadequate view of meaning. Meaning is the use of a text governed by the text itself. If this is true, historical material is not necessary to understand a Biblical *text*, which is the object of our interpretive endeavours. Historical evidence may help us to better understand the thought process of the author—if that is possible—and the original audience's

---

[1] This is the same principle used in our discussion of genre in chapter 4.

reception of the document. It cannot, however, be used to make the text say anything that is not already there. If sufficient evidence to justify the use of historical material is only present when the text says as much as the evidence is used to say, historical material is in a significant sense redundant. If we cannot appeal to historical evidence to find meaning, for the meaning we would find is no longer that of the text, then all this evidence can really do is help us see better what the text has been saying all along. So we need to ask, what good is extra-biblical evidence after all?

Before we give an answer, a secondary point needs to be made. Much use of extra-biblical material is a fallacy sometimes called *illegitimate totality transfer*.[2] That is, every word or symbol has a semantic range that is narrowed by context to indicate something specific. When a true parallel is made between an extra-biblical item and the text, this does not justify reading the whole semantic range of that item into the text. The connection is made between two specific points on the semantic range of the text and the item; such a connection does not justify expanding from there to the whole range. For example, one may argue that Paul is using the word-group παιδεια (*paideia*, education) in Galatians 3-4 in relation to the Roman views of adoption and inheritance, of which this is a key word-group. Granted that this connection is legitimate, it would be fallacious to read any more about Roman views of adoption and inheritance into the text than Paul makes clear.

If we do not allow such a jump, from one point of the semantic context to its entirety, we are then left with our initial proposition: the text must be able to make any point extra-biblical data is used to establish.

The Uses of Extra-Biblical Evidence

Our discussion so far leaves us with an obvious question: What then is extra-biblical data useful for? I want to argue that it is useful for illustration, illumination, confirmation, and application. First, it is useful for illustration, helping us preach the text. That is, we can understand how Paul used the word παιδαγογος (*paidagōgos*, guardian) in Galatians by examining the word's range of meanings within the Bible. But by drawing the connection to the broader social context of the word, we are provided with rich illustrative material to make clear Paul's point. If a preacher or teacher is able to make such an illustration without implicitly teaching his audience that this material is necessary for interpreting the text—a danger this series of books

---

[2] Cf. D. A. Carson, *Exegetical Fallacies* (Grand Rapids: Baker Books, 1996), 60–61.

have been trying to avoid—such illustrations can be very effective.

Second, extra-biblical background material is useful for illumination, useful for helping us to see the text. This is needed at times because we have cultural blinders inherited from our culture and upbringing or other limitations that prevent us from seeing what was present in the text the whole time. Historical material can unearth such things. For example, in the 19th and 20th centuries, it became popular to view the language of the New Testament as a divine language, a special Greek dialect given by God to communicate the unique content of the New Testament. However, the discovery of hundreds of Greek papyrus texts in the 20th century—letters, government documents, shopping lists, etc.—revealed that the language of the New Testament was not a divine language; it was the common language of the day, hence "Koine" or common Greek. This discovery revealed that the theories of a by-gone generation were wrong, that these theories were not rooted in anything the Bible said. This discovery was a corrective on arguing theological ideas from the absence of evidence—of violating the rule that the absence of evidence is not the evidence of absence.

Third, extra-biblical material is useful for confirmation. Sometimes there is heated debate over specific stances on interpreting a passage. There may be a case where the argument reaches a standstill and producing a piece of extra-biblical evidence will tilt the case one way or another. One instance is 1 Samuel 13:21. After telling us that the Israelites went to the Philistines to have their tools sharpened, for there was no blacksmith, we are told ... וְהָיְתָה הַפְּצִירָה פִים לַמַּחֲרֵשֹׁת (vᵉhāytāh happᵉṣîrāh pîm lammaḥărēsōt). The meaning of this verse is not immediately evident, for "פְּצִיר" (pṣîr) and "פִים" (pîm) occur only here in the Hebrew Bible. The syntax, along with the probable meaning of פְּצִיר, "fee" (from פצר, pṣr, to urge), suggests the following rendering: "and the charge was a *pim* for the plowshare...." However, the translators of the KJV attempted read פִים with פְּצִיר to mean "a double-edged (lit. double-mouthed) file," translating it simply as "a file"; this translation indicates that Israel had the ability to sharpen some of their tools themselves. However, this does not conform with the previous verse, which says that Israelites went to Palestine to have these same weapons sharpened (v. 20). Archeological evidence confirms that פִים should be understood as a Philistine measurement, weighing about two-thirds of a shekel. This supports the first interpretation over-against the KJV. The implication is that Israel was dependent on the Philistines even for their tools, showing that they had no weapons. Some commentators argue that the price suggests they were being gouged, but this is not necessary to understand the use of the term in its context.³ Thus, extra-biblical data helps us follow one interpretation over another; it may also have functioned in this case for illumination.

Lastly, it is useful for application. By bringing forth extra-biblical material we expand the sphere of application for a text: we can let the item and the text interact to shed insight on, for example, a historical question. For example, by bringing forth the discovery of an inscription reading "house of David," we can use the bible to shed light on the meaning of that phrase and its relevance.

The Challenge of Using Extra-Biblical Data

There remains a challenge in our use of such data, namely, how we can be sure that our extra-biblical evidence is being used rightly? I want to propose one test we can use and then some challenges that need to be overcome if we are to use this data rightly.

First, the test: an interpreter must ask if they could make the point for which they are using extra-biblical evidence from the text alone. This is another implication of the statement with which we began. If the historical evidence disappeared, can you convince someone from the data available in the text? If not, this is an invalid use of extra-biblical data.

Second, the use of background data is fraught with more troubles than is commonly acknowledged.⁴ 1) There needs to be a sure connection between the data and the text, but how can one establish this? What evidence can be produced to establish this connection? Many times, dating and locating are uncertain; how then can it be known that the author or audience was even aware this particular piece of background data someone wishes to employ? The problem is compounded when we add that we are unsure of the social stratification of author and audience: if the data is right concerning time and place, how do we know they had access to and then used it? 2) This data itself needs interpretation. Because the Bible claims illumination, self-sufficiency, and truth for itself, it is a better tool in interpretation than any other piece of data. Therefore, it is more appropriate to interpret extra-biblical data by the Bible than the other way around. 3) I would raise again the problem that the extra-biblical evidence can add nothing to the text. If we judge the meaning

---

³ Cf. V. Philips Long, "1 and 2 Samuel," in *Zondervan Illustrated Bible Background Commentary: Old Testament: Volume 2, Joshua, Judges, Ruth, 1 and 2 Samuel*, ed. John H. Walton, vol. 2 (Grand Rapids: Zondervan, 2009).

⁴ See the recent essay by Noel Weeks for specific examples, Noel Weeks, "Problems with the Comparative Method in Old Testament Studies," *Journal of the Evangelical Theological Society* 62, no. 2 (2019): 287–306.

of a text by its context and the meaning of the evidence by its context, by what do we judge our construal of their relationship? The only judge is the hypothesized mind of the author or audience, itself derived from one of the above. We are thus left with no standard of verification for our interpretation. We have no way of knowing if our construal of the relationship between the Bible and a piece of extra-biblical evidence is correct. However, if our use of extra-biblical data passes the test I proposed, then these challenges are no longer a problem, for our point rests in the text. Now, I can imagine that there might be some objections to the point I am making in this chapter, so in conclusion I want to consider what I think will be the most common objections.[5]

Objections

First, someone might say, "the author originally wrote to an audience, do we not need to understand what this original audience would have understood?" This same argument could be made about the author. We could answer this in two ways. First, if we accept this assumption, this does not invalidate our point. The reason is this: the text is our standard of verification, so our conception of the author or audience's interpretation must always conform to the words of the text in their literary context. Thus, such an interpretation is subject to our test for verifying extra-biblical data, given above. If our understanding of "what they would have understood' does not pass this test, it is invalid. And if it passes this test, it is redundant, we are just rephrasing "what the text says" as "what the author said," or "what the audience would hear." Second, as we have seen, the Bible was written for our sake. Thus, we are the ultimate audience of the Bible and our standard for interpreting Scripture itself, so we are back with what the text says.

Second, someone may object that such an approach de-historicizes the text. By severing its relation to the external data, have we not de-historicized the Bible, made it merely an interpretation that says nothing about the facts of history? This conclusion is unwarranted. The text speaks about history from within the flow of history—it provides the true interpretation of history—and so applies to history. Yet it is self-interpreting, written in such a way that it fully interprets history without needing external data to interpret it. It was produced in history, speaks to history, yet was shaped by God to be interpreted throughout history.

---

[5] These reflect objections I have encountered in discussions with my peers, pastors, professors, and in various articles and books concerning interpretation.

Third and finally, someone might suggest that this "disembodies" the text. That is, they might suggest that the approach given here treats the Bible as if it has fallen from heaven, free from the historical processes by which texts are usually formed. In response, we can say, first, that the points I am making are universal points of interpretation. Given a cogent text (one not meant for insiders with extensive extra-textual knowledge), the best interpretation is the one that corresponds to the words of the text. Second, though the Bible began its life in the same way as many documents written in various circumstances, these documents were reconstituted—"reembodied"—as a New Covenant document written for a community stretching 2000 years, written to be understood and used throughout the ages. We are therefore not disembodying the text, making an unearthly entity, but properly considering the way God has chosen to embody it.

APPENDIX 4 – ON EMENDATIONS AND LEXICAL MEANING[1]

This appendix was originally prepared as the introduction to a translation of Job chapter 30, prepared as part of a graduate level Hebrew-language seminar. It argues that the practice of emending the text of the Old Testament when it is found to be difficult is not justified and outlines the role of different evidential appeals in resolving such difficulties. The approach presented here is largely that taken in the commentary when dealing with *hapax legomena*, difficult syntax, and similar issues.

In a matter of days, Job lost his children and his wealth; at the hands of Satan—by God's permission—Job lost everything. Compounding this, the friends who came to comfort him fail to reckon that Job may not be suffering for his wickedness. For chapter after chapter, we read the accusations and self-styled remedies proffered by these friends. As these speeches draw to an end with the poem to wisdom in chapter 28, the narrator presents three final speeches from Job in chapters 29-31. Job moves from contemplating his past condition in chapter 29 to his present state in chapter 30; chapter 31 concludes this series of speeches with a defense of his innocence. Though each of these chapters is worthy of study, the present paper will focus on chapter 30, presenting a translation which aims to communicate the meaning of the Hebrew text to a similar poetic effect. Thus, an effort will be made to follow the form and particular emphasis of the Hebrew text in readable English, the goal not being good English literature but Hebrew literature that is comprehensible to the English reader and that achieves the emotive effect

---

[1] This appendix is adapted with permission from my paper "The Lament of the Afflicted: A Translation of Job 30," published on Teleioteti.ca 2017.

of the original.

Before considering my translation, a word on the form of evidence and argumentation employed is necessary. Like many books of the Hebrew Bible, scholarly translation and interpretation of Job regularly involves significant emendation of the Masoretic Text.[2] By their very nature, such emendations are speculative. Even on the level of explicit reasoning, setting aside theological presuppositions, one may take issue with this approach.

An emendation is only invoked when the present text is considered suspect to the interpreter, yet what is suspect to one interpreter may not be so for another. Such suspicions may be a product of the reader rather than the text, of unfamiliarity with Hebrew or an overly constrictive understanding of language (e.g. an author is not credited with the freedom to create new constructions and grammatical combinations using rules exhibited elsewhere).

Because of the speculative nature of emendation, the practice of the present author is to seek an explanation in the possible sense "awkward" texts may have when considered in light of similar grammatical and syntactical combinations found elsewhere in Scripture. Because we have no a-priori reason to doubt the Masoretic text we have received, and we have significant a-posteriori evidence to trust it, this author will accord the MT the benefit of the doubt, leaving the burden of proof on the one who seeks to prove that their emendation is better than the received text. The principle of parsimony also favours any reading that explains the text as it stands, without need of multiplying explanations. Furthermore, because it is impossible to prove that the present text is unintelligible, no one being fluent enough in ancient Hebrew to make such a definitive judgment, any proof resting on "better sense" will be rejected, for this is a subjective judgment based on limited knowledge (i.e. that it makes no sense to us says nothing about its comprehensibility for the original author or audience). According to the definition of emendation given above, such claims of awkwardness or incomprehensibility are the only possible evidence in favour of consonantal emendation, so such emendations will be rejected.

Proposed revocalizations will be considered not on the basis of "better sense," for the reasons stated above, but on the basis of analogous

---

[2] "Emendation," as used here, encompasses everything from the subtle changes of revocalization to the insertion of consonants and supposedly missing words *without manuscript warrant*. Emendation does not encompass the comparison of variant readings, which are measured by the canons of textual criticism.

misreadings in the present tradition and alternative textual evidence, thus being considered on the basis of a textual criticism as with consonantal emendation. For these reasons, the Masoretic Text will be given priority.[3]

Concerning lexica, evidential priority for the interpretation of *hapax legomena* and other rare words will be given, in order of priority, to the canonical biblical text, other Hebrew texts, Aramaic, and then other Semitic languages. The canonical text will be given priority, for it forms a single body of intelligible language and exerted an influence on itself over the course of its writing (e.g. the Pentateuch and its language influenced the following works). Because extra-biblical Hebrew texts share the same language and vocabulary where they can be compared, appeals to words that are present in these texts to explain those rare in the Biblical corpus are substantiated by this shared lexical stock. Aramaic clearly influenced the authors of the Biblical texts, including demonstrable borrowing of vocabulary, and is present in the Biblical text, so appeals to Aramaic of relatively the same period as the text under consideration are considered legitimate. Other Semitic languages yield many insightful parallels in lexical stock, yet one must tread carefully for it is impossible to be certain of the influence of a particular language and its vocabulary on the author or audience of a particular book, an issue compounded when the provenance and date of a book such as Job is unknown—despite the best speculations concerning the nature of its language.[4] On the basis of these considerations, an interpretation is to be preferred when it can be supported by the context, analogous uses of syntax and grammar,[5] and inter-biblical lexical appeals.

---

[3] A full text critical analysis of the text falls beyond the scope of this paper, yet it should be noted that many of the appeals made to alternate manuscripts and translations violate the canon of *lectio difficilior*.

[4] Cf. Aaron Hornkohl, "Periodization," in *Encyclopedia of Hebrew Language and Linguistics: Volume 1; A-F*, ed. Geoffrey Khan, vol. 1, 4 vols. (Leiden; Boston: Brill, 2013); Jan Joosten, "The Distinction Between Classical and Late Biblical Hebrew as Reflected in Syntax," *Hebrew Studies* 46 (2005): 327–339; Choon Leong Seow, "Orthography, Textual Criticism, and the Poetry of Job.," *Journal of Biblical Literature* 130, no. 1 (2011): 63–85; Ian Young, "Is the Prose Tale of Job in Late Biblical Hebrew?," *Vetus Testamentum* 59, no. 4 (2009): 606–629.

[5] "Analogy" is not restricted to identical grammatical and syntactical combinations (syntagms) but comparable uses of the same morphological (e.g. noun patterns), grammatical (clause level: e.g. a noun in a construct relationship with an adjective), or syntactical (sentence level: e.g. כִּי functioning to subordinate a clause) patterns.

APPENDIX 5 - KNOWING BIBLE TRANSLATIONS

This essay originally appeared as chapter 8 in my book, *The Gift of Reading – Part 1: Reading the Bible in Submission to God*. I have included it here because the philosophy of Bible translation outlined in it is that adopted by this commentary.

Look, all of you, among the nations and behold—
    and be astonished and astounded!
For a deed I am doing in your day;
    you would not believe it though it were told.
– Habakkuk 1:5

"Look, you scoffers,
    be astounded and perish;
for I am doing a work in your days,
    a work that you will not believe, even if one tells it to you."
– Acts 13:41

So far in this part of the book, we have considered the act of reading the Bible and the features of the Bible that we need to be aware of, with some consideration of tools we can use to read the various styles of Biblical writings. For the rest of part 2, we will consider various tools we have available in our reading of Scripture. In this chapter, we will consider bible translations. In the next chapter, the biblical languages. In chapter 10, we will consider the use of various secondary resources to check our interpretation of a text. We will conclude in chapter 11 with a consideration of how we can evaluate our own interpretation and the interpretations of others.

Whether we like it or not, we are all indebted to and reliant upon Bible translations in our study of the Bible. Even for those who will be reading in the original languages, it is often Bible translations that serve as our first recourse for interpretive help. It is essential, then, that we have a firm understanding of Bible translation in general and the translations we will be using. First, we will consider Bible translation in general, its nature and limitations. Second, we will consider general approaches to Bible translation as exhibited in the major English translations. Finally, I will offer an evaluation of several of the most significant English translations, considering their value and limitations.

Bible Translation

What is a Bible translation? Our answer to this question will have a significant impact on how we translate the Bible or how we interact with Bible translations. For example, if we say that a Bible Translations is presentation of the *content* of the original Greek and Hebrew text, we may produce or seek a very free translation that aims at communicating the ideas and truths of a text without attention to the way it communicates them. To answer this question, I want to suggest that a translation is a specific form of application or interpretation of the original texts and that there are two broad types of translation that are commonly used.

In our discussion above, I suggested that when we speak of the "meaning" of a text, we are thinking of specific ways that text could be used. "You shall not murder" means, "it is wrong to murder," "it is wrong to kill another person without God given authority," etc. We could say that these are all meanings of לֹא תִּרְצָח (lōʾ; *tirṣāḥ*) (Exod 20:13). It may be helpful to consider a translation as the communication of the meaning of a text from one language to another. Texts may mean countless things, for they apply to innumerable situations. However, there is no one-to-one correspondence between a original language, from which we are translating, and the receptor language, into which we are translating. Therefore, in its attempt to communicate the meaning of a text, a translation by necessity restricts the meanings of a text.

Consider our example of above, "You shall not murder" translates more of the text's meaning than "You shall not shoot a person indiscriminately," yet it does not replace the original Hebrew. "You shall not murder" employs the English word "murder," which is similar to but not identical with the Hebrew רצח, thus it will have a similar range of meanings but will not mean that same thing. For example, the Hebrew command includes what we would call "manslaughter," killing without pre-mediation. It also covers criminal negligence, accidental killing or negligence that results in a death. The English translation "you shall not murder" captures one set of meanings in the Hebrew but excludes others. Like application, translation attempts to communicate the meaning of a text to an audience, yet it attempts to do so in way that is analogous or as close as possible to the original. A translation may attempt to follow the word order and style of the original as much as possible, but even when this is not attempted, a translation will attempt to communicate with the same text type: we translate poetry as poetry, narrative as narrative, etc. Like an application, translation necessarily restricts the meaning of a text to communicate it to an audience, to a specific culture and language, yet generally it attempts to retain more of the **meaning potential** of the original text and tries to mirror its form to some extent.[1]

This is an important point to see. If translation is by necessity a restriction of meaning, an application, no translation will ever replace the need for the original texts. Even if we could guarantee that all translation would be perfect, there would need to be new translations as language changes and new translations as new ways we need to apply the text become apparent. In theory, then, their can be many legitimate and helpful translations in the same language; they may even complement each other where they differ (they may chose different ways of translating a text that are both legitimate). Consider, for examples, the way Paul uses Habakkuk 1:5 in Acts 13:41. Paul quote from the Septuagint (LXX), the Greek translation of the Old Testament. It is clearly different from the Hebrew represented in English translations, yet Paul's use of it indicates that it is a valid translation in one way or another. If we consider what Habakkuk 1:5 means in context, we see that it is both a declaration of God's salvific intent (e.g. Hab 3:18) and a revelation of His coming judgment (Hab 1:12). A general translation, one that seeks to convey as best as possible the full meaning potential of a text, will translate the text in such a way that allows for the text to be applied in both senses. However, a translation that seeks to make a more specific application of the text may narrow it down to either the salvific or the judgmental aspect of the text:

> The LXX ... here correctly (though restrictively) conveys the sense of the Hebrew text. If we judge the LXX here as a word for word translation, it fails. But if we consider it an application [a specific

---

[1] Meaning potential refers to all the possible applications a text could have. This is natural extension from our discussion in Chapter 5. If meaning refers to the different ways a text may apply, then any text has many meanings, as many as there are possible circumstances to which it could apply. Furthermore, these meanings are only potential, or latent, until they are met with a circumstance to which they apply. Thus, we may rightfully speak of a text's "meaning potential."

translation], it succeeds and is ideal for Paul's intended application of this text. In Hab 1:5, the Septuagint focuses on the judgment aspect of God's vision, ignoring the salvific side. Paul uses it because he is preaching that same aspect, though elsewhere he preaches Habakkuk with the salvific aspect in view (Rom 1:17).[2]

The Septuagint here is an adequate, even helpful, translation of Habakkuk 1:5, but it is not sufficient to convey all the possible meanings or applications of the Hebrew text. Other translations will be required to communicate all that God intends for His people from this text.

Translation Theories

In the history of Bible translation, both general and specific translations have been produced. The Latin Vulgate, Luther's German Bible, and the English King James Version represent *general translations* of the Bible. They attempt to communicate as much of the meaning potential of the original texts as they can. These translations are designed to be used in preaching, teaching, and general reading of the Word of God.

However, at times pastors and teachers have seen fit to produce their own translations of Biblical texts. Sometimes errors in the general translations have required it, but at other times, this has been necessary because they have needed to communicate a specific nuance or application of the original text that the broader translations do not. Sometimes these individual translations are *general translations*, trying to present the fullness of the original meaning, but often they are paraphrases or *specific translations* that attempt to narrow the meaning to a specific application.[3] In our day, this is seen especially in paraphrase or loose translations of the Bible, such as *The Message* or *New Living Translation*.

In modern translation theory, general translations are the goal, yet there are two broad approaches taken to produce general translations. On the one hand, there are translations that attempt to achieve formal equivalency, which tries to convey the form and meaning of the original text; "in its stricter form,

---

[2] See the introduction to this commentary.

[3] I have defended the appropriateness of such individual translations elsewhere. https://teleioteti.ca/2017/12/05/a-defence-of-an-authors-translation-part-1/.

this theory of translation espouses reproducing even the syntax and word order of the original."[4] The NASB and ESV—among others—are contemporary attempts at differing degrees of formal equivalency. On the other hand, some translations seek dynamic equivalency, they are not so concerned with the form of the original text (its shape, size, emphasis) but with its meaning and force. Formal equivalence does not attempt to close the historical distance between the ancient biblical texts and the modern culture; it will attempt to retain the impression of ancientness a reader of the original languages will experience. On the other hand, dynamic or functional equivalence is

> the attempt to keep the meaning of the Hebrew or Greek but to put their words and idioms into what would be the normal way of saying the same thing in English.... Such translations keep historical distance on all historical and factual matters but 'update' matters of language, grammar, and style.[5]

All contemporary translations fall somewhere between two extremes, with wooden literalness on the one hand and loose paraphrase on the other. The formal equivalency and functional equivalency of contemporary translations fall right and left of center.

We will consider how this looks in the following section, how translation theory plays out in specific translations. However, as far as theory goes, I think neither one of these theories is ideal. If our goal is to produce general translations—translations that are readable and useable for every day devotions, teaching, and preaching—then our goal should not be driven by a bare theory of how to translate but be adaptive towards the goal of translation. The goal should be to convey the most meaning-potential of the original text to a contemporary audience. The word of God is sufficient for all the Christian life; a general translation should seek to facilitate it functioning in this way for the reader. This necessitates the balance both formal and functional equivalency are trying to reach. If a translation is too awkward and foreign for the reader of English, they may not understand any of the meaning intended by the text. However, if the text is too loose and

---

[4] Leland Ryken, *The Word of God in English: Criteria for Excellence in Bible Translation* (Wheaton: Crossway, 2002).Ryken 19

[5] Gordon D. Fee and Douglas K. Stuart, *How to Read the Bible for All Its Worth*, 3rd ed. (Grand Rapids: Zondervan, 2003), 41.Fee 41.

specific, the reader may not hear the specific application the Holy Spirit would have for them.

I would endorse, then, a form of what Leeland Ryken calls "essential literalness." Ryken defines essential literalness as "a translation that strives to translate the exact words of the original-language text… but not in such a rigid way as to violate the normal rules of language and syntax in the receptor language."[6] Paraphrasing this, I would say that a general translation should seek to retain the maximum possible meaning potential of the original text by retaining its wording and emphasis—its form—, clarity, and literary force (beauty, rhythm, technicality, simplicity, etc.) in a translation that conforms to the rules of the receptor language. The goal is to stay as close to the original as possible—lest you lose some of the ways it might apply to the reader—while maintaining its ability to be understood and the more subjective effects reading produces.

These theories of translation are worked out in the many translations with which God has blessed the English speaking world. No translation adequately reproduces the original text in its totality, so we need to employ a variety of translation in our study if we are to see all that God has for us. If we are reading in the original languages, the variety of modern translations will help us to grasp better what is being said and help us learn to read and understand the original languages.

Bible Translations

There are dozens of English Bible translations available; I have chosen only to discuss below those that are most commonly used and, in my estimation, the most helpful. It should be observed that there are many unhelpful "translations" out there, those produced by various cults or by individuals without a considered approach to translation and without sufficient knowledge of the original language. For this reason, it is good to research where a translation comes from if it is not one of the more commonly recognized Bible translations. Some of those produced by individual scholars are quite helpful, but the amount of bad translations out there necessitates a comment.

From our discussion so far, it will probably not be a surprise that I recommend the moral formal equivalent translations for study while suggesting that translations on the functional equivalence side are valuable for gaining insight into the meaning and application of specific texts. The

---

[6] Ryken, *The Word of God*, 19.

following translations are given in alphabetical order, not in any way reflecting my estimation of their merit.

ESV

The English Standard Version is the translation I have chosen to employ throughout this book and other projects I have written. The ESV is generally an attempt at formal equivalence but one which seeks to maintain the literary nature of the original texts at the same time. In the translators own words, "we have sought to be 'as literal as possible' while maintaining clarity of expression and literary excellence.... As an essentially literal translation, then, the ESV seeks to carry over every possible nuance of meaning in the original words of Scripture into our own language."[7] This effort leads them, for example, to maintain cultural and historical difference where it is present in the original text.

Because of its emphasis on both the literary quality of the translation and faithfulness to the original meaning, the ESV is great study resource. It strength is in its preservation of the meaning potential of the original text, not only in what it says but also the effect its literary art conveys, such as the way narrative can draw you in and poetry can evoke various emotions. Textually, the ESV is based on the latest critical editions of the New Testament and on the Masoretic text of the Old, as much as the translators deemed possible.

KJV

The King James Version is old; it has gone through several revisions, but is rooted in the early days of the reformation. I include it on this list both because it remains a commonly used translation and has some, though limited, value for contemporary study. In its day, it represented the height of Biblical scholarship and literary quality. Though seeking to be literal in many ways, it nevertheless succeeded in communicating the beauty of Hebrew poetry, for example, in a way many modern translations fail to do. It's main value for contemporary study is the way it offers access to a different era of Biblical scholarship. Though the translators did not have access to many of the tools we have today—and this is at times evident—they also had a great knowledge of the Bible and translated on the basis of the tools they had access to and their understanding of language. For all the advances we have made in philosophy and study of language in the modern age, we have not

---

[7] ESV Preface

left the historical tradition of these things in the dust. In many ways, the beliefs that have informed modern translations are as influenced by our own culture and its deficiencies as the King James translators were influenced by theirs. For this reason, the KJV sometimes offers a superior perspective on how to interpret a text (such as is the case in Hab 3:13). However, because of its evident deficiencies, the use of the KJV needs be done carefully.

There are two major issues presented by the KJV to the modern reader. The first is that its language is outdated. That is, the English language has evolved significantly since the King James Version was produced, even since its last revisions. This means that words and grammatical structures that were once clear and understandable are no longer so, words have fallen out of our vocabulary, and some words have changed meaning (e.g. Phil 4:6, Rom 13:13, Psalm 37:14). The second issue is the quality of its underlying text. That is, though it is based on most of the same Old Testament texts as we use today (MT, LXX, and Vulgate), its New Testament text is based on a single tradition of the Greek text that today is not thought to be highly reliable. Therefore, though the KJV could conceivable have some use in study, it is not better than or to be preferred to contemporary translations.

NASB

If you are looking for very literal translation of the Bible based on the best scholarship of the years prior to its latest update in 1995, the NASB is where you would go. The goal of the NASB was to preserve the legacy of the KJV and its significant American version, the ASV, "by incorporating recent discoveries of Hebrew and Greek sources and by rendering it into more current English."[8] Thus, it sought to remedy the two significant issues that face the contemporary reader of the KJV. It is probably the closest to formal equivalency among the major contemporary Bible translations. Its close adherence to the wording of the original texts makes the NASB an invaluable tool for those beginning their journey with the original languages. It is often easy to identify how the NASB is translating the underlying Hebrew or Greek words without having to use an interlinear Bible. For these reasons, it is a valuable tool for study. I have often found in my own study that it also presents an alternative Evangelical perspective on difficult texts than what the ESV offers, so it is useful for comparing and contrasting.

As compared to the ESV or even the KJV in its own day, the NASB does not do as good of a job—in my opinion—of conveying the rich literary beauty of the original language texts. This is not a insignificant issue, for the Biblical art is essential to understanding its message. The skilled use of poetry

---

[8] From the Preface of the NASB 1995 update.

and narrative in the Bible is intended to lead the reader to the appropriate understanding and response to the text.

NET

Compared to the others, the NET is a relative newcomer to the translation scene, a whole new translation (not a revision) published in 2005. The goal of the NET is to produce a translation that is "accurate, readable, and elegant."[9] It seeks to preserve the meaning intended by the original authors in an understandable manner and to maintain the literary elegance of the original. Like the NIV, the NET attempts to achieve functional or dynamic equivalency in its printed text, however it is accompanied by extensive footnotes that explain the literal readings of texts and why they were translated the way they were.

The use of extensive translators notes makes the NET a tremendous asset to students of the Bible. For those using the original languages, its insight into the difficulties of grammar and text criticism are invaluable. For those who are not using the languages, its explanation of how they got to their translation from the original text can be helpful for resolving or at least identifying the reasons for differences between translations. The NET was produced by Evangelical scholars and so is informed by a broadly Evangelical theology in its translating choices. Though its notes are helpful for getting beyond the problems with dynamic equivalency, it still suffers from similar problem as the NIV. That is, the text is sufficiently specified for our culture today to remove much of the meaning potential the more literal translations are attempting to preserve. For this reason, the NET is a great study asset but I would recommend using a translation like the ESV or NASB as the basis for your study and Bible reading.

NIV

The NIV is the standard translation for the dynamic or functional equivalence approach to translation. It has been produced by a top-notch group of over a hundred Scholars representing many different protestant denominations. The NIV has been translated wholly from the original Greek and Hebrew texts, so it is not a revision of a previous English Bible (as the ESV, NASB, and NRSV are). It was first published in 1978 and has seen several revisions since then.[10] The NIV has sought to prioritize "accuracy,

---

[9] From the preface of the first edition of the NET.

[10] The edition I am using is from 2011.

clarity and literary quality" with purpose of creating a multi-purpose Bible translation (a *general translation* in my terminology). The translators that make up the Committee on Bible Translation which stands behind the NIV believe that the best way to attain this goal is through the functional equivalence model of translation.

The NIV is based on the latest Biblical scholarship and often represents keen insight into the meaning of the Biblical texts. For this reason, it is a great study resource, especially for checking your interpretation and seeing if other interpreters are seeing the same thing. However, as I have suggested above, it seems to me that the principles of functional equivalency do not retain the meaning potential of the original text to the same extent a more formally equivalent translation is able. The nature of a translation philosophy that seeks to be intelligible and clear throughout while communicating accurately the author's meaning often necessitates moving from the generality I have argued for to specificity, narrowing possible and potential meanings done. By "possible meanings" I mean that such a translation must often chose between mutually exclusive interpretations of a phrase or sentence in cases where an essentially literal translation will do its best to maintain the ambiguity. By potential meaning I refer to the innumerable applications a text may legitimately have. All translations will narrow this range, but functional equivalency often narrows this range beyond what is necessary for communicating the text in English. Consider a few of these examples:

> For on him God the Father has placed his seal of approval." -- John 6:27 (NIV 2011)
> for on Him the Father, God, has set His seal." – John 6:27 (NASB, cf. ESV)

> For it seems to me that God has put us apostles on display at the end of the procession, like those condemned to die in the arena. We have been made a spectacle to the whole universe, to angels as well as to human beings. – 1 Cor 4:9 (NIV 2011)
> For I think that God has exhibited us apostles as last of all, like men sentenced to death, because we have become a spectacle to the world, to angels, and to men. – 1 Cor 4:9 (ESV, cf. NASB)

> to call all the Gentiles to the obedience that comes from faith for his name's sake. – Rom 1:5 (NIV 2011)
> to bring about *the* obedience of faith among all the Gentiles for His name's sake, – Rom 1:5 (NASB, cf. ESV)

I am not suggesting that the NIV is wrong in the interpretation it presents in these passages, only that it is clearly presenting a greater restriction—a further specification—of the text than is necessary to communicate in English. Consider Romans 1:5, to translate "obedience of faith" as the NASB or ESV have communicates roughly the same range of possible meanings as the Greek phrase that stands behind it. The NIV's translation makes the meaning clear, yet the meaning they make clear is only one possible interpretation of several. 1 Corinthians 4:9 adds additional interpretive comments that are thought to be invoked by the word the ESV translates "exhibited," yet this is not what the text says nor is it 100% certain that the word would have carried those connotations. Thus, the translations is more specific than the text justifies.

A particularly significant area where this is evident is the debate over so-called "gender-neutral" terminology. There are many places in the Bible where a term can mean *either* a male or a human in general, accordingly, most Bible translations will translate one or the other (man or human being). However, there are specific words that have a component of meaning that is particularly male and yet are used to refer to both men and women. For example, υἱός (*uios*, son) means a male child yet is used to refer to male and female Christians. Should we, then, translate it "son" or "child"? It may seem common sense to translated "child" because it *refers* to men and women, yet this makes the interpretive judgment that the male component does not affect the meaning of the passages in question (cf. Rom 8:14). Therefore, if we are to leave open possible and potential meaning, we should translate what the text says (sons) not what we think it means (child). Furthermore, in many case in the New Testament, such as in Romans 8:14, the use of the word υἱός meaning son is *intentional*. That is, it is the son who inherits from the Father; it may very well be—and probably is the case—that by calling men and women together sons the Biblical authors intend to say that all of us are inheritors of God's good promises to His children. Doug Moo suggests that "son" makes an explicit connection between our status as Children and Christ's status as God's Son, a connection lost by translating υἱός as "son" in one case and "child" in another.[11] Schreiner also suggests that the use of son echoes the description of Israel as God's son.[12] For whatever reason, Paul chooses to use the more general term τεκνα (*tekna*), children, in latter verses; so if we are honour his intent—meaningful or, as is more commonly

---

[11] Douglas J. Moo, *The Epistle to the Romans*, NICNT (Grand Rapids: Eerdmans, 1996), 499–500.Moo 499-500

[12] Thomas R. Schreiner, *Romans*, Baker Exegetical Commentary on the New Testament 6 (Grand Rapids: Baker Books, 1998), 423.Schreiner 423

accepted, stylistic—we should render the two words with their more formal English equivalents (υἱός as son, τεκνον as child).[13]

NLT

So far, the translations we have considered are all around the center of the spectrum, with the NIV on the dynamic side and the ESV on the formal side. The New Living Translation moves us much farther down the line of dynamic equivalency. The NLT translators sought to "render the message of the original texts of Scripture into clear, contemporary English."[14] The goal was to be "faithful to the ancient texts and eminently readable." Where the original text was clear, this meant taking an approach that was more formally equivalent, but where the text was more difficult, they took a more dynamic approach. The resulting translation is quite a bit more dynamic than the NIV. Like the NIV, a strong team of Evangelical scholars stand behind the NLT.

The NLT has much the same strengths as the NIV, though it is harder to use for translating and understanding the original texts. In its weaknesses, it is generally the same, though by taking a more dynamic approach, these weaknesses are magnified. Thus, the NLT is useful for reference in your studies but should not serve as the basis for or primary comparison in studying Scripture.

NRSV

With the NRSV, we are back towards centre. The NRSV follows in the same English Bible tradition as the ESV and NASB but moves towards the dynamic side of things. The NRSV fares much the same as the NIV and NLT, though closer to the NIV. It is the least evangelical of the translations and this is at times evident in its translations. Overall, it makes a helpful reference but not a good basis for your study or reading.

The Message

The Message is the most dynamic of all the translations we have considered here. It is the product of the late Eugene Peterson, a popular pastor who was extensively trained in the original languages. *The Message* offers the most

---

[13] Cf. Vern S. Poythress and Wayne A. Grudem, *The Gender-Neutral Bible Controversy: Muting the Masculinity of God's Words* (Nashville: Broadman & Holman Publishers, 2000), 247–250.

[14] From the preface of the 2015 edition.

specified of these general translations; in an effort to communicate to a contemporary audience, it restricts most possible and potential meaning. This makes it unhelpful for primary use in study or for reading the Bible. Furthermore, in dozens of places, the translation adopted is down-right unhelpful and does not reflect the original text (e.g. Rom 1:26-27). However, given Peterson's writing abilities, it is probably the most readable and poetic of the translations considered. The main use to be made of *The Message* in Bible study is as a reference, to get an idea how someone has made an application of the text.

Further Reading

D. A. Carson - *The Inclusive Language Debate*
D. A. Carson – *The King James Version Debate*
Gordon Fee – *How to Read the Bible for All Its Worth*, 33-53
* Leeland Ryken – *The Word of God in English*
Vern S. Poythress & Wayne A. Grudem – *The Gender-Neutral Bible Controversy*

APPENDIX 6 - ON THE TRANSLATION OF HABAKKUK 2:2C IN THE SEPTUAGINT[1]

This appendix argues that the Septuagint text of Habakkuk 2:2c should be translated in the same way as the Hebrew text of the MT. In this way, it provides further support for the translation and interpretation of Habakkuk 2:2-4 presented in the commentary above.

Contemporary translations of the LXX text of Habakkuk, in the opinion of this author, fail to appropriately translate the last clause of 2:2. The Lexham and New English translations of the Septuagint translate αὐτα (*auta*; the things) as the object of διωκῃ (*diōkē*; he should run), resulting in translations along the lines of "so that the one who reads may pursue these things" (also Brenton). If this is the intent of the Septuagint, it would be a significant reversal—an inversion—of the sense of the Hebrew. I intend to argue that this translation is not an adequate rendering of the text. Instead, reading the Septuagint's translation according to the broader semantic ranges and uses of the respective words and in light of the Hebrew text yields a remarkably different sense.

I will argue that the LXX should here be translated, "so that the one who *reads these things* will run." That is, the LXX translator accurately renders the Hebrew text according to the regular translation of the respective Hebrew words, with a substantive ἀναγινωσκων (*anaginōskōn*: the one reading) taking the object αὐτα as the subject of the intransitive διωκω. To argue this, we will first survey the regular use of ἀναγινωσκω, followed by διωκω, then we will consider the LXX as a translation of a Hebrew text resembling the MT.

Considering the use of ἀναγινωσκω in the LXX, relevant for our

---

[1] This paper was originally published on Teleioteti.ca, 2018.

purposes is the use of ἀναγινωσκω with or without an object. According to Hatch and Redpath, ἀναγινωσκω is used 61 times in the LXX. 46 of these uses are translations of the Hebrew קָרָא (*qārā'*; to read, read aloud). In the Hebrew OT, as in Hab. 2:2, קרא often takes the object read with the preposition בְּ (*bĕ*; in, with, by). Ἀναγινωσκω nine times follows this pattern, taking the preposition ἐν (*en*; in, with, by) (Deut 17:19; 2 Chron 34:24; 2 Esd 18:3, 18:8, 19:3; 23:1, Jer 43:6; Jer 43:6, 15) for the object read. In 2 instances, Habakkuk 2:2 and 2 Chronicles 34:18, ב+object has been translated in the LXX with αὐτος (*autos*, it). There 14 instances where ἀναγινωσκω is used absolutely or with an implied object (Exod 24:7; 1 Esd 3:13, 9:41; 2 Esd 4:23, 6:1; Job 31:36; Prologue of Sirach 4; Isa 29:11; Jer 43:6, 13, 15 [x2], 21; Dan 5:17, 2 Mac 2:25). The majority of uses are with a direct object (32 times), nine of these being instances with αὐτος (there is overlap here, Jer 43 twice has the preposition referring to the book and λογος for its contents). The last six uses are five passives and one instance of reading out of a book (ἐξω, Amos 4:5). The active participle in Habakkuk 2:2 could then be transitive with αὐτα, as I will contend, or intransitive.

If ἀναγινωσκω were absolute in our context, "the reader" would refer to one who reads the vision. Many would contend, from the Hebrew, that the sense is "the herald," yet there is no support for this. There is always a concrete situation in view: ἀναγινωσκω is not used as a job description—as it would have to here. On the absolute reading then, it would read, "so that the one has read [the vision] may pursue these things." But more likely is a transitive reading. The frequency of instances where ἀναγινωσκω is followed by a direct object (2 Chron 34:18, Hab 2:2, Isa 29:11, 4 Kgdms 19:14, 22:8, 10; Jer 28:61, to this could be added the many other instances where only the subject intervenes) would lead the reader in the Greek to immediately associate αὐτα with it, not with διωκω. We will now look at the uses of διωκω to support this.

In our consideration of διωκω, it is important to first note that though frequently having the transitive meaning "pursue," it was used in the LXX with the intransitive sense "run" or "flee" as the translation of רוּץ (*rûṣ*; to run) and נוּס (*nûs*; to flee). In Rahlfs' text, διωκω appears 104 times (Swete has 110). Most frequently, it appears with an object (e.g. Gen 14:15, Lev 26:7, Deut 16:20, Josh 23:10) or with ὀπισω (to pursue *after*; e.g. Gen 31:23; Jdg 4:16, 8:12; 2 Kgdms 18:13). I have counted, roughly, 14 use of διωκω without an object. A few of these are substantives meaning "pursuer" (Isa 16:4, 31:8; Lam 1:6). The rest are a mixture of absolute and intransitive uses (Exod 15:9; Jdg 8:4; 1 Kgdms 30:10 [Swete, Rahlfs has καταδιωκω]; 3 Kgdms 25:5; Prov 28:1; Amos 2:16, 6:13; Nah 3:2; Hag 1:9; Jer 20:11, 28:31). The Minor Prophets were being treated as a unit by the time of the LXX translation, so the translators' use of διωκω here are most relevant. Διωκω appears in the Twelve 10 times: excluding Habakkuk 2:2, διωκω is found transitively four times (Hos 6:3, 12:2; Amos 1:11, Nah 1:8). Once, it is passive (Mic 2:11). This leaves four intransitive uses (Amos 2:16, 6:12; Nah 3:2; Hag 1:9). We see then that an intransitive use of διωκω is well established in the Twelve. How does this help in our reading of Habakkuk 2:2? We cannot assume that αὐτα must be the object of διωκω, it is just as likely—if not more so—to be the object of αναγινωσκω: so the frequent translation "pursue these things" is not as self-evident as translations make it seem. Furthermore, when we look at the Hebrew words διωκω is translating, an intransitive meaning becomes more likely.

The Hebrew word translated "run" in Habakkuk 2:2 is רוץ, which has a similar range of meanings as διωκω—both intransitive and transitive. διωκω is used six times in the LXX as a translation of רוץ (Amos 6:12, Hab 2:2, Hag 1:9, Jer 28:31 [x3]). In every one of these instances, other than Habakkuk 2:2, רוץ and διωκω are intransitive. It is then probable that in Habakkuk 2:2, διωκω is also intransitive.

Before turning to compare the LXX and MT texts, I will summarize what we have seen so far. Ἀναγινωσκω in the LXX is most often transitive, frequently with the subject following immediately after the verb or after the subject. The reader of Habakkuk 2:2 in Greek would, therefore, naturally read αὐτα as the direct object of the substantive participle ἀναγινωσκων. To this we can then add the evidence for reading διωκω intransitively—that is, without αὐτα as its object. We then saw that, though διωκω is most frequently used transitively or with a preposition, it is used intransitively at least 14 times. Therefore, an intransitive use must be considered a possibility. Then, in considering the Twelve, we saw that intransitive uses of διωκω are as common as transitive. Lastly, of the five other times רוץ is translated with διωκω, all function intransitively. Three of these are found in the Twelve. This should lead us to read, by default, διωκω here intransitively, and so αὐτα as the object of αναγινωσκω. Turning to a comparison with the Hebrew, this is conclusion is confirmed.

Comparing the Hebrew and the Greek text, this is what we find:

ὅπως διώκῃ ὁ ἀναγινώσκων αὐτά
so that the one who reads the things will run.

לְמַעַן יָרוּץ קוֹרֵא בוֹ:
So that the one who reads it will run.

The Septuagint has translated the Hebrew almost word for word, only translating the בּוֹ (*bô*; in it) with the 3rd neuter plural accusative pronoun αυτα. We have noted above that the Septuagint translators have done this also in two Chronicles, where the preposition likewise indicated the object being read. In the Hebrew text, רוּץ (*rûṣ*; to run) is without a doubt intransitive and בוֹ is connected with קוֹרֵא. Giving the LXX translator the benefit of the doubt—that he read the text correctly—and allowing for the translation of the preposition for object into the more regular accusative direct object, it is clear that the LXX translator intended for αὐτα to be read as the object of the participle ἀναγινωσκων, itself the subject of διωκη.

I set out to argue that the usual translation of Habakkuk 2:2 is not adequate, that it would be better to read αὐτα as the object of ἀναγινωσκω than the object of διωκω. Our examination of the lexical data and our comparison of the LXX with the MT show that my reading of the LXX is the more obvious one. In conclusion, Habakkuk 2:2c should not be translated "in order that the one who reads might pursue the things" (LES) but "so that the one who reads the things will run."

APPENDIX 7 - HABAKKUK 2:4 IN ROMANS 1:17[1]

This paper was originally prepared for a graduate seminar on the New Testament use of the Old Testament, with professor Rikk Watts. This essay provided the impetus for writing the above commentary and supplements the discussion in the introduction and notes on 2:2-4. It has been adapted for its present context.

Overview of Romans

Romans has enjoyed an eminent place in the Church's theological and exegetical discourse. Despite, or maybe because of, the attention it has received, the debates raged over it are numerous and ongoing. This is immediately apparent as one considers the purpose of the letter. For many interpreters, Romans has merely been an exegetical treatise—either with a personal letter tacked on or written to convince the Romans of Paul's credibility—but more attention of late has been paid to the practical nature of the book.[2] Far from being an abstract treatise, Romans is full of vibrant life as the wisdom of God in the Gospel is brought to bear on the issues facing the Roman Church.

Attention paid to key points of the letter reveals this. Paul is writing to a church made up of both Jews and Gentiles, yet he seems primarily to address the Gentile side as he makes plans to visit.[3] Paul wants to visit the

---

[1] This paper was originally published on Teleioteti.ca, 2018.

[2] Cf. James D. G Dunn, *Romans 1-8*, Word Biblical Commentary (Dallas, Tex.: Word Books, 1988), lvi–lvii.

[3] See the numerous references to the gentiles as the subject, e.g. 1:12-13, 15:16. So Schreiner, *Romans*, 36–37.

Roman church as part of his ministry to the Gentiles (1:1-14), yet God has thus far not allowed him (1:10, 13). Paul has been prevented by the necessity to preach the gospel to those who have yet to hear it (15:20-22), but with that ministry rounding down, his desire is to strengthen the church in Rome, to impart some spiritual gift, and to be mutually encouraged by them (1:11, 16:25-26, 1:12-13). The reason he desires to visit, and indeed for writing this letter, is to "bring about the obedience of faith for [Jesus's] name" (1:5).[4] This is a key theme throughout the letter (6:16, 15:18, 16:19, 16:25-26): from all these appearances, it is best to understand the phrase as obedience produced by faith.[5] Paul has not written his letter to save the Roman church, nor to show off his theological chops. Instead, his primary purpose is to see the Romans respond in the appropriate way to the gospel: to be united, Jew and Gentile together, and to walk in a way consistent with their new life.[6] That Paul is trying to show the obedience resulting from the gospel explains why he has begun with a large section on the gospel (1:16-11:36) and permeates this with large sections on application (e.g. ch. 6-7), concluding by expounding the behaviour resulting from the gospel (cf. "therefore" in 12:1). The outline of the letter proposed by this author is as follows,

1) <u>Salutation</u> (1:1-7)
2) <u>**The Body of the Letter: The Gospel**</u> (1:8-11:36)
   a) **Thanksgiving and Desire to Come** (1:8-12)
   b) **Inability to Do So and the Theological Foundation for the Obedience of Faith** (1:13-11:36)

---

[4] All Scripture quotations, excepting Hab. 2:1-5 and Rom. 1:16-17, are from the ESV.

[5] Paul is writing to believers and his explicit intent is to disciple them, not to convert them. So this probably reinforces that purpose: obedience produced by the faith they already have, not a new saving faith that is obedience. Contra Adolf von Schlatter, *Romans: The Righteousness of God*, trans. Siegried S. Schatzmann (Peabody, Mass: Hendrickson Publishers, 1995), 11; John Murray, *The Epistle to the Romans*, NICNT (Grand Rapids, Mich.: Wm. B. Eerdmans Pub. Co, 1995), 13; Schreiner, *Romans*, 34–35; Douglas J. Moo, *The Epistle to the Romans*, NICNT (Grand Rapids: Eerdmans, 1996), 51–53.

[6] Unity is the primary theme here, see the emphasis on the relationship between Jews and Gentiles from the Gospel in 1:16, 18; 2:6-11, 12-16; 3:1-4, 9, 19-20, 22-23, 27-31, and ch. 9-11, 14.

- *i)* Inability to come thus far, but the desires to do so to preach the Gospel for the sake of obedience (1:13-15)
- *ii)* The Gospel as the foundation for the obedience of faith (1:16-11:36)
  - *(1) Gospel Summary (1:16-17)*
  - *(2) Righteousness Needed, for all Fall Short (1:18-3:20)*
  - *(3) Righteousness by Faith for All (3:21-4:25)*
  - *(4) The Christian Life is Truly by Faith for Righteousness from the Faithful God (5:1-11:36)*
- *iii)* The obedience of faith produced by the Gospel for the Roman church (12-15:13)

3) Conclusion (15:14-16)

The passage of our focus, 1:17, stands on the precipice of Paul's grand exposition of the Gospel.[7] In two densely packed verses (16-17), Paul gives the substance of what he will unpack throughout the rest of the letter. For the purposes of this paper, we will briefly survey the redemptive-historical setting invoked by the unit within which verse 17 falls (1-17), then we will examine the verse itself and the function of Habakkuk 2:4 within it.

Introduction to 1:1-17

As with all of Paul's letters, the epistolary salutation opening Romans goes beyond merely a greeting, it is itself packed with deep theology and introduces much of what he will touch upon throughout the letter. We have already discussed the purpose of the letter as introduced here (v. 5), so we will focus briefly on how Paul prepares the reader for verse 17 and beyond by introducing the concept of covenant fulfillment.

That Paul is a covenant theologian has received more attention as of late through the work of N.T. Wright, but Wright's emphasis has focused more on Paul as a 1st century Jew than on his continuity with the inherent story line

---

[7] Some have called this verse the "thesis" of the letter, but this is not quite accurate: Paul is writing as a pastor, not a scholar. These verses are a thematic summary, the beating heart pumping the blood that flows through the rest of the letter.

of the Canonical Scriptures.⁸ This narrative—the story line unpacked across the canonical and covenantal structure of Scripture—invoked from the start of the letter illumines much of what is to follow.⁹ All of Scripture unpacks the anticipation found in the first three chapters of Genesis for restoration

---

⁸ All of Wrights works deal with this to some extent, *New Testament and the People of God* places Paul within the world of 1ˢᵗ century Judaism (for covenant, 260-262), *Climax of the Covenant* focuses on the covenant fulfillment in the NT. He is especially ardent in defending the covenantal nature of righteousness language. The focus on the narrative structure of covenant is found more within Reformed circles—such as Goldsworthy and Gentry—, with whom Wright has a lot of affinity—as he comes from an Anglican background. This distinction roughly accords with the two senses of "salvation history" described by Yarbrough. N.T. Wright, *The New Testament and the People of God*, Christian Origins and the Question of God 1 (Minneapolis: Fortress, 1992); N.T. Wright, "Translating Δικαιοσύνη: A Response," *Expository times* 125, no. 10 (July 1, 2014): 487–490; N.T. Wright, "Paul and the Patriarch: The Role of Abraham in Romans 4," *Journal for the study of the New Testament* 35, no. 3 (March 1, 2013): 207–241; Peter J. Gentry and Stephen J. Wellum, *Kingdom Through Covenant: A Biblical-Theological Understanding of the Covenants* (Wheaton, Ill: Crossway, 2012); Graeme Goldsworthy, *According to Plan:The Unfolding of God in the Bible* (Leicester, England: Inter-Varsity Press, 1991); Robert W. Yarbrough, "Paul and Salvation History," in *Justification and Variegated Nomism: Volume 2 - the Paradoxes of Paul*, ed. D. A. Carson, Peter T. O'Brien, and Mark A. Seifrid, vol. 2, 2 vols. (Grand Rapids, Mich.: Baker Academic, 2004).

⁹ "canonical and covenantal" indicates that the story line of Scripture is not independent of its canonical structure and the covenantal framework through which the story of creation-fall-redemption-consummation unfolds. The Masoretic order of the Old Testament is to be preferred here, not only for the fact that it is explicitly mentioned in Scripture (Luke 24:14), but also the internal structural clues found within Scripture (2 Chron.-Matt., Prov.-Ruth, the Twelve) and the historical evidence. Gentry & Wellum rightly emphasizes what they call "covenantal epochs" (Old covenant or New Covenant) over, though not in exclusion from, direct literary context (such as the link between Proverbs and Ruth). David G. Dunbar, "The Biblical Canon," in *Hermeneutics, Authority, and Canon*, ed. D. A. Carson and John D. Woodbridge (Grand Rapids: Academie Books, 1986); Paul R. House, *Old Testament Theology* (Downers Grove, Ill.: InterVarsity Press, 1998), 55; Gentry and Wellum, *Kingdom Through Covenant*, 95 nn.30, 135–138; Russell Fuller, "The Form and Formation of the Book of the Twelve: The Evidence from the Judean Desert," in *Forming Prophetic Literature: Essays on Isaiah and the Twelve in Honor of John D.W. Watts*, ed. James W. Watts and Paul R. House, Journal for the Study of the Old Testament Supplement 235 (Sheffield, England: Sheffield Academic Press, 1996), 86–101.

from the fall. When offered life or death, Adam and Eve chose rebellion, introducing death instead of eternal life in covenant relation with God, which is the enjoyment of creation as His representatives and children. They were exiled from the garden and cut off from Him, yet hope is introduced with the promise of an offspring who will crush the head of the serpent (Gen 3:14, cf. Rom 16:20).

These themes of land (garden, promised land and new creation), offspring (offspring, great nation, David, and Jesus), covenant (Adamic, Noachian, Abrahamic, Israeli, Davidic, Eternal), and sin are played out throughout the rest of the Bible. Genesis—referenced throughout Romans (Romans 4, 5:12-21, 8:18-25, 16:20)—anticipates God's answer to this problem in many passages. With each child born, there is an anticipation of the coming offspring; as humanity grows, the identity of the coming offspring is narrowed—Seth, Noah, Shem, Abraham—and then widened to a nation that will bring blessing to all the rest (Gen 12:2-3). Yet all with whom God has a covenant fail their obligations. Adam eats of the fruit;[10] Noah gets drunk (9:21-28) and his family receives the same indictment as those before the flood (8:21); Abraham fails immediately his mission to be a blessing (12:17). A tension builds throughout the story of Scripture: who will fulfill the covenant obligations God has imposed upon all humanity, who will crush the serpent and bring life, and how can God take upon Himself the punishment for His people's covenant failure—as is implied by Genesis 15 (cf. Jer 34:18-19)?[11] This tension is at its highest with the close of the Old Testament: the people of God are still in exile (cf. 2 Chron 36:23 in the Hebrew canon).

With all this assumed, the New Testament introduces Jesus as the one will return the people from exile through a new exodus and fulfill all of God's promises (2 Cor 1:20). In the first few verses of Romans, Paul introduces these themes by describing his Gospel as what God has promised in Scripture fulfilled through his Son (1:1-3). Particularly, it is fulfilled through Jesus as the descendant of David and so the Christ, the Messiah (v. 1, 3).[12] This is bookended with the fulfillment of Genesis 3:14 by the Church in Christ promised in 16:20.

---

[10] There is much debate over a covenant with Adam. Cf. Hosea 6:7, Jer. 33:19-26, and Gentry and Wellum, *Kingdom Through Covenant*, 177–221.

[11] Ibid., 247–258. See Appendix 8.

[12] Cf. N.T. Wright, "Romans," in *The New Interpreter's Bible*, ed. Robert W Wall and J. Paul Sampley, vol. X (Nashville: Abingdon Press, 2002), 415.

Romans 1:16-17

Before turning to verse 17, we must briefly consider verse 16 because of its close connection. Paul in verses 16-17 explains the gospel in this way:

> [16]For I am not ashamed of the Gospel, for it is the power of God for salvation to everyone who believes, to the Jew first and also to the Greek. [17]For the righteousness of God is revealed in it entirely by faith, just as it is written, "but the righteous one will live by faith."[13]

Verse 16

Verse 16 sets the tone for the rest of Romans in a clear and vivid way: Paul here explains the Gospel as God's very power to save all who believe and sets the redemptive-historical order of that salvation—to the Jews at first, but not to the exclusion of the Gentiles. The redemptive priority of the Jews appears throughout Romans (3:1-8, 9:1-11:36), being especially relevant to Paul's argument because God had promised to save the world through them (cf. Rom 4, 9-11).[14] Paul identifies his Gospel as God's very power for salvation, identifying both its primacy (it is God's means of salvation) and its efficacy (it is powerful for salvation). Before turning to verse 17, we need to identify what Paul means by salvation.

Throughout the New Testament, salvation focuses on the restoration of what was lost in Eden: eternal life with God at peace, free from judgment, in a promised land. Eschatologically, this focuses on the inheritance of the new heavens and the new earth as a people who are God's possessions, set free from death and decay and perfected in Christ to enjoy God forever (e.g. Tit 2:13-14, Rev 21:1-22:5). Throughout Romans, Paul addresses this final state (esp. Romans 8) with an emphasis on how that future salvation affects

---

[13] Unless otherwise noted, all references form 16-17 are this author's translation.

[14] For the redemptive historical, not merely historical, nature of "first", see Schreiner, *Romans*, 62; James R. Edwards, *Romans*, ed. W. Ward Gasque, New International Biblical Commentary 6 (Peabody, Mass: Hendrickson, 1992), 42; Colin G. Kruse, *Paul's Letter to the Romans*, The Pillar New Testament Commentary (Grand Rapids, Mich.: WM. B. Eerdmans Publishing Co., 2012), 68–69; Ernst Käsemann, *Commentary on Romans*, trans. Geoffrey William Bromiley (Grand Rapids, Mich: Eerdmans, 1980), 23.

us in the present—adopted children set free from sin and at peace with God, assured of a positive verdict in final judgment (ch. 5-8). Especially prominent in the letter is the final judgment; "But because of your hard and impenitent heart you are storing up wrath for yourself on the day of wrath when God's righteous judgment will be revealed. ⁶He will render to each one according to his works..." (2:5-6). The initial salvific focus of the letter, beginning in verse 18, is God's judgment against *all* humanity (1:18-3:20) and our salvation from that judgment in Christ. But the positive implications of that salvation are immediately made clear; peace with God through Christ means the inheritance of all God's promises, a new heaven and new earth set free from sin enjoyed in relationship with Him (e.g. ch. 4, 7-8).[15] In classic Reformed terminology, Paul here addresses salvation as justification, sanctification, and glorification. All these aspects are introduced here. This then brings us to verse 17, Paul's explanation of how the Gospel is God's power for salvation.

Verse 17

In verse 17 Paul writes, "For the righteousness of God is revealed in it entirely by faith, just as it is written, 'but the righteous one will live by faith.'" In verse 17, γαρ (for) is explanatory, explaining how God's power in the Gospel achieves salvation for those who believe. This verse has engendered significant debate, especially over the meaning of δικαιοσυνη θεου (the righteousness of God), but also over the meaning of εκ πιστεως εις πιστιν (from faith to faith: entirely by faith) and the use of Habakkuk 2:4. For our purposes, we will discuss briefly the meaning of δικαιοσυνη θεου and then focus on the Habakkuk quotation.

The Righteousness of God

The suggestions for understanding "the righteousness of God" are legion,

---

[15] Schreiner agrees that it involves "the fulfillment of the promises made to Israel." Most commentators agree on at least the sense of being spared from judgment through Christ, but disagree on the eschatological implications. For Moo, every spiritual need is provided. For Cranfield, we recover lost glory. Moo, *The Epistle to the Romans*, 67; Schreiner, *Romans*, 61; Kruse, *Paul's Letter to the Romans*, 68; Dunn, *Romans 1-8*, 39; C. E. B. Cranfield, *A Critical and Exegetical Commentary on the Epistle to the Romans: Commentary on Romans IX-XVI and Essays*, vol. 2, ICC (Edinburgh: T&T Clark LTD, 1975), 89.

but we can narrow these to three main positions. Since the Reformation, Protestants have often understood the genitive θεου to be a genitive of source: it is a righteousness that comes from God to the believer.[16] Others have understood it as God's righteous character: the righteousness God possesses, sometimes further interpreted as his covenant faithfulness to Israel.[17] Finally, it has been understood as an action taken by God (subjective genitive): His righteousness is His salvific action.[18] The arguments for the first are mainly grammatical and contextual, as Greek allows for this and chapters 3-5 seem to demand it; the main argument for the second is the Jewish use of the term "righteousness" in the Old Testament and Second Temple Judaism; in favour of the last is also OT usage—especially Psalm 98 (LXX 97). Instead of settling in any one of these camps, some authors have argued that Paul has all three of these ideas in mind when he speaks of God's righteousness here in 1:17.[19]

This last position seems to explain best all the evidence: for Paul, the righteousness of God is God's righteous character displayed in salvation accomplished by the provision of righteousness through Christ's life, death, and resurrection for those who believe. A defense and explanation of this position can be found in my paper "A Consideration of the Meaning of the

---

[16] The classic statement of this position is Cranfield, labelling it a genitive of origin. Cranfield, *A Critical and Exegetical Commentary on the Epistle to the Romans: Commentary on Romans IX-XVI and Essays*, 2:97–98.

[17] Wright is especially prominent here, emphasizing that in continuity with Paul's Jewish background, it is God's faithfulness to His covenant with Israel as revealed Gospel: in Jesus God has fulfilled his single plan to save the world through Israel. Wright, "Romans," 398, 403–405, 425; N.T. Wright, *Justification: God's Plan & Paul's Vision* (Downers Grove, Ill.: IVP Academic, 2009), 178–181.

[18] Käsemann's view seems to fall here, yet he wavers between God's power as transformative and saving, with the connection not being explicated. Schreiner follows suit, affirming in a confusing way this "transforming" righteousness—though he also affirms the other two understandings of righteousness. Käsemann, *Commentary on Romans*, 25–30; Schreiner, *Romans*, 64–67. Roberts argues against the transformative power view, J H Roberts, "Righteousness in Romans With Special Reference to Romans 3:19-31," *Neotestamentica* 15 (January 1, 1981): 12–33. Dunn affirms God's action and character in the phrase, with emphasis on the latter. Dunn, *Romans 1-8*, 40–41.

[19] John R. W. Stott, *The Message of Romans* (Downers Grove, Ill.: InterVarsity Press, 1994), 63; David L. Bartlett, *Romans*, First edition., Westminster Bible Companion (Louisville: Westminster John Knox, 1995), 22–23.

Righteousness of God in Romans 1:17."[20] A brief summary of the evidence presented there will suffice for our purposes here. A survey of the Old Testament uses of δικαιοσυνη (righteousness) and related words shows that righteousness is often considered as a characteristic or quality possessed by God. Though often manifest in fulfilling his covenant obligations, God's righteousness is most readily shown in judgment; a uniting idea covering much of the evidence is that God's righteousness expresses the unfailing demonstration of His character in all He does and his effort to display that character always (e.g. Daniel 9). Furthermore, Paul in 1:17 alludes to Psalm 98 [97 LXX]; in this psalm, God's righteousness is expressed in saving action. This allusion demonstrates that for Paul, God's righteous character in Romans is most clearly expressed in a saving act. From the context of Romans (3:22, 25, 4:5-6, 5:16-21) and the storyline of Scripture invoked in 1:1-3, we see that this saving act is the provision of righteousness in Christ so that all who believe can both be forgiven of their sins and be counted as those who have fulfilled their covenant obligations before God—being then inheritors of the promises to Abraham. Understanding the righteousness of God in this last sense is essential when we turn to the last part of verse 17.

The Gospel is God's Righteousness for Salvation Completely by Faith

In 17b-c, Paul explains that in the Gospel "the righteousness of God is revealed entirely by faith". This last phrase is prepositional and though it may modify "the righteousness of God" or "revealed," is best understood as modifying "revealed." Though word order is highly flexible in Greek, the prepositional phrase follows the verb and is a fair distance from "the righteousness of God"; the best explanation for this difference is an effort to link the prepositional phrase to the verb that comes immediately before it and the quote that comes after it.[21] Furthermore, the quote from Habakkuk following the phrase contains the prepositional phrase εκ πιστεως (from faith)

---

[20] Available on https://teleioteti.ca/resources/papers.

[21] Contra Moo and Schreiner. Moo suggests as evidence against the above reading the supposed connection of the prepositional phrase in the Habakkuk quote to δικαιος. He suggests following the NIV in translating the phrase independently, "For in the Gospel a righteousness form God is revealed, a righteousness that is by faith...." Moo, *The Epistle to the Romans*, 75–76; Schreiner, *Romans*, 71–72.

primarily modifying the verb—an evident parallel[22]—and the revelation of God's wrath in verse 18 is also modified by a preposition—though here the object is sandwiched between the prepositional phrase and the verb. Space does not permit us to engage the discussion around the translation of εκ πιστεως εις πιστιν (entirely by faith), but as the proffered translation indicates, this author understands it as focusing on completeness through a description of the whole process: it is completely, from beginning to end, by faith.[23] Many authors try to squeeze as much out of this phrase as possible, suggesting many different values for both prepositions. In light of the immediate context and the New Testament parallels, it is best to take it as a unit conveying the centrality and completeness of faith in salvation. In three parallels in 2 Corinthians (2:16, 3:18), the unit of εκ + noun-A + εις + noun-A has the sense "from first to last." This conveys a sense of completeness, but in these three examples, there is a discernable progression, beginning with death/life/glory and increasing towards complete death/life/glory. There is not a clear progression of faith expressed in context, nor throughout the whole of Romans, so the unit from "faith to faith" would convey the totality of that faith—nothing else intercedes to make the revelation possible: it is by faith throughout the whole.

We are now in a position to examine Paul's citation of Habakkuk 2:4—front-loading so much context will make our endeavour here that much easier. Our approach will be to go from the micro to the macro: let us first look at Paul's text form, then the function of the quote in the immediate context we have just established. From here we will then expand our horizon to determine how Paul is employing the context of Habakkuk—if he is at all—and how the quotation fits into the whole of his argument.

Beginning with the form of the quotation, it appears that Paul departed from the LXX in favour of the Hebrew:

Rom: *ὁ δὲ δίκαιος ἐκ πίστεως ζήσεται*[24] (but the righteous one

---

[22] See the discussion below of the reciprocity of this use.

[23] Cf. Dunn, *Romans 1-8*, 43; Moo, *The Epistle to the Romans*, 76; Schreiner, *Romans*, 72.

[24] In Galatians 3:11, Paul has the same text form, only dropping the δε (but). There is one variation in the text worth noting, Codex Ephraemi (C) from the 5th century has μου after δικαιος, bringing the text in line with the LXX.

will live by faith)
LXX: *ὁ δὲ δίκαιος ἐκ πίστεώς μου ζήσεται* (but the righteous one will live by my faithfulness)
BHQ: וְצַדִּיק בֶּאֱמוּנָתוֹ יִחְיֶה (but the righteous one will live by his faith)[25]

It is apparent that Paul's text form is very close to both the MT and the LXX, but the sense of his form is much closer to that of the Hebrew. In the MT, the faith in question is that of the one who is righteous; in the LXX, it is God's faithfulness. Many of Paul's quotations conform to the LXX (e.g. Romans 9:12, 13, 15), yet here he has departed. That Paul has chosen a form that differs from the LXX in as much as the LXX disagrees with the sense of the MT is telling for Paul's intention: Paul is leaving no ambiguity as to whose faith is in question; it is that of the believer.[26] Many commentators argue that Paul, though faithful to the MT in the quotation's form, intends for εκ πιστεως to modify the one who is righteous, contrary to the sense of the LXX and MT.[27] The burden of proof rests on those who would seek to show that Paul has significantly altered the emphasis of the Habakkuk quotation for his own purposes. Often arguing from the greater context of Romans, they fail to ask the key question: how is Paul using the quotation as a whole? We observed in our discussion of Habakkuk, with Watts, that there is reciprocity in this phrase found in Habakkuk's context; we could paraphrase Habakkuk 2:4b like this, "the one who is truly righteous will live by his faith." The faith making the one truly righteous is what will bring life even in the face of God's coming judgment: the emphasis lies on living, but "by faith" also describes his righteousness. Does this shed light on Paul's quote?

Turning from the text form to the immediate context, we must ask, what

---

[25] The Qumran Hab. Pesher, reconstructed from the interpretation, probably reads the same, וצדיק באמונתו יחיה.

[26] So David Andrew Dean, "The Use of Habakkuk 2:4 in the New Testament (Romans 1:17, Galatians 3:11, and Hebrews 10:38)" (Ph.D., Dallas Theological Seminary, 2008), 94.

[27] E.g. Cranfield, *A Critical and Exegetical Commentary on the Epistle to the Romans: Commentary on Romans IX-XVI and Essays*, 2:101–102; Robert H. Mounce, *Romans*, The New American Commentary v. 27 (Nashville: Broadman & Holman, 1995), 74; Moo, *The Epistle to the Romans*, 77–78; Stott, *The Message of Romans*, 64–65. Schreiner notes that if life is understood eschatologically, these two options are really perspectives on the same point. Schreiner, *Romans*, 74. Moody and Dunn take a "both and" approach, Dunn, *Romans 1-8*, 45–46. Moody 205-206

is his purpose in quoting Habakkuk? With Canfield, it is clear that the quotation is meant to support what Paul has said in verse 17a, but is Habakkuk 2:4 support for the whole of the verse or a specific aspect?[28] Moo understands the quote as confirmation that righteousness is by faith, seeing the emphasis on "the righteous one."[29] However, the emphasis in Habakkuk lies on faith. God calls for the righteous to have faith in Him that they might live: living is emphasized in contrast with the wicked who will perish, but faith is paramount as the means by which the righteous are distinguished from their oppressors and live. This focus on faith as the means by which those crying out for God's help will find themselves in right relationship with God, even in the face of judgment, sheds light on Paul's purpose with the quote.

As we have seen, Paul's Gospel is the revelation of God's righteousness in His salvific provision of a right covenant standing (righteousness) by faith: in light of this, the Habakkuk text fits perfectly.[30] In Habakkuk, faith, not perfect obedience, is the means of life before God. In Romans, it is utterly by faith, as opposed to works, that one will be right and have life; this is then explicated in terms of Christ as the one who fulfills the covenant perfectly and provides the free gift of righteousness. Though Habakkuk doesn't teach that the fulfillment of humanities covenant obligations will come from God directly, it does serve as a proof text that life before God is solely on the grounds of faith; it is then the OT support for Paul's claim that God's salvific

---

[28] Cranfield, *A Critical and Exegetical Commentary on the Epistle to the Romans: Commentary on Romans IX-XVI and Essays*, 2:100. Schreiner follows the general approach of Cranfield. Schreiner, *Romans*, 76.

[29] Moo, *The Epistle to the Romans*, 76–78. For Watts, Paul in quoting Habakkuk is confirming the trustworthiness of the revelation of his Gospel: as the Jews in Habakkuk's day would find life by the faithfulness of God's word, so now life is found in the Gospel as the expression of God's faithfulness. The quote also gives emphasis to the life that must result in response to this revelation. Our exegesis of Habakkuk argues against this interpretation, so we will not consider it in the above discussion. Rikki E. Watts, "'For I Am Not Ashamed of the Gospel': Romans 1:16-17 and Habakkuk 2:4," in *Romans and the People of God*, ed. Sven K. Soderlund and N.T. Wright (Grand Rapids: Eerdmans, 1999), 18–21.

[30] Contra Alice Ogden Bellis, "Habakkuk 2:4b: Intertextuality and Hermeneutics," in *Jews, Christians, and the Theology of the Hebrew Scriptures*, ed. Alice Ogden Bellis and Joel S. Kaminsky, SBL Symposium Series no. 8 (Atlanta, Ga.: Society of Biblical Literature, 2000), 369; Schlatter, *Romans*, 26.

provision is revealed completely by faith.[31]

This emphasis lines up with the rest of Romans and gains support from the context of judgment that verse 17 shares with Habakkuk 2:4. In Romans 1:18-3:20, all humanity is in the dock. Like the wicked of Judah in Habakkuk, they are found wanting. But like Habakkuk and those he represented who believed in God, those who believe in Jesus Christ will not only live through eschatological judgment but will also receive the promises of God in Christ—the life-before-God aspect of Habakkuk's "live by his faith," found throughout the Twelve in the promise of restoration.[32] This then provides the essential support for the whole of Romans. Paul exposits the gospel as the foundation for the Christian life lived completely by faith, with an emphasis on the obedience this faith will produce. Here in his thematic statement (1:16-17), Paul has summarized that faith is the means by which believers receive forgiveness of sins and favorable status within their covenant with God (God's power for salvation). 1:18-3:20 will show the universal need of this faith; 3:21-4:29 will show how Christ has provided salvation for those who believe; 5:1-11:36 will unpack how faith covers the whole of the Christian life and God's faithfulness in providing salvation; 12:1-16:27 will round off the letter with an application of the Gospel wrought obedience of faith to the situation of the Romans.

---

[31] It is helpful to note that Habakkuk actually leaves a deep tension: has God made the demands of His covenant lax, has He changed His character? Indeed, He has not; He has provided a way for humans to be right in Christ. Later in Romans, Gen 15:6 is Paul's main, though not exclusive, proof text for God's righteous provision. See the discussion of this passage below in Appendix 8.

[32] There are similarities between Paul's understanding of this text and that found in the later Talmud. The discussion found in Makkoth understands Habakkuk as narrowing the demands of the law to faith. Paul agrees that the one with faith will fulfill the law, but for him the demands of the law are as demanding as they ever were. For Paul, the impossible demands of the law were fulfilled by God in Christ on behalf of all those represented by Him in the New Covenant. The earlier Qumran Pesher Habakkuk understands the text to be fulfilled among those in the house of Judah who by their toil in observing the law and faith in the Teacher of Righteousness will be spared from the house of judgement (4QPHab VIII.1-2). Florentino García Martínez and Eibert J. C. Tigchelaar, *The Dead Sea Scrolls Study Edition (Translations)*, vol. 2 (Leiden; New York: Brill, 1997), 17; Florentino García Martínez and Eibert J. C. Tigchelaar, "The Dead Sea Scrolls Study Edition (Transcriptions)" (Leiden; New York, 1998 1997), 16; Rabbi Dr I. Epstein, ed., "Makkoth," in *Seder Nezikin*, trans. H. M. Lzarus, vol. 4, The Babylonian Talmud 13 (London, England: The Soncino Press, 1935), 169–173.

Conclusion

The purpose of this paper has been to elucidate Paul's use of Habakkuk 2:4 in the key thematic statement of Romans (1:16-17). Beginning with Habakkuk, careful attention to the context of 2:4 provided a reading of the text that made sense of the flow of Habakkuk's argument and the Masoretic text. In 2:4, Habakkuk provided the answer to the first of the questions arising from God's use of Chaldea in judgment—how a wicked nation could be the means of judging a more righteous one. The answer was a demonstration of those who are truly righteous, whom God would preserve: they were those who would not flee the coming judgment but would trust God for life. The faith of this remnant showed them to be those who were truly righteous, indeed it is by that faith that they would live before God—and therefore it is what has made them righteous (cf. Gen. 15:6). In the absence of an opportunity to visit, Paul writes to the Romans hundreds of years later to encourage them with the gospel towards the obedience of faith he hopes to inspire in person—an obedience primarily to be worked out in Jew-Gentile relations. The heart of his letter is God's saving gospel providing salvation attained by faith, which is the ground and motivation for the resulting life. His citation of Habakkuk 2:4 fits perfectly as he argues in favour of the primacy of faith for covenant life and escaping judgment.

APPENDIX 8– TOWARDS A BIBLICAL THEOLOGY OF IMPUTATION: A CONSIDERATION OF AN OLD TESTAMENT ROOT FOR CHRIST'S IMPUTED RIGHTEOUSNESS IN ROMANS[1]

This essay supplements the discussion in the commentary concerning the use of the Old Testament in the New Testament, Genesis 15 as it relates to Habakkuk 2:4, and the role of Habakkuk in the Biblical picture of justification.

Paul's Letter to the Romans is a treasure trove, a richly pastoral and theological letter that has fueled the fires of Christian thought for millennia. Among many of the doctrines espoused within Paul's grand exposition and defence of the gospel is justification, expounded in an effort to bring about the obedience of faith among the Romans (1:5). For 500 years, a key tenant of the Reformed understanding of justification has been Christs' imputed righteousness, yet as of late this doctrine has come under serious attack. N.T. Wright, along with dismissing the doctrine as confused nonsense,[2] attacks the 1st century foundation for imputed righteousness.[3] The purpose of this paper is, first, to show some of the contextual reasons for seeing imputed righteousness in Romans and, second, to look at Genesis 15:6 as an Old Testament proof text for God's righteousness given to those who believe. To do this, let us first look at the covenantal and redemptive historical nature of Romans and then turn to the contextual evidence for imputation in the

---

[1] This paper was originally published on Teleioteti.ca, 2018.

[2] Wright, *Justification*, 90–92; N.T. Wright, *Pauline Perspectives: Essays on Paul, 1978-2013* (Minneapolis, Minn.: Fortress, 2013), 432; N.T. Wright, *What Saint Paul Really Said: Was Paul of Tarsus the Real Founder of Christianity?* (Grand Rapids, Mich.; Cincinnati, Ohio: W.B. Eerdmans Pub.; Forward Movement Publications, 1997), 97–98.

[3] Wright, "Romans," 425.

argument of Romans. We will conclude with a look at the Old Testament foundation for imputation.

Covenant Fulfillment in the Letter to the Romans

It is fitting to start our investigation with the salutation of Romans. As with all of Paul's letters, the epistolary salutation opening Romans goes beyond merely a greeting: it is itself packed with theology and introduces much of what he will touch upon throughout the letter. In his greeting, we see Paul introduce the concept of covenant fulfillment that is woven through the rest of the letter.

That Paul is a covenant theologian has received more attention as of late through the work of N.T. Wright, but Wright's emphasis has been more on Paul as a 1st century Jew than on his continuity with the inherent story line of the Canonical Scriptures.[4] This narrative—the story unpacked across the canonical and covenantal structure of Scripture—invoked from the start of the letter, illumines much of what is to follow.[5] This story line begins, of

---

[4] All of Wrights works deal with this to some extent: *New Testament and the People of God* places Paul within the world of 1st century Judaism (for covenant, 260-262), *Climax of the Covenant* focuses on the covenant fulfillment in the NT. He is especially ardent in defending the covenantal nature of righteousness language. The focus on the narrative structure of covenant is found more within Reformed circles—such as Goldsworthy and Gentry—, with whom Wright has a lot of affinity—coming from an Anglican background. This distinction roughly accords with the two senses of "salvation history" described by Yarbrough. Wright, *The New Testament*; Wright, "Translating Δικαιοσύνη: A Response"; Wright, "Paul and the Patriarch: The Role of Abraham in Romans 4"; Gentry and Wellum, *Kingdom Through Covenant*; Goldsworthy, *According to Plan:The Unfolding of God in the Bible*; Yarbrough, "Paul and Salvation History."

[5] "canonical and covenantal" indicates that the story line of Scripture is not independent of its canonical structure and the covenantal framework through which the story of creation-fall-redemption-consummation unfolds. The Masoretic order of the Old Testament is to be preferred here, not only for the fact that it is explicitly mentioned in Scripture (Luke 24:14), but also the internal structural clues found within Scripture (2 Chron.-Matt., Prov.-Ruth, the Twelve) and the various pieces of historical evidence. Gentry & Wellum rightly emphasizes in interpretation what they call "covenantal epochs" (Old covenant or New Covenant) over, though not in exclusion from, direct literary context (such as the link between Proverbs and Ruth). Dunbar, "The Biblical Canon"; House, *Old Testament Theology*, 55; Gentry and Wellum, *Kingdom Through Covenant*, 95 nn.30, 135–138; Fuller, "The Form and

course, in Genesis. All of Scripture unpacks the anticipation found in the first three chapters of Genesis for restoration from the fall. When offered life or death, Adam and Eve chose rebellion. In doing so, they introduced death instead of eternal life to be lived in covenant relation with God, which was to be the enjoyment of creation as His representatives and children. They were exiled from the garden and cut off from Him, yet hope is introduced in the narrative with the promise of an offspring who will crush the head of the serpent (Gen 3:14, cf. Rom 16:20).

These themes of land (garden, promised land, new creation), offspring (offspring, great nation, David, Jesus), covenant (Adamic, Noachian, Abrahamic, Israeli, Davidic, Eternal), and sin are played out throughout the rest of the Bible. The whole of Genesis—referenced throughout Romans (Romans 4, 5:12-21, 8:18-25, 16:20)—anticipates God's answer to this problem. With each child born, there is an anticipation of the coming offspring; as humanity grows, the identity of the coming offspring is narrowed—Seth, Noah, Shem, Abraham—and then widened to a nation that will bring blessing to all the rest (Genesis 12:2-3). Yet all with whom God has a covenant fail their obligations. Adam eats of the fruit;[6] Noah gets drunk (9:21-28), and his family receives the same indictment as those before the flood (8:21); Abraham fails immediately his mission to be a blessing (12:17). So a tension builds throughout the story of Scripture: who will fulfill the covenant obligations God has imposed upon all humanity, who will crush the serpent and bring life, and how can God take upon Himself the punishment for His people's covenant failure—as is implied by Genesis 15 (cf. Jer 34:18-19)?[7] This tension is at its highest with the close of the Old Testament, as the people of God are still in exile (cf. 2 Chron 36:23 in the Hebrew canon).

With all this assumed, the New Testament introduces Jesus as the one will return the people from exile through a new exodus and fulfills all of God's promises (2 Cor 1:20). In the first few verses of Romans, Paul introduces these themes by describing his Gospel as what God has promised in Scripture fulfilled through his Son (1:1-3). Particularly, it is fulfilled through Jesus as the descendant of David and so the Christ, the Messiah (v. 1, 3).[8]

Formation of the Book of the Twelve: The Evidence from the Judean Desert."

[6] There is much debate over a covenant with Adam. Cf. Hosea 6:7, Jer. 33:19-26, and Gentry and Wellum, *Kingdom Through Covenant*, 177–221.

[7] Ibid., 247–258.

[8] Cf. Wright, "Romans," 415.

This is bookended with the fulfillment of Genesis 3:14 by the Church in Christ promised in Romans 16:20. Paul's use of Genesis 15:6 as a proof text for justification fits into this covenantal story that Paul invokes. Turning now to the imputation, we will look at three areas of the letter that suggest the doctrine of imputed righteousness.

Imputed Righteousness in Romans

God's Righteousness as Imputed Righteousness in 1:16-17

Our first evidence for imputation in Romans is the words of verse 16 and γαϱ (*gar*, for) in verse 17; together, they demand that the nature of God's salvific power be explained as imputed righteousness. In verse 16 we read that God's power for the salvation of all peoples is the Gospel; we are then left with the question: how is the Gospel God's power? Γαϱ signals that an answer will follow, it begins an explanation of verse 16. We would not then expect verse 17 to be merely a declaration that God has acted, or that God is faithful, but also the means by which His righteous action saves. In light of the rest of Romans, we see that the gospel is God's power for salvation because it reveals what is available through faith: in the gospel, a person finds revealed God's righteousness made available entirely by faith so that the one who believes may have life. If "the righteousness of God" in verse 17 means merely God's righteous character, how it is God's power for salvation is implicit if not obscure. If it refers merely to God's action, we don't actually have an explanation: we are told that God has acted but not how that action saves us. But if it refers to all three, the Gospel is then God's power for salvation because in it we find revealed the true nature of God manifested in His saving action on the cross, making available for us His righteousness whereby we might have life.

The wording demands us to see in "the righteousness of God" not just God's character and His salvific act, but also the provision of righteousness as the means by which He saves. So the Gospel testifies to the provision God has made for our salvation and shows us how to receive that salvation; it is the *sine qua non* of salvation (Rom. 10:14-17)—showing for what we must believe along with in whom we must believe.

Imputation in Romans 1:18-3:20

The following section of the letter also supports this conclusion. Once we are told what that the righteousness of God is manifested from faith to faith for life, we are then given a further explanation in 1:18-3:20. Paul connects this section to what proceeds with γαρ (for); this section explains why the salvation found in the Gospel is necessary. Paul in these verses lays bare the dire state of the human race. Both Jews and Gentiles have fallen short of the glory of God and have shown themselves completely unable to attain to the righteous standard set by God: they will all face final judgment and be found wanting (2:12-16).[9]

As seen throughout Romans and the NT, God's saving action—salvation—is not just saving from judgment, but the positive gifting of a new creation free from the effects of the fall (e.g. Rom 8:18-30).[10] There is a problem though: every covenant in the Old Testament leaves the reader with a tension. God guarantees that His promises will be fulfilled, yet He requires His people to fulfill the condition of faithfulness to receive His promises. Therefore, Paul's exposition of the dire state of humanity can only be good news if somehow the demands of the covenant have been completely fulfilled on the behalf of those in the covenant. Verse 17 has said that God's salvation is completely by faith, so in this verse we find that the righteousness of God must include the meeting of the covenant demands attained by faith. Believers cannot be the ones meeting His demands because the following verses make explicit that none meet the standard God has set forth. If righteousness for human beings is our meeting the demands set forth for us in relationship with God—with the covenant obligations as the standard by which we are measured—, then somehow this righteousness must be attained for us apart from our own action—for we cannot meet these demands.

Imputation in the Argument of Romans 3:21-4:25

This brings us to our last evidence for imputation in Romans, the argument from 3:21 to 4:25. These verses presuppose, as does the rest of the book of Romans, that the human side of the covenant has been fulfilled, for believers are said to receive the promises made to Abraham by faith. Though God does promise that He will do these things for Abraham, great tension is created when God seems to require Abraham's obedience to receive the promises (Gen 17:1-14, 18:19, 26:1-5). Obedience is surely required for Israel

---

[9] This section is then an exposition of the depravity of man and their need for God's intervention. In support of this, especially in light of the story of Scripture, see ch. 1 of J. Alexander Rutherford, *Prevenient Grace: An Investigation into Arminianism* (Vancouver: Teleioteti, 2016).

[10] See my larger paper on the meaning of δικαιοσυνη θεου in Romans 1:17, available at www.teleioteti.ca/resources/papers.

to obtain the promises (E.g. Genesis 6, 15:25-26, 19:5-6, 23:23-33, Lev 26, Deut 3:26, 4:1-14, 25-26, 29-31, 40, 5:23-33, 8:19-20). What then has changed to take us from the great pessimism of 1:18-3:20 to the great optimism found throughout the rest of Romans?

We read in 3:21-22 that God has made manifest "the righteousness of God through faith in Jesus Christ for all who believe." In verse 23 this is linked to 1:18-3:20 by stating that this universal application (for all who believe) is based on a universal need. God righteousness is manifest through faith because all have a need, for all sin. To be right in the final judgment and to receive God's promises, all humanity needs the forgiveness of sins *and* the fulfillment of the covenant obligations—obligations that are only stricter under the new covenant (e.g. Matt 5-7). So we read that by grace, those who believe are justified as a gift (v. 24). In chapter 5 we are told that Christ died for the ungodly (v. 6, cf. 4:5) so that those who believe may receive the free gift of righteousness and so receive eternal life—the reception of God's covenant promises which require obedience (5:16-21).[11] Jumping back to chapter 4, this is what we see Paul arguing.

What is it that we may say that Abraham has found (i.e. attained, v. 1)?[12] Though Abraham failed his covenant obligations from the beginning (Gen 12:10-20), He found a righteousness from God. God declared him righteous and so promised him the rewards of perfect covenant obedience—the promise of land and offspring in relationship with God. So God has all along had a plan to fulfill the covenant on behalf of his people (cf. Gen 15:7-21), Abraham discovered this through faith and now the gentiles have been included. We see the fulfillment of God's plan in that Jesus fulfilled the covenant obligations as the new and final Adam. Through his resurrection,

---

[11] Cf. the discussion of the free gift in Rutherford, *Prevenient Grace*, 82–88.

[12] Contra Wright, though his translation of this verse may have some merit, and if adopted, would only slightly change the emphasis found in the above reading. Contextually though, this author prefers to read ευρισκω as gained or attained—maybe with connotations of discovery—, a meaning elsewhere attested (e.g. Matt 10:39, Heb. 12:17[?]). Wright, "Paul and the Patriarch: The Role of Abraham in Romans 4," esp. 225. Johannes P. Louw and Eugene Albert Nida, *Greek-English Lexicon of the New Testament: Based on Semantic Domains*, electronic ed. of the 2nd edition. (New York, N.Y.: United Bible Societies, 1996), sec. 13.17; Henry George Liddell et al., *A Greek-English Lexicon* (Oxford: Clarendon, 1996), 729; Frederick W. Danker, *A Greek-English Lexicon of the New Testament and Other Early Christian Literature*, 3rd ed. (Chicago: University of Chicago Press, 2000), 412.

He was declared righteous and so vindicated. Therefore, He is the only perfect substitutionary sacrifice and covenant keeper, whose faithfulness results in a declaration of righteousness then received by those who are in Him.[13]

Therefore, there is a strong warrant for finding the doctrine of imputation in Romans. But, as noted above, Wright has argued that imputation is foreign to the worldview of 1st century Jews and so could not be taught by Paul. It is to the Old Testament foundation for imputation, and so the answer to Wright's objection, that we must now turn.

Genesis 15:6 as an Old Testament Root for the Doctrine of Imputation

Our answer to Wright's objection has already been foreshadowed by our previous discussions. It may be very true that Paul's understanding has no ground in 1st century Judaism, but that does not mean that he could not have taught it. To argue this way would be to make the fallacious leap from the truth that in some way Paul was a 1st century Jew to the supposition that Paul was *merely* a 1st century Jew, that is, that all his thought categories must be explained by this background. Paul was in some ways a 1st century Jew, but he was also a student of the Bible and a Christian. If Paul's Jewish background fails to yield an adequate precursor to his understanding of imputation, we can still look at the Old Testament as his source or the teachings of Jesus or the Spirit—that is, allow that God could have revealed something not yet seen.

Fortunately, we have already begun to see that there is a strong OT precedence for imputation. As noted above, God promises frequently that He will end sin (Gen. 3:15), that He will restore relationship with Him in a

---

[13] Cf. the emphasis throughout Scripture on being in Christ for the receiving of the inheritance and adoption (e.g. Eph. 1). Piper has a helpful discussion on imputation in Romans 4, Beale on the necessity and implications of Christ's resurrection for our justification—cf. Wright. John Piper, *Counted Righteous in Christ: Should We Abandon the Imputation of Christ's Righteousness?* (Wheaton: Crossway Books, 2002), 57–60; G. K. Beale, "The Role of the Resurrection in the Already-and-Not-Yet Phases of Justification," in *For the Fame of God's Name: Essays in Honor of John Piper*, ed. Sam Storms and Justin Taylor (Wheaton: Crossway, 2010); N.T. Wright, *Paul and the Faithfulness of God*, vol. II, Christian Origins and the Question of God 4 (Minneapolis, Minn.: Fortress, 2013), 943.

new land (Gen 12:1-9, 17:8); but He expects obedience from His covenant partners. A great tension arises, how can God maintain a promise that depends on the obedience of those who are by nature disobedient? This is where Paul's favorite Genesis quote is central; Abraham's faith was reckoned as righteousness (Gen 15:6). In this text, after the narrator tells us that Abraham's belief that God would indeed be faithful to His promises was reckoned for righteousness, this vague statement is unpacked. God, in verse 7, reaffirms his promise, but Abraham in verse 8 responds with what almost appears to be doubt; "how am I to know that I shall possess it?" What happened to his faith; does he now doubt God's ability to fulfill his promise?

Abraham is not looking for a sign that God can fulfill His promise; he has already expressed faith that God can. If we are already told that Abraham is assured of God's faithfulness (v. 6), the only room left for doubt is in Abraham's ability to uphold his side of the bargain. This is exactly what the following verses address. God leads Abraham through the covenant making ceremony, one involving a self-maledictory oath (that covenant failure will result in the death of the one who fails) (9-11, cf. Jer 34:18-19), yet when the time comes for both covenant makers to walk through and affirm their obligations, it is God alone who walks through in a fiery theophany (v. 17). In verse 18 God then affirms that He will indeed give the land to Abraham's offspring. So we see that the answer to Abraham's question has been given. What was it? Because only God walked through the line of severed animals, He is saying that He will take upon Himself not only the penalty of His hypothetical covenant failure but also the failure of His covenant partner. YHWH is also affirming that all obligations placed on Abraham will find their fulfillment by His hand. This leaves another unresolved tension through the OT: how can God Himself die for the covenant failure of men?[14] Both of these commitments then find their resolution in Jesus Christ who died for the sins of man and, as the new Adam, did what Adam and Abraham could not: He perfectly fulfilled God's covenant obligations so that all those found in Him might receive the fullness of God's covenant blessing. If this interpretation is accurate, the Old Testament gives a background for the doctrine of Imputation—even though Paul's Jewish background does not.[15]

---

[14] Cf. the discussion in Gentry and Wellum, *Kingdom Through Covenant*, 248–258; Stephen G. Dempster, *Dominion and Dynasty: A Biblical Theology of the Hebrew Bible*, New Studies in Biblical Theology 15 (Leicester: Downers Grove: Apollos; InterVarsity, 2003), 80.

[15] Though not discussed in this paper, Habakkuk 2:4 presents a vital pathway

Excurse: Is Imputation Confused Nonsense?

What about Wright's claim that imputation is confused nonsense?[16] Wright explains the Jewish law court as a basic setup featuring a plaintiff, defendant, and judge. Within this law-court, a righteous status for the plaintiff or defendant is to have the courts rule in their favour, for the judge it is judge rightly.[17] For Wright, it is then a category error for the judge to give his righteousness to the plaintiff or defendant: the "righteousness" in each case is a completely different thing.[18] Though there has often been great confusion in the language used to describe imputation, not all accounts of imputation fall prey to this criticism.

For imputation to make sense, both the covenantal and law court imagery of righteousness must be kept in view. We saw earlier that humanity needs both the forgiveness of sins—law court imagery—and right covenant standing to inherit God's promises; imputation explains the latter (though probably still within the forensic sphere). From 1:18-3:20, we see that man is in the dock. Considering the legal need, God as a judge must rightly render the verdict against sinful humanity: He would be unrighteous to ignore their sins. So Jesus died for the sins of men and women so that He may be just *and* the justifier of the ungodly (3:25-26).

Turning from the law court, in which we no longer have an accuser (8:33-34), the covenantal imagery makes sense of imputation. Imputation is not receiving Christ's righteousness in the sense of the right judging character of a just judge. Imputation speaks of receiving His righteousness as He who is fully God, able to fulfill God's commitment in Genesis 15, and fully man, able to step in and lead a renewed humanity as the new Adam and covenant head. Jesus' righteousness is then the righteousness of a covenant head, like Abraham and Adam, who has perfectly kept His covenant obligations. Christians are those whom He represents in covenant relationship and imputation is the reception of the benefits of His covenant faithfulness: because He fulfilled the covenant obligations on our behalf, we can receive God's promise of land (New Creation) and, more so, relationship with Him.

---

between Gen. 15:6 and God's provision of righteousness in Romans.

[16] Wright, *Justification*, 90–92; Wright, *Pauline Perspectives: Essays on Paul, 1978-2013*, 432; Wright, *What Saint Paul Really Said*, 97–98.

[17] Wright, *What Saint Paul Really Said*, 97–98; Tom Wright et al., *The Great Acquittal: Justification by Fatih and Current Christian Thought*, ed. Gavin Reid (London, England: Fount Paperbacks, 1980), 14–15.

[18] Wright, *What Saint Paul Really Said*, 98; Wright, *Justification*, 90–92.

From what we have seen, Paul in Romans teaches that God's salvific act revealed in the Gospel involves the provision of righteousness through Christ to those who believe. Furthermore, we have seen that this doctrine is not without OT precedence: Genesis 15:6 and the tension found throughout the Biblical storyline anticipate this doctrine. Given more space, Paul's quote of Habakkuk 2:4 in 1:17 could be shown to support this. Habakkuk anticipates this when he speaks of the righteous one living before God by faith, but only in Christ do we see the fullness of how this works. God has not changed and lowered His covenant demands; He has become a man to fulfill them. Because this righteousness comes by faith through union with Christ, the fullness of the Christian life—salvation and the resultant behaviour—is grounded in faith, as Paul argues with Habakkuk 2:4.

BIBLIOGRAPHY

Alter, Robert. *The Art of Biblical Poetry*. New York: Basic Books, 1985.

Andersen, Francis I., ed. *Habakkuk: A New Translation with Introduction and Commentary*. 1st ed. Anchor Bible 25. New York: Doubleday, 2001.

Armerding, Carl E. "Habakkuk." In *The Expositor's Bible Commentary: With the New International Version; Daniel and the Minor Prophets*, edited by Frank E. Gaebelein. Vol. 7. Grand Rapids: Zondervan, 1985.

Baker, David W. *Nahum, Habakkuk and Zephaniah: An Introduction and Commentary*. Tyndale Old Testament Commentaries 27. Nottingham; Downers Grove: Inter-Varsity Press; IVP Academic, 2009.

Barker, Kenneth L., and D. Waylon Bailey. *Micah, Nahum, Habakkuk, Zephaniah*. The New American Commentary 20. Nashville: Broadman & Holman, 1999.

Barr, James. *The Semantics of Biblical Language*. Oxford: Oxford University Press, 1961.

Barré, Michael L. "Newly Discovered Literary Devices in the Prayer of Habakkuk." *The Catholic Biblical Quarterly* 75 (2013): 446–462.

Bartlett, David L. *Romans*. First edition. Westminster Bible Companion. Louisville: Westminster John Knox, 1995.

Beale, G. K., ed. *The Right Doctrine From the Wrong Texts? Essays on the Use of the Old Testament in the New*. Grand Rapids: Baker Books, 1994.

———. "The Role of the Resurrection in the Already-and-Not-Yet Phases of Justification." In *For the Fame of God's Name: Essays in Honor of John Piper*, edited by Sam Storms and Justin Taylor. Wheaton: Crossway, 2010.

Beckwith, Roger T. *The Old Testament Canon of the New Testament Church and Its Background in Early Judaism*. Grand Rapids: Eerdmans, 1986.

Bellis, Alice Ogden. "Habakkuk 2:4b: Intertextuality and Hermeneutics." In *Jews, Christians, and the Theology of the Hebrew Scriptures*, edited by Alice Ogden Bellis and Joel S. Kaminsky. SBL Symposium Series no. 8. Atlanta, Ga.: Society of Biblical Literature, 2000.

Ben Zvi, Ehud. "Twelve Prophetic Books or 'The Twelve': A Few Preliminary Considerations." In *Forming Prophetic Literature: Essays on Isaiah and the Twelve in Honor of John D.W. Watts*, edited by James W. Watts and Paul R. House, 125–156. Journal for the Study of the Old Testament Supplement 235. Sheffield, England: Sheffield Academic Press, 1996.

Berlin, Adele. *The Dynamics of Biblical Parallelism*. Bloomington: Indiana University Press, 1985.

Blaising, Craig A., and Darrell L. Bock. *Progressive Dispensationalism*. Grand Rapids: Bridgepoint Books, 2000.

Boda, Mark J. "A Deafening Call to Silence: The Rhetorical 'End' of Human Address to the Deity in the Book of the Twelve." In *New Form Criticism and the Book of the Twelve*, edited by Mark J. Boda, Michael H. Floyd, and Colin M. Toffelmire. Ancient Near East Monographs 10. Atlanta: SBL Press, 2015.

Boice, James Montgomery. *The Minor Prophets: An Expositional Commentary*. Vol. 2. 2 vols. Grand Rapids: Zondervan, 1986.

Bomgaars, Dennis Leroy. "Habakkuk: Some Introductory and Literary Issues." Master's Thesis, Reformed Theological Seminary, 1984.

Brannan, Rick, Ken M. Penner, Israel Loken, Michael Aubrey, and Isaiah Hoogendyk, eds. *The Lexham English Septuagint*. Bellingham, Wash.: Lexham Press, 2012.

Bratcher, Dennis Ray. "The Theological Message of Habakkuk: A Literary-Rhetorical Analysis." Doctoral Dissertation, Union Theological Seminary, 1984.

Brown, Francis, S. R Driver, Charles A Briggs, James Strong, and Wilhelm Gesenius. *The Brown-Driver-Briggs Hebrew and English Lexicon*. Peabody: Hendrickson, 1996.

Brown, WIlliam P. *Obadiah through Malachi*. Louisville: Westminster John Knox, 1996.

Brownlee, W.H. *The Text of Habakkuk in the Ancient Commentary from Qumran*. Journal of Biblical literature: Monograph series. Society of Biblical Literature and Exegesis, 1959.

Brownlee, William Hugh, ed. *The Midrash Pesher of Habakkuk*. Monograph series - Society of Biblical Literature ; no. 24. Missoula, Mont.: Scholars Press, 1979.

Bruce, F. F. "Habakkuk." In *The Minor Prophets: An Exegetical and Expository Commentary*, edited by Thomas Edward McComiskey. Grand Rapids: Baker Book House, 1992.

Calvin, John. *Commentaries on the Twelve Minor Prophtes; Habakkuk, Zephaniah, Haggai, Zechariah, Malachi*. Translated by John Owen. Vol. 4. Calvin's Commentaries XV. Grand Rapids: Baker, 1996.

―――. *Daniel I: Chapters 1-6*. Translated by T. H. L Parker. Vol. 1. 2 vols. Calvin's Old Testament Commentaries 20. Grand Rapids: Eerdmans, 1993.

Campbell, Douglas A. "The Meaning of Δικαιοσύνη Θεοῦ in Romans: An Intertextual Suggestion." In *As It Is Written: Studying Paul's Use of Scripture*, edited by Stanley E. Porter and Christopher D. Stanley, 189–212. Society of Biblical Literature Symposium series 50. Atlanta, Ga.: Society of Biblical Literature, 2008.

Carson, D. A. *Exegetical Fallacies*. Grand Rapids: Baker Books, 1996.

Carson, D. A., and John D. Woodbridge, eds. *Hermeneutics, Authority, and Canon*. Grand Rapids: Academie Books, 1986.

―――, eds. *Scripture and Truth*. Grand Rapids: Baker Book House, 1992.

Cathcart, Kevin J., and Robert P. Gordon, trans. *The Targum of the Minor Prophets*. The Aramaic Bible 14. Wilmington, Del.: Michael Glazier, Inc., 1989.

Chisholm, Robert B. *Interpreting the Minor Prophets*. Grand Rapids: Zondervan, 1990.

Clark, David J., and Howard Hatton. *A Translator's Handbook on the Books of Nahum, Habakkuk, and Zephaniah*. Helps for translators. New York, N.Y.: United Bible Societies, 1989.

Cleaver-Bartholomew, David. "An Alternative Reading of Hab 1 and 2." *Proceedings, Eastern Great Lakes and Midwest Bible Societies* 24 (2004): 45–59.

Clendenen, E Ray. "Salvation by Faith or by Faithfulness in the Book of Habakkuk?" *Bulletin for Biblical Research* 24, no. 4 (2014): 505–513.

Clines, David J. A., ed. *The Dictionary of Classical Hebrew*. Vol. 6. Sheffield, England: Sheffield Academic Press, 1993.

———, ed. *The Dictionary of Classical Hebrew*. Vol. 1. Sheffield, England: Sheffield Academic Press, 1993.

———, ed. *The Dictionary of Classical Hebrew*. Vol. 5. Sheffield, England: Sheffield Academic Press, 2001.

———, ed. *The Dictionary of Classical Hebrew*. Vol. 7. Sheffield, England: Sheffield Phoenix Press, 2011.

Craigie, P.C. *Psalms 1-50, Volume 19: Second Edition*. Edited by M. Tate, B.M. Metzger, D.A. Hubbard, G.W. Barker, J.D.W. Watts, J.W. Watts, R.P. Martin, and L.A. Losie. Electronic. Word Biblical Commentary. Grand Rapids: Zondervan, 2018.

Cranfield, C. E. B. *A Critical and Exegetical Commentary on the Epistle to the Romans: Commentary on Romans IX-XVI and Essays*. Vol. 2. 2 vols. ICC. Edinburgh: T&T Clark LTD, 1975.

Craven, T. "Habakkuk 1:1-11." *Interpretation* 61, no. 4 (October 1, 2007): 418–420.

Culver, Robert D. "Ḥāzâ." Edited by R. Laird Harris, Archer Jr. Gleason L., and Bruce K. Waltke. *Theological Wordbook of the Old Testament*. Chicago: The Moody Bible Institute, 1980.

Danker, Frederick W. *A Greek-English Lexicon of the New Testament and Other Early Christian Literature*. 3rd ed. Chicago: University of Chicago Press, 2000.

Dean, David Andrew. "The Use of Habakkuk 2:4 in the New Testament (Romans 1:17, Galatians 3:11, and Hebrews 10:38)." Ph.D., Dallas Theological Seminary, 2008.

Dempsey, Carol J. "Harrowing Woes and Comforting Promises in the Book of the Twelve." In *New Form Criticism and the Book of the Twelve*, edited by Mark J. Boda, Michael H. Floyd, and Colin M. Toffelmire. Ancient Near East Monographs 10. Atlanta: SBL Press, 2015.

Dempster, Stephen G. "An 'Extraordinary Fact': Torah and Temple and the Contours of the Hebrew Canon Part 1." *Tyndale Bulletin* 48, no. 1 (1997): 23–56.

———. "An 'Extraordinary Fact': Torah and Temple and the Contours of the Hebrew Canon Part 2." *Tyndale Bulletin* 48, no. 2 (1997): 191–218.

———. *Dominion and Dynasty: A Biblical Theology of the Hebrew Bible*. New Studies in Biblical Theology 15. Leicester: Downers Grove: Apollos; InterVarsity, 2003.

———. "From Many Texts to One: The Formation of the Hebrew Bible." In *The World of the Aramaeans*, edited by P. M. Michèle Daviau, John William Wevers, Michael Weigl, and Paul-Eugène Dion. Journal for the Study of the Old Testament 324–326. Sheffield: Sheffield Academic Press, 2001.

———. "The Prophets, the Canon and a Canonical Approach: No Empty Word." In *Canon and Biblical Interpretation*, edited by Craig G. Bartholomew, Scott Hahn, Robin Parry, Christopher Seitz, and Al Wolters, 293–332. Scripture and Hermeneutics Series v. 7. Grand Rapids: Zondervan, 2006.

DiMattei, Steven. "Biblical Narratives." In *As It Is Written: Studying Paul's Use of Scripture*, edited by Stanley E. Porter and Christopher D. Stanley, 59–96. Society of Biblical Literature Symposium series 50. Atlanta, GA.: Society of Biblical Literature, 2008.

Dockery, David S. "The Use of Hab. 2:4 in Rom. 1:17: Some Hermeneutical and Theological Considerations." *Wesleyan Theological Journal* (October 1, 1987).

Dumbrell, W. J. *Covenant and Creation: A Theology of Old Testament Covenants*. Exeter, Devon; New South Wales: Paternoster; Lancer Books, 1984.

Dunbar, David G. "The Biblical Canon." In *Hermeneutics, Authority, and Canon*, edited by D. A. Carson and John D. Woodbridge. Grand Rapids: Academie Books, 1986.

Dunn, James D. G. *Romans 1-8*. Word Biblical Commentary. Dallas, Tex.: Word Books, 1988.

Dunson, B. C. "Faith in Romans : The Salvation of the Individual or Life in Community?" *Journal for the Study of the New Testament* 34, no. 1 (2011): 19–46.

Dyck, Elmer H. "Canon and Interpretation: Recent Canonical Approaches and the Book of Jonah." Doctoral Dissertation, McGill University, 1986.

Edwards, James R. *Romans*. Edited by W. Ward Gasque. New International Biblical Commentary 6. Peabody, Mass: Hendrickson, 1992.

Ego, Beate. "The Repentance of Nineveh in the Story of Jonah and Nahum's Prophecy of the City's Destruction - A Coherent Reading of the Book of the Twelve as Reflected in the Aggada." In *Thematic Threads in the Book of the Twelve*, edited by Paul L. Redditt and Aaron Schart, 155–164. Berlin, Germany: Walter de Gruyter GmbH & Co., 2003.

Emerton, J. A. "The Textual and Linguistic Problems of Habakkuk II. 4–5." *Journal of theological studies* XXVIII, no. 1 (1977): 1–18.

Epstein, Rabbi Dr I., ed. "Makkoth." In *Seder Nezikin*, translated by H. M. Lzarus. Vol. 4. The Babylonian Talmud 13. London, England: The Soncino Press, 1935.

Evans, Craig A., and James A. Sanders, eds. *Paul and the Scriptures of Israel*. Journal for the study of the New Testament 83. Sheffield, England: JSOT Press, 1993.

Everson, A. Joseph. "The Canonical Location of Habakkuk." In *Thematic Threads in the Book of the Twelve*, edited by Paul L. Redditt and Aaron Schart, 165–174. Berlin, Germany: Walter de Gruyter GmbH & Co., 2003.

Fee, Gordon D., and Douglas K. Stuart. *How to Read the Bible for All Its Worth*. 3rd ed. Grand Rapids: Zondervan, 2003.

Fitzmyer, Joseph A. *The Aramaic Inscriptions of Sefire*. Biblica Et Orientalia 19. Rome: Pontifical Biblical Institute, 1967.

Floyd, Michael H. *Minor Prophets. Part 2*. The Forms of the Old Testament literature v. 22. Grand Rapids: Eerdmans, 2000.

Fokkelman, J.P. *Reading Biblical Poetry: An Introductory Guide*. Translated by Ineke Smit. First edition. Louisville: Westminster John Knox, 2001.

Frame, John M. *The Doctrine of God*. A Theology of Lordship. Phillipsburg: P&R Publishing, 2002.

———. *The Doctrine of the Knowledge of God*. A Theology of Lordship. Phillipsburg: P&R Publishing, 1987.

———. *The Doctrine of the Word of God*. A Theology of Lordship. Phillipsburg: P&R Publishing, 2010.

Freedman, David Noel. "Another Look at Biblical Hebrew Poetry." In *Directions in Biblical Hebrew Poetry*, edited by Elaine R. Follis. Journal for the Study of the Old Testament 40. Sheffield: JSOT Press, 1987.

———. "Pottery, Poetry, and Prophecy." In *Pottery, Poetry, and Prophecy:*

Studies in Early Hebrew Poetry, 1–22. Winona Lake, Ind.: Eisenbrauns, 1980.

———. "The Broken Construct Chain." In *Pottery, Poetry, and Prophecy: Studies in Early Hebrew Poetry*, 339–342. Winona Lake, Ind.: Eisenbrauns, 1980.

Freeman, Hobart E. *Nahum, Zephaniah, Habakkuk; Minor Prophets of the Seventh Century B.C.* Everyman's Bible commentary. Chicago: Moody Press, 1973.

Fuller, Russell. "The Form and Formation of the Book of the Twelve: The Evidence from the Judean Desert." In *Forming Prophetic Literature: Essays on Isaiah and the Twelve in Honor of John D.W. Watts*, edited by James W. Watts and Paul R. House, 86–101. Journal for the Study of the Old Testament Supplement 235. Sheffield, England: Sheffield Academic Press, 1996.

Futato, Mark D. "Ezra-Nehemiah." In *A Biblical-Theological Introduction to the Old Testament: The Gospel Promised*, edited by Miles Van Pelt. Wheaton: Crossway, 2016.

García Martínez, Florentino, and Eibert J. C. Tigchelaar. "The Dead Sea Scrolls Study Edition (Transcriptions)." Leiden; New York, 1998 1997.

———. *The Dead Sea Scrolls Study Edition (Translations)*. Vol. 2. 2 vols. Leiden; New York: Brill, 1997.

Gentry, Peter J., and Stephen J. Wellum. *Kingdom Through Covenant: A Biblical-Theological Understanding of the Covenants*. Wheaton, Ill: Crossway, 2012.

Gentry, Peter John, and Stephen J. Wellum. *Kingdom through Covenant: A Biblical-Theological Understanding of the Covenants*. Wheaton: Crossway, 2012.

Gesenius, Friedrich Wilhelm. *Gesenius' Hebrew Grammar*. Edited by E. Kautzsch and Sir Arthur Ernest Cowley. 2d English ed. Clarendon, 1910.

Gesenius, Wilhelm. *Gesenius' Hebrew and Chaldee Lexicon to the Old Testament Scriptures*. Translated by Samuel Prideaux Tregelles. Bellingham, WA: Logos Bible Software, 2003.

Godfrey, Robert W. "Biblical Authority in the Sixteenth and Seventeenth Centuries: A Question of Transition." In *Scripture and Truth*, edited by D. A. Carson and John D. Woodbridge. Grand Rapids: Baker, 1992.

Goldingay, John, and Pamela J Scalise. *Minor Prophets II*. Peabody: Hendrickson, 2009.

Goldsworthy, Graeme. *According to Plan:The Unfolding of God in the Bible*. Leicester, England: Inter-Varsity Press, 1991.

———. *Gospel-Centered Hermeneutics: Foundations and Principles of Evangelical Biblical Interpretation*. Downers Grove: InterVarsity Press, 2006.

Graham, William Creighton. "A Note on Habakkuk 2:4-5." *The American Journal of Semitic Languages and Literatures* 42, no. 2 (1926): 128–129.

Gruenthaner, Michael J. "Chaldeans or Macedonians?: A Recent Theory on the Prophecy of Habakkuk (1)." *Biblica* 8, no. 2 (April 1927): 129–160.

Haak, Robert D. *Habakkuk*. Supplements to the Vetus Testamentum XLIV. Leiden: E.J. Brill, 1992.

Hailey, Homer. *A Commentary on the Minor Prophets*. Grand Rapids, Mich.: Baker Book House, 1972.

Henderson, Ebenezer. *The Twelve Minor Prophets*. Grand Rapids: Baker, 1980.

Henry, Matthew. *Matthew Henry's Commentary on the Whole Bible: Complete and Unabridged in One Volume*. Peabody, Mass.: Hendrickson, 1994.

Hiebert, Theodore. *God of My Victory: The Ancient Hymn in Habakkuk 3*. Edited by Frank Moore Cross. Harvard Semitic Monographs 38. Atlanta: Scholars Press, 1986.

———. "The Book of Habakkuk." In *The New Interpreter's Bible*, edited by Leander E. Keck and et al. Vol. VII. Nashville: Abingdon Press, 1996.

———. "The Use of Inclusion in Habakkuk 3." In *Directions in Biblical Hebrew Poetry*, edited by Elaine R. Follis. Journal for the Study of the Old Testament 40. Sheffield: JSOT Press, 1987.

Hill, Andrew E., and John H. Walton. *A Survey of the Old Testament*. 2nd ed. Grand Rapids: Zondervan Publishing House, 2000.

Holt, John Marshall. "So He May Run Who Reads It." *Journal of Biblical Literature* 83, no. 3 (September 1964): 298–302.

Horgan, Maurya P. *Pesharim: Qumran Interpretations of Biblical Books*. The Catholic Biblical Quarterly Monograph Series 8. Washington, D.C.: THe Catholic Biblical Association of America, 1979.

Hornkohl, Aaron. "Periodization." In *Encyclopedia of Hebrew Language and Linguistics: Volume 1; A-F*, edited by Geoffrey Khan. Vol. 1. Leiden;

Boston: Brill, 2013.

House, Paul R. *Old Testament Theology*. Downers Grove, Ill.: InterVarsity Press, 1998.

———. "The Character of God in the Book of the Twelve." In *Reading and Hearing the Book of the Twelve*, edited by James Nogalski and Marvin A. Sweeney. SBL Symposium Series no. 15. Atlanta, Ga.: Society of Biblical Literature, 2000.

———. *The Unity of the Twelve*. Edited by David J.A. Clines and Philip R. Davies. Bible and Literature 27. Sheffield, England: The Almond Press, 1990.

Hunn, Debbie. "Habakkuk 2.4b in Its Context: How Far off Was Paul?" *Journal for the Study of the Old Testament* 34, no. 2 (December 2009): 219–239.

Ito, Akio. "The Written Torah and the Oral Gospel: Romans 10:5-13 in the Dynamic Tension Between Orality and Literacy." *Novum testamentum* 48, no. 3 (2006): 234–260.

Janzen, J Gerald. "Eschatological Symbol and Existence in Habakkuk." *The Catholic Biblical Quarterly* 44, no. 3 (July 1982): 394–414.

Janzen, J. Gerald. "Habakkuk 2:2-4 in the Light of Recent Philological Advances." *Harvard Theological Review* 73 (1980): 53–78.

Johnson, Marshall D. "The Paralysis of Torah in Habakkuk 1:4." *Vetus Testamentum* 35, no. 3 (July 1985): 257–266.

Joosten, Jan. "The Distinction Between Classical and Late Biblical Hebrew as Reflected in Syntax." *Hebrew Studies* 46 (2005): 327–339.

Josephus, Flavius. "Against Apion." In *The Works of Josephus: Complete and Unabridged*, translated by William Whiston. Peabody, Mass.: Hendrickson, 1987.

Käsemann, Ernst. *Commentary on Romans*. Translated by Geoffrey William Bromiley. Grand Rapids, Mich: Eerdmans, 1980.

Keil, C.F., and F. Delitzsch. *Commentary on the Old Testament in Ten Volumes: Minor Prophets; Two Volumes in One*. Translated by James Martin. Reprint. Vol. 10.2. 10 vols. Grand Rapids: Eerdmans, 1978.

Keller, Timothy. *Center Church: Doing Balanced, Gospel-Centered Ministry in Your City*. Grand Rapids: Zondervan, 2012.

Kidner, Derek. *Tyndale Old Testament Commentaries : The Proverbs*. Downers Grove, Ill.: InterVarsity Press, 1983.

Kleinert, Paul. "The Book of Habakkuk." In *The Minor Prophets: Exegetically, Theologically, and Homiletically Expounded*, edited by Johann Peter Lange and Philip Schaff, translated by Charles Elliott. New York: Scribner, 1874.

Kline, Meredith G. "Kingdom Prologue," 1993.

Koehler, Ludwig, Walter Baumgartner, M. E. J. Richardson, and Johann Jakob Stamm. *The Hebrew and Aramaic Lexicon of the Old Testament*. Electronic ed. Leiden; New York: Brill, 1999.

Kraus, Wolfgang. "Hab 2:3- in the Hebrew, Septuagint, and New Testament." In *Septuagint and Reception: Essays Prepared for the Association for the Study of the Septuagint in South Africa*, edited by Johann Cook. Supplements to the Vetus Testamentum v. 127. Leiden ; Boston: Brill, 2009.

Kruse, Colin G. *Paul, the Law, and Justification*. Peabody: Hendrickson, 1997.

———. *Paul's Letter to the Romans*. The Pillar New Testament Commentary. Grand Rapids, Mich.: WM. B. Eerdmans Publishing Co., 2012.

Kugel, James L. *The Idea of Biblical Poetry: Parallelism and Its History*. New Haven: Yale University Press, 1981.

Lenski, R. C. H. *The Interpretation of the Acts of the Apostles*. Augsburg Publishing House, 1961.

Liddell, Henry George, Robert Scott, Henry Stuart Jones, and Roderick McKenzie. *A Greek-English Lexicon*. Oxford: Clarendon, 1996.

Lints, Richard. *The Fabric of Theology: A Prolegomenon to Evangelical Theology*. Grand Rapids: Eerdmans, 1993.

Lloyd-Jones, D. Martin. *From Fear to Faith: Studies in the Book of Habakkuk*. London: Inter-Varsity Press, 1970.

Long, V. Philips. "1 and 2 Samuel." In *Zondervan Illustrated Bible Background Commentary: Old Testament: Volume 2, Joshua, Judges, Ruth, 1 and 2 Samuel*, edited by John H. Walton. Vol. 2. Grand Rapids: Zondervan, 2009.

Louw, Johannes P., and Eugene Albert Nida. *Greek-English Lexicon of the New Testament: Based on Semantic Domains*. Electronic ed. of the 2nd edition. New York, N.Y.: United Bible Societies, 1996.

Lugt, Pieter van der. *Cantos and Strophes in Biblical Hebrew Poetry: With Special Reference to the First Book of the Psalter*. Vol. I. 3 vols. Oudtestamentische studiën 53. Leiden; Boston: Brill, 2006.

Lust, Johan, Erik Eynikel, and Katrin Hauspie. *A Greek-English Lexicon of the Septuagint: Revised Edition*. Deutsche Bibelgesellschaft: Stuttgart, 2003.

Martínez, Florentino García, and Eibert J. C. Tigchelaar. *The Dead Sea Scrolls: Study Edition (1Q1-4Q273)*. Vol. 1. 2 vols. Leiden: Brill, 1997.

McComiskey, Thomas Edward, ed. *The Minor Prophets: An Exegetical and Expository Commentary*. Grand Rapids, Mich: Baker Book House, 1992.

McConville, Gordon. "Old Testament Laws and Canonical Intentionality." In *Canon and Biblical Interpretation*, edited by Craig G. Bartholomew, Scott Hahn, Robin Parry, Christopher Seitz, and Al Wolters, 259–281. Scripture and Hermeneutics Series v. 7. Grand Rapids: Zondervan, 2006.

Moo, Douglas J. *Galatians*. Baker Exegetical Commentary on the New Testament. Grand Rapids: Baker Academic, 2013.

———. *The Epistle to the Romans*. NICNT. Grand Rapids: Eerdmans, 1996.

———. *The Epistle to the Romans*. NICNT. Grand Rapids: Eerdmans, 1996.

Moody, R M. "The Habakkuk Quotation in Romans 1:17." *The Expository Times* 92, no. 7 (April 1981): 204–208.

Moriarty, F. L. "The Habakkuk Scroll and a Controversy." *Theological Studies* 13 (January 1, 1952): 228.

Motyer, J. Alec. "Stricken for the Trangression of My People." In *From Heaven He Came and Sought Her*, edited by David Gibson and Jonathan Gibson. Wheaton: Crossway Books, 2013.

Mounce, Robert H. *Romans*. The New American Commentary v. 27. Nashville: Broadman & Holman, 1995.

Mounce, William D. *The Crossway Comprehensive Concordance of the Holy Bible: English Standard Version*. Wheaton: Crossway Books, 2002.

Muraoka, T. *A Greek-English Lexicon of the Septuagint*. Rev. ed. Louvain ; Walpole, MA: Peeters, 2009.

Murray, John. *The Epistle to the Romans*. NICNT. Grand Rapids, Mich.: Wm. B. Eerdmans Pub. Co, 1995.

Neufeld, Waldemar. "An Exegetical and Theological Study of Habakkuk 2:4-5." *Master of Art Theology Thesis* (May 1, 1990). http://scholar.csl.edu/ma_th/10.

Nietzsche, Friedrich Wilhelm, and Walter Kaufmann. *Basic Writings of*

Nietzsche. Modern Library ed. New York: Modern Library, 2000.

Nogalski, James D. "Book of the Twelve." In *The New Interpreter's Dictionary of the Bible: A-C.* Vol. 1. Nashville: Abingdon Press, 2006.

———. "Guest Editorial: Reading the Book of the Twelve Theologically." *Interpretation* 61, no. 2 (2007): 115.

———. "Intertextuality and the Twelve." In *Forming Prophetic Literature: Essays on Isaiah and the Twelve in Honor of John D.W. Watts*, edited by James W. Watts and Paul R. House, 102–124. Journal for the Study of the Old Testament Supplement 235. Sheffield, England: Sheffield Academic Press, 1996.

———. *The Book of the Twelve: Micah-Malachi*. Smyth & Helwys Bible Commentary. Macon, Ga: Smyth & Helwys Publishing, 2011.

———. "The Day(s) of YHWH in the Book of the Twelve." In *Thematic Threads in the Book of the Twelve*, edited by Paul L. Redditt and Aaron Schart, 192–213. Berlin, Germany: Walter de Gruyter GmbH & Co., 2003.

Orelli, C. Von. *The Twelve Minor Prophets*. Translated by J. S. Banks. Reprint. Minneapolis, Minn.: Klock & Klock Christian Publisher, 1977.

Patterson, Richard Duane. *Nahum, Habakkuk, Zephaniah*. The Wycliffe Exegetical Commentary. Chicago: Moody Press, 1991.

Perry, Edmund F. "Meaning of 'emuna in the Old Testament." *Journal of Bible and Religion* 21, no. 4 (October 1953): 252–256.

Petersen, David L., and Kent Harold Richards. *Interpreting Hebrew Poetry*. Guides to Biblical Scholarship. Minneapolis: Fortress, 1992.

Peterson, David L. "A Book of the Twelve." In *Reading and Hearing the Book of the Twelve*, edited by James Nogalski and Marvin A. Sweeney. SBL Symposium Series no. 15. Atlanta, Ga.: Society of Biblical Literature, 2000.

Pinker, Aron. "Historical Allusions in the Book of Habakkuk." *The Jewish Bible quarterly* 36, no. 3 (July 1, 2008): 143.

Piper, John. *Counted Righteous in Christ: Should We Abandon the Imputation of Christ's Righteousness?* Wheaton: Crossway Books, 2002.

———. *Desiring God: Meditations of a Christian Hedonist*. 25th anniversary reference ed. Colorado Springs: Multnomah, 2011.

———. "The Demonstration of the Righteousness of God in Romans 3:25, 26." *Journal for the Study of the New Testament* 7 (April 1980): 2–

32.

———. *The Future of Justification: A Response to N.T. Wright*. Wheaton: Crossway Books, 2007.

———. *The Justification of God: An Exegetical and Theological Study of Romans 9:1-23*. Grand Rapids, Mich.: Baker Book House, 1983.

Poythress, Vern S. *Understanding Dispensationalists*. 2nd ed. Phillipsburg: Presbyterian and Reformed, 1994.

Poythress, Vern S., and Wayne A. Grudem. *The Gender-Neutral Bible Controversy: Muting the Masculinity of God's Words*. Nashville: Broadman & Holman Publishers, 2000.

Pritchard, James Bennett, ed. *The Ancient Near Eastern Texts Relating to the Old Testament*. 3rd ed. with Supplement. Princeton: Princeton University Press, 1969.

Redditt, Paul L., and Aaron Schart, eds. *Thematic Threads in the Book of the Twelve*. Berlin, Germany: Walter de Gruyter GmbH & Co., 2003.

Rendtorff, Rolf. "How to Read the Book of the Twelve as a Theological Unity." In *Reading and Hearing the Book of the Twelve*, edited by James Nogalski and Marvin A. Sweeney. SBL symposium series no. 15. Atlanta, Ga.: Society of Biblical Literature, 2000.

Renz, Thomas. "An Emendation of Hab 2:4a in the Light of Hab 1:5." *The Journal of Hebrew Scriptures* 13 (2013).

Roberts, J H. "Righteousness in Romans With Special Reference to Romans 3:19-31." *Neotestamentica* 15 (January 1, 1981): 12–33.

Robertson, O. Palmer. *The Books of Nahum, Habakkuk, and Zephaniah*. NICOT. Grand Rapids: W.B. Eerdmans, 1990.

Robertson, O Palmer. "'The Justified (by Faith) Shall Live by His Steadfast Trust': Habakkuk 2:4." *Presbyterion* 9, no. 1–2 (1983): 52–71.

Rutherford, J. Alexander. "A Consideration of the Meaning of the Righteousness of God in Romans 1:17," 2016. https://teleioteti.ca/resources/papers/.

———. "A Critical Review of Stephen Dempster's Dominion and Dynasty." Teleioteti, 2017. Accessed January 23, 2018. https://teleioteti.ca/2017/10/13/a-critical-review-of-dempsters-dominion-and-dynasty/.

———. "Do Not Say in Your Heart: An Exposition of Romans 10:1-8." Teleiotēti, 2016. Accessed January 1, 2018.

https://teleioteti.ca/resources/papers/.

———. *Prevenient Grace: An Investigation into Arminianism*. Vancouver: Teleioteti, 2016.

———. *The Book of Habakkuk: An Exegetical-Theological Commentary on the Hebrew Text*. A Teleioteti Old Testament Commentary 1. Vancouver, BC: Teleioteti, Forthcoming.

———. *The Gift of Knowing: A Biblical Perspective on Knowing and Truth*. God's Gifts for the Christian Life Part 1 Vol. 1. Vancouver: Teleioteti, 2019.

———. *The Gift of Reading - Part 1: Reading the Bible in Submission to God*. God's Gifts for the Christian Life Part 1 Vol. 2a. Vancouver: Teleioteti, 2019.

———. *The Gift of Reading - Part 2: A Biblical Perspective on Hermeneutics*. God's Gifts for the Christian Life Part 1 Vol. 2b. Vancouver: Teleioteti, 2019.

Rutherford, James. "God's Kingdom through His Priest-King: An Analysis of the Book of Samuel in Light of the Davidic Covenant." ThM Thesis, Regent College, 2018.

Ryken, Leland. *The Word of God in English: Criteria for Excellence in Bible Translation*. Wheaton: Crossway, 2002.

Sailhamer, John H. *Introduction to Old Testament Theology: A Canonical Approach*. Grand Rapids: Zondervan, 1995.

Schenker, A., and et al., eds. *The Twelve Minor Prophets*. Biblia Hebraica Quinta 13. Stuttgart: Deutsche Bibelgesellschaft, 2010.

———, eds. *The Twelve Minor Prophets: Introduction and Commentaries on the Twelve Minor Prophets*. Biblia Hebraica Quinta 13. Stuttgart: Deutsche Bibelgesellschaft, 2010.

Schlatter, Adolf von. *Romans: The Righteousness of God*. Translated by Siegried S. Schatzmann. Peabody, Mass: Hendrickson Publishers, 1995.

Schreiner, Thomas R. "A Biblical Theology of the Glory of God." In *For the Fame of God's Name: Essays in Honor of John Piper*, edited by Sam Storms and Justin Taylor. Wheaton: Crossway, 2010.

———. *Galatians*. Edited by Clinton E. Arnold. Zondervan Exegetical Commentary Series on the New Testament 9. Grand Rapids: Zondervan, 2010.

———. *Romans*. Baker Exegetical Commentary on the New Testament 6.

Grand Rapids: Baker Books, 1998.

Scott, James M. "A New Approach to Habakkuk 2:4-5a." *Vetus Testamentum* 35, no. 3 (July 1985): 330–340.

Seifrid, Mark A. *Christ, Our Righteousness: Paul's Theology of Justification.* New Studies in Biblical Theology 9. Downers Grove, Ill.: Apollos/Intervarsity Press, 2000.

———. "Romans." In *Commentary on the New Testament Use of the Old Testament*, edited by G. K. Beale and D. A. Carson. Grand Rapids, Mich.: Baker Academic, 2007.

Seow, Choon Leong. "Orthography, Textual Criticism, and the Poetry of Job." *Journal of Biblical Literature* 130, no. 1 (2011): 63–85.

Silva, Moisés. *Biblical Words and Their Meaning: An Introduction to Lexical Semantics*. Rev. and Expanded ed. Grand Rapids: Zondervan, 1994.

Smith, George Adam. *The Book of the Twelve Prophets*. Edited by W. Robertson Nicoll. The Expositor's Bible. London: Hodder and Stoughton, 1898.

Smith, Ralph L. *Micah-Malachi*. Word Biblical Commentary 32. Waco, Tex.: Word Books, Publisher, 1984.

Southwell, P. J. M. "A Note on Habakkuk Ii. 4." *Journal of theological studies* XIX, no. 2 (1968): 614–617.

Stott, John R. W. *The Message of Romans*. Downers Grove, Ill.: InterVarsity Press, 1994.

Sweeney, M.A. *The Twelve Prophets*. Edited by David W. Cotter. Vol. 2. 2 vols. Berit Olam. Collegeville, Minn.: The Liturgical Press, 2000.

Sweeney, Marvin A. "Form and Eschatology in the Book of the Twelve Prophets." In *New Form Criticism and the Book of the Twelve*, edited by Mark J. Boda, Michael H. Floyd, and Colin M. Toffelmire. Ancient Near East Monographs 10. Atlanta: SBL Press, 2015.

———. "Sequence and Interpretation in the Book of the Twelve." In *Reading and Hearing the Book of the Twelve*, edited by James Nogalski and Marvin A. Sweeney. SBL Symposium Series no. 15. Atlanta, Ga.: Society of Biblical Literature, 2000.

———. "Structure, Genre, and Intent in the Book of Habakkuk." *Vetus Testamentum* 41, no. 1 (January 1991): 63–83.

Thayer, Joseph Henry, Carl Ludwig Wilibald Grimm, and Christian Gottlob Wilke. *Thayer's Greek-English Lexicon of the New Testament*. Peabody,

Mass.: Hendrickson, 1996.

Theodore. *Commentary on the Twelve Prophets*. Edited by Robert C. Hill. The Fathers of the Church: The Writings of Augustine 108. Washington D.C.: Catholic University of America Press, 2004.

Thomas, Heath A. *Habakkuk*. The Two Horizons Old Testament Commentary. Grand Rapids: Eerdmans, 2018.

Tsumura, David Toshio. "Hab 2:2 in the Light of Akkadian Legal Practice." *Zeitschrift für die alttestamentliche Wissenschaft* 94, no. 2 (1982): 294–295.

———. "Ugaritic Poetry and Habakkuk 3." *Tyndale Bulletin* 40, no. 1 (1989): 24–48.

———. "Vertical Grammar of Parallelism in Hebrew Poetry." *Journal of Biblical Literature* 128, no. 1 (2009): 167–181.

Turner, Geoffrey. "The Righteousness of God in Psalms and Romans." *Scottish journal of theology* 63, no. 3 (August 1, 2010): 285–301.

Van Pelt, Miles. *A Biblical-Theological Introduction to the Old Testament: The Gospel Promised*. Edited by Miles Van Pelt. Wheaton: Crossway, 2016.

Waltke, Bruce K., and Michael Patrick O'Connor. *An Introduction to Hebrew Syntax*. Winona Lake, Ind.: Eisenbrauns, 1990.

Waltke, Bruce K., and Charles Yu. *An Old Testament Theology: An Exegetical, Canonical, and Thematic Approach*. 1st ed. Grand Rapids: Zondervan, 2007.

Walton, John H., Victor Harold Matthews, and Mark W. Chavalas. *The IVP Bible Background Commentary: Old Testament*. Downers Grove, Ill: InterVarsity Press, 2000.

Ward, William Hayes. "A Critical and Exegetical Commentary on Habakkuk." In *A Critical and Exegetical Commentary on Micah, Zephaniah, Nahum, Habakkuk, Obadiah and Joel*. Edinburgh: T. & T. Clark, 1965.

Watson, Wilfred G. E. "Poetry, Biblical Hebrew." Edited by Geoffrey Khan. *Encyclopedia of Hebrew Language and Linguistics*. Leiden; Boston: Brill, 2013.

Watts, Rikki E. "'For I Am Not Ashamed of the Gospel': Romans 1:16-17 and Habakkuk 2:4." In *Romans and the People of God*, edited by Sven K. Soderlund and N.T. Wright. Grand Rapids: Eerdmans, 1999.

Weeks, Noel. "Problems with the Comparative Method in Old Testament Studies." *Journal of the Evangelical Theological Society* 62, no. 2 (2019): 287–306.

Westerholm, Stephen. "The Righteousness of the Law and the Righteousness of Faith in Romans." *Interpretation* 58, no. 3 (July 1, 2004): 253.

Whitekettle, Richard. "Like a Fish and Shrimp out of Water: Identifying the Dāg and Remeś Animals of Habakkuk 1:14." *Bulletin for Biblical Research* 24, no. 4 (2014): 491–503.

Williams, Ronald J., and John C. Beckman. *Williams' Hebrew Syntax*. 3rd ed. Toronto: University of Toronto Press, 2007.

Williamson, Paul R. *Sealed with an Oath: Covenant in God's Unfolding Purpose*. New Studies in Biblical Theology 23. Downers Grove: Apollos/InterVarsity Press, 2007.

Williamson, P.R. "Covenant." Edited by T. Desmond Alexander and Brian S. Rosner. *New Dictionary of Biblical Theology*. Leicester; Downers Grove: Inter-Varsity Press, 2000.

Willis, John T. "Alternating (ABA'B') Parallelism in the Old Testament Psalms and Prophetic Literature." In *Directions in Biblical Hebrew Poetry*, edited by Elaine R. Follis. Journal for the Study of the Old Testament 40. Sheffield: JSOT Press, 1987.

Woodbridge, John D. *Biblical Authority: A Critique of the Rogers/McKim Proposal*. Grand Rapids: Zondervan, 1982.

Wright, Benjamin G., and Albert Pietersma, eds. *A New English Translation of the Septuagint: And the Other Greek Translations Traditionally Included Under That Title*. Oxford: Oxford University Press, 2007.

Wright, Christopher J. H. "Response to Gordon McConville." In *Canon and Biblical Interpretation*, edited by Craig G. Bartholomew, Scott Hahn, Robin Parry, Christopher Seitz, and Al Wolters, 282–292. Scripture and Hermeneutics Series v. 7. Grand Rapids: Zondervan, 2006.

Wright, N.T. *Justification: God's Plan & Paul's Vision*. Downers Grove, Ill.: IVP Academic, 2009.

———. *Paul and the Faithfulness of God*. Vol. II. II vols. Christian Origins and the Question of God 4. Minneapolis, Minn.: Fortress, 2013.

———. *Paul and the Faithfulness of God*. Vol. I. II vols. Christian Origins and the Question of God 4. Minneapolis, Minn.: Fortress, 2013.

———. "Paul and the Patriarch: The Role of Abraham in Romans 4."

Journal for the study of the New Testament 35, no. 3 (March 1, 2013): 207–241.

———. *Pauline Perspectives: Essays on Paul, 1978-2013*. Minneapolis, Minn.: Fortress, 2013.

———. "Romans." In *The New Interpreter's Bible*, edited by Robert W Wall and J. Paul Sampley. Vol. X. Nashville: Abingdon Press, 2002.

———. *The New Testament and the People of God*. Christian Origins and the Question of God 1. Minneapolis: Fortress, 1992.

———. "Translating Δικαιοσύνη: A Response." *Expository times* 125, no. 10 (July 1, 2014): 487–490.

———. *What Saint Paul Really Raid: Was Paul of Tarsus the Real Founder of Christianity?* Grand Rapids, Mich.; Cincinnati, Ohio: W.B. Eerdmans Pub.; Forward Movement Publications, 1997.

Wright, Tom. *Romans: Part 1: Chapters 1-8*. Vol. 1. 2 vols. Paul for Everyone. Louisville: Society for Promoting Christian Knowledge, 2004.

Wright, Tom, John Tiller, George Carey, and Tony Baker. *The Great Acquittal: Justification by Fatih and Current Christian Thought*. Edited by Gavin Reid. London, England: Fount Paperbacks, 1980.

Yarbrough, Robert W. "Paul and Salvation History." In *Justification and Variegated Nomism: Volume 2 - the Paradoxes of Paul*, edited by D. A. Carson, Peter T. O'Brien, and Mark A. Seifrid. Vol. 2. Grand Rapids, Mich.: Baker Academic, 2004.

Young, Ian. "Is the Prose Tale of Job in Late Biblical Hebrew?" *Vetus Testamentum* 59, no. 4 (2009): 606–629.

ABOUT TELEIOTETI

Teleioteti (Τελειοτητι, te-ley-o-tey-tee)—meaning "unto maturity"—is dedicated to faithful, thoughtful ministry. We create resources for Christian discipleship, resources that address theological and pastoral concerns from a Biblical worldview. Our purpose is to see Christ's Church mature in its understanding of God and His Word. We do this through the production of Gospel-centred materials that connect the Bible with the heads, hearts, and minds of Christians. We hope to enable Christians from all walks of life to better understand and glorify God through service in His Church.

To achieve this purpose, Teleioteti publishes books researched with academic rigor yet based upon Biblical presuppositions. That is, we are neither academic nor lazy. We use methods, or epistemology, informed by the Bible along with the hard work usually associated with professional research and study. We produce resources directed towards all Christians, but most of our resources are directed towards students, pastors, and theologically inclined lay Christians.

To learn more about us and what we are doing, please visit us at https://teleioteti.ca or contact me at jalexanderrutherford@teleioteti.ca. If you have found this resource helpful, prayerfully consider supporting us by giving a review on the web (e.g. Amazon, Goodreads, etc.), praying with and for us, or giving financially so that we can produce more resources like this one. For more information on how you can support us, visit us at https://teleioteti.ca/about/partner/.

Other Books by J. Alexander Rutherford

Prevenient Grace: An Investigation into Arminianism (Teleioteti, 2016)

When a building is built on a poor foundation, the inevitable result is its collapse. But this isn't a book on architecture; foundations are found in thought structures as well as in material structures. In theology, a bad foundation will produce results as catastrophic as a bad foundation in architecture. How we think about God and His work in the world will profoundly affect how we live and work out our Christian faith; is your foundation strong? This book evolved from the conviction that a prominent theological system rests on fragile foundation.

Believe the Unbelievable: A Study in the Book of Habakkuk (Teleioteti, 2018)

What would we do if our prayers for justice, our prayers that God's will be done in our nation, were answered with a vision of desolation, of utter destruction?

When Habakkuk prayed for salvation, a prayer for justice amid chaos, violence, and suffering, that was God's answer. He revealed in a vision the invasion of the vicious armies of Babylon. God's answer contradicted everything Habakkuk thought he knew. Yet in the end, he praised God and trusted Him for this horrid salvation.

What do we do when God's actions or words contradict our understanding, contradict what we have believed? The book of Habakkuk answers this question in the face of the Babylonian invasion of Judah. Habakkuk is a book of discipleship, a book written to bring its reader to a deeper faith in Yahweh in the presence of His unthinkable deeds.

Using study questions addressing the text, theology, and application of Habakkuk and explanatory comments on difficult themes, *Believe the Unbelievable* seeks to realize this purpose for the contemporary reader.

Endorsements:

> James Rutherford is a capable and creative thinker, well equipped to tackle tough projects, such as the book of Habakkuk. In this study guide, Rutherford has produced a very useful resource for individual or group study. He combines theological acumen and well-honed linguistic and literary skills to discover and then to present, in highly understandable fashion, the riches of this not so "minor" Minor Prophet.

- V. Philips Long, PhD Cambridge
  Professor of Old Testament, Regent College

My good friend, James Rutherford, has given the church a gift. He has taken his love for God's Word and focused it on an Old Testament book that most Christians know very little about. The result is a study in Habakkuk that brings together deep insight and real relevance. Habakkuk is a voice among the Biblical chorus that believers need to hear today. Thank you, James, for helping us to hear it clearly and faithfully.

- Fredrick Eaton
  Pastor, Christ City Church, Kitsilano

The Gift of Knowing: A Biblical Perspective on Knowing and Truth (Teleioteti, 2019)

To any attentive observer, the Western world is in serious trouble. It shows the signs of languishing under a devastating disease. This is clearer nowhere else than in the realm of epistemology, the study of truth and how we attain it. Here, the belief in human autonomy—the freedom of individual men and women to interpret the world and live within it as they see fit—has slowly eroded any foundation for knowledge or morality. The result is a society adrift, floating wherever the tide might take it.

If the disease ravaging our society is the belief in human autonomy, the cure is submission once again to the God who created this world, at least that is the argument of the Gift of Knowing. The author argues that apart from submission to God as He has revealed Himself in the Christian Bible, there is no firm foundation for truth or a trustworthy way of attaining it. However, through His revelation in Scripture, God has given His people a foundation for knowing the world He has created and living within it.

God's Kingdom through His Priest-King: An Analysis of the Book of Samuel in light of the Davidic Covenant
Endorsements:
In the present environment of high interest in the Book of Samuel, this

contribution by James Rutherford is most welcome. Rutherford is well versed in current scholarship on Samuel, but his work moves well beyond this scholarship to contribute fresh insights, not least in respect of the priestly character of King David. And concerning its structure, Rutherford argues that the Book of Samuel as a whole is arranged and narrated so as to draw attention to the centrality of the Davidic Covenant of 2 Samuel 7. Having myself studied 1 and 2 Samuel for decades now, I was nevertheless benefitted at numerous points from Rutherford's creative interpretive suggestions. His is a work well conceived, well written, and worthy of a serious read.

- V. Philips Long
  Professor of Old Testament, Regent College

This thesis argues that by weaving references to God's promises made to King David throughout his narrative, the author of Samuel reveals God's will to strip away all human pretension by bringing his promises to fulfillment through a lowly man whose ascension to kingship and endurance therein is entirely owing to God. In this way, the Samuel author fulfils his purpose of demonstrating God's sovereign working in history to establish his kingdom on earth through his chosen priest-king, a descendant of David. The thesis represents an excellent piece of work that does a great job of bringing together into one coherent argument, focused on the Davidic covenant, much of the best recent narrative-critical research on 1-2 Samuel, and from this point of view represents a distinctive contribution to the field of Samuel studies.

- Iain Provan
  Marshall Sheppard Professor of Biblical Studies, Regent College

www.ingramcontent.com/pod-product-compliance
Lightning Source LLC
Chambersburg PA
CBHW030229100526
44583CB00013BA/629